E

Ever since I met David in about 20 _____ *and reaching others in need. His heart for those incarcerated is overwhelming, birthed from his own time spent in the federal penitentiary. By sharing his life experience within the pages of Jet Ride to Hell, Journey to Freedom, David has literally made himself an open book. In finding his freedom, he has opened doors for others to find the same peace. I am privileged to know him as a minister but even greater, as a friend. This is a wonderful story of God's love, forgiveness, and redemptive power, and I gladly recommend it to all.*

Prophet Rob Sanchez
Prophet Rob Sanchez Ministries
Author, Life is Very Good Devotional

David's life has been spiritually marinated between the extremes of excessive worldly ambition and being broken, and then immersed in the humility and love of Christ. He's lived a life tempered by 20 years of a jet ride through Hell and a redemptive journey into freedom! David's life testimony told in his inspiring style will put you on the edge of your seat while illuminating God's redemptive nature!

Michael L. Mathews
Ordained Minister and Global Education Strategist,
Oral Roberts University

I've known David for years and knew some snippets and details of his life but when I started reading the entire story I've got to admit I was flabbergasted. David's journey is movie material! He gets arrested trying to steal a jet for the Columbian cartel, he receives a visitation in his Leavenworth prison cell, he faces persecution, revival break out, etc. If you want a page-turner, this is it. If you want an amazing story of God's grace, this is it. Either way, you should read this book.

Jackie Macgirvin
Editor/Ghost Writer - ChristianBookDoctor.com
Author, The Designer Bag at the Garbage Dump

I have witnessed first-hand over several years the consistency of David's walk with Christ, and the anointing that has graced his life. It has been a privilege to experience and participate in the powerful working of the Holy Spirit as David has looked beyond his circumstance and daily reaches out to those around him to expand the Kingdom of God. David's life story is a narrative of God's grace and redemption and the power of the love of Jesus Christ which provides hope for all.

Reverend Michael Longanecker
Federal Prison Chaplain (Ret.)
FCI Waseca, MN

My friend, David Hairabedian, is a shining example of God's transformative and saving grace. His story is, aside from many things, one of the most unique and interesting I have ever heard. I encourage you to dive into this inspirational read.

David Diga Hernandez
Evangelist, Author, TV Host
DavidHernandezMinistries.org

Additional Endorsements in the back.

JET RIDE TO HELL

★★★

JOURNEY TO FREEDOM

DAVID HAIRABEDIAN

Publisher: Virtual Church Publishing
© Copyright 2015 – David Hairabedian

A NOTE FROM THE AUTHOR

"Guilty as charged!" Those words used to haunt me, but not any longer. I heard them loud and clear from the judge. I didn't 'pass go' and I didn't collect $200. This wasn't Monopoly, this was the Feds who play for keeps, and I was headed to jail for 20 years without parole.

Considering how I was raised, how did I go so far down the road of darkness that I tried to steal jets for the Colombian Cartel? What possessed me to do the things I did?

We've all been prisoners in one form or another, whether it's a physical, spiritual, emotional, relational, mental prison or even a religious one. Whether incarcerated or free, bondage comes in many forms – sometimes apparent, sometimes not. You may secretly be wearing the *Shackles of Shame*. Others may be successful in their jobs, but are privately held captive on their computers in the *Lockdown of Lust*. Another could be stuck for years in the *Underground of Unforgiveness*, held *Captive by Condemnation*, trapped in the *Dungeon of Depression* or even bound in the *Bastille of Bitterness*. Whether it's the *Penitentiary of Pride*, the *Handcuffs of Hatred*, or something else, there is hope and freedom. I am living proof.

Although I made many mistakes, I am humbled and encouraged to have learned first-hand that God chooses to use each of us, in spite of our past, our habits, and even our strongholds. I think of Jacob, Joseph, and David in the Bible, all who had many rough edges yet God used them mightily. He wants to use us all.

Out of dozens of amazing moments where I've been privileged to see God honored, I've only included those the Holy Spirit highlighted to tell the true story of my rebellion, redemption, and the miraculous journey for myself and others into God's glorious freedom. I chose to write in short vignettes to highlight what God was doing to bring freedom to me, and to capture men's hearts during the almost 20 years and in the nine different facilities where I served.

Over 75% of prisoners end up incarcerated again. Often pursuing Him is the one thing that keeps prisoners from returning. Whether I was behind bars as a free man in Christ, or out of prison, also as a free man in Christ, I saw God going after my heart and always after others. God has a miraculous life of freedom for each of us, and He wants to use us wherever we are for His glory.

Although some in the body of Christ do not believe in or rarely experience miracles, I was taught by my mother that "God said it, and that makes it final." I believe that healings, visitations, hearing God, and all that I read in God's Word is meant to be "normal" abundant life, and that is the journey I've experienced. My reason for writing this book is to help inspire you to take your own *Journey to Freedom*.

David C. Hairabedian

DEDICATION

To my wonderful parents, Tom and Susan, I bless you with gratefulness for laying your lives aside for me when I was in prison. You say it's been a privilege to have me as your son. The privilege has truly been all mine.

To my siblings, Cary and Carron, you've been supportive in more ways than can be described. Without your love and all you've done, I would be only a portion of who I am.

To my friend Koren, you were stalwart and unbending while helping disciple me during the early years of my journey to freedom. Thank you for all the timely and God-ordained discipleship books, letters, words of encouragement and annual prison visits while I was behind bars that helped in my spiritual formation. May God bless your house and family with a Lion's share of the harvest.

To Brother Kent, a friend, prayer warrior, and faithful partner with this ministry for more than 25 years. May the street that leads to your eternal home in Heaven be fully paved with gold. You deserve it!

To Jeff, my ministry partner, and friend, who single-handedly helped edit and co-author more than 30 of my teachings and booklets while I was behind bars. Thank you for your innumerable prison visits and for undergirding, strengthening and growing HEART prison ministry the last 20 years. Your labor of love and leadership has enabled more than 1,000 prisons to receive discipleship teachings and the Word of God, *"Helping Change Lives…One Bible at a Time."* May Heaven shine upon your legacy.

To Ray, Pam, and Tammy, who believed God, and then helped facilitate the birth of a church after my release from prison, a church that is now reaching around the world. Your family is amazing!

To the countless others who have tirelessly supported this ministry, and this minister, silently behind the scenes. You know who you are. May God reward you openly for what you have done in secret.

And finally, to my beautiful Proverbs 31 wife, Joanna. Your name and life truly mean *Gift from God*. You inspire me daily with your love for God, and the ways you seek His Presence through prayer, worship, warfare, and desire to release His miracles. The Father's heart in you for the lost shines through all you do. Thank you for partnering with me in life and the eternal vision to see God's message of hope reach around the world.

CONTENTS

FOREWORD

I have read many books. This one is extraordinary. It could be used in a movie to inspire those who are still bound, confirming that every chain can be broken through the blood of Jesus Christ. It demonstrates that the power of God overcomes your past and the past holds no power over your future.

David's life is an example of the power of the cross and the miraculous power at work in his life. He is a modern day Paul, who was Saul, whose life was changed while killing Christians. David was on the way to Hell, but God had a great plan for his life, He saved him. He is a living epistle and true witness on the grace of the Lord Jesus Christ.

I believe this book is a MUST read. It has brought tears to my eyes and will transform your life.

Having met David and his wife, Joanna, I encourage you to meet him. I recommend this book. David has passion to see the captives free, with a strong anointing to heal the broken hearted and sick.

The book you are holding is an answer to those who want to know the power of God. Read on.

Dr. Gershom Sikaala
President, His Presence Fire Ministries/USA/South Africa
www.GershomSikaala.org

TIMELINE AND ABBREVIATIONS

Timeline
Before prison
USP Leavenworth, Kansas (1990)
FCI Englewood, Colorado (1990-94)
FCI Miami, Florida (1994-95)
MCFP Springfield, Missouri (1995-98)
USP Terra Haute Penitentiary, Indiana (1998 7 days)
FCI Waseca, Minnesota (1998-2001)
USP Terra Haute Prison Camp, Indiana (2001 7 days)
FCI Florence Prison Camp, Colorado (2001-2003)
USP Leavenworth Prison Camp, Kansas (2003-2008)
Post-prison

COMMON ABBREVIATIONS

BOP = Bureau of Prisons
CCO = Community Corrections Officer
FCC = Federal Correctional Complex
FCI = Federal Correctional Institution
FPC = Federal Prison Camp
FTC = Federal Transfer Center
MCFP = Medical Center for Federal Prisoners
USP = United States Penitentiary

1

ARRESTED WITH A STOLEN JET

It was 9:05 in the morning. The sun was shining as our crew drove the silver Mercedes to meet the pilot of the Cessna Citation II jet taxiing toward us on the tarmac of the executive airfield in Florida. The pick-up was Boca Raton, the delivery location, Virgin Gorda in the British Virgin Islands, where the plane would be repainted, data plates changed and then used in the cocaine trafficking world by the Cali Cartel. This was our second plane in a month.

I looked up and down the runway. Based on last night's dream, I couldn't shake the feeling that something seemed off, but it was too late for the four of us to abort the mission. We were committed.

The plane's door opened and the pilot I'd met two days earlier at a Kansas City hotel stepped off. He had agreed, for a price, to deliver a jet that was on the list of planes we were stealing from the US and delivering to South America. Later I would discover *two things*, Boca Raton is translated, *Mouth of the Rat*, and a big rat was among us. I carried a bag filled with cash and climbed the steps to meet the pilot and hand over partial payment. The rest would be delivered once the plane was safely in the air.

An unmarked police vehicle sped down the tarmac toward us. Unsure of what was happening I thought maybe I'd run interference, and my friend could get the plane off the ground. I was moving toward the vehicle. Almost before it came to a complete stop the car door flew open, the driver popped out and stuck a chrome 45 caliber pistol in my face. I quickly assessed the roof situation -- two snipers with beads drawn on our other two crew members still in the Mercedes. There was no place to hide.

"Get your hands up, YOU ARE UNDER ARREST!" yelled the agent, still waving a gun in my face. My hands flew up to display the international sign of surrender and at that moment, my life changed forever. Amidst every other emotion and thought, it came to me, it's *finally over*.

Everything was happening so fast. My head was spinning. In a matter of seconds, 20 plus heavily armed federal agents descended on us from all four sides, some on foot and others in unmarked vehicles.

As I looked into the morning sunshine streaming down on my face, I realized I was going to jail. This would not be an orange juice morning in South Florida. Rather, this was the beginning of, *My Journey to Freedom…*

2

ARRAIGNED IN FEDERAL COURT

We were arraigned in federal court later that morning in West Palm Beach. The female judge read the charges. Then the prosecutor added, "Your honor, we believe these same defendants may have been involved in the theft of the King Air 300 in Ft. Lauderdale about 30 days ago."

My thoughts narrowed as I fixated on one question, *how much do they really know?*

Upon hearing the judge's words, my partner-in-crime and friend Vic tapped me on the arm and said, "Dave, Dave."

"Not now, I'm trying to listen." Vic hit me harder to fully get my attention.

"Dave! Look around, it's just like your dream!"

His words stopped me cold. *He's right!* I thought.

The judge was a woman, and she was wearing a Tag Heuer black anodized aluminum watch. I had dreamed the day before that not only were we getting caught, but I saw the judge, and she was wearing the same watch. I knew watches because I owned five watch stores.

Vic pointed, "There's the reddish-orange haired guy." I looked at the disheveled agent. "He even has mud on his boots." I was too stunned to say anything.

"How'd it end? Did we get convicted or acquitted?" prodded Vic.

"Don't know, I woke up."

"Well, go back to sleep and find out!"

We were taken to the county jail; a bond hearing was scheduled for the following day. I called my mother on a monitored phone. When she answered, I was overwhelmed with shame. For the first time in many years, I found myself choked up, tears dropping down my face. *What are these? Tears? That's not who I am. Where are these coming from? Get a hold of yourself, David.*

I reminded myself to stay focused. I lived in a world where I had to be tough and there was no room for tears. My thoughts had no bearing on my emotions. I had stained the family name.

Mom didn't chastise me, rather, she encouraged me, affirming that she loved me. She went into motherly protection mode and refrained from asking questions because the call was recorded. I gave her specific instruction on whom to call to post my bail. I was still using my worldly contacts to help me, with absolutely no thoughts to trust God.

This, however, would prove to be only the beginning of sorrows for me and of course, my family. The breaking process was long and arduous, and this was merely the first phase. Little did I know that I was being drawn down a path that led back to a forgiving God, where both my mother's prayer and Vic's grandmother's prayers were being answered! Years later, I would learn that at the direction of the Holy Spirit, many interceded for us through these difficult times, none of whom knew one another.

Our lawyers flew in the next day and Vic and I were bonded out after another hearing. Vic's family put up property as collateral, and a well-respected millionaire friend of mine from Kansas City put up my $50,000 dollar cash bond. I'll always appreciate his vote of confidence in me at that time. He made it clear to me, "David, I see in you what was in me at your age." He communicated to me that although I was making wrong choices leading me down a very wrong path, I had respectable character traits and was well-liked. (I attributed this to my upbringing and by the grace of God.)

He believed in me and my potential. In fact, I later learned that the lead Customs agent showed up in my friend's office, unannounced, questioning why he would put up my bail. I learned how the conversation went.

"Because he's my friend, that's why."

"Yes, but what collateral did David give you?"

"No collateral."

"And you gave him 50 grand, just like that?"

"I would have given him 200 grand if he needed it. Now here's my attorney's card. Speak with him if you have further questions."

Now that we were out on bond, it was time to prepare our defense. The Feds didn't know anything about the cocaine yet, and without any witnesses, they lacked sufficient evidence of our involvement on the King Air 300. The Cessna II jet fell under the "attempted theft of a vehicle" statute. It carried a maximum of five years.

"What's the worst case scenario?" I asked my lawyer.

He laughed. "Dave, as a first-time offender and with no real loss of property, probably 18-24 months. Probably at "Club Fed" so don't worry." These guidelines have since changed dramatically since 9/11.

Relieved, I thought, *if I get sentenced to 24 months I'll do 20. I'm a little out of shape, so I'll use the time to get in shape, and I'll come out a hero since I didn't snitch[1] on anyone.*

We were sitting on $450,000 of cocaine from the first jet we'd stolen the month prior with which we hadn't yet been charged, and my share would have been $150,000 cash. My legitimate business - five watch stores - was estimated by my accountant to be worth $1,000,000 on Dunn and Bradstreet at age 24.

I'll have a bag of cash waiting, go legit, and get back to my watch business. I sighed in relief, certain this was just a bump in the road.

Our defense teams hoped to beat the case. They pointed out that the discovery file showed that the Feds had done a very poor job on this one. Some of the undercover tape recorders failed. Their undercover pilot, a U.S. Customs agent, delivered a different plane. Also, he appeared to have a drinking, and potential drug problem, some of it recorded on tape, and other undercover tapes were strangely missing. Moreover, the flight instructor turned informant, who knowingly introduced me to an undercover agent, seemed to be mentally off and had second thoughts about testifying.

A ray of light seemed to appear on the horizon when our attorneys told us news of the government's weakening case against us. Encouraged by this, we paid our lawyers some additional money, trusting them to get us off the hook. Soon, however, the noose would again tighten. Through interagency intelligence reports from Florida and New York, the Missouri prosecutor discovered that this white-collar stolen vehicles case was just the tip of the iceberg.

Journey Insights

For the first time, I was ashamed of my actions and it was the beginning of a long, arduous breaking process of the "old man." The Bible says God disciplines those He loves, although at that time I had no idea who I was yet to become. Who are you right now?

---

1   A snitch is an informer for law enforcement usually with questionable motives. A regular witness would simply tell the truth in a court case, but a snitch is motivated by personal gain. He often uses questionable testimony and follows the prosecution's script to achieve a conviction. Sometime this involves altering facts or creating stories, i.e. tilting or withholding the facts. The motivation can be early prison release, financial reward, or simply getting even. A snitch can also be called a canary, fink, stool pigeon, stoolie, sneaker, chiva, snitcher, rat, or rat-on.

3

THE INDICTMENTS KEEP COMING

Pandora's Box was open. Our attorneys now feared what the Feds would uncover next, and this news concerned Vic, the Colombians, and me. Vic and I were out on bond, but things were far from over. As it turned out, the jail cell the Feds tossed Vic and me into for the night would not be our last. More indictments followed.

Instead of calling out to the God I was told about while growing up, and by Vic's grandmother just a few weeks earlier, I decided to go it on my own. *You got you into this mess, now get yourself out. God's not going to help you anyway.* The devil effectively uses this same lie, often delaying our journey to freedom for months or years, other times, forever.

We all agreed on a trial strategy, which means we "bent the truth" to the story we thought would work. I would plead guilty and take the heat for the case, and Vic and Alex would go free. I would only serve 18-24 months, do my time at Club Fed and come home a hero for refusing to squeal.

My first conviction occurred in June of 1990. I pled guilty right before our trial started. My lawyers told me we had a verbal agreement that I wouldn't be called to testify, and I'd do 18-24 months.

Vic proceeded to trial with Alex, the 45-year-old ex-military fighter jet pilot who was part of our team, and I refused to testify. The second day of trial Alex took the stand on his behalf, and told our fabricated story, untrue although plausible. All we needed was "reasonable doubt" before the jury to be acquitted. He denied knowing anything illegal was going on. His defense claimed he'd been hired at the last minute and didn't know Vic or me until that morning when arriving at the airport to fly a chartered plane. "It's common for pilots to be hired this way. Stuff like this happens to pilots in South Florida all the time."

The jury heard Alex say that I called him, claimed to get his number from a previous client at a bar and hired him to fly a private plane out of Boca Raton on that date. His intention was to convey that I'd duped him. My refusal to testify made his story plausible and all he needed was "reasonable doubt" in front of the jury to go free. Everything was going as planned; our behind the scene trial strategy was working flawlessly.

Vic testified in his own defense and dumped the case on me, the guy who already pled guilty. This was our strategy. Vic claimed he knew me, but was unaware of any illegal transaction. Vic's Florida trial lawyer told the jury Vic was a licensed chiropractor who'd simply given a friend from Kansas City a ride to the airport at Boca Raton. He further told them that Vic had been duped, and the guilty party pled guilty because he is guilty. His client was going to trial because he is innocent. We all had agreed on this plan before I pled guilty. God, however, had other plans.

Alex was known as "Einstein" in our group for his education, tactical planning, and exceptionally high IQ. Things were going well for the defense until the prosecutor caught Alex in a simple lie. Einstein must not have been thinking clearly because this mistake was the beginning of the end.

Alex and a Columbian were piloting the first stolen plane. The United States Air Force was flying the high-level surveillance plane, called an AWACS, alongside Alex as he flew the plane out of the country. He and the Columbian were wearing masks of Nixon or Reagan. At trial, the prosecution brought up the fact that in his trunk was a cash receipt for the purchase of two masks. Alex claimed he purchased the masks for Halloween. The problem? The receipt showed a November date which was *after* Halloween. He was caught in that lie. The prosecutor held up a woman's wig and a toupee they had also found in a briefcase.

"What were you going to use these for?"

"Uhh, wear it to the beach to impress the women."

"Show me," said the prosecutor, handing Alex the toupee.

Alex put it on backwards. Laughter rippled through the jury. Alex's lie about the masks cracked the dam, it crumbled as the jurors continued laughing, and then the water of guilt flowed onto Alex and Vic. Lies have a way of being found out. The jury convicted them both.

A few months later at sentencing on my first case, instead of 18-24 months, the judge departed outside of the recommended guidelines to the maximum allowed under the statute, 60 months without parole. Five years, no parole? I was furious. *This isn't the agreement between my lawyer and the prosecutor! What the heck did I plead guilty for? I couldn't have received a day more time if I'd gone to trial!* Then the Judge added, "And three years of supervised release."

This is like an eight-year sentence! I screamed inside. *The feds tricked me into a bait and switch plea agreement.* This made me even angrier. It was unjust, regardless of the crimes I'd committed because they didn't keep their word.

Now I was even more committed to beating the system because of what they did to me. My freedom depended on it. Little did I know that God allowed this injustice by the court, to teach me a lesson, and I was reaping what I'd sown. The same way I tricked a pilot out of his jet, I was getting tricked out of my freedom. None of my reasoning was helping. Being upset made no difference, and my hands were tied (in more ways than one!). I needed to come to the end of myself.

Vic and Alex got the same penalty of five years. The judge's reason for departing to the maximum allowed was because he believed the stolen jet was to be used in drug trafficking by the Columbian cartel. Vic remained out on bond while Alex and I were sent to a very old county jail in rural Missouri. It was here we would await our final designation[2] to serve our time. This jail lacked cameras or other security systems. They were used to prisoners who had DUI's or had written hot checks. They weren't trained to work with federal prisoners yet, but because of a recently signed contract they were being paid significant money to temporarily house this type of criminal. It was big news in the town and when I arrived the press took photos. My photo ended up on the front page of the town newspaper the next morning.

To visit a prisoner, a visitor has to go through a thorough approval process including photographs, fingerprints, Social Security number, driver's license, background check, etc. But this jail didn't even have a visitor's system in place. I was surprised when I was told, "Hairabedian, you've got a visitor" and looked through the window to see some college-aged girl smiling at me. I didn't know my photo was in the paper, and I thought maybe I was being set up. Paranoid, I requested no further visitors, except for immediate family.

There were 11 men in our pod. Two gang members arranged to have metal files smuggled to them inside boom boxes. It took them a week to file through the lock. In the middle of the night, they escaped. The rest of us had the opportunity to leave, but none of us did. The thought crossed my mind, but I hadn't been sentenced yet and never thought I'd do more than 24 months, so I just stayed.

The next morning the guard came to count, and we were down by two. Both escapees were eventually caught, one doing a cocaine transaction. He was sentenced to 60 years total. The other was caught in California and given a total of 20 years.

Two other prisoners made a false statement against the prison guard to get a

---

2   The Bureau of Prisons (BOP) designates a specific facility where an offender is to be confined based on the level of security deemed appropriate for that individual. Prison facilities are designated as either minimum, low, medium, high, or administrative.

reduced sentence. They accused him of taking payment to bring in the boom boxes and stated that he hadn't properly inspected them. He was inadequately trained, and he didn't do any of this, but he ended up in federal jail. One day on the way to court I privately pulled aside a federal marshal who was a decent guy.

"Can I tell you something, off the record?"

"Sure, what is it?" he responded.

"The guard is innocent and they need to look more into this case." I wasn't a snitch, but, I couldn't allow false witnesses to send an innocent man to jail, even if he was a cop.

The guard responded like I thought he would. "Yeah. We know there's something not quite right here." Unfortunately, six months later, they convicted him anyway. Life isn't always fair.

Two Christians were present in our 12-man cell. Alex was a devout atheist, who'd read the Bible three times and was well-educated on world religions. He used to fly the Hajj, (an annual Islamic pilgrimage), for Braniff Airlines to Mecca during Ramadan. Once he was the captain of a 747 loaded with Arabs making their annual pilgrimage to Mecca and he was quick to tell me he had no respect for Muslims or Christians. He talked about how they were idiots, and he said criminals who became Christians inside jail were "born-again 'till they're out again."

"David," Alex warned, "Whatever you do, don't go joining the God Squad on me!"

Vic arrived four months later. He'd given his life to Christ a couple of months earlier at his grandmother's home in New Jersey. This occurred one evening after a church service he attended, and it made Alex very uncomfortable. He no longer trusted Vic. Two months later Vic and I were indicted a second time and charged with cocaine trafficking. Alex escaped this indictment. He had always stayed away from cocaine trafficking, and now it seemed to be protecting him from a harsher sentence.

Since Alex appeared to be in the clear, he was designated by the BOP and transferred to Eglin Air Force Camp in Florida to serve his five years. His parting words to me were, "David, always exercise your right to go to trial. If you lose, win on appeal, and never cooperate with the government." We all filed appeals in our first case. Alex was still very clearly innocent in his mind, and fighting this travesty of justice in the 8th Circuit Court of Appeals. We were upset about the judge departing from the guidelines, enhancing our sentence from 18-24 months to 60, the maximum allowed by law, and without parole.

For Vic and me, things were getting much worse. The new case involved cocaine and the potential penalty stunned us. We were now looking at a minimum of 10 years and as much as life without the possibility of parole!

What? I screamed internally. I began wearing a "V" on the floor from pacing.

Ten years? Life? No parole? Impossible! No way could this happen to me.

It was confusing that when I mentioned this to Vic, he wasn't moved. *How in the world,* I wondered, *can you not be worried? What do you know that I don't? Are you cooperating with the government?* I glared at him as the thoughts raced through my head. I was still in denial, and I refused to believe this was a reality.

Serving all this time cannot happen, period.

With a confidence that made no sense to me, Vic said, "Dave, don't worry. God's got everything under control." Then he shared with me how he'd been born again. I guess I was happy for him, especially because his new spiritual status seemed to have a calming effect on him, but I wasn't interested. I didn't understand, and besides, Alex's words rang in my head about "not jumping on the God squad."

I'm not doing THAT, I told myself as I paced. *Besides,* I reasoned, *I have a case to fight, and this time, I'll be fighting for my life!* Given the nature of our case, the prosecutor requested the U.S. Marshals transfer Vic and me to Leavenworth for secure holding.

It was January 1990, another prisoner and I were in the van. When it stopped, I looked up at this ominous stone and brick building with the huge dome. It was the infamous "big house" with 42 steps leading up to the massive facility. We were going in to a place from where there's rumored to be no return.

Leavenworth was filled with prisoners serving life sentences. I looked at the other prisoner, back to the penitentiary and then back to him. Looking for a word of hope, I realized I was nervous. He rounded his shoulders, ducked his head, laughed and squeaked "home." I failed to see the humor.

I was "welcomed" to Leavenworth with my first real strip-search, and it was thorough. Then I put on a prison uniform, and that was the last time I wore street clothes until release. Prison guards escorted us, in cuffs, to Building 63 where the infamous Birdman of Alcatraz had his canaries in the 1950's.

As we were walked down the tier, we were bombarded with prisoners shouting "greetings."

"Hey, good looking. Need a roommate?"

"Welcome to Heavenworth."

"No, welcome to hell. People check in, but they don't check out."

"I'm serving eight life-consecutives."

"Hunker down in our nice little roach motel."

The metal clanged as the guard shut the door. An empty feeling gripped me; I felt like I'd been slugged in my stomach. The only other time I felt this low was when I had to call my mom and tell her I'd been arrested.

Assessing the stark, three-man cell that I would call home for the next nine months, there were few positives. It was eight by 16-feet with 16-feet ceilings, a shower and a stainless steel prison toilet which was freezing cold. Flaking paint littered the floor. I later realized that the infestation of large, black, hard-shell cockroaches was accelerating the wall paint's decay. At any time, there were 50-200 of these disgusting pests in the cell.

At night, the cockroaches crawled intermittently over any part of my body. I'd feel something on my foot and wake up. It was pitch dark, it was cold, and cockroaches were crawling on me. The more I smashed, the more seemed to take their place. They'd climb high on the wall and then drop on me as I slept. Building 63 was swarming with cockroaches, but worse, there was an overwhelming feeling of evil. The sickening darkness seemed to permeate the atmosphere no matter the time of day. Later I learned this place was filled with a hundred-year history of malicious criminals serving time for some of the most heinous crimes imaginable, and their demons seem to remain even after they were gone. *Welcome to Heavenworth, David.*

To deal with vicious criminals, guards sometimes chose to fight fire with fire and it wasn't pretty. It's said, "There's standard operating procedure, and then there's the Leavenworth way." They had their own rules here, made up as "needed." If a prisoner was disrespectful to the guards, they would get even. One time I saw the guards throw a guy in a cell with three homosexual rapists and provide them all with alcohol. Nature took its course. Prisoners were always on pins and needles knowing anything could happen at any time.

Night and day I overheard prisoners talking, swearing, yelling, and telling dirty jokes. The complaining was constant whether it was about snitches, wives leaving, lawyers, or sentences. People were picked on, abused, or raped. There was a hollow, cold and miserable gloom here; this was no Heavenworth. The reality of being sentenced to a couple of decades or more in prison crushed down on me.

What in the world happened? How'd I get here?

I realized that I could be spending almost the same amount of time in prison as I'd been alive. *Is this where the second half of my life will be spent before I see the light of day? I'll get out and have no children. I'll miss my sister's wedding, my nieces and nephews birthdays. Will my parents still be alive?*

I stared at the ceiling and had all night to wonder, *How'd I end up in Leavenworth Penitentiary, looking down the barrel of a gun loaded with a bullet labeled, "life without parole?"* Those words wouldn't leave my head. I fluctuated between despair and denial.

Somehow I've got to beat this. Round and round my thoughts went, examining the details of my case. There were holes in the case. The new witness for the government perjured himself at my expense and his benefit, to the tune of $200,000 in cash. My incarceration seems unjust because the prosecutor promised I'd get 18-24 months if I pled guilty.

My conclusion? *I can outsmart the system. Come on, David. Find a way. There's GOT to be a way.*

While I was reasoning ways out of my predicament, my thoughts strayed to a deeper place. *What led me to make the choices I did?* I thought about my life. My family had always been fine, maybe even great. Eventually, I made friends. Our family wasn't particularly poor. I had positive attributes including excellent focus, a sharp mind, an entrepreneurial spirit, and what others described as charisma that would take me a long way in legitimate business. A bright future should have awaited me.

I rolled over on my lumpy mattress and flicked a cockroach off into the darkness. Although I couldn't see it at the time, God was using this to bring me to a final breaking point so I would call on Him and He would build character in me. I was a character, but I significantly lacked character!

One thing I had was a lot of time on my hands. I continued to more seriously reflect on my life. *I was raised in a good home with a good family. How did I end up in prison facing life without parole? Where was the fork in the road that I obviously took?*

I began examining my journey, starting with my childhood years. *Who am I? How did I become a federal prison convict?*

Journey Insights

Instead of calling out to God, I decided to do it my way, but God has a way of allowing things to happen to get us on our knees. Lies got exposed to the jury; I faced the possibility of life without parole. All I could think about is how I got here. Have you thought about what has got you to this point in your life?

4

SEARCHING FOR ANSWERS

Reflecting on my childhood isn't quite enough, I thought. Deeply engrossed in my musings, I was determined to figure out how I ended up in such degradation. I racked my brain, willing to look into my history. *I'm going back even further, back to my parents. Maybe their lives will help provide me with a clue.*

I knew that my father, Tom, was full-blooded Armenian, and his mother survived the Armenian genocide. My mother, Susan, was full-blooded Hebrew, and her relatives survived the German Holocaust. *I can survive prison,* I acknowledged.

"No, I WILL survive prison." I was adamant as I proclaimed this out loud.

These words strengthened me as they came out. I repeated them. "I will survive prison and live to tell about it." Something inside me came alive, and I began to believe what I'd spoken. A small ray of hope came.

I reflected further remembering the story of how my parents met while my Mom was visiting Los Angeles. Dad was a healthy and good looking swimming instructor and life guard. Mom was smart and charismatic, blessed with stunning good looks as a young woman in New York City. They were a magnificent couple, good-hearted, and simply good citizens. They fell in love quickly and married. A few years later, during a stirring sermon at a small congregation in Phoenix, they gave their lives to the Lord.

My brother, Cary, was the first born, and then my sister, Carron. My parents felt they had the perfect family, one boy, and one girl, but about five years after my sister was born the Holy Spirit said to my mother in a dream, "I want you to have another child;" soon after she received another confirmation. As a young girl, my mother had several supernatural encounters and did not doubt when she heard from Heaven. This time was no different. Though she was far from perfect, when Mom heard the Lord, she always obeyed. Thinking about how she heard that she was to have me, I was confused because here I sat in prison.

As I contemplated my family history, searching for clues to the mess I was in, I remembered an example of God unmistakably showing up in my Mom's life. In the early 1940's Mom walked to school daily with several girlfriends. One day when she was about 12 years old, the Holy Spirit interrupted this habit, instructing her to leave for school immediately. She wanted to wait, but when she heard Him the second time, she got her coat and left, telling no one because she knew others wouldn't believe her. Along the way, she saw many men walking to the Long Island Railroad. Suddenly a rabbi in dark clothes appeared. He had a beard and the bluest eyes she'd ever seen on a Jew.

"Maidala (Pretty Maiden)," he called to her in Hebrew, "Come." Across the street she went, and everything seemed to disappear during the encounter with the rabbi. He said he'd been walking the streets all night and couldn't get home. "Maidala, can you spare some money?" Without hesitation, she gave him her lunch money, a dime, and nickel.

"Because you did this, I will bless you." He laid hands on her head and spoke a Hebrew blessing. At this point, everything reappeared, and the rabbi was gone. He seemed to vanish into thin air and there was no natural way of explaining his disappearance. She was clear, even at a young age, that God had orchestrated it.

That experience burned into her memory as a defining moment in life because she was certain, even as an adult, that God sent the rabbi who, in turn, prayed she would one day find the Messiah, and she did. Another time the Lord once impressed on her that He had a serious message for her. He spoke to her that she was to meet Him at the end of a pier. Testing him along the way, she heard nothing yet the moment she arrived at the end of the pier, *as He had instructed,* she instantly heard, "You are not to marry Larry." My mother knew God's voice, and she obeyed, leaving that relationship right away. Afterwards she met and married my father; unfortunately, Larry died one year later.

The three of us kids came along and my mother had similar meaningful encounters as we grew up, whether impressions, visions, or dreams, so it was no surprise in 1987 when one of these involved me. Before I actually ended up in prison, God gave me a chance to avoid being arrested in another matter. He used my mother and her obedience saved me from an indictment and prison *that time.*

I received a cryptic message from her on my answering machine. "Meet me for breakfast on the same day, location, and time we met the last time. It's important."

What the heck is going on? Warning bells were going off but I ignored the serious implications, and didn't see God trying to get my attention. Instead on the specified day, I parked my car away from the restaurant to make sure I wasn't followed, and headed inside. When I arrived for breakfast, Mom was sitting in the back booth with a menu covering her face. I recognized her by her wrist watch.

As usual, she wasted no time. "David, God gave me a dream two days ago. There's a tanned man with blonde hair who wears a gold medallion around his neck. He drives a car like that one." She pointed to a Porsche 911 parked in front of the restaurant. "Except his is brown with California plates. He's about to be arrested by federal agents for cocaine trafficking, and he's going to tell on everyone in exchange for his freedom." My stomach contracted, and I just stared at her.

"Do you know anyone like that?"

"Maybe," I replied in a non-committal manner. I knew exactly who he was, and everything she said was accurate. I left after breakfast and at a stoplight he pulled up next to me in the brown Porsche.

He held up his pager and said, "Let's get together and do some business." I smiled outwardly and waved. He drove off and because of Mom's warning dream, I never made that phone call. Two weeks later he was arrested with 99 pounds of cocaine. It was the largest drug arrest in Kansas City up to that time, and he told on everyone he'd sold drugs with, in exchange for a sentence reduction. He served just two years. Because I heeded my mom's warning, I avoided going to jail. After the smoke had cleared, I recruited the cocaine dealer's leftover clientele, expanding my market share.

Hmmm, maybe God was trying to get my attention on that deal, so I would head in another direction, and I would have avoided getting sent to prison now.

I remembered one of my mom's favorite Scriptures, where Jesus said, **"My sheep hear my voice, and I know them, and they follow me"**[3] (John 10:27). Hearing from God was common to her throughout her life and she did follow Him. Even so, I could only imagine her reaction to having the dream that she was to have another child, and now that child was in prison. When she told my father of her dream and the confirmation, at first, he rejected the idea because that wasn't their plan, but then he agreed knowing how accurately she heard from God. Mom became pregnant with me shortly after that.

While pregnant, the Holy Spirit spoke again. This time, He directed them to move the family over a thousand miles from Arizona to Missouri, much to

---

3   My ability to hear the Lord in dreams, visions, etc. obviously has little to do with my obedience; God graciously gave this gift through my family's bloodline. I believe in this current season God is pouring out His Spirit on all flesh, just as He promised in Acts 2:17-18, and you can hear His voice. To learn more, I encourage you to read an e-book entitled, "25 Biblical Ways You Can Hear from God", at www.HearingGod25Ways.com (also available on Kindle).

their dismay. Missouri? Why would we want to live in Missouri? Years later, around the dining room table, we would joke about the Lord sending them off to the extreme summers and bone-chilling winters in *"Mis-ery."* It was a monumental reckoning as I thought about my birth being initiated by the Lord, not to mention my parent's sacrifices to be obedient.

Our family has a rich heritage in God. How then did God let me end up in this nightmare? None of this made sense.

Mom was born and raised in New York City and Dad in Los Angeles. Dad had been offered a job teaching athletics at Central Missouri State University ⁴ (CMSU) and simultaneously he was offered a job in Southern California where he would make five times what the Missouri job would pay. Dad and Mom prayed, and the prompting from the Holy Spirit never changed. They received God's peace and packed up for Missouri with two children and one in the womb.

They arrived in the small town of Warrensburg, population 9,125, where Dad began teaching at CMSU in May of 1964. I was born later that month and, as I was coming down the birth canal, my mother knew I was a boy, and she consecrated me to the Lord. Dad and Mom agreed to name me David Caleb. David, because Acts 13:22 taught that David was a man after God's own heart, and Caleb because he was one of the only two Israelites who made it from Egypt to the Promised Land (Joshua 14:14). Little did she know that I would end up like Joseph, in prison for many years (Genesis chapters 37-41).

When I was still a baby I came down with double pneumonia, lost a third of my body weight and nearly died. My parents were alarmed and prayed over me, re-dedicating me to the Lord. My health was miraculously restored. Mom always believed I had a destiny in God because of the dream she received and how I was healed during this crisis.

My parents were steadfast in attending church with their three children. Sunday morning services, Wednesday night prayer and testimony meetings, plus summer church retreats and vacation Bible school were part of my upbringing. Stories of David and Goliath, Samson's great strength, Noah's Ark and the big flood, etc. were familiar to me, and I even learned to recognize God's promptings when they came my way. That was about it. I didn't see God as having much bearing on my life at this point.

At age eight I made a profession for Christ with several other friends. We were water baptized the following week and confirmed by the elders. The

---

4   CMSU; now known as University of Central Missouri

confirmation involved the elders laying hands on us and praying to release a spiritual blessing. Something odd happened; the head elder suddenly began to tremble as the spirit of prophecy fell on him. The prophetic word was rare at our church, and the elder added that he'd never had an experience quite like this. He then prophesied about my future, the words bubbling out of his mouth about God's call on my life.

He warned, "Never smoke a cigarette. Don't even put a stick in your mouth and play like you're smoking!"

How strange, I thought, but I respected how serious he was. I understood smoking would lead to addictions and much worse things so I decided to steer clear of this vice. I'd be offered cigarettes many times, but would remember this prophetic cautioning and always decline. When asked why, I would share my warning and the response always seemed to be in agreement. "Weird, but you better stay away from these," or "hey, forget it then," or just "never mind," and they'd leave me alone. I remember one occasion where my response caused a smoker to instantly decide to quit.

One evening in my early twenties, to impress a girl at a bar, I took a cigarette from her hand to light it. I flipped the cigarette into my mouth like I'd seen seasoned smokers do. I briefly inhaled to light the cigarette. With a raised eyebrow, I handed it back to her. She smiled and invited me to sit down. My debonair persona was crushed when I began to cough and gasp for air, like a true amateur. Then I experienced a dizzy feeling that was addictively pleasant. I immediately wanted to take another drag, but the prophetic warning sobered me. I left the bar immediately and renewed my vow never to smoke.

After probing this part of my history, I was clear that somehow God was involved. I was intrigued and mystified. *If I have such a call on my life, how did God let me end up here? Okay,* I admitted, *maybe I was at fault and not God, but I still don't get it.*

Journey Insights

We all have a destiny that God will reveal if we pay attention. Signs are being given to us all the time, but do we recognize them or ignore them? Jesus said that His sheep would hear His voice, but can you hear Him if you don't really know Him?

5

CHILDHOOD REJECTION

Around age nine I got really angry with God. He'd given my mother prophetic dreams, and I got them too. These dreams were usually about "little kid things" i.e. losing a toy, knowing I'd catch a rare butterfly during a school outing, or simple warnings to stay away from certain children who would lead me into trouble. I usually remembered these dreams when it was too late.

Unfortunately, like Joseph, I liked sharing some of the dreams, and it led to ridicule and rejection. Some of my peers intensely disliked me for claiming that God spoke to me. They weren't used to it so it must not be true. After getting burned repeatedly, I was determined to prove my dreams were accurate. My pride was hurt, and I fell headlong into the enemy's trap. **"Pride goes before destruction and a haughty spirit before a fall."** (Proverbs 16:18).

To vindicate myself I told some school kids that the next time I had a serious dream, I would tell them. Before going to bed that night, I asked God to give me something *really* big. Nothing happened that night or the next.

Terese, who was very vocal, often mocked me, "Did God talk to you last night? Tell me my future, dreamer boy!" Matters only got worse and by the third night, I was pretty miserable. I told God that I needed Him to give me a dream about something that the kids would know came from Him. I went to sleep and had a horrible dream about my third-grade teacher, Miss Kerry.

In the dream, Miss Kerry was seriously injured in an automobile accident on a Thursday. The dream indicated we would have a substitute teacher on Friday who didn't seem to know anything about the accident. The next scene was Monday morning, and we had a new male teacher. He announced that Miss Kerry was in the hospital alive, but wouldn't likely be back for the remainder of the school year.

When I woke up, I didn't know what to do. I liked Miss Kerry, and I felt sick to my stomach.[5] Reluctantly, I went to school to face my peers. Terese came running up to the group. "Well dreamer boy," her voice dripped with sarcasm, "did God show you anything about the future?"

---

5   Dreams are often warnings of the enemy's plans (Job 33:14-18). Later I learned that through our prayers, these plans can be thwarted, and God's plans released (Amos 7:1-6; Matthew 16:18-19; Matthew 6:10-11).

I foolishly blurted out, "Actually, I did have a dream last night of something that is about to happen this Thursday." The dream indicated *a* Thursday, but not necessarily *this* Thursday.[6]

Terese rolled her eyes, "Oh, tell us more, David." With mixed emotions, I proceeded to share the dream. The other children were shocked. One visibly shaken girl said, "That's a terrible thing for you to wish on someone."

"I - I don't wish this on her," I stammered. "It's just something that's going to happen. I can't control it."

Several students agreed that at least I should warn her and tell her to be careful driving. Terese chomped on her gum and declared, "His dream won't happen, he's a liar, and by Friday morning we'll all know it!"

Thursday came and I was nervous. I didn't want anything to happen to Miss Kerry and I felt an obligation to warn her. At the close of the school day, I quietly approached her. Staring at my feet, I mumbled, "Miss Kerry, please be extra careful driving tonight."

She sweetly said, "Oh David, I'm always careful when I drive." After I had repeated the warning, more urgently this time, she raised her eyebrows and leaned in closer to me. "David, did someone you know get hurt in a car accident?"

"No, why?" I was confused. She looked in my eyes.

"You seem scared about people driving for some reason." I assured her I wasn't scared, and another teacher entered which ended our conversation.

I felt like I was failing with this dream stuff, even though I still believed. Disgusted and feeling rejected by everyone, I told God I didn't like His dreams, and I wanted them to stop.

The following day I got to school early and was waiting in the classroom when Miss Kerry walked in. It was bittersweet. I was glad she was fine, but my dream looked inaccurate at best, or worse yet, from my wicked imagination.

Dejected I headed to the playground to endure the abuse that I knew awaited me. *Why'd You even give me this dream, God?* I even told Him maybe he allowed me to be tricked by the devil. I was miserable and told God it certainly shouldn't be happening to me, but there was no response. At that point in my life, I'm not sure I even knew how to listen, but, I sure was mad.

---

6 Prophetic words involve three parts: (1) Revelation, (2) Interpretation and (3) Application (and timing). As a child, I didn't realize this, that when God gave dreams He is often looking for someone on the earth to agree with Him in prayer to release His will in Earth as it is in Heaven (Matthew 6:9-10) or contend with Him in prayer to change the outcome (Amos 7:1-5). I learned the importance of writing down dreams and visions, and asking God for each dream's purpose (Habakkuk 2:2-3; Daniel 7:1).

When I walked by the teeter totter, Terese taunted me loudly in front of the other kids. "Well, dreamer boy, Miss Kerry's fine, and this proves you're a liar." She smirked, "Looks like your dreams are from watching too many horror movies!" The laughter of all the students reverberated in my head.

A sweet girl named Abagail told me, "David, I trusted you. I stood up for you. You made me look stupid." I didn't know what to say so I just walked away.

The following Friday Miss Kerry was absent. The principal took us to the gymnasium. Forty-five minutes later we returned to our classroom and a substitute teacher was there. She didn't seem to know anything. "Hello children. I'm Mrs. Foster. I was at home when I received a call from the principal, so I grabbed my purse and came. Miss Kerry will probably return on Monday."

But, Monday morning a Mr. Crossley introduced himself as our new teacher. "Miss Kerry was in a bad car accident last Thursday. She's still in the hospital. She could use your good thoughts and prayers." He cleared his throat and told us, "I'm sure she'll be fine." Several kids stared at me as we were released for recess.

I didn't know if I was I vindicated or if they'd label me a devil, but I couldn't wait to see Terese eat crow. I confidently approached the group and to my shock Terese began spinning my words, "You said she died, and she's not dead!" My jaw dropped in silence. The other kids were confused.

Abagail looked right at Terese, "No, this is how David told us he saw it, and you all know it!" The others nodded and looked back at Terese.

Now on the defensive, she said, "Well, that dream couldn't have come from God because something bad happened. It had to come from the devil!" She pointed her finger at me and hissed, "David's a devil person!"

I had no idea how to defend myself. First I was a liar, and now I was "a devil person." Little did I know, but this was my first encounter with a Jezebel spirit.

As I was walking back to class, Abagail caught up with me, "David, I believe God speaks to you in dreams. Don't worry what *they* say. If you see me in a dream, tell me 'cause I definitely wanna' know." Her words were a ray of light in an otherwise gloomy experience.

That night I told God I still wanted Him to speak to me through dreams as long as they were good. Years later He showed me the life of Joseph and his gift of dreams and interpretations. While Joseph was in prison he accurately interpreted the dreams of the baker and cupbearer; one resulted in a good outcome and the other, a bad outcome. In three days, Pharaoh restored the cupbearer but hanged the baker (Genesis 40:8-22). Through this, I learned that God requires us to deliver His messages, whether blessings or warnings. Usually with a warning message, God also gives a strong word of hope, or a way to lessen the detrimental effect if the person repents. For the messenger, this is often a difficult test, especially when sharing words of admonition, warning, correction, or a call to repentance, and it causes prophetic people to either run to God or from Him.[7]

Journey Insights

Unhealed hurt, rejection and disappointment—plus spiritual gifts that are misunderstood by others or yourself—can send you in the wrong direction. The choice is running to God for healing through the many steps we journey in this lifelong process or running away from Him. Where are you in this process?

---

7   I later learned that most of God's prophetically gifted servants were ostracized, imprisoned, beaten and even stoned to death for speaking His message. Rejection is part of the two-fold cup: the cup of the anointing and the cup of suffering. The real litmus test of our commitment to God is whether we find ourselves running to God or from Him through the many steps we journey in this lifelong process.

6

LEARNING TO OBEY GOD

I was still trying to figure out how I ended up in prison. As a young boy I knew God had a call on my life and He was communicating with me, but I wasn't really interested. It didn't occur to me that He was trying to help me, and the ridicule and rejection left me feeling like I had to fend for myself.

At age 11, while attending church camp, I skipped out and hid in my cabin. I was happy to be free from the enslavement of another dreary service. The Holy Spirit convicted me with a clear message to attend, but I didn't care.

"No way am I going. Too boring."

What happened next was chilling. Within seconds of my decision, a paralyzing darkness descended, so thick and tangible it seemed to suck the oxygen from the room. I could see the sun shining outside, but the light wouldn't penetrate my cabin and I sensed a frightening evil presence. Panicked, I cried out, "Save me, Lord!"

At first, nothing changed. I fell on my knees. "God, I promise I'll go to the service and I won't miss another one all week!" With this, the horrid darkness departed. The sun shone through the windows again, and once again I felt happy, even joyful.[8] I knew God had answered my prayer.

Quickly exiting the cabin, I ran toward the service. Looking up, I noticed it was a perfect day.

There's not a cloud in the sky. I get it, God. You're warning me and I'm going to obey You!

This was a defining moment in my life, receiving a warning, hearing, and obeying. I didn't miss a single service the rest of the week. But all these years later, as I sat in my prison cell contemplating how I'd made that decision to obey, I thought how unfortunate that the obedience lesson didn't stick. *If it had, I bet I could have avoided prison,* I thought.

It was 1975 and for Christmas vacation, my parents decided to go to an exclusive aquatic resort in Mexico. It was a great vacation, I ate all kinds of new foods, hung out with lots of Spanish-speaking Mexican kids, and played

---

8   Later my mother showed me a passage in Exodus 10:21 (NIV), **"Then the LORD said to Moses, 'Stretch out your hand toward the sky so that darkness will spread over Egypt-- darkness that can be felt'."**

in the natural hot springs and mineral pools. Surprisingly, I picked up the language rapidly during this 10-day hiatus.

The following summer my parents received an unexpected call from the father of one of the children I met at the resort. In broken English, Alberto Valdez asked my parents to send me to his home outside of Mexico City for two weeks. All my expenses upon arrival would be paid. We would only have to pay for airfare. My mother told my father it would be crazy to let me go to Mexico and stay with a family they hardly knew. My parents politely thanked Mr. Valdez for his generous offer but declined. Kidnapping and child trafficking was far less common then, but it was still clearly a legitimate concern!

Later, when my mother prayed, the Holy Spirit showed her that it was His will that I go and promised that I'd be safe. She arose from prayer, carefully pondering these words. After all, her very strong Jewish mother's voice said *no*, but the Holy Spirit said *yes*. She obeyed, deciding if Dad agreed, I was to go. Then she realized that at age 11, I could travel for half fare. This was just good business sense to her. I've learned over the years that God has different ways to convince each of us to obey. Based on past experiences my dad knew my mom heard from Heaven, so he agreed.

Two weeks later, just before my 12th birthday, I was boarding my first airplane flight alone, flying coach to Dallas, then to Mexico City -- El Ciudad de Mexico. Before we took off, one of the attendants bumped me to first class to watch out for me. Midway through the flight she returned from the flight cabin and told me the captain wanted to see me. I choked, "What'd I do?"

She chuckled, "Nothing. Have you ever seen a cockpit?" Relieved, I told her about being in my dad's Cessna 172, but never in a big jet like this 727. "Well, you're about to!"

I jumped up and shouted, "Cool!"

When I entered the cockpit, the captain welcomed me, and the co-pilot gave me his seat. (This was 1975 and safety procedures were far less stringent.) The captain showed me all the buttons, gauges, toggle switches, etc. He looked at me with a smile. "Do you want me to show you how I fly this bird?"

Thrilled, all I could think to answer was, "Yeah!" He explained a few things then banked the plane to the right and the left. I got nervous when I saw a giant white cloud ahead. "What about that cloud?"

"We're going to fly right through it." Not wanting to object, I still had to double check.

"Is it safe?"

"Usually, unless it's a storm cloud." He smiled at me. "Let's find out."

We entered the cloud and everything turned white for a couple of seconds, then became clear again.

"Cool, what about that cloud?" He navigated through it too, and the same thing happened. I'd never experienced anything like this. When the captain asked me if I wanted to try and fly the plane, I gulped.

"But I don't know how to fly." That didn't faze him. He promised to make it simple and reassured me by putting his hand on my shoulder.

"Don't worry. We'll turn on autopilot first to make sure everyone is safe." Then he directed my hand to a switch between the two seats.

"Watch this." He slowly turned it to the left, and the plane banked to the left, then to the center and the plane evened out and then he banked right and straightened out the plane a second time.

"Now, you try it." I was a little nervous, but when he told me the autopilot would keep everything safe I took his words to mean that I wouldn't be making any difference in the plane's flight. I grabbed that switch and turned it hard to the right. Much to my surprise, the plane banked sharply! The pilot had to grab my hand to straighten things out! Then, he quietly said, "Not so hard son. Try it again and gently this time." Gradually I turned the plane to the left, evened it out, and banked it to the right and back to center. "You're going to make a good co-pilot someday." I smiled. My dad was a pilot and sometimes took us on small four seater plane flights. The thought of one day flying like Dad delighted me.

When I saw a cloud ahead, I asked, "Can I fly through that?" He nodded and pointed toward the large cloud approaching our right.

"Point the nose of the plane toward that big one, my junior pilot!" Being overly cautious I under-banked the plane. Most of the cloud passed by us on our right. I was disappointed. The captain just said, "Don't worry about it, try again."

This time, I lined up the plane and everything became white. I blurted out, "Is this what Heaven's like?" The captain grinned.

"I don't know, but I'm looking forward to finding out when I get there." The co-pilot returned and said some of the passengers were complaining about the jerky ride. He'd assured them that everything was okay, and he'd head back to the cockpit to help the captain out. The co-pilot stared at the captain shaking his head and then politely asked me for his seat. I thanked them and then exited the cockpit. I thanked the flight attendant for all the first class treatment. What a memorable experience for a kid my age!

When the captain announced, "Welcome to Mexico City," the flight attendant told me to wait and then escorted me through customs with the crew. Mr. Valdez and his three boys were there to greet me. The flight attendant compared Mr. Valdez's letter of confirmation to hers, then smiled and said, "Mr. Valdez, you take good care of my friend David!"

I had no idea at the time but in retrospect I saw that God was instilling in me a lesson I would deeply need later in life. God wanted me to be confident in Him, and to realize that He cares for and highly favors His children.

Journey Insights

Evil spiritual forces are very real and come in different forms and situations to lead us down a bad path. When we cry out and repent to God, He hears us. Some opportunities come to us once in a lifetime, but we have to recognize them and set aside our fears. What fears do you need to face that could alter the course of your destiny?

7

MEXICO

The Valdez family was hospitable, friendly and accommodating. I liked that. There were some things that were very different from my lifestyle. For instance, they never went or took me to a church service, instead, we went to the martial arts and Judo studio on Saturday morning. Mr. Valdez announced, "This is our church for the week."

Being a puny kid, I liked these classes because they taught me some defense against bigger kids. The first class, the more experienced kids tossed me around the mat like a sack of potatoes. I kept getting back up. Eventually, with the instructor's guidance, I learned to toss around a few of the others that were my size. It was a start and a much-needed confidence builder. This weekly class helped establish an early understanding for wrestling, which would come in handy later in life.

On Sunday morning, sleeping in appeared to be the family tradition. Everyone was very nice, but none of them expressed much interest in God. I also noticed Mr. Valdez had unusual business practices, contrary to anything I understood. He appeared to have partial ownership of a few gas stations but never actually worked there. One morning while his wife, Lachina, was serving us breakfast I asked Mr. Valdez why he never seemed to work. He looked offended, and as Lachina and he exchanged glances, they remained silent.

Is this a normal thing to do down here? Something seems weird. Finally, he broke the silence, telling me he was on vacation. Puzzled, I innocently kept pushing, "Oh, when do you go back to work?" He said that he worked when people called him. His wife just looked at me like I shouldn't be asking such questions. Being forthright and inquisitive was my nature, and I wondered about many things I experienced.

The Valdez' family lived in an upper-middle class neighborhood, and everyone in the area seemed to know and respect them. Mr. Valdez received phone calls and would rush out the door to meet other business people at various times of the day. He seemed stressed at times from financial problems and then the following day he would seem to be on top of the world again. He'd be out of money one moment and have a pocket full of cash the next.

One morning Lachina gave me one peso (the equivalent of about eight cents) with instructions to go buy tortillas. The woman at the tortilla stand charged me "un peso, veinte centavos" (one peso and twenty centavos). I handed her the peso. Though she adamantly told me, "Veinte centavos mas," (twenty centavos more), I stood my ground because I knew that I was correct. She was indignant and demanded full payment. I didn't understand everything she was saying, but I knew I wasn't going to let her overcharge the "stupid American." Everyone waiting in line fell silent. The woman flailed her arms, told me the price was *un peso veinte centavos,* and she didn't need my business.

I told her that I wasn't just some estupido gabacho del Estados Unidos (the stupid white boy from the U.S.), pero Mexicano en mi Corazon (but Mexican in my heart) and I called her "tramposa" (swindler). Fire shot through her eyes at my very public accusation in front of the neighborhood mothers who witnessed our interchange. As she grabbed the tortillas from my hand and ordered me never to come back, I heard her ask, "Whose boy is this anyway?" One of the women in the line told her that I was Lachina's guest.

When she realized that no one had informed Lachina that the price for tortillas had increased earlier this week, she went from hot anger to sidesplitting laughter. She looked at me with a twinkle in her eyes, smiling from ear to ear. She handed me back the tortillas, patted me on the head and told me to "Take the tortillas de gratis hoy (for free today)." Everyone in line chuckled.

I returned to the Valdez' home and handed Lachina the peso and the tortillas. Because of my limited Spanish, I still didn't fully understand what happened at the tortilla stand and Lachina was having difficulty understanding me. She wanted to make certain the Valdez name had not been damaged because I didn't pay for the tortillas but rather inadvertently stole them. She walked with me back to the tortilla stand.

About 100 feet from the stand a conversation ensued in Spanish between the tortilla lady and Lachina. Within a few seconds, everyone in line was laughing again. Lachina took "un peso, veinte centavos" from her purse. The tortilla lady refused, saying that the morning's experience not only gave her a much-needed laugh but also clarified the price increase for everyone in the neighborhood. She smiled at me and said in broken English, "Mijo (my son), the tortillas are free para ti (for you) today. But tomorrow, *un peso veinte centavos!"*

Everyone hooted, including Lachina, and we returned to eat breakfast with the rest of the family. Even from a very young age, I had a fascination with finances, and at times seemed over-confident in my understanding how to make and manage money. This time was no different and I was actually proud that I had stood up to the lady over the money issue. Soon after, Mrs. Valdez asked me in broken English if I wanted to extend my visit for another few weeks with their family. I responded, "I miss my Mom and Dad."

Trying to make the situation better, she said, "Well, you can go home later this week if you want, or we can all go to Acapulco for a week." I thought about it and decided to ask my parents. I told Mom about the opportunity. She asked a few questions to make sure this was something I wanted to do, then said she'd talk to my father. Later that evening my parents called back and agreed to let me stay for another two weeks.

After the month-long summer vacation, Mr. Valdez took me to the airport, and I returned home. The Spanish language slowly evaporated from my memory, but my life experience in Mexico would later prove to be of significant value. I've come to realize that God does everything with divine purpose even though we may be totally oblivious to it at the time. He graced me with this full submersion experience in Mexico with a Latino family. It helped to nurture an appreciation for this wonderful culture, its people, their familial values, and expressive language. It later proved helpful in prison and beyond enabling me to communicate better God's love and the journey to freedom with Latinos.

Later in international business classes, I drew on this experience with the Latino culture. Although there were some puzzling things about the Valdez family, I was most impressed by their love and respect for family. I actually felt an odd kinship to Alberto Valdez and the way he did business. In his case, it seemed questionable. In my case, it was just flat out wrong.

By age 12 my church experience was so dry that I began to look for other things to fill the void in my soul. To compound matters, my thoughts now included another country and the new culture I'd experienced. When I shared with my school friends how the captain of the 727 allowed to me to fly the jet, they just said, "Yeah right!" Once again I wasn't believed, which was often the pattern, and their rejection hurt.

Whether my friends didn't believe me, or I was bullied, I searched for acceptance and satisfaction, but could find neither. Although I experienced many amazing adventures, rejection was a familiar theme. I was always picked next to last for school sports activities. The only student picked after me was physically disabled. I never seemed to be good at basketball, football or softball. I didn't have good hand-eye coordination or timing, and it was particularly embarrassing to be the only kid who could "strike out" in kickball. How does one miss a ball the size of home plate three times in a row? It was demoralizing.

We had a professional size trampoline in our front yard, and it was there I realized I had some physical skill. I seemed to do well at swimming, diving, trampoline, and gymnastics thanks to inheriting some of Dad's genes and his ability to focus. My dad taught athletics at the local University, and he was the swimming and diving coach. He had been a four-year letterman at the University of Southern California (USC) with a full ride scholarship, placing second at Nationals on the three-meter diving board his senior year in 1950.

He would go on to win more than 160 national and international titles, be featured in Sport's Illustrated and Faces in the Crowd, and become inducted into the International Swimming and Diving Hall of Fame. By age 90 he would be the oldest living diver still competing 10-meter tower (32 feet). His brother Ara won the National Floor Exercise Championship two years in a row during his junior and senior years at USC. Our cousin would become the Armenian Olympics champion in several events. Their success wasn't easy to live up to and although later in life I was able to excel in several sports, at the time I was frustrated.

Within our small town school at Warrensburg, there was no swimming, diving or gymnastics offered for students. I was like a beached starfish, unable to find my niche in sports, and never fit in. During these pre-teen and early teen years I rode my bicycle to the university and was allowed to use the gymnastics equipment along with the college gymnastics team. Unfortunately, due to my age, I never fit in there either and so I limped along socially. Purpose and significance seemed to evade me, but God had a plan in all this that would unfold later.

Journey Insights

We search for significance and rejection hurts. Hurtful experiences through other influences or people can cripple our identity of who we are in Christ. When we seek God for our identity and purpose, He works all things together for good in our lives. Do you see yourself through God's eyes, or eyes from the painful experiences of the past? The Lord wants to heal your identity.

8

THE ARAB WORLD

When I was three, Adiba Hadad came from Kuwait to the United States as a young college student to attend Central Missouri State University. Dad first met him on campus. When he discovered Adiba's Middle-Eastern background, he told my mother, who comes from a Jewish family bloodline. She immediately invited him to dine at our home, the first of what became numerous, delicious middle-eastern feasts that she prepared.

My parents offered our basement apartment for Adiba to rent his final two years of school. Until Adiba's graduation a few years later, he and my mother debated tirelessly about the 4,000-year-old Arab/Israeli conflict. They would "argue" politics for hours and then we would eat. Adiba would pray over his food in Arabic to Allah and my parents prayed in the Name of Jesus.

Adiba enjoyed my mother's personality and New York outspokenness. She said things to Adiba that many women in his nation weren't allowed to speak to men. We later learned and experienced his wife enjoying the same type of freedom to speak her mind. In some Muslim cultures, women are often taught to submit to men in what can be perceived by some Americans as demeaning. Women in some cases are even thought of as property, similar to cattle. So, for my Jewish mother to speak in such a direct manner to Adiba shocked him at times, yet he loved her for it. Mom was older than Adiba and was in some ways like a mother to him. He also treasured her allowing him to cook the food of his homeland as it was culturally unacceptable for a man to cook in his country at that time.

He loved calling me his "little Daoud," (Arabic for David) and he seemed a type of godfather to me. He returned to Kuwait and over time became a wealthy business person. When I was 15, we received an incredible invitation. Adiba wanted to extend his appreciation to our family, and introduce us to his culture and nation, so he sent us plane tickets to Kuwait for a 10-day fully paid, first class vacation. My brother and sister were living on their own now, so Adiba sent tickets for just the three of us. Adiba and his Kuwaiti wife had three children.

We flew to Kuwait on a 747 in mid-December 1979. Upon arrival, we headed toward Customs, but before it was our turn we noticed a man who looked like Adiba. He waved at the Customs officers. As it turned out, it was Adiba's brother, who was head of the Customs Department for the entire country of Kuwait. At Adiba's request, he greeted us at the gate, ordered his officers to carry our luggage to his office and served us Turkish coffee at four o'clock in the morning.

Adiba was also there to greet us. He wore what looked like a dress (called a "dish-da-sha") and on his head he had a turban called a "ghu-tra." Everyone seemed to be wearing this attire, looking like something out of the movies, but these people weren't actors! Some of the dishdashas glimmered in the light and I asked Adiba about it. "That is the silver, gold and platinum threads woven through the materials."

"It's not real gold, right?"

He assured me, "Oh yes, 18 to 22 kt. gold in most cases. It is a form of status, like a Rolex watch, or similar to you wearing Nike tennis shoes while other children wear Keds." The thought of having real gold woven into my clothing seemed like an extremely opulent use of money. I thought of all kinds of other things for which that money could be spent. Little did I know that this was only the beginning of the opulence the Kuwaitis would demonstrate daily while we visited this oil-rich land of sand, salt-water, and Muslim Arabic culture.

I was 15 and it was here I was first introduced to earthly riches. Kuwait was in the "Golden Era" of prosperity driven primarily by oil - and my fascination with wealth grew exponentially. Later I would see that one of the purposes God created me for was to learn, understand, and help teach others how to produce wealth to meet the needs of others. At the time, however, all I knew was I liked the lavish affluence. Kuwait had two classes of people, the rich and those who served them. It's difficult to become a Kuwaiti citizen, but there are benefits. Police rarely pull you over for speeding and the government provides special loans as capital to start businesses, invest in new businesses, and to play the stock market. In 1979, Kuwait was the richest per capita income country in the world, and Kuwaiti citizens were given vast opportunities by the government to make money.

Kuwait is a nation-state covered by socialized medicine, meaning that all medical bills for Kuwaitis and foreigners are covered by the government. If a person landed in Kuwait and suffered a heart attack, their bills would be paid by the government, including their hospital stay, surgery, and even a heart transplant. Dental work is also covered. I found this very interesting as a 15 year old. In fact, I was enthralled by the wealth and opulence.

We discovered that Adiba owned several very lavish homes, and he was building another in a more affluent area. Land at that time cost half a million dollars per lot and Adiba and his friends were all purchasing double lots. One of Adiba's homes had a swimming pool made of marble on the ground floor. He rented this home to a couple from the U.S. Embassy. To put things into perspective, our entire home in Warrensburg, including our lot, was worth about $35,000.

Adiba took us directly from the airport to our hotel. It was a small hotel but elegantly dressed out in marble from floor to ceiling. Arriving at 5:00 a.m., the front clerk was waiting for us and immediately loaded our belongings into the elevator. A special key was necessary for each of the three floors on the elevator. He let us in and gave us each a key to access the third floor. We asked if these keys would also open the door to our room. He laughed and said, "This is the door to your room." We didn't fully understand that the whole floor was our hotel room! When the elevator doors opened, we saw a beautiful house full of flowers and magnificent baskets of fresh fruit waiting for us on the dining room table. I marveled at how Adiba treated us like royalty the entire vacation, even providing a chauffeured vehicle at our disposal.

Being raised in a middle-income family from a small town in the Midwest, this was quite an impacting experience. It was my first taste of the life of luxury, and I liked it. This seed would later prove to be the breeding ground for the adversary of my soul to seek the same types of luxuries, but the wrong way. As the days of vacation continued I would see opulence beyond my imagination.

One of Adiba's friends invited us to a party. His home was huge and had several floors. On the ground floor, there were three living rooms, each with a different décor, Traditional Kuwaiti, Ancient-Chinese, and Contemporary-American. Servants were available by simply ringing a bell. Many of the Kuwaiti wives would regularly "fly the Concord" with their children to London for the day, returning with bags and bundles of purchases from the finest stores in England. It was common for them to order catered food flown in from around the world for their parties a couple of times a month. Many of the Kuwaitis we met seemed to have nothing but time on their hands to experience all the finer things in life along with what appeared to be inexhaustible bank accounts.

It was at this time that I was exposed, full submersion, to Muslim culture in this wealthy nation. On the side of the road, five times a day, the majority of vehicles would pull over and businessmen wearing dishdashas and ghutras bowed toward Mecca and prayed on ornate prayer rugs. We were very careful not to share with anyone that my mother was of Jewish bloodline. When Adiba's Kuwaiti friends discovered that we were from the United States, they began having expensive catered dinner parties for us each night. Specialty foods were flown in from around the world, there was live music, and several of Kuwait's elite attended. Adiba told these people that we were VIPs from the University where he graduated. He painted a picture of my dad as a special professor with great expertise in his field and that the Kuwaiti University was hoping to hire him to train their new Olympic Diving Team.

We were welcomed with open arms by everyone. At one party, however, a finely-dressed, attractive, and well-educated woman approached my mother, inquiring about her nationality. I had an uneasy feeling. My mother lied to her, which was uncharacteristic. She carefully constructed her answer -- she was part Russian and educated in England before coming to the United States where she married my father, who is full-blooded Armenian. The portion about Dad was true. As the woman looked across the room at my father, she seemed appeased, and my mother politely ended the conversation.

My mother whispered, "David, be very careful with that woman. Don't tell her I'm Jewish or that you are Jewish by bloodline."

Minutes later, this same woman introduced herself to me. She announced that she was from Palestine-Israel and then asked me what nationality I was. I told her I was American. Pressing further, she asked, "I know you are from the United States, but what is your nation of origin?" To say I was uncomfortable would be an understatement. A dark feeling enveloped me, similar to what I'd encountered as an 11 year old inside my cabin at church camp. Everyone else in Kuwait was so nice to us, but this woman's intentions seemed evil. She was obviously on the hunt for something which I couldn't figure out.

Who is this woman? I wondered. *What does she want?*

I told her a second time, "I am an American."

She obviously wasn't satisfied and continued with her interrogation. "Where did you attend school?"

When I told her the United States, her deliberately slow and sinister response was eerie. "Yes, but what nationality, I mean, you have an accent when you speak. Where were your parents born originally?"

Remembering my mother's word of caution, I smiled politely and lied, "Because of my father's job at the University, we sometimes travel. I went to school in England for one year, my father was from Armenia originally, and my mother's family was from England."

This seemed to satisfy her momentarily but she wasn't finished. For the third time, she ominously mentioned that I had "another blood" in me that she couldn't quite determine.

My reply was mannerly and polite. "I'm not sure what you mean. You'll have to speak with my mother who knows better than me." I began to look for my mom to alert her.

I saw this woman go to a room where many of the adults were getting drinks from the bar and lounging around. (Although Kuwait is a "dry state" the alcohol flowed like water at almost every party.) Neither of my parents were drinkers and they avoided the bar area. My mother conveniently sidestepped the woman the remainder of the evening.

We left the party early and I told my mother about the uneasiness I experienced. "David, the Holy Spirit told me that woman is a member of the Palestinian Liberation Organization. She would love to have us killed right here if she could." I was startled. Adiba and his close friends weren't like her. Adiba's best friend, Diya, who owned the majority of the photography studios in the Middle East, graciously invited us to his lavish home the night before and was aware of my mother's Jewish background. He didn't have any problems with and certainly no personal hatred toward Jewish people.

Years later I would learn more about the Palestinian/Israeli conflict and the Five Commitment Levels of Islam. Similar to deepening commitment levels in Christianity, where at the most committed level a person is willing to *die for Jesus*. The most committed level in Islam is when a Muslim is willing to *kill for Allah*. At the time, to me it felt like this woman harbored a loathsome hatred for anyone who isn't a Muslim and especially toward Jews, and would be willing to have us killed or kill us herself. My fascination with the extreme wealth was tempered by a growing understanding of the abhorrence for Jews that some felt in this part of the world.

On the way home, my mother communicated to Adiba that she wanted to visit her homeland, Israel. Although he loved and respected our family, Adiba was not supportive. His countenance changed in a subtle way. He told my mother that because he was an Arab Muslim, he couldn't pay our way to Israel, but if we wanted to visit any Arab countries he would help.

Mom didn't relent and Adiba compromised by paying our way to Jordan. From there we were on our own financially. From the minute we left Kuwait, we went from first-class living on someone else's tab to second-class tourist living out of our own pockets. Later in life, I was grateful to have experienced the Israeli culture and to walk where Jesus walked. At the time, although

I enjoyed the visit, I was acutely aware of no longer reveling in first-rate treatment.

As an adult, I learned more about Adiba's home country. Kuwait was invaded by Iraq in 1990, just over 10 years after we visited. Over half the citizens fled the country and most Kuwaiti families at the time lost family members to torture and execution. It was an unbearable time with so much loss including the looting of food, equipment, and supplies from schools, businesses, stores and hospitals. Men between the ages of 15 and 40 were forced to join the Iraqi military, the lack of medical care for Kuwait's ill and wounded was atrocious, and the arbitrary arrest and murder of Kuwaitis was rampant. Adiba told my parents that the Iraqis beheaded many Kuwaiti men on a single rock not far from his home. Thankfully, Adiba and his family were saved from that horror. Interestingly enough it was an American-led coalition that saved the Kuwaitis from the invasion by Saddam Hussein and Iraq.

At 15 years old, I'd become enthralled by immense wealth. I liked it. I embraced it. I wanted it. I was intrigued that there had to be a way to live like this. Thinking back years later, from my prison cell at Leavenworth, I started getting a sense of the temptations taking root as a 15-year-old that would eventually urge me to take a doomed jet ride that was heading for a crash. My disdain for being rejected, seeing the wonders of the world, and experiencing the power of incredible wealth were all seeds being planted that would influence future decisions.

Journey Insights

The seeds of being rejected by my peers, yet treated as royalty and living in luxury would later prove to be the breeding ground for the enemy of my soul to set a trap later in my life. I wanted the same types of luxuries, but would seek them the wrong way. What types of seeds have been planted in your life that are taking you down the wrong path?

9

ISRAEL

We flew to Jordan first. The old airport at that time was filthy. Arabs leading two or three goats on ropes through the airport was commonplace. People that looked like they hadn't showered in weeks were everywhere. It was hot and sticky, dust was rampant, and there was a certain angst among the people. We waited for what seemed like an eternity at customs only to be harassed by the officers as they looked through our luggage. They even closed our suitcases on some of our clothing. They seemed to want a bribe to expedite us through their checklist. We just waited patiently. Finally, we were released from customs.

We immediately got into a cab and headed toward the bus station. The cab driver spoke broken English and drove like a New Yorker. He almost hit some animals crossing the roads. Instead of slowing down he just honked his horn, drove into the herds, around them, on the shoulder of the road, or wherever he could to get us closer to our destination. Driving this way seemed normal to him but as passengers, we were terrified. It gave us the same anxiety we felt at the airport.

Finally, we arrived just in time to catch a bus going to Israel. Dad was shelling out money for this and for that, and all the native Arabs here seemed to love U.S. dollars. On the bus from Jordan to Israel, the ride seemed like it would never end. Then we saw it, what my mother referred to as "the beautiful land of Israel." What I witnessed looked more like a military zone! The landscape was barren at best.

What beauty could she see in this? Barbed wire, row after row, covered the border. A dozen or so 'slow down fences' were strategically placed to stop potential terrorists on the hillside. Security was the highest of any place I'd imagined or witnessed, including what I'd seen on television. The bus ride had taken another 45 minutes before we arrived for check-in at Israeli customs.

The Israeli Defense Forces (IDF) were present everywhere. We waited in line and then an IDF officer asked me to remove my dress shoes. I remembered the movie *The Ten Commandments*. God told Moses to "take off his shoes because he was standing on holy ground." I quickly surmised my present situation was clearly different than Moses'.

The officer took my shoes and ran them through a screening machine to check for weapons, explosives, and drugs. I thought how fortunate I was to live in the United States, free from fear of Islamic terrorists and maximum-security airports. Little did I know that less than 25 years later Islamic terrorists and Homeland Security would be in our country with similar actions. At the time, however, what I witnessed was confusing. *We are friends of Israel, not your enemies,* I thought. *We're Americans.*

Our passports, however, indicated we had just come from two Arab countries, Kuwait, and Jordan. We were pointedly asked what business we had while in Kuwait. My dad answered for us, telling them he was a college teacher and that we were vacationing there. Then my mother broke into the conversation telling the officer that this was her third time in Israel. "I'm Jewish and I'm from New York City." She looked directly into the eyes of the woman officer who had just walked up to assist, and that woman looked deeply back into my mother's eyes.

She then looked briefly at my father and me, smiled warmly, and said, "Shalom. This is the Israeli greeting for peace that is often used to communicate hello, goodbye and everything in-between." She then welcomed us to Israel in English. They politely and neatly closed our suitcases and quickly shuffled us through customs.

Later, after 9/11 and the addition of Homeland Security, I would remember this experience. It caused me to understand why the Israelis would remain light years ahead of us in fighting terrorism. They use trained people looking into the eyes of people to determine intentions, in addition to state of the art technology.

Arriving at our hotel in Tel Aviv for our brief 24-hour stay in the Holy Land, I was ready for a quick bathroom break and a much-needed nap. Something I ate in Jordan from a street vendor didn't agree with me. The first thing I noticed different about the hotel bathroom was the toilet paper. The color was an ugly green, and the paper was uncomfortably coarse. It felt like sandpaper. I asked my mother if she would call down to the front desk and get some replacement toilet paper because obviously someone had made a mistake.

"What's wrong with it?" she asked. I told her. She laughed and said, "That's the way they make it in Israel. Things are very expensive here, and they cut costs wherever they can. Just grin and bear it for the next 24 hours."

"If I'd known this" I replied, "I would have brought a couple of rolls of Kuwaiti toilet paper." How easily I had grown accustomed to the finer things in Kuwait, including their toilet paper.

We took an hour nap and then went to grab a bite to eat in the hotel restaurant. The next day we went to Jerusalem. My father wanted to go to the Armenian Orthodox Church, the original denomination of his ancestors. He told me that Armenia was the first fully Christian nation in the world. In Jerusalem, we found the Armenian Orthodox church. Inside it was like an ancient mausoleum, cold and almost a little creepy to me. Statues of saints were everywhere. An Orthodox priest speaking in English greeted us. My father spoke to him in Armenian, and he immediately welcomed us in and asked what he could do for us. My father switched back to his primary language, English, and explained that we were in Israel for only 24 hours and wanted a brief tour of Jerusalem.

The priest immediately locked up his office and took us for a quick tour of the famous sites pointing out various high points. We went to the Shroud of Turin and saw the alleged burial site of Jesus before his resurrection. It seemed commercialized to me. My mother said she wanted to visit the Wailing Wall. This wasn't her first time in Israel, and she knew her way around. We thanked the priest, my dad made a small cash donation to the church, and the priest returned to his parish.

Upon arriving at the famous Wailing Wall, Rabbis in black hats and wearing yarmulkes, the Jewish religious head coverings, were everywhere. Some Rabbis were walking around with open prayer books and others were sitting and discussing the Torah. I even noticed some answering questions from tourists. The most intense Rabbis, however, were swaying back and forth, loudly reciting Jewish prayers in front of the wall. I asked my mother why they rocked. She said that was referred to as "davening" which some Jews do when they pray.

The three of us agreed to meet in half an hour, and we split up. I approached one of the rabbis praying at the men's section of the wall. His head was covered with a blue and white prayer shawl, and as he finished his prayers, he closed his book and uncovered his head. Noticing me standing next to him he looked at me and kindly said, "Shalom." I replied in kind and then marveled as he immediately began speaking fluent Hebrew. When I explained that I didn't understand him, and I was an American, he immediately switched to English and asked why a good Jewish boy like me didn't speak Hebrew. I couldn't think of a good answer, so instead I told him that my mother is Jewish, and my father is Armenian.

He patiently responded, "If your mother is Jewish, the children are Jewish. You're a Jew. You need to learn Hebrew!" He then asked me if I'd ever been bar mitzvah'd.

"No." He looked at me with what seemed like disgust and wasn't the least bit cautious as he chastised our family.

"Shame on your parents; yes, both of them! You need to be bar mitzvah'd'; you are of age." Intrigued and taking it all in, I thanked him for his concern. He asked me what I was asking God for at the Wailing Wall.

I told him, "Nothing really, we just came to see it."

He didn't mince words as he insisted, "Nonsense! No one, especially a Jew, should come all the way from the United States to Israel's Wailing Wall without asking God for something special. He pulled a piece of paper and a pencil from his black coat and said, "Here son, write down a prayer on this piece of paper and put it in a crack in the wall. God will answer. I guarantee it!"

I seriously thought about it, then inquired, "What should I ask for?"

The rabbi didn't hesitate, "If you are really wise you will ask something for someone else, and God will answer your prayer for them and give you a blessing." I thought for a moment and then wrote down a prayer asking for long life and good health for my mom and dad.

He told me to fold it up and wedge it into a crack in the wall. The wall was full of papers like these, different colors and various sizes. I located an available crack, wedged in the paper and turned to him. Suddenly a wind blew in and my paper fell out of the wall.

"The devil is fighting your prayer. Pick up the paper and place it back in the wall in a more secure spot." I found a spot up higher, and it stayed. I don't know if I bought the idea that the devil was involved in any way in my life, but I did feel an unusual peace flood over my soul. I somehow knew in my heart that my parents would live a long life with health from God. The old rabbi smiled, patted me on the head, then rested his hand on my head speaking a blessing over me in English and Hebrew. As he turned to walk off he affectionately reminded me, "Now, get yourself Bar Mitzvah'd." Someone bumped me from behind, I turned briefly, and then turned back, the old rabbi was gone.

I joined my parents, and we walked around Jerusalem until late in the afternoon, purchased handmade souvenirs from Jewish vendors, and ate Israeli food. Our entire time in Jerusalem, I experienced a supernatural peace that to this day is difficult to describe. I asked my mom about this and affirming my feelings she said, "Israel is a very dangerous place, but God's Shalom (peace) protects the people from those who want to do the Jewish people harm."

She explained that Jerusalem means the City of Peace. She also told me that Jesus, Yeshua, is the Jewish Messiah and is called the Prince of Peace. He protects this city even though most Jews don't yet realize that Jesus is their Messiah and the One protecting them. Mom quoted from the book of Psalms 121:4, **"He will not allow your foot to be moved; He who keeps you will not slumber. Behold, He who keeps Israel shall neither slumber nor sleep."** She went on to say, "This is the reason you're feeling the peace of God in His city." We left Israel to return to Jordan, but I never forgot her poignant words.

So maybe, I thought, all those years later in my nasty prison cell, *maybe God had wanted to give me a peaceful life and I chose something different?* That seemed to be another clue and gave me much to think about.

Journey Insights

The peace of God is in His special city even though the enemy lurks. Shalom (peace) is your heritage. I put in my prayer request at the Wailing Wall and the devil tried to fight it, but I pressed in and God answered. Did you know Jesus, Yeshua, protects us when we don't even know it?

10

HIGH IMPACT CULTURES

Before returning to the United States, Mom wanted to show Dad and me one of the wonders of the world, a breathtaking archeological site called Petra. Once again my thoughts were stimulated as I viewed this ancient city that at one time had been the epicenter of commerce and wealth. We left Israel and went back to Jordan where we secured a tour guide who arranged bus tickets to Petra, the famous city cut from a giant rock (the word Petra means "Rock").

Petra is a mile long and a half a mile wide, located about 50 miles south of the Dead Sea in the highlands of the Transjordan. The rock town itself lays in a basin surrounded by mountains, and the main entrance is through a twisting Siq (narrow gorge) between cliffs that tower 500-feet high. To enter and view Petra, it was necessary to travel the mile long Siq with our tour guide. Horses were also available at an additional cost.

Dad decided that we should walk, telling us, "We all need the exercise after our lavish eating in Kuwait." Mother and I laughed, as we were pretty certain he was just watching the budget. We set off on foot and found Petra to be an unforgettable sight. Much of the city was comprised of rose-red structures from the rock walls. I scaled one of the structures in my tennis shoes and entered a small dwelling where the temperature inside was much cooler than outside. I could see how a family, if necessary, could reside in one of these cave type homes. As I exited, I looked around the canyon of rock cliffs and immediately noticed innumerable similar cave homes. This city could hold tens of thousands of people in a time of need or war.

The tour guide told us the Bible references a place hewn from the rocks. Many believe the Israelis will flee to this place and be protected by Yahweh during the end times. He also showed us the high points of Petra, which I found to be fascinating. He pointed out an aqueduct that gathers rainwater for its inhabitants, a rock theater seating 4,000, and a wide colonnaded street laid out Roman style.

Next we saw the temple face. It was magnificent. Carved into the rose-red cliff, it towered nearly 150-feet high. The entrance door alone was 23 ½-feet high. We entered and looked around. The tour guide told us this was thought to be an ancient worship center for the Nabateans, who worshiped a god called Dushara. I didn't ask who Dushara was but knew he wasn't Christian.

Locals were selling what they called "original artifacts" to the gullible tourists. I held one of these carved rock statues and discovered it to be made of hard plastic. When I pointed this out to the vendor, he cursed me in Arabic and walked off. A few minutes later I saw him approaching another tourist. I yelled to her in English sharing what I'd discovered earlier. The Arabic boy cursed me again, took back his "artifact" and ran off. The tourist smiled and waved thanking me for this warning. I've learned that regardless of culture, bloodline or background people everywhere are the same when it comes to human nature.

Sitting in my prison cell I was fascinated with who I was as a teenager. I saw that most people look for the short cuts in life, and I definitely took many myself. This Arabic boy was looking for quick money at a tourist's expense. The tourist was looking for an ancient artifact at a low price—one that would be illegal to remove from the Petra site. I thought, *when it comes right down to it, we all need redemption from ourselves because humans are bent toward sin.* As I was searching for answers I couldn't have imagined that a few months later in prison, I would come face to face with my critical need for redemption. But at the time I was just trying to rationalize what in the world I'd done to end up in prison. I realized as a 15-year-old I was wrestling with what I seemed to know was right and wrong in others, but wasn't about to take a look at myself!

As I thought more about the impact of these two weeks in the Middle East, I saw God planting seeds that would crack open a door to understanding the Arab and Israeli people. First, it reinforced the multi-colored, high impact family cultures of the Arabs and Jews, much like the Mexicans I met three years earlier. I discovered great emphasis is placed on eye contact and facial expressions for communications, but Western culture places less emphasis on non-verbal communication while emphasizing words as its primary mode of communication.

In Western cultures, people say what they mean and mean what they say, whereas, in Middle-Eastern and Latino cultures, people express what they mean and mean what they express. In high impact cultures expressing what one means can occur through hand gestures, physical touch, face expressions, tone of voice, clarity, verbal expressiveness, posture, eye contact, body language, etc. This intrigued me and I somehow knew that caring about a culture would open a door of communication.

Next, I learned there are many religions in the world, and I experienced the cultures of Arab/Muslim, Israeli/Jewish, Armenian Orthodox Christian, and scores of Christian tourists from various denominations from around the globe. It began to make sense to me why Jesus declared, **"…I am the way, the truth, and the life. No one comes to the Father except through Me."** (John 14:6).

Finally, the full submersion experiences in these Middle East and Mexican cultures helped me grasp the Scriptures years later when I finally began reading the Bible. Comprehending Jewish culture adds understanding when reading the life of Jesus and the biblical parables. This became especially significant when viewing the lives of many of the prophets and studying God's language of symbols, dreams, visions, and other prophetic forms of communication.

On the way home, Dad lamented that we spent more money in 24 hours living second-class in Israel than during the entire 10 days we lived first-class in Kuwait. Mom joyfully countered, "It was the best money we've ever spent!" Years later, this brief trip to Israel would prove to be monumental for me, along with providing me a better understanding of Scripture, Jewish custom, and a deeper more methodical study of the Bible. But a grave deviation from God's best will for me would occur first as I allowed Satan to slowly sift me like wheat during the next few years of my life.

Journey Insights

Little did I know the seeds sown in Israel would give me a foundational understanding of Scripture, Jewish custom, and the Bible. Later it would help me better understand the various religions of the world as well as why Jesus declared, "I am the way, the truth, and the life. No one comes to the Father except through Me" (John 14:6). How can you get better understanding for others?

11

SLOW REBELLION AGAINST GOD

I was still looking back at my life trying to figure out how the heck I got here. I was raised in a loving Christian home, my mom definitely heard from the Lord since she was a little girl, and I did too, in dreams from time to time. In fact, I experienced at that church camp the presence of evil and never wanted to experience it again. So I knew the difference between good and evil. I began to feel rejected by my peers, I despised it and was determined to protect myself from being hurt by people. God gave me understanding of various cultures beyond the United States and He showed me I had a natural ability with money. I experienced opulence with the Arabs and began to desire that kind of a lifestyle. Thinking about this, it was starting to make sense how I ended up on the wrong road.

Returning from my trip to the Middle East, my high school friends began to drink. Most of their parents were drinkers, smokers, or both. Since my parents neither drank, smoked, nor allowed either of these things in our home, alcohol didn't appeal much to me. However, because of high school peer pressure, I experimented with it several times. I'm grateful it never seemed to grab me like it did with the other kids.

I believe there are generational curses inside a person's DNA that draw certain people like metal to magnets. One person can take a drink of alcohol, and they are seemingly addicted overnight, whereas another person can drink alcohol sporadically and it never seems to gain a stronghold. I also believe there are generational blessings that insulate a person from certain addictions and sins. A child may be completely immune to alcohol or drugs because of the generational blessing and completely consumed in sexual addiction because of a generational curse.

In the area of alcohol, it appears I was under the generational blessing. There was, however, a generational curse called, "the love of money" that came from my mother's ancestors and attached itself to my life and I perpetuated it. This addiction tripped me up later, bringing with it all kinds of evil. Later in life, I would learn the power of how to break these curses and release the blessing of superior DNA that God wants to give each one of us for the asking; (DNA: the Divine Nature of the Almighty).

Since I couldn't seem to find the fun that the "in group" experienced with alcohol, I sought out sports, another form of acceptance from popular groups in school. A friend had suggested I try out for the wrestling team. About this same time, I was growing colder and colder toward church activities because it utterly bored me. I wasn't reading the Bible or hearing from God through dreams anymore, and my rebellion course was set.

The saying by the French Philosopher Blasé Pascal that "we all have a God-shaped hole in our hearts that only Jesus Christ can fill" rings true here. During this season, I started filling this hole with everything but Jesus. Once the wrestling team accepted me, I felt like I belonged. Suddenly I experienced fresh purpose in life and immediately began sleeping in on Sunday mornings to avoid church. This caused me to get farther away from God and my mother was distraught. After much prayer and repeated words of admonishment, she finally left me to my own devices.

I focused more on wrestling. Initially, I was a slow learner. In fact, my unorthodox wrestling style was laughable to the other wrestlers and the coach. This lasted the first couple of months, but then something happened. I started pinning my opponents with my unconventional moves. Soon the majority of my wrestling matches resulted in unexpected and unusual pins. I soon moved from junior varsity to varsity and continued to win my matches. My senior year the team members voted me in as co-captain. I won Conference, District, and Regional and then went to State.

Later that season one of the untraditional wrestling moves my coach initially said would never work was nicknamed after me. This occurred after I was somehow able to pin 11 opponents (including that year's state champ) with this move. The following year my coach started teaching this move to other wrestlers and eventually to other coaches. By age 17 my confidence was building, and girls that paid no attention to me before were now expressing increased interest. I worked 10-hour shifts on the weekends at a local convenience store. The manager of the store, Jeff Gay, and I became good friends. Fifteen years later Jeff renewed his commitment and life to Christ and a few years later became president of Heart of America Prison Ministries., providing first quality study Bibles to prisoners who wrote in their testimony and got on the waiting list.

Working at Quik-Trip on the weekends made dating problematic. Even though I could now get a date, I was unable to do so because of my job. Worse, everyone who was out and about on Friday and Saturday nights stopped in the store, often telling me about how much fun they were having. A seed of resentment took root with repeated resentful thoughts.

They're all out having a good time. Here I am dressed in a stupid looking Quik-Trip shirt with my name embroidered on the front. I'm waiting on them, stocking shelves, and cleaning the ice cream machine. They're enjoying life.

And to throw salt in the wound, by the time I got off work at 2:00 a.m. everyone was going home for the night. I longed to be part of the popular crowd but never seemed to have the time or enough money apart from working to participate.

After I had graduated from high school, my parents paid for my first year of college tuition and books at CMSU where my dad worked. I majored in business management and lived at home. All the other kids were living on campus. I continued to work at the convenience store while many of my friends joined fraternities and sororities. Their parents always seemed to be giving them things that made me envious: a college allowance, a car, or payment of various expenses for which I had to work or go without. I had an entitlement attitude and my resentment built, both toward my peers and my parents. I saw myself even more as the one standing on the outside and looking in.

It was at this time I became involved in a martial arts class offered on campus. My wrestling experience gave me a ground fighting style that felt natural to me, and I quickly excelled. The rest of my martial arts style, however, was unorthodox just like my wrestling. At first, this also seemed out of place and laughable. Over time, however, my style became increasingly effective and within a year, I started winning tournaments and stacking trophies in the closet.

A couple of older students with advanced belt ranks took me under their wings and taught me techniques beyond my rank. With their acceptance and mentoring, I felt included for the first time in my life. Many were graduating and going into business. They continually spoke of how the real world was different than the academic world. Repeatedly hearing this caused my interest in academic business to wane while my interest in actual world business accelerated.

As I searched for answers as to why I was trapped in a federal penitentiary, I saw myself searching for significance. There was something growing stronger and stronger in me that was dissatisfied with the status quo. I felt I was born for more than what I witnessed in the lives of my peers in this small mid-western town. The thought of a lavish lifestyle similar to the Kuwaiti's had taken root in my heart in the four years since I'd experienced my Middle East adventures. I was just 19-years-old yet I craved the jet set lifestyle and the money to go with it.

Journey Insights

Slow rebellion against God began from a root of rejection in my heart. Even though I was being accepted for the first time in my life, something in me was still dissatisfied with the status quo. I thought that if I had more money and prestige, I'd be more important and my life would be better. It was the beginning of a false identity. What are some roots that may have created a false identity for you?

12

THE SEDUCTION OF THE DRUG BUSINESS

I was an entrepreneur by nature so whatever appeared most profitable appealed to me. I'd sold magazines door to door, worked at a grocery store and Wal-Mart, taught swimming lessons during the summer, life guarded, cut lawns, shoveled snow, etc. One day I discovered I could make a profit in selling a new product that many in my now expanding circle of friends seemed to want, cocaine. My overwhelming desire to make quick money to do the things I wanted trumped the inward conviction that selling drugs was wrong.

It started with an upper belt rank buddy named Darren telling me how we could make an extra $50 each week by selling off an "eight ball" (three and a half grams, adding a half gram of cut and making it into four grams) of cocaine. We would purchase this for $300 and sell the grams at $100 each and split $100 profit. Finally, I was able to take a night off from work and go out on a date!

Darren had a contact in the coke business, an assistant karate instructor at our dojo. I knew only one person who bought and used cocaine and his name was Colby. He had just received a large insurance settlement which meant he had money to spend. In the drug business, anyone can be a dealer overnight with two simple things, a supplier, and a buyer, and Colby was my buyer.

My first transaction took place inside Colby's brand new Corvette in the parking lot at the grocery store where I worked. I was nervous and prayed I wouldn't get caught. Colby looked at the cocaine, tasted it and then handed me two crisp one hundred dollar bills.

Did I just make $50 in 60 seconds? I just made more in 60 seconds than I'm going to make as a supermarket checker in the next two days.

My conversations with myself were in full force as I got into my vehicle and drove off. I looked carefully and was certain no one was following me. *You did it, David!*

My conscience, however, prodded in a different direction. *What have you just gotten yourself into? Maybe you'd better not do this again.*

This was a defining moment for me. I had a choice to do it God's way, but I shrugged Him off. I clutched the two Ben Franklins, thinking that this was too easy not to do again.

I'm going to take $150 of this to my buddy, take Saturday night off work, and go out on a date like everybody else.

The next day, Colby called and said he wanted more. I called Darren, and he had a gram and a half left. I picked it up and met with Colby, who gave me another $150 and asked when he could get more. I said, "Don't you think you need to slow down on this stuff?"

I could see him thinking, "Maybe you're right. I'll give you a call in a few days."

I brought the $150 to Darren. I was too excited to sit. "We need another eight ball. I sold three and a half grams and you only sold a half-gram, but it's okay. We'll still split the profits."

Darren looked away, "I didn't sell it, I snorted it."

I glared at him, "I thought this stuff was for earning money, not to use."

"I was testing the quality."

A bartender doesn't drink on the job, I thought, and a good drug dealer doesn't get high on his own supply. I decided that I needed a better business partner or perhaps no partner. I asked Darren if he minded if I did business directly with his supplier and he said sure because he was graduating college soon and he didn't need to be in the business anyway.

I knew Darren's "low level" supplier, a guy named Greg, who lived in Kansas City. He taught at the main martial arts dojo. Greg eventually started selling to me directly and at a lower price. I sold to Colby and then picked up another buyer who was a local bar owner, and then another, a bartender, who sold to others. Soon I was making $500 a week, triple my supermarket salary, and it only took a couple of hours. I quit that job, started dating on Friday and Saturday nights, and realized that getting dates simply required time and money.

As I look back, I see how one wrong choice led to another, and each time it bothered me less. As I stopped caring what God thought, the enemy gained legal rights to fuel my decisions, continuously beckoning me in the wrong direction, and I just kept going. Ephesians 4:18-19 (ESV) says, **"They are darkened in their understanding, alienated from the life of God because of the ignorance that is in them, due to their hardness of heart. They have become callous and have given themselves up to sensuality, greedy to practice every kind of impurity."** This began at age 19, and my journey darkened. Two years later at age 21, I moved to Kansas City, Missouri. I started a small cleaning company (residential and small office buildings) and sought financial success as the answer to all things. Little did I know how seeking such things first instead of seeking God would eventually pierce me through with many sorrows.[9]

As the cocaine business took off, I received an unexpected invitation to Easter church service from my mother. Since the service was several weeks off I agreed, just to get her off my back. My hope was that she would forget about it. One of us did forget, but it wasn't her. Easter morning my phone rang.

"Hello David. Just giving you a little reminder."

"I, uh, want to go but I have a commitment. I'm sorry. Let me promise to go another time because I can't get out of the meeting I'm needed for..." She didn't buy a word of it.

"I raised you to be a man of your word. Are you coming?" I paused and then agreed to drive the 70 minutes from Kansas City to the little church congregation of 50 people in Knob Noster, Missouri.

Arriving late I tried to sneak in and slip into one of the back pews, hoping to go unnoticed. My plan was to be present at the service, slip out during the final song, and take a church program with me to document my attendance. God had different plans. As I slid into the pew, I was stunned as the preacher suddenly stopped the song service, pointed to me, and began to prophesy.

"David Caleb Hairabedian, son of Tom and Susan, God is calling you back to Himself. It is time to return to the Lord and fulfill the calling He placed on your life from before the foundation of the world and confirmed through the elders through the laying on of hands and prophecy. Today is the day of salvation."

During his delivery, I felt as if the preacher's pointer finger was on the end of my nose, even though I was in the back pew and he was in the pulpit more than 40 feet away. He finished, and the church was so silent that you could hear a pin drop. Everyone stared at me. I was convicted of my sinful lifestyle and for the first time I saw the drug trafficking as wrong. It was as if a dark cloud of confusion lifted off my brain.

I'm out of control, I thought. *I need to return to the Lord.* My thinking was crystal clear. *I'm selling poison to people for profit and destroying lives.* As these thoughts flowed through my mind, the minister began to preach the Easter message. I don't remember any of it.

---

9   For the love of money is a root of all kinds of evil. Some people, eager for money, have wandered from the faith and pierced themselves with many griefs. (1 Timothy 6:10 NIV).

All I could think about was the word spoken to me. *What am I going to do? Obeying means leaving behind "the good life" that I have just started to build. Disobeying means returning to a lifestyle I know beyond a shadow of a doubt is displeasing to God and could result in my going to hell for eternity.* I knew at this moment that no one went to hell by accident. It was a choice.

The next 30 minutes were incredibly uncomfortable. *I need to get out of here so I can go back to my apartment and think clearly.* As the final song began, I made my move, slipping quietly towards the back door, and heading toward my car.

Just as my vehicle came into view, I saw an elderly lady in a dress and tennis shoes running in the same direction. I walked faster, hoping to drive off before she tried to engage me in any conversation. I failed. As I tried to put the key in the ignition, she arrived huffing and puffing to catch her breath. She smiled brightly and said, "Oh my, what a wonderful prophecy was spoken over your life today."

I looked at her and thought, Wonderful prophecy? My sins were exposed before the congregation!

Then she said, "I wish the Lord would speak to me like that," and it hit me! *She didn't know what the prophecy really meant. God's been merciful to me after all.* For those who didn't know my secret lifestyle of drug trafficking, the prophetic word appeared to be very encouraging. However, these words pierced me to the heart because I knew the truth. God was calling me on the carpet.

I nervously smiled at her and said, "Well, maybe you have already heard from God and are doing what He's called you to do, so He doesn't need to speak to you this way."

She smiled brightly and said, "Oh, you're such a nice young man to say that. Will you be back next Sunday? I'd like to get to know you and so would several others, I'm sure." I was, of course, not interested as I responded with the first thing I could think of, to get her off my back.

"Well, I'll have to think about it." Then, making up several excuses (the distance to drive, busy schedule, etc.), I told her that I would see how things worked out.

Her welcoming kindness continued, "How about staying for the Easter luncheon? The food is all home-cooked, and you'll be able to meet everyone." I told her I couldn't join them due to a previously scheduled appointment.

She looked discouraged for a second and then perked up, "Well, maybe next time. Our door is always open for you."

Finally sitting in the car, I waved, then turned the key. Nothing happened, not even a click. I turned it again. Nothing. *This isn't happening to me,* I thought. After the third attempt, I uttered my first prayer in years. "God, I know I'm in sin. If You let this car start, I'll go to church and get my life right with You." I turned the key, and immediately the engine roared to life! Relief flooded me. I put the vehicle in drive and pulled from the church parking lot. The farther I got away from the church, the farther I also seemed to get away from the conviction of the Holy Spirit and my quickly made promise to God.

My pager beeped. I looked at the number and saw it was one of my cocaine customers. I pondered as I drove, knowing I was at a crossroads.

What am I going to do? Should I call him back?

The pager went off again. I made a conscious decision to shake off the Holy Spirit's conviction. Within two hours, I was back in the drug business. This time, there would be no looking back. Jesus had stepped in my path to stop me, but I refused Him.[10]

Journey Insights

The Preacher's words pierced my heart with truth and in that moment I knew that no one went to hell by accident. The deep seated love of money caused me to shake off the conviction of the Holy Spirit. Jesus had stepped in my path to stop me, but I rejected Him. Later I would find out what it meant to be pierced with many sorrows from the love of money (1 Timothy 6:10). What is God speaking to you right now?

---

10   Audio CD available: "No One Goes to Hell by Accident": NoOneGoesToHellByAccident.com

13

GOING OFF THE DEEP END

At age 21 business was uppermost in my mind. My internal compass moved toward making money. At every chance, I started some new endeavor. It's just the way I saw life based on what could make a profit. One day I was in a billionaire's home in Mission Hills, Kansas, supervising a cleaning job. After several conversations with others in the room, he looked at me and said, "If you have a few minutes I'd like to talk to you. Meet me in my green room."

I was honored and a little overwhelmed, but mainly excited. I always felt like I was supposed to make money and it seemed like he recognized something in me. There I stood, feeling a bit like a favored son in the king's court. I commented on his impressive fireplace. He didn't seem interested in impressing me, very unlike the way I always felt the need to impress others.

"This fireplace belonged to Napoleon." How casual he was as he shared this "tidbit" with me. *Napoleon Bonaparte?* I tried not to drop my jaw. I was impressed with everything about this man.

"Cost me $800,000 at auction."

"That's a lot of money for a fireplace. What if lightning strikes it?"

He chuckled, "I wish it would," and then paused. "It's insured for a million." Then it dawned on me. Wealthy people appreciate the value of items, but instead of just spending money on stuff, they invest in what they can use that also makes money for them. Rich people have a different mentality. They are ambitious, they aren't afraid to risk, and they know how to quickly seize opportunities. They seem to find the fun in investing, and they watch their money like a hawk.

The talk I had that day could have sent me in the right direction, making money legitimately, and from what he told me, I had what it took, and it seemed like I had an advocate. Instead, of humbling myself by asking for his mentorship, and going through the learning process, I took the shortcut. I remained on board the "jet bound for hell," and paid no attention to the choices I was making. Greed has a way of blinding you to everything except the quickest way to make a profit.

Cocaine sales supplemented my cleaning business. Before long, I was traveling to South Florida to buy from my supplier's, supplier's supplier. I was also taking monthly vacations, enjoying what I thought was the good life. I was dating five nights a week, meeting different girls at parties, bars, and fine restaurants in Kansas City. I also dated whenever I traveled abroad. Dating turned into a conquest, and I felt as if I'd found some significance, acceptance, and purpose, yet these activities left me feeling empty the next day.

The Christian values taught to me as a child melted away while a hardening toward God and my fellow man took hold in my heart. I had tunnel vision where money was concerned. My language became harsh as did my actions toward people. Slowly, but surely the enemy of my soul was gaining more control of my life, and my morals were deteriorating. Unbeknownst to me, I was becoming totally demonized.

Late in 1987 I was making about $20,000 a month, tax-free. The median household income was $28,999. I'd purchased all the latest clothing, furniture, and guy toys, and now my thoughts turned to investing in something legal with my ever increasing influx of money. I was smart enough to know that if I stayed in the cocaine business, it would eventually lead to prison or death, but not smart enough to simply stop at this point.

Vic, whom I'd met a few years earlier when he attended Chiropractic College in Kansas City, invited me for a Bahamian gambling vacation. He was my best friend and primary cocaine supplier. I noticed some exquisite fashion watches in the various shops. These were similar to the watches I'd purchased in New York City from illegal street vendors, but with one major difference. These inexpensive watches didn't bear the Gucci, Rolex, Piaget names. Instead, these were labeled Acura, Visage, Monnett, etc. Such watches were known as knockoffs. They looked like the real thing but were not illegal counterfeits like those on the streets of New York City. I concluded the cocaine business was just a temporary stepping-stone to raise capital for something legal and began laundering my money into this new budding adventure. I went into the watch business the next week, opening my first small store in a shopping mall in Kansas City the day before Thanksgiving in 1987.

I was surprised that I was the first in the Midwest to open a specialty store offering inexpensive fashion watches. It appeared I was on the cutting edge of this new fad. I called the first location, "Times Up!" Soon one store turned to five, and in the process, a wholesale company was added named, "Universal Time." I began wholesaling to other Kansas City stores as the fashion watch craze began to take off in the late 80's. Then unofficially, I added a division I called "Time Labs" as a creation company for my ideas. My first project was engineering a prototype of the first hologram watch on a 30mm dial. This reduced the size of the hologram to that of a dress watch.

Before this, the hologram watch was only being produced on a bulky 50mm watch, selling exclusively at novelty stores, mostly to teenagers. Reducing the size of the watch and hologram effectively opened an untapped demographic of adult consumers, the sky being the limit in what could now be produced and sold. The hologram manufacturer I worked with engineered more than 100 different images to fit on the new Movado style watches. This process took approximately 18 months and considerable money. Time Labs also developed personalized picture and caricature watches with a diversity of logo watches for catalog, business and point-of-contact sales in the stores.

Two holographic images that sold like wildfire in Christian bookstores stumped me. One was the image of Jesus Christ on the Cross (often purchased by Catholics), and the other was the face of Jesus Christ (usually purchased by Protestants). I thought this duel-demographic of religious people were mostly just fanatical Christians and failed to understand their thinking. *Who would want to pay $60 for a watch bearing a three-dimensional image of Jesus?*

We continued manufacturing the Jesus images simply because they sold. In fact, they sold so effectively Christian bookstores couldn't seem to keep them in stock. Conversely, when trying to wholesale these Jesus images to non-Christian stores, the owners didn't have any interest in even displaying them on consignment.

What a paradox, I thought. This would later prove to be yet one more ignored signpost in life that pointed me to Jesus. A signpost from the Lord that I couldn't seem to read even though it was being manufactured and sold through my own hands! Later, I would discover the reason I missed the message was because, **"The god of this age has blinded the minds of unbelievers, so that they cannot see the light of the gospel of the glory of Christ..."** (2 Corinthians 4:4 NASB).

In a continued state of spiritual blindness, I purchased and resold cocaine to finance the expansion of the watch stores, my lifestyle and my ever-burgeoning ego. The proceeds also paid for ongoing research and development of the latest new watch concepts that came to mind. My initial intent of shifting to the watch business was to get out of the cocaine business, but now I needed more and more money to fuel my legal enterprises.

Someone once told me "the road to hell is paved with good intentions." I was redoubling my efforts while having lost focus of my original goal. To others, things appeared to be going pretty good for me. It was about this time the coastal international watch importers were referring to me as "the watch guy in the Midwest." It seemed I was on the cutting edge of everything to do with fashion watches in the center of the United States. Internally, however, there was great turmoil in my soul. Eighteen months later, I would discover the verse in Isaiah that succinctly described what I was experiencing, **"There is no peace for the wicked..."** (Isaiah 57:21 HCSB).

Journey Insights

Even though I was living "the good life" via money, businesses and dating, my soul was in turmoil and blinded to the Christian morals with which I had been raised. "...the god of this age has blinded the minds of the unbelievers so they cannot see the light of the gospel of the glory of Christ..." (2 Corinthians 4:4 NASB). I had no peace, "There is no peace for the wicked..." (Isaiah 57:21 HCSB) and "the road to hell is paved with good intentions." Is your soul in turmoil and have you lost your peace? There is a way out...

14

AERO GRAND THEFT

In the fall of 1988, a new opportunity presented itself from Vic, buying and selling small airplanes to the Colombian Cartel by delivering them to South Florida. I had an ex-military helicopter pilot associate named Elliot Bails, whom I met during my six years in martial arts. We'd advanced in the belt ranks and were both assistant instructors at the dojo where we worked out. Coincidently, just one month earlier, Bails mentioned how he could turn a profit by reselling planes purchased inexpensively in the Midwest.

At the time, Bails was working as a helicopter pilot for a local sheriff's department in rural Missouri. He'd been hired and deputized to fly around spotting patches of marijuana. These finds were then reported to the DEA. Bails had a wife and three children and was making a meager salary. He began looking for ways to increase his income. Initially, he offered to notify me when he spotted a patch of high-quality marijuana so I could harvest it, sell it and we could split the profits.

I pondered the scheme, "Sounds risky."

"The Feds don't know it's there unless I tell 'em."

"It's not the Feds. Growers have been known to kill people who steal their harvest. Sometimes the bodies are never found."

Bails didn't know any marijuana buyers, so he decided the plane idea was better, safer and it was legal. With Bails' contacts for purchases and my contacts for sales in Southern Florida, we could make a little money together—probably $15-25,000 per plane divided among us—with little additional time on my end.

Also, I wanted to purchase a small twin-engine plane for personal and business use. This would be a perfect opportunity to learn more about the aeronautics business while simultaneously getting the best possible deal on my own plane.

The following week we received the Colombian's laundry list of planes from Vic. Every plane was either a business jet or a twin turboprop capable of carrying payloads of a ton or more long distances – Columbia, South America to the United States. Each used plane sold for between one and five million.

These were way out of our league, and Bails wasn't even rated on most of these planes. I told Vic no and focused back on watches.

During a watch-buying trip in Miami, Vic approached me a second time on the airplane issue. He was drawn to this scheme by the potential of raising quick capital for his new chiropractic office. This would place him in his own legal business, and he would be able to get out of the drug trade. Up until this point, Vic had spent the majority of his profits on gambling, primarily professional football on the weekends with a local bookie, and an occasional trip to Las Vegas for blackjack at Caesar's Palace or to the Bahamas for Roulette, or a combination of all three.

Almost everyone has a potential vice, although it varies from person to person. The enemy of our souls is very shrewd and constantly positions temptations in front of us hoping to lure us away from the right path. About the same time the Colombians, from whom Vic bought wholesale cocaine, offered him a large amount of cash for the delivery of *any plane on the laundry list.* They didn't want us to buy the plane and resell it to them at a profit. Instead, they wanted us to steal a plane and deliver it to Florida for their own pilot to fly to South America for use on the coca plantations.

The Colombians had several crashed planes on their land, and they couldn't claim insurance losses due to the shady nature of their business. They simply wanted to switch the data plates in the stolen planes with the data plate from their crashed planes of the same model. Since they already had legal titles for these no one would ever know the difference.[11] The Colombians would end up with a replacement plane, saving a couple of million dollars each.

This whole scenario is insane, I initially thought. However, with persuasion from Vic in Florida and Bails back in Kansas City, I was convinced.

This will be easy and benefit all parties involved. Bails wanted to buy a small helicopter and start his own crop-dusting business. Vic's dream was his own chiropractic clinic. I wanted to further expand the watch business and put drug trafficking behind me forever. *Our money problems will be solved. Finally, we're going to catapult to easy street. It's a real "Godsend,"* I surmised.

Bails assured me he could fly at least two of the planes on the list, so we were ready to go. All we had to do was steal a plane and get it to an airfield in South Florida. The Colombians' pilot would take it from there, and we'd get paid. It seemed simple enough.

We decided that Bails would handle the plane theft on our end, and Vic would handle the Colombian end. I was the middleman. In my assessment, this was

---

11   Tracking numbers for planes and plane parts have changed radically since 1988.

the safest position. Little did I know that the safest place would later become a pressure sandwich.

The following day Bails and I purchased a "Trade-a-Plane" publication for a few dollars, and I shelled out about a grand for a cutting-edge portable Loran[12] system. We planned to use this for piloting the plane to the airfield in South Florida.

We located several planes from the list and prepared to steal a King Air 300 Twin Turbo Prop in Florida. This was pre-9/11, and although not a common crime, it wasn't unheard of. In fact, while we were stealing the King Air in Ft. Lauderdale, an Aero Commander 980 we had scoped out the week before in Kansas City, was lifted by another group 11 hours later! Somebody stole the next plane we were planning to steal if the King Air 300 didn't pan out.

A month earlier, another group working for the same Colombians botched a King Air 300 theft worth about two and a half million dollars at Ft. Lauderdale Executive airport. While attempting to steal the plane at 2:00 a.m. one of the crew failed to open the hanger door completely. The pilot tore off the plane's wing. They fled leaving the damaged plane on the tarmac. Later I would learn that this pilot was also our pilot for the King Air 300 at the same airport. I would soon be making the acquaintance of Alex Oswald.

Bails and I flew to Naples, Florida. Trade-A-Plane listed a pair of King Air 300's, recently parked at a plane dealership. By the time we arrived an Arab oil sheik has purchased both planes in Saudi Arabia. We weren't about to go to Saudi Arabia and steal our planes back. *That's where they cut the hands off of thieves!* I thought. The trouble signs should have captured our attention, but when you're determined, you just keep pressing on.

We looked in the Trade-A-Plane again. *This is it!* We both were hopeful. *Another King Air 300 is available in Tampa and it's ours!* There were only 187 of these manufactured at the time, and most of them were located out of the country. Every time one went on the market, it sold a few days later to some wealthy businessman. We had our eyes locked on that bird and we wanted it.

The Executive Airport had all kinds of security fences, cameras, and checkpoints. We saw the King Air 300 parked behind the tall safety fence. This was my first time seeing in person and it was truly a beautiful plane. Now I understood why the Colombians wanted it.

While in the parking lot admiring the plane we were startled by the abrupt arrival of a police officer. He turned on his security flashers and approached

---

12   Similar to present day GPS systems that now cost about $100.

quickly. "You're going to need to show me some identification." He wasn't kidding around. The tension was thick. Handing over our driver's license, we exchanged nervous looks while the officer ran a background check.

We came up clean, but he wasn't finished with us. "What are you two doing in this parking lot?" he demanded.

Bails shamelessly handed the officer his military I.D. "We just wanted to watch some of the planes as they took off."

His attitude changed. "Several car stereos have been stolen in the last few months. We're on the lookout for any suspicious activity."

"Thanks, officer. We appreciate that you're doing your job."

"Well don't hang here too long unless you want to be harassed by the other officers!"

That was our cue to take off. Bails laughed out loud. "The cop thought we were there to steal a $500 car stereo. 'Uh, no officer, we aren't here to steal car stereos. We're casing the airport and planning to steal that three million dollar twin turboprop instead!'" We should have taken it as another warning sign, but we began to think we were invincible. Our egos were out of control.

Journey Insights

Just one more gig, stealing the jet felt like a quick answer. It was easy capital and we just needed one more. Tampa's airport security precluded us from stealing the King Air 300 parked there. It was a warning sign we should have backed off, but chose not to because we thought it would take us to easy street. Are there warning signs God has given that you've chosen to ignore?

15

PLAN "C"

Tampa's security precluded us from stealing the King Air 300 parked there. Plan C came next. Bails boldly made a call directly to Beechcraft in Atlanta, inquiring about purchasing a used King Air 300. He concocted a story about working for IBM out of New York City. The Beechcraft rep went into full sales mode.

He told Bails that the King Air 300 was a really hot plane that was worth the asking price. "Consider purchasing a new one. It holds its resale value." This was an offer we couldn't refuse.

For the next four days, Bails spoke to the sales rep working out the details. He convinced the rep to send a brand new, three and a half million dollar King Air 300 twin turboprop, with a pilot, to Ft. Lauderdale for his boss to view and fly into New York for potential purchase.

At 6:00 a.m. the next morning the bird was airborne from Atlanta to Ft. Lauderdale Executive Airport. Simultaneously Vic and I, the Columbians and their co-pilot were meeting in the Hilton Hotel parking lot less than a mile from the airport to discuss final plans. Alejandro, Vic's cocaine supplier, was a Colombian national with a wife and two children who moved an average of 100-200 kilos of cocaine a month in the United States. Alex Oswald was their pilot. We were one hour from the transaction.

My job suddenly became transporting the incoming pilot to a pre-rented room at the airport Hilton Hotel, while Alex would fly off in the plane, in broad daylight. The Colombians would then "take care of the pilot." A chill ran up my spine. *Surely they can't be serious. I deal drugs, but I'm not a murderer. No amount of money is worth this.*

I understood that if I knowingly escorted an innocent man to his death, there would be no turning back for me. I can't fully explain it, but it was somehow made clear to me at that moment. Once I stepped over this clear and definite line, I would be done for eternity.

I turned toward Alejandro, "This isn't part of our deal. No one's getting murdered on my watch." I leaned in closer. Alejandro looked at me with fury in his eyes.

For a Colombian drug dealer to order one of his workers to kill an American was no big deal. Alejandro knew, after all was said and done, he could just fly back to Colombia. His attitude was, "Business is business; nothing personal."

Moreover, Alejandro wasn't even his real name. He had a fake passport and a fake green card. During that time in South Florida both were commonly sold to the Cali cartel through the black market or corrupt U.S. government workers. I believe there is a different point of no return for each one of us. In this situation, because of my upbringing, murder was the dark line for me. I knew better. Maybe the Colombians who were present in this scenario did not. God can forgive anyone, but there is a price to pay for the choices we make.

Desperate to do the right thing, I offered Alejandro an alternative. "I'll take the pilot to breakfast while Alex gets the plane off the ground. If he picks anybody out of a police lineup, it'll be me. You're clear." They knew me and agreed to this arrangement. I breathed a silent sigh of relief.

At 6:45 a.m. I was parked, waiting for the plane in Alex's silver Mercedes just off the tarmac. At 7:00 a.m. our plane landed. I drove onto the tarmac to meet the pilot and waved him to the vehicle. Grabbing his briefcase, he waved back with a friendly smile and headed to my car.

He turned out to be a retired military colonel, married with grown children. He was now flying for Beechcraft in his spare time. Eight hours earlier the Beechcraft rep called him at his house around 11:00 p.m., requesting he fly a plane to Ft. Lauderdale, then to New York for a test flight for a high-level IBM executive. During the earlier week's phone calls, Bails represented himself to the Beechcraft rep as the IBM boss's executive assistant, who handled all their plane and hotel arrangements.

The pilot was relieved to see me. He said the Beechcraft rep provided him with unusually sketchy instructions for the test flight, and he had no idea who would be meeting him. "I don't even have the name of the potential buyer," he told me.

"It's been a crazy week for us too," I replied. Directing him to the Mercedes, I told him my boss was waiting in the hotel room. The pilot had been up since 2:00 a.m. and was tired. "Hey, you want to grab a cup of coffee?" I asked. We headed to the hotel restaurant and ended up ordering breakfast, conversing the entire time as we waited for my boss to come down for his flight to New York.

While we were eating, I excused myself to the lobby when my pager buzzed. Vic was there at the pay phone looking inconspicuous. He told me he needed the keys to the Benz to get everyone to the airport. I nodded my head and tossed him the keys. He darted out the door. I returned to the restaurant.

I told the pilot that it was my boss with a courtesy call from upstairs letting us know he would be delayed about 20 minutes. "He apologizes for the inconvenience."

"It's no problem. This is a common thing."

During this time delay, Alejandro drove the Mercedes onto the tarmac. Prepayment for refueling was already taken care of by Vic. Alex and a Columbian co-pilot exited the Mercedes and boldly boarded the plane, preparing it for takeoff. Alex was a seasoned pilot, ex-military, and well decorated for his piloting exploits during the Viet Nam war. He had a history with both the Cali cartel and local American drug dealers importing from Jamaica and he primarily flew loads of marijuana, refusing to fly any cocaine, calling it poison.

Alex did, however, unknowingly fly tons of cocaine from Colombia to the United States for the CIA during the Iran/Contra era. Later, while we were in the county jail together, he told me about a job he had as a DC-8 pilot flying 35,000 pounds of seafood and flowers several days a week for a local import company. One day after flying in a load of seafood he took a five-pound box of frozen jumbo shrimp from the pallet load marked with blue X's on the outsides, thinking these were the higher quality boxes. Then he went home to shower and eat. Upon opening the box to prepare dinner, he found a couple of pounds of shrimp in ice, surrounding a kilogram of cocaine. He realized what was going on. Daily loads of cocaine were secreted away in the shrimp, lobster, and flower boxes, and he was flying it in.

He put the kilo back in the box, along with the shrimp, and returned to his boss's office. He walked in, put the box on his boss's desk and apologized for the mistake. His boss looked at the blue X, looked at Alex and realized he knew the truth.

Alex told his boss, "Don't worry, I won't say anything, I just wanted some shrimp, I don't mess around with the other stuff."

His boss laughed as he slid the box of shrimp into a desk drawer and took Alex to the warehouse. He handed Alex two five pound boxes of shrimp, without the X, and said, "Anytime you want shrimp, lobster, flowers or anything else you're flying, just ask me. You can have as much as you want for free. Just don't touch anything with the blue X's on them. His boss then said, "I guess I need to give you a raise too."

Alex smiled and muttered, "Yeah, that'd be nice."

A couple of weeks later Alex quit this job saying that he was moving out of state. He told me his real reason was he didn't want to end up dead, (indicating the CIA operatives are more unpredictable and dangerous than the Cartel), plus he hated cocaine trafficking.

This was the same pilot who was now helping us steal a plane to be sold to cocaine traffickers. Once in the plane, Alex confidently radioed the tower for clearance and after obtaining it, he headed for Virgin Gorda first, and then to Cali, Colombia.

About an hour later I received the pager call from Vic confirming the plane was airborne and our part of the transaction was complete. After paying the breakfast bill, I excused myself from the table, to make a brief phone call to *my boss* again. I was planning on calling Vic to pick me up since I was now without transportation.

The colonel went to the phone also. He said he had to update his flight plan and call the airfield to let them know he would be late.

I swallowed the lump in my throat, "Is that normal procedure?"

"Only when your plane is sitting for an hour, and you told the flight tower that you'd be flying out in 45 minutes." He laughed and noted, "I just have to give them a courtesy call. Don't want to block any planes." I smiled weakly and told him that it seemed like the polite thing to do. Then I said, "Go ahead and make your call, I'll be in the lobby."

I knew that he'd soon discover his plane wasn't blocking anything. It was already airborne to South America with the transponder device turned off! With my heart pounding, I stepped outside the hotel, flagged a cab, and within seconds, I was out of there.

Did we really just pull off stealing a jet? Were they really going to kill that pilot? Did I save his life or put him in harm's way? Is this going to come back to harm me? That pilot could pick me out of a police lineup! Either way, I'm glad he's not dead.

I headed to Vic's condo to meet up with the crew, glad that it was over. Forty-five minutes later, police were everywhere. By this time, however, our plane was already out of the country, and we were celebrating at a local club. We then returned to our own cities, never to be seen by any witnesses again, or so we thought.

Journey Insights

There's a point of no return for each of us, where there is no turning back. This was mine. I refused to go there and made sure the pilot was protected. We returned to our own cities after our "success," never to be seen by any witnesses again. Or at least that was my plan at the time but...our sins have a way of finding us out. Are you at a crossroads of something in your life that could be a point of no return? It's not too late to stop and turn away.

16

PAYLOAD MEETS CONVICTION

Between selling my first three and a half grams at age 19, and stealing multi-million dollar jets at age 24, I'd picked up some expensive tastes and become increasingly addicted to the power that came with this kind of easy money. I'd also taken on the responsibility of an expanding fashion watch business, including paying the salaries of several employees each week, and all of this demanded more money.

Vic, on the other hand, had picked up a gambling habit that was costing him several thousand dollars a month. I watched him lose $25,000 one weekend in Las Vegas when the price to mail a letter was still 19 cents and gas was $1.25 a gallon!

These Scriptures were accurate, **"Those who love money will never have enough,"** (Ecclesiastes 5:10 NLT) and, **"For the love of money is the root of all kinds of evil…"** (1 Timothy 6:10). What a powerful seductress money was in our lives. The prisons, graves, and hell are full of men and women who fell prey to this trap of the enemy.

A few days after stealing the jet I met Vic in New York to pick-up the payment for Bails and me. Everything seemed to be going well. Overnight we were in special graces with the Colombians. They wanted more planes and were offering bonuses.

But, Vic and I were looking forward to going straight. Our justification for entering at this higher level was to raise capital for other legit ventures. We were ready to retire from the world of cocaine when a minor twist occurred. In New York, the Colombians offered Vic cocaine instead of cash as payment. (I learned later that once you're trapped in this world, it's almost impossible to get out!) Vic told Alejandro we could wait to receive cash, and we headed to Vic's family home an hour away in New Jersey to relax and wait for a pager call.

Vic is of Italian descent, and he told me part of his family had been involved with the New York/New Jersey crime families. When Vic was just a child, his grandmother requested that he would not be involved with the family business. She wanted him to become a doctor or a lawyer, something legal. So after high school Vic went to a well-respected chiropractic college in Kansas

City, becoming one of its youngest graduates in its history.

We lived in the same high-rise apartment building, saw each other at bars and after-hours parties, and along the way we became friends. One thing led to another, and three years later we found ourselves in our current situation. No one on either side of Vic's family was aware of this. First Corinthians 15:33 says, **"Do not be deceived: "Evil company corrupts good habits,"** and in our case, both of us were increasingly bad influences on the other.

Vic's grandmother fixed us lunch. She shared what she referred to as "her testimony," and went on to say she had experienced "the new birth." In her words, she was, "born again." Her words intrigued me.

"Would you like to have one of my company's Jesus Hologram watches?" I asked.

"That's kind of you, David, but no. Thank you for the offer." Her decline was respectful and I took it as a good sign.

Okay, now she doesn't seem quite as nutty as she first did, I thought.

Sitting at the kitchen table, eating roast beef sandwiches, I learned that she and her husband came to Christ 15 years earlier, and it was only then that he broke ties with the east coast crime families. Her eyes glistened, "He got out just in time. Several of his business associates died violent deaths in the following years."

Her husband died of natural causes several years later during one of their vacations together. "David, he simply stepped into eternity to be with Jesus." This happened shortly after they began their mornings with Bible devotions and prayer over breakfast.

Crying tears of joy, she told me, "We will see each other again. I *know* it." I was genuinely moved.

Because of her husband's past lifestyle, she understood the look Vic and I had in our eyes, the pager calls, private conversations, etc. She didn't ask questions, but she knew we needed to get off the road we were on, or we would soon end up in prison, dead, or in hell for eternity.

Her manner was very gentle. She smiled broadly and began to share the love of God through her story. Vic had heard it all before. He rolled his eyes and departed to make an important phone call.

"David, when my husband came to Christ he had a hard decision to make." She took a sip of coffee and looked into my eyes. "The family business was extremely lucrative."

I listened intently. Her message was clear, accept Christ, go straight, and live.

Her words interested me, but I didn't realize them as Heaven reaching out to me with a teachable moment. I now attribute Heaven's messengers sent in an effort to redirect and rescue me to my praying mother's love for her wayward son.

When Vic returned 15 minutes later, he broke into our conversation, "Grandma, stop bothering David, he doesn't want to hear that stuff!" Vic's disrespectful tone took me by surprise.

"She's not bothering me."

Vic grumbled an apology then blurted, "I've got business with David. We need privacy."

She picked up her coffee cup and stood, "I'll be praying for both of you. God has a plan for your lives. I'm believing and expecting He will bring you both to salvation soon." She exited and left us to our own devices. Her words both encouraged and scared me. I wasn't quite sure what salvation meant in my situation, and it made me a bit nervous.

Although Vic's grandmother didn't realize it, that brief meeting over a roast beef sandwich had positively impacted my life. *Am I missing something?* I wondered. *Would a relationship with Jesus make a difference?* Vic interrupted these new thoughts.

"I just got off the phone with Alejandro...." There was a new plan to pick up our payment. Jesus and eternity would have to wait until another day. Business first!

The new plan involved me flying back to Kansas City, and then Bails and me driving to Houston. We would each receive our individual shares of the money for the Florida theft at a hotel in Texas.

Journey Insights

"Whoever loves money never has enough..." (Ecclesiastes 5:10 NIV). Bad friends will ruin good habits; the love of money seduced us into all kinds of evil. The prisons, graves, and hell are full of men and women who have fallen prey to this trap of the enemy. Vic's grandmother's message to me was clear; accept Christ, go straight, and live. Her words both encouraged and scared me. Have you fallen into the trap of bad friends and bad decisions? God can help you get out if you ask.

17

COMPLICATIONS CONTINUE

Bails and I arrived in Houston at the designated location on Christmas Eve, 1988. Vic had arrived a day earlier. When we knocked on Vic's door, he was grinning like the cat that ate the canary. He pointed to a large shoebox, and two suitcases on the bed. The shoebox was full of cash, and the suitcases were both overflowing with kilos of cocaine!

"The cash is a partial payment for the first plane," Vic explained. "The cocaine represents the remaining payment for getting the King Air 300, plus partial payment for the next plane they want us to steal!"

He told me that Alejandro took him to the garage of a suburban Houston home containing hundreds of kilos of cocaine, stacked from the floor to the ceiling. Alejandro told him, "Take the cocaine at a discounted price then make even more money." It was like reinvesting his money from the plane theft into the cocaine business to double our profits.

Alejandro assured Vic that if we sold the additional cocaine we could just pay him back and not worry about another plane. Or if we had trouble moving the coke right away, we could sit on it, sell it in smaller quantities and make even more money. If all else failed, we could just steal another plane, pay off the fronted coke, and they would owe us even more cash.

Things were getting complicated… again. Just when we thought we were out of the business, circumstances seem to pull us right back in. This is normally the way the devil works, and it seemed to be the story of my life.

Troubled but determined, I asked Bails, "What do you want to do?"

"Take the cash and coke and steal another plane." He didn't waiver.

"Okay, but I'm out after this one!" I meant it. He agreed and comforted me by saying he had a friend in St. Louis who would take all the cocaine for cash. This would solve our problem and make us even more money. Now we were getting somewhere. I felt invigorated! Vic looked at me; I looked at him, and we both laughed. This was beginning to resemble something out of a Miami Vice episode. We both liked that show because the drug dealers often came out on top.

"Vic, things are going our way; 1989 is going to be an excellent year!"

Vic's face brightened and then he acknowledged ominously, *"Yeah, things are going really good…almost too good!"*

We stared at each other, and I swallowed the lump in my throat, "You've got a point." We both thought for a brief moment in silence and then quickly shook off the strange feeling of impending doom.

We finished our transaction. Vic flew to New Jersey to celebrate Christmas with his family. Bails and I loaded the cocaine-filled suitcases into our vehicle. Stopping at an Oklahoma mall, we picked up gifts for Bails' wife and kids, had them wrapped, and stuffed them in our back seat, ready for Christmas. The presents would help conceal the suitcases in the event we were pulled over.

We arrived back in Kansas City on Christmas morning, singing, "I'm Dreaming of a White Christmas." Secreted beneath the presents were two suitcases full of our "white Christmas," soon to be turned into green Benjamin Franklin, 100 dollar bills. Bails dropped me off at my townhouse and he headed home to spend Christmas with his family.

I met my parents for brunch at an elegant restaurant at a Kansas City hotel overlooking the famous Country Club Plaza. My father and sister greeted me warmly, but my mother gave me a long searching look. She intuitively knew I'd been up to something bad! Mothers always seem to know.

As a young child, she told me she had eyes in the back of her head. One day I climbed onto a chair searching through the back of her long black hair for her "extra set of eyes" while she washed dishes. She caught me and told me I couldn't see her extra eyes because I wasn't an adult. I believed her!

This particular day, 20 years later, my mother strongly admonished me to stop doing whatever I was doing that was illegal and return to the Lord. It sounded eerily similar to the warning I'd received three and a half years earlier at that little church in Knob Noster, Missouri. I denied all wrongdoing (of course), told her I loved her, and we all settled in to enjoy Christmas brunch.

Journey Insights

Things got complicated fast and yet we didn't stop because we had to finish just one more job. It was always doing just one more. On this day my mother looked me in the eye and strongly admonished me to stop and turn to the Lord, much like the warning I had received in the church. Strange feelings of impending doom wouldn't leave me and once more, I had a choice. Is it your time to stop what you're doing and turn to God?

18

MY SIN REACHES FULL MEASURE

God is patient but at that point, I believe He'd had enough of my antics. I'd been given continual opportunities and warnings. Two and a half weeks later, the Holy Spirit directed my mother to give her son fully into His hands. Her prayer went something like this, "God, all I ask is that you spare his life and bring him into Your service for the Kingdom." This was January 9, 1989. My mother didn't know it but 48 hours later her prayer was answered.

Like Abraham sacrificed Isaac, my mother spiritually sacrificed me to the Lord in prayer, fully laying me on the altar. This is one of the most difficult prayers a parent can pray, but often proves the most effective. It is heart-wrenchingly painful for a parent. The consequences that often follow can appear disastrous as God accomplishes His goal **"…To root out and to pull down, To destroy and to throw down, To build and to plant."** (Jeremiah 1:10).

The following week, Bails' St. Louis friend lost all his money on a very large cocaine deal gone bad. On the exact highway we'd traveled back from Houston, their transport car was pulled over with so much cocaine that it made national news. This meant Vic or I had to either liquidate the cocaine for cash, front it to this guy on credit and risk losing it, or we had to steal another plane to satisfy our outstanding debt.

"Vic, I don't want to go back to the cocaine business." I was adamant.

His response was quick. "Well, I don't know buyers in Kansas City for that kind of weight."

We finally decided to steal another plane to resolve the debt. Like Alejandro had suggested, we would simultaneously make even more money in the process. Interestingly, there always seemed to be an accompanying temptation to go along with the additional pressure. The only problem was that Bails wasn't ready to steal another plane. He wanted to relax.

"Just go and sell the cocaine," Bails told us, "and pay the Colombians instead." Bails now claimed that he never wanted the cocaine, and it wasn't on his credit line but ours. The responsibility was all on Vic and me. Vic called Alejandro from a pay phone and told him we'd have another plane on his list within seven days.

"Alex will be ready to fly it to Colombia just like last time," Alejandro assured us.

About the same time another Kansas City pilot I knew contacted me in hopes of finding an opportunity that would provide him enough money to purchase his own small aircraft. I flashed a superior grin, confident our present dilemma was about to be solved by the end of the week.

This pilot was employed locally at an executive airport as a flight instructor. His position provided full access to all the business jets, plus their regular flight-use schedules. He could easily take any plane during its off time providing a window of several days before anyone would notice. We met to discuss the details. I provided him and his co-pilot cousin who he introduced me to at a Kansas City hotel room with a down payment for the delivery in cash. This plane stealing business was starting to get easy!

Early the next morning I was awakened with a start from a vivid and horrifying dream. In this detailed dream Vic, Alex, and I were all arrested at Boca Raton Executive Airport. The Feds descended on us from all sides. In the next scene, we were being arraigned in federal court in front of a woman judge in a black robe, wearing a Tag Heuer black anodized aluminum watch. The lead agent was a country-looking man in his early 30's with reddish orange hair and he was wearing mud-covered cowboy boots. The judge read the charges. Then the prosecutor told the judge they had additional information that we may have stolen a King Air 300 in Ft. Lauderdale about 30 days earlier.

While lying in bed processing this dream, the phone rang. It was the pilot's cousin telling me he was ready on his end. Still startled from the dream I tried to delay the deal, telling him I would call him back. I had to rethink this whole matter. I showered and went to a payphone to gather my wits. Vic and I were under pressure to produce, the pilot was ready, the Colombians were ready and we'd already given them our word. It was time for action.

I flew to Florida and met Vic at his condo later that day, hoping to get some advice. We always discussed things when we were unsure or if someone or something made us uncomfortable. In this case it was both, plus a third component; a warning dream that I couldn't shake off.

Vic met me as I was exiting my rent-a-car. He saw my downcast face and said, "What's wrong?"

"Nothing, why?"

"Something's wrong. Tell me."

I finally admitted, "Vic, I had a horrible dream this morning."

"A nightmare?"

"More than a nightmare, *we got busted!*"

"Busted?" Stress lines formed on his brow. He looked in both directions and grabbed my arm, "Let's go inside and talk."

I shared my dream and its stark details. Vic chewed his lip as I told each vivid scene: the jet's markings, color, dented left wing, its late arrival, Vic driving the Mercedes onto the Tarmac with the Colombian's co-pilot, etc. I even shared the décor of the courtroom describing its walnut walls, details of what was spoken during the arraignment hearing, by whom, and so on.

"Wow, that's wild. My grandmother has warning dreams like that! Paying attention to those dreams saved my grandfather's life on more than one occasion." We both agreed to try and cancel the deal. Two hours and several pager and phone calls later, no one called us back. We were frustrated, but we had already given our word to do this deal and it was in progress.

We talked more about the dream, pointing out its improbability factors with the details. We nervously laughed at how the dream couldn't come to pass for several reasons, beginning with the jet's color. The plane we ordered was a new blue and white Cessna Citation II, not the older brown and white model. The Mercedes-Benz in the dream wasn't even going to be on the tarmac. Also, Vic was staying at a hotel two miles from the transaction, but in the dream, Vic was arrested with Alex and me. Finally, the plane was scheduled the next morning at 6:00 a.m., not 9:05 a.m. like the dream indicated.

Relying on our own understanding we threw caution to the wind, and both said simultaneously, "Aaaah, what's in a dream?"[13] After convincing ourselves we would be okay, we laughed off any foreboding and said, "Let's do this thing!"

As I twisted the door knob leaving the condo, I turned to Vic and affirmed our decision by concluding with, "Whoever heard of a woman judge in federal court, let alone a reddish-orange haired agent sporting muddied boots in South Florida?

The next day we learned, albeit too late and not without God's advanced warning, that the Kansas City pilot was working undercover and he'd turned us in. He did this in trade for a government reward in hopes that he could

---

13   Sixteen months later I was surprised to discover these Scriptures, **"For God speaks again and again, in dreams, in visions of the night when deep sleep falls on men as they lie on their beds. He opens their ears in times like that, and gives them wisdom and instruction, causing them to change their minds, and keeping them from pride, and warning them of the penalties of sin, and keeping them from falling into some trap." "Yes, God often does these things for man-- brings back his soul from the pit, so that he may live in the light of the living."** (Job 33:14-18, 29-30 TLB).

buy his own plane with the money. The co-pilot's cousin was an undercover U.S. Customs agent. The transaction was a reverse sting operation. On January 11th, 1989, Vic, Alex and I were arrested on the tarmac of Boca Raton Executive Airport in South Florida. The undercover pilot delivered an older model brown and white Cessna Citation II jet with a dented left wing, just like the one shown in the dream! The plane was delayed until exactly 9:05 that morning.

Earlier that day the Mercedes-Benz arrived, driven by Alex. Because of the delays, we all ate breakfast at a local Denny's and then drove to the airfield together in the Mercedes to await the plane's arrival. The electric driver's seat mysteriously malfunctioned at 9:00 a.m., leaving the seat in the "all the way back position." My legs were too short to comfortably reach the pedals. Vic, being taller, said, "I'll drive!" The rest is history. Twenty federal agents hiding in parked cars and planes swooped down on us with loaded guns ordering us to the ground.

How has my life spiraled to this? I had known something was off, but I didn't stop. Yet hearing, "Get your hands up, YOU'RE UNDER ARREST!" stopped me dead in my tracks.

The next few days were a swirl. The arraignment was just as I'd seen in my dream. *My dream? Who gave me that warning? Why didn't I heed it?* County jail for holding and that shame-filled call to my mother. I had no idea that her prayers were, in a way, being answered and my sorrows were just beginning.

My determination to outsmart the system was uppermost in my mind, but then, Pandora's Box opened with more indictments. Still, I fought against needing any help from God. *I HAVE to beat this! There will be no "God Squad" for me, just strategize, David. Focus!* My rebellion remained firmly intact.

Back and forth I went, unwilling to admit to my obvious need for God. Faced with appeals, increasing sentences, and a new case involving the cocaine, I could not believe what was happening. *WHAT DO YOU MEAN, 10 YEARS TO LIFE? God's got everything under control? Ha! No thanks, I'VE GOT TO FIGHT THIS.* With all these thoughts spinning in my head and everything happening beyond my control, I was transferred to Leavenworth for secure holding.

Journey Insights

God gave me advance warnings, dreams, opportunities to repent, even messengers with prophetic words, but I continued to do the wrong thing. There comes a time when God says that's it, then allows the consequences to come crashing down. My mother prayed "God, spare his life and bring him into Your service for the Kingdom," and God heard. My world was crumbling to pieces yet I continued to say, "I don't need God, I'm going to fight this my way!" Are you still trying to do it your way?

19

WELCOME TO "HEAVENWORTH"

In January of 1990, Vic and I were locked in different cells in the most secure pre-trial holding facility in the nation at that time, Building 63 at Leavenworth. After a thorough strip search, the guard handed me some prison khakis and a T-shirt, cuffed me behind my back, and along with another guard escorted me to my three-man cell in the lockdown unit. We'd hit the big time. My "journey to hell" education had begun.

A prisoner in an adjacent cell proclaimed, "Welcome to Heavenworth!" *Did I hear him right? Is this sarcasm,* I wondered, *or does he like it here?* I'd heard of people who liked prison better than the free world, but never actually met one. This place seemed more like hell to me: poor lighting, cockroach infestation, and paint falling off the 16-foot high walls. *This was the flagship facility of the Federal Bureau of Prisons? Seems more like it ought to be condemned,* I thought, and found out that this unit was at a later date.

The average sentence at Leavenworth at that time was 35 years, and 25 percent were serving life sentences. Billy, in the cell across from me, was serving eight consecutive life sentences. He had tried to escape on so many occasions at different penitentiaries that he was now locked down for several years, which meant he was confined to his cell. This is how Billy ended up in the "hole" (separation and solitary confinement) with the rest of us who were placed there for safe keeping.

Billy was the "tier tender" during the daytime, and allowed to roam the tier (different levels of cells built above one another) for a couple of hours daily. He would help the guards clean and pass out food trays. Having one of our family members send money to Billy's commissary account would ensure we received extra food when it was available. Vic and I did this, and we were eating in the top five percent of the lockdown population the next day. We were still striving for any available creature comforts. We didn't realize just how far we'd fallen. The oversized cockroaches running rampant in our cell should have been the first clue.

Lockdown is usually 23 hours a day in a small cell. Food is delivered on Styrofoam trays three times a day through a small slot in the door that locks and unlocks with the guard's key. Recreation is offered five times per week, 30 minutes to one hour per day (or less often if the guards can get away with it). Double guard escorts were present as well, and from recreation, we were handcuffed behind our backs and the guards grasped the chain to our handcuffs and pulled upward to impart discomfort as they opened a fenced-in recreation cage with a pull up bar and a basketball goal inside.

We called these the "squirrel cages." The top of the cage wasn't high enough to use an arched shot; challenging when trying to shoot a basket. It seemed everything in prison was like this, controlled and awkward. At least we were out of our cells and saw some semblance of sunshine a few days a week. For many, this was the highlight of the day!

God's hand of discipline was upon us, which I didn't yet recognize. I thought I was fighting against the Feds, when in reality, I'd been fighting against God. It would be several months before I would open a Bible and discover what the Lord was doing in my life because He loved me and was answering my mother's prayers.[14]

Looking from an earthly perspective, this was a place of little hope. Violence could erupt anywhere at any time on the compound, yet I still wanted out of the lockdown unit and into general population where I had access to the law library, typewriters, telephones, exercise facilities, etc. I put in a written request to be released from segregation, but my request was denied. In retrospect, I was right where I needed to be for introspection on what got me here.

Shortly after my arrival at the infamous Building 63, 14 men were locked down for an incident that started with someone cutting in line at the washing machine in the main prison. Things progressed from there; someone was stabbed, and then two more, culminating with 11 others getting involved, all wielding prison shanks (illegal knives). A prisoner told me something that stuck with me that day, "David if you're not right with God in Leavenworth, you're always just one heartbeat away from hell."

Through this simple statement, God began to speak to me about my eternity. Someone else said, "Tomorrow isn't promised. No one knows the day he will step into eternity." Vic tried to share the Gospel with me. This time, the Holy Spirit slowly removed my blinders. God also sent other witnesses which were prisoners from various cultures and criminal backgrounds. I listened to each,

---

14   **"For the Lord disciplines him whom he loves, and chastises every son whom he receives. It is for discipline that you have to endure. God is treating you as sons; for what son is there whom his father does not discipline? If you are left without discipline, in which all have participated, then you are illegitimate children and not sons. Besides this, we have had earthly fathers to discipline us and we respected them. Shall we not much more be subject to the Father of spirits and live?"** (Hebrews 12:6-9 RSV)

sometimes arguing, other times mocking.

A parole violator in his late twenties was placed in our cell by the name of Jarrod Paxton. He was from Kansas City and we soon discovered we knew a lot of the same people. I'd seen Jarrod several years before at nightclubs when I was sneaking in with a fake ID at age 19. He was a big cocaine dealer, busted by the Feds five years earlier. Jarrod had moved hundreds of kilos of cocaine for the Cali Cartel. A friend of his set him up, and he went to prison on a half-pound of cocaine transaction, with a five-year sentence.

His case was "old law"[15] and that made him eligible for parole, and he was out in three years. Now, 10 months later he was back in prison for coming up dirty at a urinalysis, testing positive for cocaine use. Jarrod was looking at another 12-18 months in prison.

He was only 28 years old, but his back was hunched over so badly he could barely walk. He told us he was in a one-car accident and broke his back in five places. We asked about medical treatment. Jarrod smirked. "This is a prison. They don't give you medical treatment for these things; you just have to tough it out."

We asked if he'd received medical treatment on the outside. His face was downcast. "The doc fitted me with a back brace and pain pills to hold my back in place."

"Where is it?" I asked.

Jarrod said, "It had metal strips for support, so the guards mailed it to my home for when I get out. In the maximum-security lockdown unit, hardback books aren't even allowed; let alone something with metal strips that could be made into a shank to kill someone."

How awful, I thought and then asked, "So, what did they give you instead?" When he told me that they didn't give him anything, my heart sank. I hardly wanted to keep questioning him, but I continued, "And for the pain?"

Jarrod just smiled a bit, and said, "My pain medication was also taken from me upon arrival and replaced with 800 mg Motrin." Quietly he said, "It doesn't even touch the pain." Vic and I were shocked.

Vic assessed Jarrod's situation quickly, then pulled me aside, "Whatever you do, don't tell this guy I'm a chiropractor. There's nothing I can do for him; without an X-Ray machine, adjusting table, or my equipment I may do more

---

15   "Old law" was a reference to federal criminal laws put in place through 1987, where receiving parole was common and sentences could be greatly reduced, i.e. serving 1/3 to 1/2 before being paroled. In 1987, new sentencing guidelines were implemented, eliminating parole, and stiffening penalties for almost everything. New law, which I was under, is 85% with good time, no exceptions.

harm than good."

Turns out Jarrod was a born again Christian too and he and Vic hit it off. They started studying the Bible together, asking me to join in, and out of a combination of boredom and curiosity I agreed. I didn't know it at the time, but the Holy Spirit was at work.

They talked while I listened. Jarrod was a different breed of Christian. He referred to himself as a Charismatic, who spoke in tongues. He shared how he came to know Christ and how God delivered him from his drug addiction three and a half years ago in the county jail. He included how God healed him miraculously from a chronic neck problem and how God delivered him from what should have been a life-sentence considering his criminal conduct with the Colombians for four years before his arrest.

Then Jarrod explained how he backslid six months after being released. It started with tooth pain one night. He called his dentist on a Friday afternoon, but couldn't get treatment until Monday. This opened the door for the enemy. He was out with some friends at a barbecue later that evening, when an old acquaintance offered him cocaine to numb the pain. Jarrod's response was, "I don't do that stuff anymore."

"Your dentist sometimes uses *pharmaceutical* cocaine to anesthetize his patients. Put a little on the tooth to see if it helps." These seemingly reasonable words were the perfect justification Jarrod needed. The devil's words are usually reasonable in one form or another.[16]

Because of the pain Jarrod yielded to his friend's words. Relief came instantly and the lie seemed true. Every hour or so Jarrod put more cocaine on the tooth. His original intent was not to get high but to gain relief from the pain. The cocaine taste, however, was in his mouth again for the first time in years which triggered memories from his old lifestyle. Next, someone offered him a drink, then another, and another.

Jarrod woke up the next morning with a girl he'd met at the barbecue. He had a hangover, and the tooth pain was back with a vengeance. He called his dentist to get some medication authorized through the pharmacy. He went to church on Sunday, but couldn't seem to break through into the Presence of God. On Monday, his tooth was repaired, but the real damage was yet to be seen. The enemy had gained a stronghold in Jarrod's life. He returned to work for the week and then, on Friday night, Jarrod found himself drinking again.

16　When Jesus was hungry at the end of a 40 fast the devil reasoned with Him, **"If you are the Son of God, tell these stones to become bread."** (Matthew 4:3 NIV). Jesus refused to reason with Satan. Instead, he responded with God's written Word, saying, **"It is written: 'Man does not live on bread alone, but on every word that comes from the mouth of God.'"** (v. 3 NIV).

This led to a lifestyle of carousing with more women and using cocaine one night a week. God had delivered Jarrod from demons during his first prison sentence yet they had returned with a vengeance![17]

Three months' time and nine girls later, Jarrod had the one-car accident that broke his back. God saved his life, but it seemed He was chastening Jarrod for his waywardness. Interestingly enough, inside Leavenworth Penitentiary Jarrod happily proclaimed, **"...the goodness of God leads you to repentance."** (Romans 2:4)

Shocked, I asked, "You call this place good?"

His face brightened, "It's better than hell for eternity. If you have to go to jail to avoid going to hell, it's worth it!" His words hit me hard and have had a lasting impact on my life. This began to be a recurring theme: no one goes to hell by accident.

Journey Insights

I thought I was fighting against the Feds when in reality I had been fighting against God. His hand of chastisement was upon me. The words, "David if you're not right with God, you're one heartbeat away from hell" never left me. "For the Lord disciplines the one he loves, and chastises every son whom he receives" (Hebrews 12:6 ESV). It would be months before I'd begin to understand what those words meant and how much God loves me. Have you been fighting God, thinking you are fighting someone else?

---

17 "This evil nation is like a man possessed by a demon. For if the demon leaves, it goes into the deserts for a while, seeking rest but finding none. Then it says, 'I will return to the man I came from.' So it returns and finds the man's heart clean but empty! Then the demon finds seven other spirits more evil than itself, and all enter the man and live in him. And so he is worse off than before." (Matthew 12:43-45 LVB).

20

HEALING MIRACLES

The Jewish Rabbi arrived at our cell and wanted to talk to me. He heard through my intake screening that I was Jewish by bloodline. Being Jewish is both a religion and a bloodline. You can be an Orthodox Jew, a Hasidic Jew, a Reformed Jew, an atheist Jew, or a Buddhist Jew, and still be recognized as a Jew in Israel because of your mother's Jewish bloodline. For some reason, the only thing you can't be is a Christian Jew, without being ostracized to some degree by other Jews for believing in Jesus as Messiah. I later learned Jesus' 12 disciples were all Jewish, and their first 3,000 converts to Christianity in the Book of Acts on the Day of Pentecost were all Jewish (Acts 2:17-41). Moreover, the majority of the New Testament was written by Jews.

Since I wasn't a practicing anything, the Rabbi approached me with a question that seemed more like an instruction. "David, you want to be bar mitzvahed, don't you?"

I remembered the Rabbi at the Wailing Wall telling me I needed to be bar mitzvahed, so I told the Rabbi I was interested. That's all it took. Right away he showed me how to wear tefillin[18] and read the Hebrew prayers as they were sounded out in English phonetics. He taught me the details of the bar mitzvah ceremony, and when I was ready, I was officially bar mitzvahed. Returning to my cell, I was keenly aware of the commitment I'd made to the God of Abraham, Isaac and Jacob. Although I felt no significant difference in my life, I sensed something important had begun.

During the next few weeks, Jarrod's back went from bad to worse. Regardless of the circumstances, or how badly Jarrod felt, he kept proclaiming that God was going to heal him, but Vic didn't believe it for a minute. *Jarrod is just hoping against hope. I feel sorry for the poor guy.*

I noticed that every night Jarrod and Vic listened to an international evangelist on the radio. At the end of the 15-minute broadcast, this preacher prayed the prayer of faith with the radio audience. Jarrod would pray the prayer, but nothing would happen. This went on for a couple of months. I felt badly for

---

18 Tefillin: two small leather black boxes that hold scrolls of parchment inscribed with verses from the Torah. They are worn by observant Jews during weekday morning prayers.

him. Vic finally confessed to Jarrod that he was a licensed chiropractor and agreed to examine Jarrod's back. Vic told me that out of the 100 patients a week he'd been seeing before being arrested, Jarrod's back was one of the 10 worst cases he'd seen. The prognosis wasn't good, five compression fractures and three blown discs. His spine was irreparably damaged, and the skin was white and pink just micro inches apart, indicating blocked circulation. Vic could do nothing for Jarrod given our present circumstances, so he just put ice on Jarrod's back when a guard or the "tier tender" inmate would provide a few cubes.

Vic sadly gave Jarrod his discouraging long-term diagnosis, "Jarrod, I'm sorry, you have the back of an 80- year-old man in poor health. Even with medical treatment, you'll have back problems and chronic pain the rest of your life. It'll never be right."

Jarrod just looked at Vic and boldly declared, "I don't receive that report. Jesus is my healer, and He is going to heal me!"

The look Vic gave him spoke volumes. Jarrod seemed like a fanatical Christian and Vic rolled his eyes and walked off. Thirty minutes later "Doctor Vic" was about to learn a lesson from the Great Physician above.

I began to listen to the same radio preacher they had and liked his storytelling style. There was always a miraculous healing testimony, and I started to wonder if these stories might be true or if he was just making it all up to sell books or get donations. Like a lot of people, I wasn't too sure about these "faith preachers" but they sure were entertaining.

Long after the radio was off, the same thought began to swirl in my head. *What if it's true?*

That night I saw Jarrod getting ready to pray the prayer of faith *again* with this radio preacher. Pity came over me for how much he hurt, and how much he wanted to be healed. I found myself offering my first prayer for healing, not out loud but in my head.

God, if You're up there, and You still heal today, I'm asking You to heal my friend Jarrod. I'm not asking for myself, because I don't know You well enough for You to do a miracle for me. I'm asking for him because he's a child of Yours, and he needs a miracle that only You can give him.

I finished my brief prayer and then looked over at Jarrod, who was less than four feet away. I saw something supernatural before my eyes. The only way I can describe it is something like clear liquid gel descended over Jarrod's head and shoulders, and down his back. Over the next 10 to 12 seconds, I simultaneously heard popping and cracking, pop, pop, pop, crack, pop, crack, pop, crack. Jarrod slowly began to twist his back to the left, then the right.

He pulled off his headphones and ecstatically began to cry out, "Hallelujah! I'm healed! Hallelujah!" He wasn't embarrassed or afraid, he just kept shouting, "Praise God! I'm healed! Thank You, Jesus!" Then he began speaking in tongues, praising God.

Startled, Vic took off his headphones, looked at Jarrod and asked, "What's going on?"

"Vic, David, I'm healed. Jesus healed me!"

Jarrod quickly got off his bunk, stood upright, bent over, then back up again, and repeated the motion until he could touch the floor with his hands. "Dr. Vic" was amazed. So was I! I told neither of them about my prayer or the supernatural clear gel substance that I saw a few seconds earlier. I simply continued to watch what was happening.

Jarrod was incredibly excited, confident that he was better. "Hey, I want to work out with you guys. Let's do some push-ups! Come on. I can do some dips. I know I can do jumping jacks right now!"

Vic, on the other hand, was extremely cautious. Assessing the situation, he said, "Jarrod, let's examine your back first. If this is psychosomatic, I don't want you to hurt yourself."

Heavenly fire suddenly appeared in Jarrod's eyes as he countered, "You're not going to steal my healing." Every word became stronger and more pronounced. "Neither is the devil. You told me earlier I would have back problems and pain the rest of my life, but that's not true. God is my healer. Get away from me you doubter!"

Jarrod meant business and Vic was clearly taken aback and humbled. "Jarrod, I believe God has healed you. I don't want to cause you to lose your healing because I believe God still heals today. Just 30 minutes ago, I was repenting for my lack of faith and for what I said to you. Just let me look at your back to see if there are any physical changes. God's healings can stand the test of a physician, can't they?"

Jarrod thought about it for a second and said, "All right." Then he laid down on the bed so "Doctor Vic" could examine him. I looked over Vic's shoulder. We were stunned. Miraculously, the vertebrae were back in alignment with no sign of discoloration and circulation was restored.

Jarrod worked out with us that night. The following morning we went to the squirrel cages and Jarrod did pull-ups and played basketball with us. Vic and I were still astonished. The other inmates immediately noticed and asked what was going on.

Jarrod smiled broadly and confidently proclaimed, "Jesus healed me last night!"

The responses were a mixture of surprise to unbelief. "Oh really, well, let's see how you feel tomorrow!"

Tomorrow came, and the next day and the next, and Jarrod remained healed. It was evident that he felt great. Eventually, this miracle opened a door for Jarrod to share the Gospel with others and all the while, I remained stunned. These miracles are happening, right before my eyes! God had my attention.

Journey Insights

For the first time as a non-Believer I prayed, "God I don't know You, but if You still heal today, will You heal my friend?" Seconds after that prayer, I saw a gel like substance flow over my friend's body and his back made loud popping sounds. Jarrod cried out, "I'm healed!! Jesus healed me!" I was stunned. God had answered my prayers and now had my attention. Have you prayed to God yet? If not, is it time for you to ask?

21

THE MOMENT THAT CHANGED EVERYTHING

In Biblical days, miracles got people's attention and this one sure had mine. I finally reached out to Heaven with a prayer, "God, if You're up there…" Over time, God took me from curious to convinced, and finally to committed. I had finally begun to understand what Jesus told Nicodemus, **"…You must be born again."** (John 3:7) I realized my heart needed to change and there was something to this idea of trusting in Jesus' Name.

As I took a close look at myself, I began to understand what the Apostle Paul said about the matter. **"As for you, you were dead in your transgressions and…the spirit who is now at work in those who are disobedient."** (Ephesians 2:1-2 NIV) Jesus told him the way to enter His Kingdom was to be born again.

It dawned on me that I needed to ask forgiveness and go a new direction, which I learned was called repenting. I actually needed God to help me go His direction which was something my pride did not want to acknowledge. My best thinking had landed me in federal prison. It was time to give up my great ideas and the ways of the world and finally accept the mind of Christ.

Coming to the realization that I was a sinner in need of the Savior, Jesus Christ, was monumental. It became clear that God *wanted* to forgive me and help me. He was inviting me to Himself, not because I earned anything but because Jesus Christ paid the price for my sins. Romans 10:13 says, **"For 'whoever calls on the name of the Lord shall be saved.'"** I was the "whoever."

In April of 1990, I made what I later would learn was a covenant agreement with God, giving my life, case, and future totally to Jesus. No bells went off, no fireworks exploded, but I just knew. Vic and Jarrod led me in a prayer of salvation, "Jesus, I give You my life. I surrender all to You. I believe You are the Son of God and that You died on a cross 2,000 years ago, were buried in the tomb, and on the third day rose from the dead. Come in and make me new from the inside out. Write my name in the Lamb's book of Life. Cleanse me with Your shed blood now. Amen."

That single decision was the turning point in my life. The jet that up until now had been heading to hell was recalculating its course to begin a new journey, this time to freedom.

I asked Jarrod and Vic, "When's our next Bible study?" They told me that I needed to read the Bible on my own. "I'd rather just listen to you guys, and I'll be able to repeat it to others."

Vic spoke to me with great compassion and fervor, "You can't just be a parrot, you've got to let the Holy Spirit illuminate the Scriptures, and lead you personally into truth. That truth is being revealed to you for your personal walk with God." He quoted 2 Timothy 2:15 (NET), **"Make every effort to present yourself before God as a proven worker who does not need to be ashamed, teaching the message of truth accurately."**

He told me to read the first book in the New Testament, Matthew. I did, and an hour and a half later I asked, "What's next?"

"You've got to study to remember, not just speed read. Finish Matthew."

"Finished it."

He leaned back, with his arms folded. "Okay, what's in it?" I gave names, places, miracles, etc. Jarrod was a good Bible teacher who spent four to five hours a day studying. Neither he nor Vic could believe I'd never read the Bible before, but I've learned that God does things differently to capture us and bring us into an ongoing personal relationship. In my case, He knew what would be effective in getting my attention, which was not only listening and remembering (something I'd been able to do since a child) but now reading and comprehending.

I hungered for more. I searched for preachers on my little transistor radio. I believed, even expected, that I'd hear from God, and I began dreaming things that I hadn't read but would later find in the Bible.

The Lord used an old convict named Sam in the cell across from me to help me clean up my language. Sam had been a heroin addict and was tattooed almost everywhere on his body. He'd been in and out of prison on the "installment plan" and was now serving a fresh 20. This time, however, Sam had finally given his heart to Jesus.

"Hey, you got to discipline your speech, man. Each time you curse, drop and do 25 pushups to help you remember you've got a new life in Christ."[19] Sam told me once I could do that, then start paying attention to my thoughts. If I even thought something filthy I was to do the pushups! This helped get me in physical shape rather quickly while new character was developed inside me. I

---

19   Colossians 3:8 (ESV) says, **"But now you must put them all away: anger, wrath, malice, slander, and obscene talk from your mouth."**

was actually becoming accountable.

I began having a recurring dream about chewing gum which is against prison rules to possess because it can jam locks. In each dream, the scene always started with me blowing bubbles with a little harmless gum, but before long it was stuck to my teeth and gums. My efforts to remove it left gum stuck to my fingers and hands. It just kept growing and I couldn't get it out of my mouth. I'd almost choke.

After calling a friend who was gifted in dream interpretation, she said, "David, it's something with your mouth. It seems fun but turns into a big mess, and you can't clean it up." The next thing she said shocked me.

"Coarse joking, that's what it is." She quoted the same verse old Sam had about getting rid of filthy language.

As she spoke, the Holy Spirit brought to mind another verse, **"But among you there must not be even a hint...of any kind of impurity... because these are improper for God's holy people. Nor should there be obscenity, foolish talk or coarse joking, which are out of place, but rather thanksgiving."** (Ephesians 5:3-4 NIV)

Prison. It's like a men's locker room here. Everywhere I go there is jeering and crude joking.

Maybe it was just the culture. But, I saw a picture in my mind of putting a boat in the water. That was okay, but it wasn't okay to let that water in my boat or you'd risk sinking. I knew it started as harmless verbal banter or even sparring, but it quickly becomes a sticky mess that is not pleasing to the Holy Spirit. That much I knew!

God was teaching me that I must be cleaned up from the inside. Not only my language but my pride, my impatience, and something I learned was exhibitionism. These are more than bad habits, there is a spirit behind these behaviors. I found out that exhibitionism, or a performance spirit, is a desire to be seen and it often comes from a root of rejection. I was grateful that God began revealing, and still does to this day, the areas of my life that need to be cleansed.

Jarrod and I were talking a couple of weeks later. "David, now that you've given your heart to God do you want to receive the infilling of the Holy Spirit, along with a personal prayer language in tongues?"

"Sure, I want everything the Lord wants to give me, even if I don't yet understand it all."

This was another time I was grateful my mother modeled an openness to

God, His miracles, and His teachings that sometimes seem odd to the world (and even to Christians). If God said it, then I wanted it. I have since learned that some people feel like speaking in tongues is not for today. It's not an issue to divide over, but rather we should have grace for each other. We can agree to disagree agreeably, and agree always to agree on the critical essentials of our faith.

Jarrod laid hands on me and prayed that I might receive the baptism of the Spirit. Vic agreed, and so did I. Nothing seemed to take place, so I said, "Well, maybe one day I'll receive this gift of tongues."

Jarrod confidently replied, "You received, you just don't realize it. It will manifest!"

Strange, I thought, *but a lot of things have been strange lately!* For some reason, I believed Jarrod. He spoke with a certain confidence and authority and everything else he proclaimed by faith seemed to be coming to pass.

A few weeks later I was listening to a Christian radio station while lying in bed. Jarrod asked, "Have you been thanking the Lord for giving you the gift of tongues?"

I said, "I pray for it from time to time and believe He'll give it to me one day."

Jarrod shot straight up in bed and said, "You don't yet understand faith. You already received it when I laid hands on you. Now you have to *believe you've received,* and the Holy Spirit will give you the supernatural utterance to speak in tongues."

"Jarrod, I don't understand."

Jarrod opened his Bible and showed me this verse, **"Therefore I say to you, whatever things you ask when you pray, believe that you receive them, and you will have them."** (Mark 11:24) He explained, "You have to believe you've already received, and then you'll have it. To believe it is to take it. Start praising and thanking God as if He has already given it to you because the Bible says you already have it. Why? Because we prayed and asked for it." Then he flipped a few pages and showed me another verse that encouraged me, **"So I say to you, ask, and it will be given to you; seek, and you will find; knock, and it will be opened to you. For everyone who asks, receives; and he who seeks, finds; and to him who knocks, it will be opened."** (Luke 11:9-10 NASB)

Jarrod continued, "The context of this passage concerns those asking God for the Holy Spirit." Pointing to the page, he told me to keep reading.

"Now suppose one of you fathers is asked by his son for a fish; he will

not give him a snake instead of a fish, will he? "Or if he is asked for an egg, he will not give him a scorpion, will he? "If you then, being evil, know how to give good gifts to your children, how much more will your heavenly Father give the Holy Spirit to those who ask Him?" (Luke 11-13 NASB)

Jarrod closed his Bible. "See, God gives you the Holy Spirit when you ask Him. Simply believe Him."

"Okay, I'll try it, but what you're telling me isn't logical." Jarrod just smiled and lay back down on his bed. I liked that about him. He was prepared to give an answer or a reason for the expectation of God's goodness and that he did it with gentleness and respect.

I went back to listening to the Christian radio station on my headphones and started acting on this faith principle. I said out loud, "God, I uh, thank You for already giving me the spiritual gift of tongues." I sounded ridiculous but following Jarrod's advice, I said the same thing a second time. A droplet of faith suddenly came into my spirit and I no longer felt foolish. Something was changing. I repeated this a third time, with more boldness. This time, something happened, and I believed I had received this gift.

I couldn't explain it, but something had just occurred in my spirit deep down on the inside and I now felt confident about this matter. I slowly drifted off to sleep with a supernatural peace upon my heart and soul. Ten minutes later I woke, and my mouth was moving! It wasn't uncomfortable, but it did startle me. My mouth was a little numb as if some supernatural energy was on my lips. I got Jarrod's attention, and asked, "Hey, is this what happens when you receive the gift of tongues?"

"It's a little different for everyone, but this is the beginning of it for you. Say the word 'Hallelujah.' God inhabits the praises of His people (Psalm 22:3). When you say 'Hallelujah,' God's Presence will come upon you more tangibly in response to your praise."

I raised my hands to God, "Hallelujah." Instantly my mouth started moving again as if this jump started something. I was speaking words that I'd never learned, and they were bubbling upward from my inner man, my spirit. The audible portion of these words was weak at first and sounded like little puffs of air making different sounds.

Jarrod said, "Now speak the words out loud. Just keep yielding to Him and eventually a full language will bubble forth. Keep speaking by faith."

Smiling, he laid back down on his bed. He began praising God as he muttered, **"...being confident of this, that he who began a good work in you will**

carry it on to completion until the day of Christ Jesus"[20] and "'Well done, my good servant!' his master replied. 'Because you have been trustworthy in a very small matter, take charge of ten cities.'"[21]

The very next morning Jarrod was transferred from *Heavenworth* penitentiary to the adjacent prison camp about a mile away. His work and assignment with us were complete, and he had received his healing from the Lord in front of a licensed chiropractor who confirmed it. Grateful for his encouragement and teaching, I was finally beginning to understand the simplicity of having faith like a child. If God, my Father, says it's true, then we can believe it. We can know that He will bring it to pass in time if we just have a little patience and trust Him at His Word.

Journey Insights

Miraculously my heart started changing. Then it dawned on me that to repent means turning away and going the other direction. I could only change with the help of Jesus and my commitment to God was given. The words Jesus spoke to Nicodemus, that "…you must be born again" (John 3:7), became real for the first time and I asked to receive my prayer language. It felt foolish at first, but I was told to thank God for giving it to me even though I hadn't experienced it yet. "Therefore I say unto you, all things whatsoever ye pray and ask for, believe that ye receive them, and ye shall have them" (Mark 11:24 KJV). Is it time for you to turn away, go the other direction, and start a new journey?

---

20   Philippians 1:6 NIV
21   Luke 19:17 NIV

22

JESUS APPEARS IN A DREAM

USP Leavenworth, Kansas (1990)

Two weeks later Jesus appeared to me in a dream. He put His right hand on my shoulder and opened my paperback Bible to Luke Chapter 5. As I stared at the page, He said, *"Do not be afraid. From now on you will catch men."*

When I woke up, I protested. *How can this be, God calling me to catch men for Him? I'm too sinful; I could never be worthy to preach to others!* I grabbed my paperback Bible and opened it to Luke 5. I'd never read this passage before, and I stared in disbelief.

> **"When He had stopped speaking, He said to Simon, "Launch out into the deep and let down your nets for a catch.**
>
> **"But Simon answered and said to Him, "Master, we have toiled all night and caught nothing; nevertheless at Your word I will let down the net." And when they had done this, they caught a great number of fish, and their net was breaking. So they signaled to their partners in the other boat to come and help them. And they came and filled both the boats, so that they began to sink. When Simon Peter saw it, he fell down at Jesus' knees, saying, "Depart from me, for I am a sinful man, O Lord!"**
>
> **"For he and all who were with him were astonished at the catch of fish which they had taken; and so also were James and John, the sons of Zebedee, who were partners with Simon. And Jesus said to Simon, "Do not be afraid. From now on you will catch men." So when they had brought their boats to land, they forsook all and followed Him."**
> (Luke 5:4-11)

I was startled. Here I was barely saved 30 days. *How could Jesus expect me to catch others for Him?* I pondered the dream all night and shared it with Vic for an understanding of what Jesus was calling us to do. I assumed Vic was going to tell me we were called to catch others out of the dirty waters of humanity and get them in the boat of salvation. I awaited his response.

Vic replied in a matter of fact tone, "It's clear to me that God wants us to catch men for the government, he wants us to snitch, to reduce our prison sentences." When Vic said this, my body recoiled. My head was shaking *no*. "That's not what it means!" I blurted.

"Well then, what do you think it means?" He spit out the words with contempt.

What a defining moment in my walk with Christ! I hesitated at first. And then a boldness rose up in me, "Jesus wants us to catch men for His Kingdom with the Gospel! He wants us to preach to others."

Vic's demeanor changed for a moment, and he asked, "Maybe, but how are we going to do this in prison? These men aren't interested! We need to get out first, and that means we have to catch others for the government to reduce our sentences. Then we can catch men for Jesus on the outside." He seemed convinced; I, on the other hand, remained dismayed for somehow I *knew* what the Holy Spirit meant and it wasn't what Vic was saying.

"That may be what it means to you, Vic, but that isn't what it means to me. Let's pray and trust God to confirm which interpretation is accurate."[22]

The next day God began sovereignly placing men who were ripe for harvest in our cell. Most men came to Christ within a few days to a couple of weeks. God would then move them out, saved, and send others who were about to be saved, in. It stunned me to realize He was giving me the boldness to share the Gospel. Vic, who knew more Scripture, supported me where I floundered. Where I had looked at other things and activities for gratification before, I found myself immensely enjoying sharing my testimony and what I knew to be true. It was a wonderful work of co-laboring in the Lord, and God's grace abounded during this time with many men repenting from their old lifestyle and accepting Jesus as their personal Savior.

Years later, I received letters from two of the men God placed in our cells, neither of whom came to Christ while we were cellmates. One was a committed Muslim, and the other a fervent Satanist. They both shared how they were now Christians and that the time we spent together impacted them with Gospel seeds that helped bring them to salvation.

Looking back, I see how God gave lots of grace to encourage me in this first season of catching men. They were handpicked, low-hanging, ripened fruit. Most of them were only a prayer away from salvation. When we shared a few

---

22 We all interpret dreams, visions, and life-circumstances differently based on our callings, missions and assignments from God, and even the idols in our own hearts. We're directed to seek God for interpretation, remembering He says that His sheep hear His voice. Occasionally only time and fruit will indicate the correct interpretation. In addition, we have different assignments. A single wrong decision can cost us additional years "in prison," yet rarely can a single decision disqualify us for service. God has a way of repositioning us back on the path that leads to our eternal destination. In the process, character is built in us, and we bear fruit with others, as God works to perfect us.

Scriptures, they "fell off the branch into the basket of salvation." The prayers of family and friends and numerous seeds sown by others had gone ahead of us, preparing their hearts and the way for their conversions.

The Holy Spirit later showed me the following verse that provided more understanding of what occurred during that season. **"I planted, Apollos watered, but God gave the increase."** (1 Corinthians 3:6) I've since learned a person in the United States is exposed to the Gospel an average of 7.6 times before receiving Jesus. Regardless of how poorly and immaturely I may have done things, God allowed me to be number 7.6 each time! As I was obedient, the Holy Spirit revealed Jesus and ushered these men into His Kingdom. These first months after the Luke 5 vision encouraged me to continue to win souls, "catching men" for Jesus.

Journey Insights

Barely saved 30 days Jesus appeared to me in a dream. He told me to win souls to Him, but how could Jesus expect someone like me to catch others for Him? Vic's interpretation of the dream was to snitch and catch men for the government, to reduce our prison sentences. It was a defining moment in every way. As I was obedient to pray and trust God for understanding, the Holy Spirit revealed Jesus and ushered many of the prisoners into His Kingdom right in our prison cell. What are some of your defining moments?

23

THE HANGING JUDGE GOT OUR SECOND CASE

USP Leavenworth, Kansas (1990)

The first time we went to court was for stealing a jet. This time, Vic and I headed back to court for the two suitcases of cocaine we received as partial payment for that jet. Our attorneys advised us to enter our pleas in front of a judge known for his leniency. This way, we would get away from the hanging judge who was threatening to give us life if we were convicted at trial.

"It will limit your potential sentencing exposure," we were told. "The government knows there's a problem with their witness, and they want this case off their docket." We listened carefully to every word, contemplating what we should do. "They've agreed to recommend five years concurrently to the judge in chambers, and he's likely to go with it." You won't do a day more time.

"But the plea agreement didn't specifically say five years," I pointed out, concerned with this issue.

He responded adamantly, "David, I swear on the blood of my children, I'm not screwing you. Sign the plea."

When a Jew swears on the blood of his own children I figured he must be telling the truth. As I handed his pen back to him, he smiled, seemingly relieved, and told me, "Things will get better from here. Trust me."

It was March of 1990. The month before I had given my life to Christ, Vic and I pled guilty to this drug case. Our judge was known for leniency. The "plans of man," however, failed to foresee the lenient judge dying of a heart attack two weeks later and the prosecutor refusing to keep his word behind the scenes with the new judge.

Everyone got amnesia concerning the five-year plea deal except for Vic and me. That's when the Lord illumined truth from the Book of Psalms, **"Do not put your trust in princes, Nor in a son of man, in whom there is no help. His spirit departs, he returns to his earth; In that very day his plans perish…Who executes justice for the oppressed…the Lord gives freedom to the prisoners…"** (Psalm 146:3-7). God was telling us to trust Him as our judge and not put our trust in princes (lawyers) nor in a son of man (judge).

Shortly after the lenient judge died, to our shock and dismay, the hanging judge from our first trial picked up our case. He was the judge that sentenced us to the maximum allowed under the statute, more than doubling the recommended guidelines to five years without parole! He even said that if there was any legal way he could give us more time he would.

When we pled guilty on the second case to a five to forty-year statute in front of the lenient judge, we'd hoped to get the five years minimum sentence, and for it to run concurrently. The hanging judge, vastly more severe, now had the authority to sentence us to anything between five and 40 years. To say this was an ominous turn of events would be a gargantuan understatement.

Our attorneys were suddenly nervous and no longer responded to our letters. As I sat in my cell, my situation seemed hopeless. I realized that although I was a newborn Christian, not everything was "coming up roses." The probation officer was by reputation, an outspoken, seemingly bitter lesbian who hated men, especially womanizing drug defendants, and especially those who claimed to turn to Christ while incarcerated. Her sentencing recommendation within the court-ordered pre-sentence investigation report was more than 20 years! What happened to my attorney's guarantee of five years to run concurrently? The probation office recommended 15-18 years for Vic.

We turned to our cellmate, Big Rich Bruno, a veteran of the federal prison system. He was facing double life for a large meth-manufacturing charge, and he'd served 26 of the last 30 years in maximum-security penitentiaries.

Twenty years earlier Big Rich had been on the FBI's top 20 Most Wanted list. After he had been released, he resumed criminal activities. Although unarmed, the Feds shot Big Rich in the leg, coming out of a grocery store while arresting him. He ended up in a county jail and they refused him medical treatment. After the untreated bullet wound had become severely infected, he wrote a letter from the county jail on toilet paper to a federal judge asking for help.

The "toilet paper letter" was effective. The judge ordered Big Rich to be transferred to a medical facility. Upon arriving, however, the doctors said, "We have to amputate!" Big Rich refused and opted to pray instead. A few hours later an ex-military doctor, who had served field-side in Vietnam told Big Rich he could try to operate, but there were no guarantees he could save the leg. Only with Heaven's intervention would his leg ever be fully restored. Big Rich's 'mustard seed faith' kicked in and he said, "I believe God sent you to me in response to prayer. I trust you; where do I sign?"

Surgery went surprisingly well. God intervened, and Big Rich was grateful. He thanked the doctor as he headed to seven months of rehabilitation. Big Rich acknowledged amongst the prisoners that God did this miracle for him, restoring the leg and he eventually became the number one handball player on the compound. Upon release, Big Rich allowed his two legs to take him running off into the ways of the world again. Arrested, as a fourth-time offender, he was facing the rest of his life in prison on a new case.

Big Rich studied the Bible with us a few nights a week. He believed in Jesus and the Bible, but also believed in a book called *Urantia*, supposedly given to an earthling by an alien from a more advanced planet in 1934. The book alluded to Jesus, the Bible, etc., but spoke of "other worlds" and ethereal interpretations of Scripture. Big Rich never seemed to yield his life fully to the Lord, but continued to pray with Vic and me whenever we asked. By prison standards, Big Rich was a "good convict," and someone you wanted on your side if at all possible. He was also very prison wise.

I asked him about my situation and the probation officer's sentencing recommendation of 20 years. He told me, "David, you need to get as much on the transcript at the sentencing hearing as possible to prepare for an appeal. If you don't get things on the record at sentencing, you don't have an 'ice cube's chance in hell' of winning your appeal. The prosecutor and the probation officer are working together behind the scenes to ratchet up your sentencing guidelines and muddy up your pre-sentence investigation report to get the judge to hammer you."

He went on to tell me they were doing this as part of a plan to get me to cooperate because they thought I knew people they wanted to put away. Big Rich casually told me, "Their goal is to get you to help them make new cases, going to grand juries, debriefing, testifying at trials, etc."

I was already dumbfounded, but Big Rich wasn't finished. "They want to turn you into their prize government witness. In their eyes, you are their potential meal ticket for their promotions. The 20 year, non-paroleable sentence they're trying to give you--after they agreed to five years concurrent--is the main way they do things." He continued with his lesson, as I stared in stunned silence. "It's a tool they use to apply as much pressure as possible to get you to cooperate, resulting in more indictments and convictions. It's called a bait and switch plea agreement."

Vic and I listened intensely to the wisdom from Big Rich's 26 years behind bars. He explained that they knew I would never plead guilty for 20 years as a first offender, and they knew they had me in a bind. "If you didn't know anything that could help them then your sentence probably would be no more than 10 years." What he said made sense. The question was, what to do with this knowledge?

Big Rich later pulled me aside while Vic was in the shower, "I don't want to talk negative about your friend, but I believe he's going to turn on you to get himself out of the 15-18 years they're recommending."

I adamantly disagreed, "No, Vic would never turn on me. We've been friends for years, and he's my brother in Christ that helped lead me to the Lord. Even if he were to turn against everyone else, he would never turn against me."

Big Rich looked at me and simply said, "I hope you're right."

Journey Insights

"Do not put your trust in princes, nor in a son of man, in whom there is no help." (Psalm 146:3). Even though I was a new Christian, not everything was coming up roses! God used Big Rich to educate me with a better understanding of my terrible plight and give me a warning. God is merciful, even when we can't see it. Despite what my circumstances looked like I had to trust God. What have you been trusting in?

24

THE NIGHT THE POWER FELL

USP Leavenworth, Kansas (1990)

The night before my sentencing in the drug case, June 5, 1990, one of the most stunning happenings in my life took place. I was in Leavenworth's Building 63, and the Lord visited me in my cell. There were two witnesses. Even as of this writing, I remain amazed and eternally grateful for God's mercy and kindness to come to me in this way. Not only was I a new Believer, but my sentencing the next day was a monumental moment in my life. So, for God to give such a visitation of His Spirit tremendously humbled me. Even my best explanation leaves much to be desired, but I'll try.

For some reason, I was scheduled to be sentenced alone. They scheduled Vic for his sentencing at a later date. I didn't feel like praying, but out of some religious duty, I decided to get off my bed and ask Vic and Big Rich if they'd pray with me.

They said, "Sure." I felt compelled to get on my knees, humbling myself before God. The cement cell floor was cold, but it didn't matter. Vic and Big Rich prayed with me. I felt nothing. I sensed nothing. God seemed miles away.

Then, something in the atmosphere altered. At first, the change was slight, then a surge of God's Presence began to fill the cell. Suddenly I began speaking in tongues loudly and fluently for the first time, and then singing in tongues. Vic received the interpretation of my words in his mind from the Holy Spirit. He heard in fluent English. This went on for about two hours. *Then Jesus appeared in front of us clothed in an iridescent white robe.*

In John 14:21 Jesus tells us that when we love Him, He will manifest Himself to us, and He did. Over the years, I've learned not to depend on others' understanding and experiences, and never to back down from the promises in God's Word and the standards Jesus set. God tells us we're all pre-qualified by Him, and our job is to lean into God and not away from Him.

Jesus didn't say anything. He just stretched out His arms in love and stood before us. His tangible Presence filled the room, and everything else just faded into the background. Jesus' appearance lasted for about 15 minutes. It's hard to put into words, but I experienced what seemed to be a supernatural love and peace emanating from Jesus. Somehow I knew that Heaven was in total control of all that was taking place. His holy Presence caused worry and anxiety about my sentencing scheduled for the next day to dissipate.

The sounds coming down the tier from inmates in other cells yelling and cursing, which were regularly very noisy, seemed to be muffled as if God's Presence was keeping the world out of our cell for this special time together. Vic and I kept praying. I prayed in English and then in tongues, and then Vic interpreted. Almost everything that came into Vic's mind to pray about would suddenly flow out of my mouth in prayer in English. The Holy Spirit brought us into "one mind, one accord." We experienced for the first time what I believe to be the mind of Christ in prayer and intercession. It was an incredible visitation of God's Spirit that had a profound effect on us.

After Jesus had disappeared from our midst, something else occurred. A small white cloud appeared on the cell floor in front of me. The Holy Spirit reminded me to "test the spirits." I pointed at this cloud and declared, "DO YOU KNOW JESUS?" When I said the name, JESUS, the cloud sparkled with small shimmering gold and platinum flashes of light. I repeated this again, and the same thing occurred. Then I spoke, "Jesus, Jesus, JESUS!" Each time I spoke the name, JESUS, the cloud sparkled with these gold and platinum flashes of radiant light. Then Vic and I began singing about the sin-cleansing blood of Jesus. When we did, the cloud increased in size, height, and depth and then I was standing in the cloud, up to my knees. It was like energy. The gold and platinum flashes felt like electric energy on my legs, like static electricity, but not painful in any manner. It tickled.

The cloud was tangible; it could both be seen and felt. I put my hand into it, so dense and thick that my hand disappeared. The cloud itself felt like warm energy, somewhat electric in nature. I was cautious, but not fearful. Amazed, I felt God's peace. Like a child experimenting, I put both my hands into the cloud, and then pulled them out, scooping a small portion of the cloud into my hands and pulling it upward before my eyes to get a better look at it. The cloud remained in my hands until I raised it to my chest level, and then it would slip out of my hands, and then spring back into the rest of the cloud. I did this several times.

The Spirit of God prompted me to "drink from the cloud." Initially, I hesitated, but obeyed as I again felt God's peace. Kneeling down, I cupped my hands and "drank" from the cloud. I felt led to do this three times. With each drink of the cloud a feeling of warm, healing energy filled my lungs and sinuses. Before that, I had horrible allergies and chronic sinus problems. That night I was miraculously healed of this problem, and to the date of this writing, these problems have never returned.

One day in 1991 I received a Christian magazine from an international ministry. In this issue, the minister taught on the Glory of God. His testimonial experiences and Bible examples helped me better understand my experience a year earlier. After reading this article, I then began discovering numerous places in Scripture where God's tangible and visible Presence manifested in similar ways. One example occurs on the Mount of Transfiguration:

> **"Now it came to pass, about eight days after these sayings, that He took Peter, John, and James and went up on the mountain to pray. As He prayed, the appearance of His face was altered, and His robe became white and glistening…[23] While he was saying this, a cloud came and overshadowed them; and they were fearful as they entered the cloud."** (Luke 9:28-29, 34)

Another example occurs in the Old Testament during Solomon's reign as they worshiped during the temple dedication:

> **"…and praised the Lord, saying: 'For He is good, for His mercy endures forever,'" that the house, the house of the Lord, was filled with a cloud, so that the priests could not continue ministering because of the cloud; for the glory of the Lord filled the house of God."** (2 Chronicles 5:13-14)

In addition to what occurred in the cell that night, God miraculously answered almost all that we prayed within the next 48 hours. His Presence was astonishingly powerful. In one of my lowest times, He showed me the wonder of His love. After this experience, it took me nine months of searching the Scriptures before I could biblically understand it. Rare, yes, but it was a powerful reminder never to limit the Holy One of Israel (Psalm 78:41).

After the life and perspective-altering glory cloud experience, we all went to bed at about 2:00 a.m. and experienced a perfect night's rest. The following morning the U.S. Marshals escorted me to federal court for sentencing. I moved to withdraw my plea making the prosecutor and judge angry. Sentencing was delayed, and new hearings were ordered. A new sentencing recommendation was given to the judge by the probation officer, increasing my sentence. Vic was unexpectedly moved from the cell shortly after that. I continued to share the Gospel with each man God placed in my cell, helping catch men for Jesus.

---

23 The word Luke uses for glistening is the Greek word exastrapto, Strong's NT #1823, which translates: To send forth lightning, to flash out like lightning, to shine, be radiant. The flashes of gold and platinum that came from the cloud when we spoke the Name of Jesus were a type of this exastrapto or glistening.

Journey Insights

Jesus appeared to us in the cell. He just stretched out His arms in love and stood before us. His tangible Presence filled the room, and everything else just faded into the background. There are no words to describe the pure love and peace that radiated from Him to touch my soul to the core. Jesus wants to touch your soul and fill you with a love you have never known. Will you let Him appear to you? (John 14:21)

25

"DAVID IS NOT YOUR FRIEND"

Communication between Vic and me became difficult after he was moved out of the cell. The temperature was heating up in the non-air conditioned lockdown unit, and large fans were brought in to combat the stagnant heat. It seemed as if everything I tried to yell down the hall became distorted. Vic heard me say things that I didn't say. I tried to pass notes to him about how I was continuing to grow in the Lord. I prayed and continued trying to communicate, but things seemed only to get worse. I couldn't understand what was happening and it became a dark time between us.

One day in the squirrel cages at recreation, Vic and I were placed in adjoining cages. He was very cold toward me. I asked him what was wrong. He looked angrily at me through the cage and said, "Earlier this week I heard an audible voice saying, 'David's not your friend!'" The look in his eyes appeared evil.

"Where do you think this voice came from?"

He answered with a bitter snort, "I believe God spoke to warn me about what you're planning to do against me. You've always gotten me into trouble. In fact, if it weren't for you I wouldn't be in prison right now!"

A sudden burst of adrenaline shot through my veins. "Do you believe it was God telling you that I'm not your friend? Could it be the devil trying to turn us against each other? Let's pray about this together."

I could see his muscle tensing and the veins in his neck bulging. Then he threatened me. I took a step back to assess the situation. Vic was much bigger than I was and he was a disciplined body builder who worked out in his cell regularly. He also had some martial arts training.

I had experienced Vic being filled with the glory of God just months earlier, but the look I saw on his face now seemed the exact opposite. Some of his family were still involved in the mob, and he threatened to use them against me. *Is this my best friend and Christian Brother?* The darkened look in his eye seemed unearthly.

I was utterly confused. "What's gotten into you? For two weeks, you haven't been thinking rationally." I pleaded, "Please, rebuke Satan in Jesus' Name,[24] and let's talk about this."

His face pinched with resentment. "Get away from me," he growled. Then he leaned in closer and spit on me!

Vic and I were both young Christians. Through the evil one's deception, we became divided and took different paths. He refused to communicate with me. Several weeks later we were heading to court for sentencing. We were both cuffed and shackled in the marshal's van. I turned to Vic and said, "Vic, what about the cloud of God's Presence we experienced? What about Jesus appearing to us in a glistening robe? What about the wonderful things that happened that night? What about prayers that were answered miraculously within a couple of days? Do you deny that experience was from God?"

A look of turmoil clouded his face. He shook his head violently and said, "I don't know what to believe anymore. I don't know what I saw that night. Leave me alone and don't talk to me!"

Later that day, September 6, 1990, the judge announced his sentencing. Vic received 15 years 8 months. I received 262 months. *How much is this?* My head was spinning. It took four hours before my brain would allow me to calculate it. *Nearly twenty-two years with no parole!*

In the federal system, parole wasn't allowed under current guidelines; they would only deduct 54 days a year for good conduct. Without supernatural intervention on my 22 year sentence, the Feds would make me serve 19 years and 6 months before release to a halfway house. Vic and I were sent to different prisons. He went to Memphis, and my new "home" was FCI Englewood, Colorado.

This was another crossroads for me, a defining moment in my life. The stark reality of my future started to set in and on top of that, I couldn't believe that my best friend and brother in Christ had suddenly turned his back on me. How could this happen? *It makes no sense. We've been in this together from the beginning, and now we're brothers in Christ.* Then the haunting words of Big Rich came flooding back in living color, "Be careful David; Vic will betray you."

My frame of mind was still disbelief that God would allow me to spend twenty years in prison. A new born-again Believer, in the process of learning and growing, I was still letting pride be my guide. *Surely, God, You're going*

---

24   The Bible commands us to **"…test the spirits, whether they are of God…"** (1 John 4:1). Seven primary origins of voices contend for our attention: (1) God, (2) Satan, (3) the world, (4) our flesh, (5) our soulish desires (emotion-driven), (6) the false voice of the dead, and (7) religion. It is important we follow the voice of God above all these other voices.

to rescue me somehow. You placed an anointing on my life because of my mother's prayers, right? You had a covenant with her before I was born. You're using me in the lives of others. You're not mean. You deliver people. No matter what I reasoned, I remained shocked, reeling to think God would allow me to spend all that time in prison.

One morning I had a dream. A tiny tree sapling sprouted up from the ring finger of my right hand. The scene changed, and the sampling erupted upward with exponential growth and an uncontrollable force like a Jack in the Beanstalk movie! The next thing I knew books began falling from this full grown tree down to prisoners below who were catching them. Each prisoner was elated to receive his or her book.

When I awakened from the dream I shook my head "no." Defiantly and adamantly I spoke out loud. "I do *not* want to be a writer; I don't even like to read!"

The audible voice of the Lord spoke back to me, "Just as it was told to Joseph it shall be done!"

The Holy Spirit inside of me responded out of my mouth with two words, "Yes Lord!" I sat stunned in my cell. I'd heard the voice of the Lord! And I knew the Holy Spirit had brought forth my response. But thinking it through, the Lord's declaration confirming the dream bothered me. *What just happened? Don't I get a choice?* I knew not to say anything more.[25]

The next step that made any sense was to explore more about this Joseph in the Bible. I had to search for two days in the Bible before I found him in Genesis chapters 37-50. The unpleasant similarities between Joseph, the dreamer, and myself troubled me. My thoughts raced. *He was a prideful dreamer, and, well, so am I. People continually turned against him, and that happens to me as well. Joseph spent many years in captivity; from what I gather he was a slave or prisoner from age 17 to 30. No way I'm spending that kind of time in captivity. God, You can't possibly be requiring me to serve 13 years in prison before I'm out of here.*

Little did I know it would take a lot of time, even more time than Joseph had spent in captivity, for God to properly break, rebuild, and prepare someone as messed up as me before sending me out to full-time ministry. I simply could not, and would not believe that He would allow me to serve all of my long sentence.

In retrospect, God was developing much-needed character in me. He knew my journey to freedom. He knew what He wanted to do with my life, both in prison and out. He loved me enough to make sure I didn't end up back

---

25　The full account of this Tree of Books dream is included in Chapter 38.

in prison. He was setting me free on the inside before He opened the actual prison doors to set me free on the outside.

If you have to go to jail to avoid going to hell, it's worth it. Even if you have to do all of your time, so you don't "fail jail," and have to repeat the class, it's worth it! Whatever God allows, I've learned to trust Him because He is the perfect Teacher, loving each of us and dedicated to helping us out of the pit and into our destiny.

Journey Insights

The stark reality of my future (22 years without parole) started to set it in. The words of Big Rich came flooding back about Vic betraying me. I couldn't believe that my best friend and brother in Christ was threatening me, accusing me of evil and turning his back on me. He claims a voice said, "David is not your friend." What voice was that? The Bible commands us, "…test the spirits, whether they are of God…" (1 John 4:1). Has someone betrayed you or have you betrayed someone else? Jesus wants to heal you and is waiting to give you forgiveness. Will you let Him?

26

FIRST PRIORITY

I was transferred to FCI Englewood, a medium-security facility near Denver, in the fall of 1990. Once outside on the compound, I experienced quite a moment as I gazed on the Colorado foothills through the prison fence.

The sun is out, shining on my face, and there's a rainbow glistening in the sky. It's 60 degrees, and I see emerald green foothills outside here at my new compound. I can walk on the half mile track. God's beauty is a long, long way from those Leavenworth cockroaches. For a moment I actually had the thought that if I had to, I could serve my entire sentence in this kind of beauty. That thought, however, was short-lived. Reality struck. *Prison is prison, David, and you're not going anywhere fast.*

Genesis 50:20 speaks of what the enemy meant for harm, God was turning for good.[26] For the previous nine months, God had my full attention in the place where I had first come to know Him. He had secreted me away in the belly of Leavenworth Penitentiary and I was a captive audience. I'd been constantly studying, sharing the Gospel, had read through the entire Bible, and experiencing God in amazing ways. I was in the early stages of my growth in God, yet as I moved to this new compound, I remained perplexed about my extra-long sentence and my Christian brother's betrayal.

God, I'm convinced You don't want me to serve such a long sentence. There's got to be a way out and I trust You for the answers.

My thoughts swirled in expectation of some kind of deliverance from my situation. No answers came. I knew, however, I was on the right track with God and that He knew my needs. I'd read the Scripture, "And my God shall supply all your need according to His riches in glory by Christ Jesus" (Phil 4:19) and I believed it. He did supply my needs but not in the way I expected.

Upon arrival, I was introduced to a strong Christian named Charles Martin. I'd seen him on Oprah Winfrey and in the Business Magazines when he was in his prime at age 18-21. Charles was the infamous "Wonder Boy of Wall Street" of the 1980's, who swindled people out of tens of millions of dollars with his fraudulent carpet cleaning company. Now, Charles was a born-again

---

26   Genesis 50:20

soul-winner.

We both had Jewish backgrounds because one of our parents was Jewish. We had one more thing in common, we were both serving 20 plus year sentences in the federal system. We instantly became good friends, fellowshipping, talking about Yeshua (Jesus) our Meshiach (Messiah), and winning souls together. Charles was a conservative evangelical, and I was more interdenominational in my belief about Jesus. If you believed in Jesus as your personal Lord and Savior, that was enough for me to call you brother and we could easily fellowship together.

We followed the advice of Peter Lord, who said, "The main thing is to keep the main thing the main thing." Because of this we refused to divide ourselves, or anyone in the congregation, over the gifts of the Spirit, eternal security, Calvinism versus Arminianism, forms of water baptism, worship styles, the exact timing of the rapture, etc. All these things were secondary to knowing Jesus. In following this rule, we experienced great fellowship, and genuine brotherly love and as a result, God brought gang members, Muslims, Buddhists, Hindus, Jews, Satanists and many others to Christ. We encouraged each one to begin reading the Bible and continue on their journey to freedom.

Parole was eventually granted to Charles. He was transferred to a camp facility, serving only seven of his 25 years before release in 1993. He was able to get out that quickly because he was under the "old law" which allowed for parole. I was under the "new law", where there was no parole and instead, a prisoner had to serve approximately 85% of their sentence. Charles had a 25 year sentence and served seven. I had a 22 year sentence and although the law said I'd serve a little less than 20, I remained certain that God would intervene.

Next I met Kent Hodges from Liberal, Kansas. Kent was in prison for an oversized firecracker he made in his basement. He lit the mini-bomb and tossed it out his car window one night on his way to the bar with a girl. The homemade firecracker proved more potent than he'd anticipated, and he quickly learned that more is not always better when it comes to gunpowder. The device caused nearly $20,000 in damages to two new cars. No one was injured, thankfully. After a short investigation in this small town of 16,470, the girl told on Kent. Because this case involved explosives, the Feds got involved, and Kent was indicted and arraigned in federal district court.

While out on bond Kent gave his life to Christ at a Full Gospel Church in Liberal. God delivered him from a 25-year alcohol addiction, and he began whole-heartedly serving the Lord. Kent grew rapidly in the Lord for the 20 months he was out on bond. The judge imposed 27 months and ordered him to pay full restitution. Kent arrived at this medium-security facility instead of a camp because of the violent nature of his explosive.

Just as Charles had, Kent proved to be a wonderful blessing to me which furthered my conviction that God would supply all my needs. We were accountability partners and prayer partners for the two years he spent behind bars. His church family supported him with prayer, letters, discipleship books, and Christian materials. Kent's heart was always to share this abundance with me. Through these discipleship materials, the Holy Spirit began to teach me more about evangelism, the ministry of deliverance and the gifts of the Holy Spirit. Eventually, Kent was released, but two years later Kent would make contact with me at the direction of the Lord and would help birth and fund a ministry of Bibles to prisoners.

Finally, God brought another brother into my life named Robert. He was a seasoned, Spirit-filled Christian in on a small parole violation. He and I spent an hour every night in prayer over the compound. God opened numerous doors for the two of us to share the Gospel, including studying with brothers, praying together, healing the sick, and casting out demons. The Lord was faithful during these early months at Englewood to strengthen my own faith and ability to minister through my fellowship and co-laboring with Charles, Kent, and Robert.

I'd assumed God would meet my needs in the way I thought He should but I was wrong. He had different priorities. He was most committed to my long-term character development. He accomplished this by giving me precisely what I needed most: friendships, fellowship, discipleship, and ministry opportunities. This proved critical in my early walk by giving me roots to know Him and enduring faith to sustain me during my journey to freedom.

Journey Insights

Learning to trust God to supply what He says we need and when we need it is important. Proverbs 27:17 (ESV) says, "Iron sharpens iron, and one man sharpens another." The betrayal from Vic was devastating, but during this time, God brought me incredible brothers in Christ. Together we supported and prayed for each other, grew in our faith, and won countless souls for the Kingdom. It was a healing to my heart. Do you need a healing to your heart and friends to come alongside you? Jesus, bring them strong Believers in Christ to minister to them.

27

TRUSTING GOD AS MY ALARM CLOCK

FCI Englewood, Colorado (1990-94)

Early in my experience with God, He asked me to trust Him in even the little things. One of these things was to trust Him to awaken me instead of trusting my alarm clock. At first, this was difficult, because if a prisoner sleeps through work call, the guards can instantly toss him into solitary confinement.

After you serve a year of your time, the Feds have a policy of giving you 54 days of good time. This means you serve only 85% of your sentence; however, any infraction can cause you to lose a portion or all of your 54 days for the year. The system was designed to help maintain order and to incentivize inmates to follow rules.

Time violations were non-negotiable. Mistakes were costly as we could lose a portion of our 54 days per year good time. We could also forfeit other earned privileges such as our prison job, seniority we may have established, increased pay grades, room assignments, commissary and phone access, plus we could be assigned extra duty, such as cleaning toilets, picking up trash, etc.

I realized the Holy Spirit was inviting me to a deeper personal relationship with Him so I would learn to hear His voice and learn to trust Him for bigger things. Proverbs 3:5-6 was quickened to my spirit: **"Trust in the Lord with all your heart, and lean not on your own understanding; in all your ways acknowledge Him, and He shall direct your paths."** Trusting Him in this time thing was challenging because of the possible penalties. But God wanted me to keep my eyes on Him and He was using this to teach me about trust.

I sighed and accepted the challenge. *Okay, Holy Spirit, Jesus said He sent You to us for several reasons, including being our Helper. I need Your help on this one. You always know what time it is, You're much better than a rooster, Your battery never runs out, and You are smarter than any alarm clock I could buy. From this day forward I commit myself to trust You to wake me up instead of my alarm clock.* I felt like I was drawing a line in the sand, stepping over it, and determining, with the help of the Holy Spirit, to absolutely trust God in this forever.

The first morning was interesting. I felt a tap on my shoulder. I opened my eyes and no one was there. The time was 5:55 a.m. *Who touched me,* I wondered? I prayed for a few minutes and then the 6:00 a.m. lights came on in the unit. *Hmmm, was this the Holy Spirit, or one of the angels He sent, or did I imagine it? Maybe it was just a dream.*

The next morning, I heard a gentle voice in my right ear, "David, time to get up." Instantly, I was wide awake. The time again was 5:55 AM. *Was this a dream? Maybe it was my body clock. The number five is the number of grace. God, is this a sign of Your triple grace operating in my life, or am I imagining it all?* I decided not to share this experience with anyone and just leave it between God and me, for now.

Each morning was a little different. Some mornings I would be awakened with a song in my spirit that became my focus for the day. **"...God my Maker, Who gives songs in the night"** (Job 35:10). Other mornings He would awaken me with a Scripture to meditate on that day. **"...He awakens me morning by morning; He awakens my ear to hear as the learned."** (Isaiah 50:4) But each day I was awakened in time and was never late for work.

One day I was dog tired from being up late sharing about Jesus with a couple of inmates. We were short on work duties that day, and my boss gave me permission to return to my unit before the lunch hour. I took a much-needed nap and fell into a deep sleep. I felt a tap on my thigh that awakened me with a start. No one was in my two-man room and the door was closed. I was so tired I didn't know what day it was, let alone the time. Looking at my watch with groggy eyes I was shocked to discover it was 12:50, a good twenty minutes after the final lunch call to return to work. My heart pounded and I jumped to my feet.

The unit doors were locked, and I was surely in trouble. I panicked. *How could this be? Why didn't the Holy Spirit wake me?* I scrambled to locate a guard who would grant me grace and let me out the front door so I could slip back to work. I located one and he said, "No one is going anywhere; it's a census count."

I hung my head, "Not a census. This is the worst! I'll get thrown in the hole for sure," I muttered to myself.

The sudden voice over the loudspeaker startled me, "Census count clear, everyone return to their work assignments."

As it turned out, the special census was called while I was asleep and safe in my assigned location. The Holy Spirit knew all this, and He allowed me the extra sleep until five minutes before it was time to return to work. He knows the future and is much, much better than any alarm clock.

The Holy Spirit then began waking me up at odd hours of the night to intercede for others. He would either speak to me in the still small voice, give me a dream in the night that revealed potential disasters and how to pray for these to be averted, or I would just quietly pray in tongues and He would give me the interpretation. These spontaneous prayer times would last as little as a few minutes or as much as a few hours.

From that day until now, nearly 25 years later, He has never failed me. Learning to trust God in the smallest of things helps us build history with Him so when the big stuff comes we don't panic. I've learned God wants us to ask Him what He is inviting us into so we can learn to trust Him.

"The steps of a good man are ordered by the LORD, And He delights in his way" (Psalm 37:23).

Journey Insights

My whole life I had trusted in myself and my own abilities which landed me in prison. Now it felt like I was drawing a line in the sand, stepping over it, and determining, with the help of the Holy Spirit, to absolutely trust God to wake me up every day forever. Isn't it time for you to start trusting God and make the decision to never look back?

28

SPIRITUAL RAIN IN A MOP CLOSET

FCI Englewood, Colorado (1990-94)

God didn't just ask me to trust Him in the little things like waking me up each day. He also met me in stunning ways similar to how I experienced His tangible Presence in my Leavenworth cell the day before I was first sentenced. It's an understatement to say prison life is difficult, yet I found that God wanted to encourage me in the midst of challenge to bring me hope.

It was important for me to learn that I needed to rely on Him instead of my own reasoning. God was helping me with this along with driving home the message to never, never, never limit Him.[27] While at FCI Englewood, he taught me this lesson again. Several times a week, I secreted away to a sour-smelling mop closet to spend time alone with God. It reminded me a bit of reading about Corrie ten Boom at the horrific Ravensbruck concentration camp during the Holocaust. Corrie's sister Betsie insisted they be thankful for being covered with fleas. Why? Because those fleas kept the guards away at night and the sisters could worship freely.

"My" mop closet allowed me temporary freedom from prying eyes, interactions, requests, random orders from guards, or any of the interruptions that kept me from my time with God. I'd take my Bible into that musty space, sit on a folding chair, and pursue God, usually praying in the Spirit.[28] God was showing me that if I sought Him with all my heart, I would find Him.[29] These were some of the most intimate and life-changing moments in my early walk with the Holy Spirit.

I'd go at 9:00 p.m. and stay one hour, getting back to my cell just in time for the 10:00 p.m. count. One night after praying in tongues for about 30 minutes it appeared as though tiny shards of light were raining down from the ceiling and right through the floor. At first, I thought there was something wrong with my eyes. I rubbed them for a moment and looked again to discover the light shards continued. I thought, *the fluorescent lighting in the room is malfunctioning. Is there a ballast going bad?*

---

27 "They… limited the Holy One of Israel" Psalms 78:41 (KJV).

28 Praying in the Spirit can be in your native language or in tongues.

29 Jeremiah 29:13

The Presence of God was tangible, and the energy in the room felt electric. I continued to pray in tongues, and a new level of fervency rolled upward from deep inside my belly and out of my mouth. Within a few minutes, the light shards began to increase in size. These were no longer tiny and clearly not caused by a lighting issue.

No one had ever taught me anything like this. But God had been teaching me to approach Him with the faith of a child. Mark 10:15 says, **"Assuredly, I say to you, whoever does not receive the kingdom of God as a little child will by no means enter it."** So before my reasoning could get in the way, with trusting faith I reached my hands out into this rain, palms-up. I could feel the shards of light go directly through them.

God, this tickles. It feels like static electricity, like the night at Leavenworth when the glory cloud appeared. I remembered how I had seen flashes of gold and platinum sparked each time I said the Name of Jesus. This time is was just clear shiny shards of light, and to me, this was just as amazing.

In the mop closet, I put my feet out, and the same electric feeling occurred. I felt it another 10 minutes or so as I experimented and the only way I can explain it is the Holy Spirit and I had fun together. We were briefly interrupted when an inmate opened the door. He started to walk inside, but suddenly it was if he ran into something that was odious to him, and it wasn't the smell of sour mops, but God's Presence. He spun around and shut the door as quickly as he came in.

God, what just happened? Then the Lord reminded me of 2 Corinthians 2:16. **"To the one we are the aroma of death...and to the other the aroma of life leading to life..."** I realized that God's Presence is refreshing to people drawn to serve Him, and offensive to those who aren't. I have also learned that a religious spirit can keep some Christians from acknowledging the Lord showing up in any way except those with which they feel comfortable, so God meets them in a way that they can receive him.

While God was ministering His love to me, He began to show me His love and heart for others. He wanted me to carry this same Presence He was imparting to me during our prayer time in the mop closet, outside, to others in their dark places. Jesus said that we are to be salt and light in the earth[30] and carry His love to others. I've learned that He usually does it to us before He does it through us.

These extraordinary times in God's Presence were refreshing and invigorating.

---

30   Matthew 5:13-14

They accomplished many things including God ministering to me, which I deeply needed. He strengthened me there, as I dealt with the cold reality that I was in prison serving a long sentence. I was reminded that Heaven was my home, the prison was a temporary destination, and there was life beyond the bars. The Bible says that God blessed his children with, **"...the days of heaven upon the earth"** (Deuteronomy 11:21 KJV). For me, God made this Scripture real inside a sour mop closet in federal prison.

Journey Insights

The mop closet is where God would meet me and fill me with His Presence. Here God ministered deeply to my soul and spirit, giving me strength and refreshing. Without it, my situation would have been pretty unbearable. What is giving you strength, refreshing and ministering to your soul in an unbearable situation? Jesus is waiting to fill you with His Presence too. Will you say yes?

29

THE SIN OF OMISSION

About a year after Vic and I were sent to separate facilities, I received a letter from Big Rich. He had been sentenced to life plus 90 years. Without God's intervention, he'd be in prison for the rest of his life. He'd heard Vic had snitched on me and was still working for the government and wanted to know if it was true. Big Rich said that there was a hit on Vic and wanted to know if I wanted him to use his influence to lift it, or just leave things alone, and let "Heaven keep the books."

I knew that Vic was catching men for the government, but I didn't know what to do. If I left things alone, Vic could end up shanked in the shower and possibly die. If I intervened through Big Rich's contacts, it could reflect badly on me down the road, for protecting a known snitch. This was when the Holy Spirit showed me the difference between the *sin of commission* and the *sin of omission*.

The sin of *commission* occurs when we do something contrary to the will of God. The sin of *omission* occurs when we fail to do something that we know is God's will. The person who ordered the hit on Vic was committing the sin of commission. **"You shall not murder."** (Exodus 20:13) My situation was different. I knew Vic was in trouble, and if I chose not to intervene, I would be guilty of the sin of omission. **"If anyone, then, knows the good they ought to do and doesn't do it, it is sin for them."** (James 4:17 NIV) In Christ, we become responsible for our actions and inactions.

I wrote Big Rich and said, "Vic never testified against me." This was true at the time, even though the "jury was still out" on the matter due to the negative turn of events in our friendship. I asked Big Rich to let the appropriate people know that Vic did me no harm. Big Rich intervened through the internal convict prison communications system.

Because of things Vic had done—things I was unaware of--he eventually had to be placed in protective custody. He was again living on the edge, playing both sides of the fence, a convict working for the cops. Vic would be a government witness against several recently indicted drug importers that were at higher levels than either he or I. I knew several of these people from the outside, and would see them again on the inside. They would lament that Vic's statements forced them to either plead guilty or be convicted. Others claimed they had never even met Vic, and he was testifying against them as if he knew them. Whether this was true or not, I don't know.

Vic had been involved in illegal activities with some of them, including cocaine trafficking and marijuana, grow houses. It was like a brotherhood, albeit an evil one. When our pilot, Alex told them that Vic had joined "the God squad," and become a snitch they were furious. I never was able to lead any of them to Christ. *God, you saved me, save them too.*

Lord, why not? I wondered. *What's going on with these guys?* Are their hearts just hardened? This Scripture from Proverbs helped answer my question, **"A brother offended is harder to win than a strong city, and contentions are like the bars of a castle."** (Proverbs 18:19)

I prayed for each of these men and tried to demonstrate the love of Jesus during the months, and even years we spent together. Sometimes it was tough, and at other times, it seemed impossible. God did open the door for me to at least pray with the majority of them. From this experience, I realized that our actions, whether perceived as good or evil, have a great influence on those around us and who we claim to serve. This impact is either for, or against the Kingdom of God. As representatives of God's Kingdom, we are called to "re-present Christ" in all we do. People's eternities can depend on it.

I had always appreciated the comradery Vic and I shared as friends, first when we were involved in criminal activities, and later through worship and experiencing the powerful Presence and love of God. It was disheartening the way our friendship ended as we took different forks in the road on our journeys to freedom. I always held an interest in his life and hoped for reconciliation because of our common ground in Christ. Throughout my journey, the Holy Spirit has directed me off and on to fast and pray for Vic. In October of 1991, the judge reduced Vic's sentence from 15 years 8 months to only 27 months for his ongoing substantial assistance with the government.

Journey Insights

Vic had become a Christian and a snitch. He gave Christians a bad name and under these circumstances, winning others to Christ became more difficult than overtaking a strong city. Our actions, whether perceived as good or bad, have a great impact on those around us. We are called to "re-present Christ." People's eternities depend on it. There will be disappointments with relationships on the way. What do your actions say about you?

30

DAVID AND GOLIATH

FCI Englewood, Colorado (1990-94)

New prisoners arrived on the compound about once a week, flown in by U.S. Marshals on what we referred to as CON Airways. One week in 1991, an unusually large prisoner named Garrett walked in with the other normal suspects. He was 6'5", had nearly an 80-inch reach, and he was without a pound of fat on his chiseled body. Garrett was a former gang member doing time for cocaine trafficking.

There was something different about him that went far beyond his physical appearance. It was spiritual. I watched from a distance over the next few days as he gravitated toward a few black Muslims that had been shipped in from Leavenworth. When prisoners come in from higher level facilities, it's often like a high school senior showing up at middle school. They can indoctrinate and manipulate others into their way of thinking and quickly begin wreaking havoc on the compound, or peacefully integrate and just do their time.

This Leavenworth crew appeared bent on evil and indoctrinating others to their mindset. They carried what I can only describe as a spiritual dark cloud over them. They were planning something, but I couldn't exactly put my finger on it. *Why does it matter to me anyway?* I wondered. Normally this wouldn't be any of my business, but for some reason, I couldn't shrug it off.

Garrett was placed in our housing unit and began attending private studies of The Nation of Islam, also known in the prison system as Black Islam. As I would walk by their four-man cube, they would stop talking and stare at me as if I was their arch enemy. Their aversion to me, which I didn't understand, went on for weeks.

One of the more bizarre doctrines within the Americanized *Nation of Islam* is their belief that 6,000 years ago the white race was created by Yakub, a rogue black scientist. Yakub was one of the Council of 24 black scientist-gods. He rebelled against Allah and the council, causing havoc and was noted for creating the white race as a race of devils to strike back at the blacks. Elijah Muhammad[31] said that black people are not sinners, but that the white man

---

31 This teaching is not in the Koran or believed by historical Islam but is a more recent teaching from Elijah Muhammad who led the Nation of Islam from 1934 until his death in 1975. Other Muslims, as a general rule, do not acknowledge the Nation of Islam as Muslims.

is at fault for their problems. According to NOI doctrine, Yakub's progeny was destined to rule for 6,000 years before the original black peoples of the world regained dominance, a process that had begun in 1914. I knew nothing of this doctrine at that time.

One afternoon while walking just outside the dining hall I ran across Garrett, who had a job in the area. I'm not sure exactly what happened to spark things off, but the next thing I knew we were squaring off against each other. It was 6'5" Garrett against 5'8" David. We circled each other like we were in a boxing ring and he glared down at me with fierceness in his eyes.

"You better go on, little man, before you get hurt real bad."

A Holy Spirit boldness rose up in me, and I glared back, fully committed. Before I could think I heard myself say "My name is David, and I run to the battle against Goliath!"

He looked down at me shocked, and said, "Man, you're either crazy, a fool, or I don't know something." He cocked his head to the side, looked at me again and then laughed out loud.

"Just go on little man, I mean David." He waved me toward the door. I took the cue and hurried away. The boldness left me as quickly as it came. I later learned that Garrett was one of the former sparring partners for the 1978 heavyweight champion Ken Norton, who broke Muhammad Ali's jaw to win the title.

Garrett continued to show up at the private Nation of Islam study. One day I saw him with a Bible in his hand, arguing with the leader who was yelling, "That's the white man's book! I don't trust nothin' in it!" It was none of my business and I just kept walking.

That night I had a dream. It was a five-on-five basketball game. My team was multi-racial, and we wore matching uniforms. Garrett was on the other team, comprised of all black players. Their uniforms were also matching but a different color. Garrett's attire was mixed. His top represented their side, his shorts represented ours.

Each time our player got into trouble, he would see Garrett's shorts and pass him the ball. Garrett would then pass the ball to one of his team members to move toward their basket. Then I would run down and steal the ball and pass it back to our team to try and score.

As the dream continued, one of Garrett's team would pass the ball to him and Garrett, looking at his shorts and then at his shirt, confused at which team he was on, would pass the ball to one of our team members. His team would yell and curse him. At one point, both teams waved their hands wildly for Garrett to pass them the ball. He kept looking at his mismatched uniform unsure what to do.

I finally said, "Garrett, you're wearing the wrong uniform top, you've been playing on the wrong team. You're one of us!" I pointed to his shorts representing his true foundation.

Garrett's eyes were opened to the dilemma, and he looked up to God for an answer. Within a split second, the color of his top changed to match our team and he seemed restored and complete. When he realized his true identity, he became a one-man team and drove the ball to our goal and dunked it. With his size, stature, and newfound determination, he was unstoppable! Then I woke up.

I knew I needed to talk with Garrett. He was standing in the same location where we had squared off. I didn't have supernatural boldness this time and I was hesitant to even talk to him. How was I supposed to tell Garrett, part of an extreme Black Muslim group that hates white people, that he was playing on the wrong team? I prayed for strength.

I approached Garrett and said, "Hey, I had a dream about you this morning, and I need to share it."

He looked at me in disbelief and said, "I had a dream about you too. Tell me yours first."

I recounted my dream, expecting an explosive reaction, but as each scene progressed he humbly looked at me and nodded. When I finished, he began choking out his life story.

"David, I used to be a Christian. I came out of a gang, complete with all the violence and everything that goes with that life. I served God on the real. I was in church two, three times a week. I carried my Bible with me to work to read on break, I became an elder, and helped others get out of the gang life. Then I got tricked at a church service when I heard a false voice that said, 'This is your wife, marry her.'"

He admitted he didn't submit to authority. Thinking she looked good and that he was hearing from God, he married her. She wasn't a Christian but had infiltrated his church from a cult.

"It messed me up. We got divorced. Man, was I am angry at God! Money was short which sent me back to the gang and I started slingin' dope again. Then I caught this case in the Feds. I've been angry with the white man -- the prosecutor was white, the judge was white, and the probation officer was white."

"What color was the informant?"

He paused for a moment and then whispered. "He was black." Then he quickly added, "But the white man made him snitch on me." I just looked at him; he looked away and reluctantly admitted, "If I weren't dealin' and was still in church I wouldn't be here. It's my own sin and choices that landed me in prison."

It was easy to agree with him regarding my own situation, and I said, "Yeah, me too," then inquired, "What was your dream?"

He seemed eager to tell it but cautioned that we needed to make sure we weren't being seen. "It's serious. The Black Muslim guys I study with have said they want to kill you."

That probably shouldn't have surprised me, but it did. Alarmed, I asked, "What for?"

"One guy says back when you were together at Leavenworth you was payin' protection of $50,000 a year. He says you're a big money jet thief and drug kingpin for the Colombian Cartel. They say, 'you gotta pay to live.'"

I protested, "I never paid a dime. That's a lie from the devil." Then I asked again, "Garrett, what was your dream?"

"Jesus appeared to me and you were standing off in the distance with a glow on your face sharing the Gospel with someone. Jesus pointed at you and said, 'Garrett, this is my servant. If one hair on his head is harmed, I will hold you personally responsible.' Then I woke up!" Stress lines formed on his brow. "My job is to protect you. Your job is to pray for me. They got shanks and are prepared to kill you, or me if I stand in the way."

Although I didn't actually think it would have helped, I asked, "Did you try to talk with them?"

He insisted he did. "Yeah, I went to them this morning with my dream. They told me it was Shaytān (Satan) deceiving me like he tricked me into marrying." I said, "No, this is different. I may be backslidden, but I know the voice of Jesus and He appeared to me in the dream. I have to obey God and not man." He leaned in closer. "These guys are hell bent on pressing you for the $50,000, or shanking you!"

We went to my room and prayed together. Then I prayed over him for about 45 minutes for God's protection and safety. He recommitted his life to Jesus and received a fresh set of spiritual clothing like Joshua in the Old

Testament.[32]

Garrett beamed. He told me he felt clean for the first time since receiving Jesus years earlier. Then the Lord filled him afresh with the Holy Spirit and he began to pray in tongues. As he prayed all the rage against the prison system and the white man and black man who had snitched on him washed away. Garrett was filled with joy and his face began to glow which was a sight to behold. We became good friends that day. Garrett became a powerhouse for Jesus on the prison compound, winning many gang members to Christ the next two years before his release.

When we emerged an hour later ready to face this problem we learned that a guard did a random shakedown where the Black Muslims lived. He found three shanks, one was a 10-inch copper water faucet handle with a jagged edge. We'd all seen a variety of them before, but this was unique and would be deadly in the right hands.

All three men were immediately removed from the compound and placed in solitary. Through this, we discovered that when we pray, God often takes care of our business by the arm of the Spirit, instead of us having to battle with the arm of the flesh.

Two of these three men were shipped back to Leavenworth. The other was serving 30 years and on appeal. While in the hole, he won his appeal and was unexpectedly released. Many of the black men on the compound started to go to the Nation of Islam services believing that if they went maybe they would be released from prison also until news came that the released prisoner was killed by another gang member only 18 days later.

Journey Insight

When Garrett and I prayed, God intervened and protected us in ways we could never have protected ourselves. It's possible for anyone who seeks Jesus to become a powerhouse for Him, winning souls into the Kingdom. How long has it been since you have prayed? Perhaps it's time to start and ask God to defeat your Goliath.

---

32 **"Then he showed me Joshua the high priest standing before the Angel of the LORD, and Satan standing at his right hand to oppose him. And the LORD said to Satan, "The LORD rebuke you, Satan! Is this not a brand plucked from the fire?" Now Joshua was clothed with filthy garments, and was standing before the Angel. Then He answered and spoke to those who stood before Him, saying, "Take away the filthy garments from him." And to him He said, "See, I have removed your iniquity from you, and I will clothe you with rich robes."** (Zechariah 3: 1-3)

31

NEW AGE AND THE GOLDEN THRONE

FCI Englewood, Colorado (1990-94)

The New Age movement has a seductive appeal to those who have an interest in the power of the mind and the metaphysical or supernatural realm. New Age brings with it a vast conglomeration of beliefs that can include psychic power, spirit guides, phenomenon, paranormal, telekinesis, channeling, astral projection, automatic handwriting, reincarnation, karma, cosmic consciousness, shamans, gurus, and the list goes on.

Beliefs usually involve God being in everything, all things are one, we are God (divinity), and we create reality with our mind. Sorcerers recognize that guided imagery and contact with "spirit guides" is powerfully intriguing to the gullible, and the enemy loves fueling this confusion. God warned about religious deception and where He, His Word, and the Gospel are not the central focus deception is often rampant.[33] The good news is that most New Ager's hold Jesus in high esteem as a renowned spiritual teacher or guru, so there is an open door back to the truth.

The New Age leads to much confusion that I saw up close and personal in Steve. He was raised in a Christian home, but after trying psychedelic mushrooms at a high school party, he found himself tripping and liked the altered state of consciousness. He decided there had to be more to the spirit realm than he'd experienced in his denominational church. So he spent the next 20 years on a journey that included a variety of hallucinogenic drugs and natural things from the earth, such as marijuana and even, as strange as it sounds, licking a type of toad that secretes a hallucinogenic toxin when it's scared. When I met Steve, he was about 40 and was serving a seven-year sentence for growing marijuana.

Steve was regularly at the chapel, usually in the Buddhist room, sitting in silence, cross-legged on a pillow accompanied by the smell of burning incense. Robert and I liked Steve. He liked us too. He was a nice guy who was usually upbeat and positive, but he couldn't seem to overcome a streak of cynicism that he admitted was rooted in anger and unforgiveness. He tried repeating

---

33   God tells us in Matthew 7:13-14 (NIV) **"Enter the narrow gate. For wide is the gate and broad is the path that leads to destruction, and many enter through it. But small is the gate and narrow the road that leads to life, and only a few find it."**

affirmations for half an hour each day, but these just held the anger at bay. He was always on a path of what he called, "higher truth," and his meditation times were ascending the "vertical reality." This vertical reality was when Steve communicated with what he called his spirit guides vertically and received what he referred to as *special revelation and wisdom* during meditation.

One day Robert asked Steve if he ever saw Jesus when he ascended into the second heaven. Steve replied, "I've never run across Him."

Robert queried, "Don't you think it's strange that you've never run into Him? Would you ask your guides if any of them know Jesus or has seen Him?"

Steve shrugged, "Okay." He returned from the session a couple of hours later and said, "My main spirit guide got angry when I mentioned Jesus. He said he was training me, and I didn't need Jesus. He told me not to mention His name again."

Robert and I looked at each other and asked, "Doesn't that sound a little strange?"

Steve reasoned, "Well, I don't want to lose my most powerful guide."

"Steve, think about it. What if he's trying to keep you from an even stronger guide?" Steve's face scrunched in thought. I continued, "Are you familiar with the three heavens?"

"What do you mean three?" Robert explained that the Bible points to *three* heavens. The first is the atmospheric realm where man lives. The second heaven is where fallen angels, such as principalities and powers reside, and the third Heaven is where God and the angels are.[34]

We encouraged him to ask permission to go to the third Heaven to meet Jesus. We reminded him of his earlier words to us about seeking "higher truth." Steve agreed to try. Robert and I went to the sour mop closet to pray, asking God to reveal Jesus, who is the Way, the Truth and the Life (John 14:6). We sensed God had inspired our conversation and prayer and Jesus was about to answer it.

The following day Steve came to us, a little freaked out. "I need to talk. I saw something in a vision that I've never seen before. It was amazing but scary."

"You have our full attention; let's hear it." We were curious how God had met Steve.

"I was ascending into the vertical reality, and as I looked up I saw several spirit guides, each offering to give me wisdom and guidance, but instead of talking with any of these I just felt like I was to keep going higher, like you said, into the third Heaven. As I kept looking higher and higher, I saw a powerful guide

---

34   See 2 Corinthians 12:2, Revelation 12:10, and Romans 10:6.

seated above all of these, he was on a golden throne and looked awesome!"

Adamant about what he was telling us, he continued. "When He looked at me I felt power, knowledge, wisdom and something I'd never experienced before from any of the other guides, an immense love emanating from His very being. Then, I was instantly taken above all the other guides, directly in front of His throne. He looked at me face-to-face. He didn't say anything, but His immense love, like nothing I've ever felt, filled my being. And when I came out of the vision the anger and unforgiveness that I've been struggling with were somehow gone. I can't explain it."

He finished, emphatically saying, "I knew this was Jesus. He is above all the others, the Most-High guide!"[35] Steve's explanation opened the door for us to pray with him and give him a couple of books that helped explain the differences between the New Age spirit world (the second heaven) and the spirit realm of God and His angels (the third Heaven). He read them and then we discussed accepting Jesus. It was a defining moment for Steve. Unfortunately, he said *no*.

He decided he didn't want to accept Christ because, in his words, "I don't want to quit my drugs." When Steve decided to reject Jesus as the one true God, the following day his anger *returned with a vengeance*. Steve combatted this anger and bitterness by doubling his daily affirmations from 30 minutes to an hour. Eventually, his wife divorced him because of his unresolved anger, and then he became more embittered. The last I heard Steve was released from prison, broke his parole by leaving the country to live where marijuana and hallucinogenics were legal.

God loves those immersed in New Age and is always planting seeds. It may not result in immediate fruit, but we are to pray and share the love of Christ. Giving a clear salvation message, when God opens the door, is important. Jesus said He is the Son of God (John 11:4). Jesus said that He and the Father are one (John 10:30). Jesus said He is the way, truth, and life and no one comes to the Father except through Him (John 14:6).[36] He asks us to chose, and our choices have life-altering consequences.

Jesus was either a liar defrauding the masses, or the Son of God He claims to be (John 10:27-30). It is impossible that Jesus was just a good man and great teacher. He didn't leave us with this option. He's either a Liar, a Lunatic or the Son of God. We must choose, and our choice will determine our eternity.

---

35 In New Age you have to qualify, to move ahead by works. Jesus just tells us to ask and believe. Steve didn't have to qualify to get taken before Jesus.

36 John 11:4, John 10:30, John 14:6.

Journey Insights

Steve met Jesus and experienced His love like nothing felt on this earth. Jesus healed him of deep seated anger and bitterness, yet Steve was unwilling to lay down his addiction and it caused him to lose his healing. Isaiah 1:19-20 says "If you are willing and obedient, you shall eat the good of the land; But if you refuse and rebel, you shall be devoured by the sword; For the mouth of the Lord has spoken." Where are you being devoured? Are you ready and willing to lay down your vice at the feet of Jesus to receive freedom today? He's waiting for you to choose.

32

JESUS' NAME HAS POWER

Jimmy was a career criminal, in and out of prison for nearly 40 years. I later learned he was only 58, but at first glance, he looked about 70. He was a quiet, small-framed, thin man who minded his own business. He was just doing his time.

I later found out he was a heroin dealer and long-term addict. When I met him at the medium security prison, he couldn't wait to finish his short parole violation, get out and score some heroin, get high and return to his old life. For Jimmy, prison time was just the price of doing business. He called it a delay between highs, deals, women, expensive Cognac and money. Money and heroin represented power to him. He'd get people to do just about anything for these, and he always had plenty of both between prison bits.

Jimmy lived in Chicago most of his life. He'd recently moved to Denver for a change of scenery, but shortly after transferring to the mountain state he violated federal parole for coming up dirty on a urine specimen. He didn't yet know a new network of criminals, or anyone locked up in the federal system in Colorado, so he didn't have any of the normal props or people to help him do his time.

He watched me at mail call as letters from family and friends came in. The officer called my name "Hairabedian, #27530-004," several times and passed back letters. Jimmy watched to see if I had any yellow slips. Those slips indicated you'd received money from the outside, good for commissary shopping, i.e. food, hygiene items, hand-held radios, headphones, sweats, fruit, tuna, rice, chips, soda, and other assorted items, including pints of ice cream. Jimmy was broke, and he knew from my yellow slips that I wasn't.[37]

One day he followed me to my cell after mail call and asked, "Uh, could I speak with you?"

"Sure, what's up?"

"You got a yellow slip today. You seem to get lots of 'em. I was wondering if I could borrow a few dollars to get some toothpaste and shampoo until my

---

37   The Feds have since changed the way they process and notify inmates about money received into their prison accounts.

money comes in."

I looked at him, sensed a *yes* from the Lord, and said, "Sure. Here's a commissary slip, just fill it out and also add an ice cream for yourself."

He eyed me skeptically, "Just like that?"

I gave him a big grin, "Yeah, just like that." He wanted to know what the catch was and I assured him, "No catch. You don't even have to pay it back. It's a gift to you from Jesus."

His body shuttered and he stammered, "Jeee...suuss! That name! Oooh, thaaat name. I'll get it from somewhere else." He hurried away. *Strange response,* I thought. The Holy Spirit prompted me to buy the hygiene supplies for him anyway -- and the ice cream.

Most prisoners love ice cream. It's the only frozen food you can buy. It's a weekly treat with which you can reward yourself if you have money. What's even better is no one asks for a bite because your spoon has already been in it, and they don't want to eat after you.

An hour later I arrived back with my groceries in a prison-issued, see-through mesh bag. I spotted Jimmy as I walked in. He glanced at me and then averted his eyes. I put his items on a chair. After locking my groceries away, I searched for Jimmy and found him walking down the hall. "Hey Jimmy, I've got those items for you."

He squirmed as he replied, "What are you talking 'bout? I didn't give you no commissary slip!"

I gave him a welcoming grin, "Just get in here." He followed somewhat reluctantly.

Sitting on the chair was double the hygiene items he requested, plus a Ben and Jerry's Cherry Garcia and a clean spoon. He eyed me suspiciously, "Why'd you do this? I'm black. You're white."[38]

"It's a gift, no strings attached. Jesus prompted me to do it."

He just stood stunned again when I said *JESUS*. I continued, "Consider it, uh, like an answer to your silent prayers at night." He looked bewildered and I could see his mind spinning. I respectfully waved toward the chair as I took my first bite, "Sit. Let's have ice cream." A confused look clouded his face, but he slowly picked up the spoon." Since he was still standing, I moved the

---

38   In 1992 the FBOP was pretty segregated, especially at Englewood. When I arrived two years earlier the guards wouldn't even house a black inmate with a white inmate in the same four man cube, unless it was temporary. Racial tensions relaxed within a few years, or maybe I just didn't notice it as much, or just refused to participate, or maybe a combination of the three. Over the years I would have a variety of cellmates; White, Black, Hispanic, Native American, Arab, Jewish, etc. God loves everyone the same.

hygiene items and said, "Let's dine together on the commissary's finest!"

He sat and between bites he gradually opened up. "I don't know why I'm telling you this. I keep to myself. I don't trust no one."

I laughed and held up my carton, "Maybe it's the sugar high!" He thought about it for a second and almost chuckled. After several more bites, details of his life as a Chicago heroin dealer and addict, came out -- fancy cars, fur coats, wine, women and the clubs. I just listened while I enjoyed my ice cream.

The next day Jimmy came to me, "I need you to pray for me. You have a real connection with God."

"Sure Jimmy, what do you want from the Lord?"

He got right to the point. "I need some money!"

I laughed and replied, "The Bible says that **'...my God shall supply all your need according to His riches in glory by Christ Jesus.'"** (Philippians 4:19) When I said *JESUS*, he shuddered, again.

I was really curious. "What is it about that name?"

His face turned troubled. "I can't tell you, I don't know you well enough. Can you just pray for me to get some money?"

I thought about it for a second. "Sure, give me your hand. Matthew 18:19 says, **'...if two of you agree on earth concerning anything that they ask, it will be done for them by My Father in heaven.'** Father, lay it on the heart of one of Your children to bless Jimmy with some money." As I ended the prayer in the Name of Jesus, I experienced what I would call a short film clip vision. This was Monday and I saw Jimmy receiving a yellow slip at mail call for $50 on Thursday. Jimmy looked at me like I was playing games with him when I shared this. I told him, "You'll see!" and he walked out of my cell shaking his head.

Jimmy's negative response was an understandable lack of faith since he didn't know how to hear from God. I was confident as I declared what I had seen in the vision, but pondering his response, doubt began to settle in. *God, what if it doesn't happen?* I was double-minded for a moment, but I went to God, and He reminded me that my job was to listen to Him and obey; His job was to bring it to pass.[39] His peace replaced my doubt.

Thursday during mail call I was in my room reading my Bible and Jimmy knocked on my door. He was grinning from ear to ear, waving a yellow slip

---

39 It makes me think of Philippians 4:6-7 which says, **"Be anxious for nothing, but in everything by prayer and supplication, with thanksgiving, let your requests be made known to God; and the peace of God, which surpasses all understanding, will guard your hearts and minds through Christ Jesus."**

for $50.

"David one of my old girlfriends sent me $50. It may not have been from Jee-sus, but I gotta' say, it did arrive on Thursday, just like you prayed. Can't wait to read this letter, we did a lot of heroin together. She's probably trying to reconnect!"

He returned to my cell about 30 minutes later with a confused look on his face. "I need to talk."

The old girlfriend had given her life to Jesus. She had been clean for three years, attending church, and had become an evangelist. She wrote that Monday night Jesus appeared to her in a dream and told her Jimmy was in federal prison and to send him $50. She called the BOP to confirm the dream, located Jimmy, and sent the money the next day!

"That's amazing, Jimmy. Really. Jesus is answering your prayers. He loves you!"

Then he told me about the phone call he had just made to her, "I thanked her and tried to talk about old times and getting together when I get out. She told me *no* because she wasn't the same girl anymore! I said, 'Come on baby; you remember when we used to...' and she immediately started calling on the Name of Jesus and speakin' in tongues! Then she commanded the devil to come out of me. I started sweating; something happened, I feel different."

This whole encounter with Jimmy was remarkable. I explained what I could. "Jimmy, the Name of Jesus is all powerful. It's the Name above every other name. The Bible says **"that at the name of Jesus every knee will bow,"** whether in Heaven or in Earth and to **"...confess that Jesus Christ is Lord..."**[40] You're going to do it one way or another, now or later, why not now?"

He just looked at me, but I could tell he was thinking. He leaned in close to me, "I'm going to tell you something I never told anyone. I've killed a lot of people and never been arrested for any of 'em." He was quiet and somber. "A lot of people died who refused to pay me, who stole from me, or were going to snitch on me. EVERY time I went to kill someone, and they called on the Name of Jesus, it didn't work, they wouldn't die."

I was stunned, "You mean you had mercy on them?"

He flailed his arms. "Mercy, #*%! no! I tried to kill 'em anyway. It made me even madder that this heroin addict would try and call on Jesus after they'd been doin' heroin, stolen my money, my dope, or tried to snitch on me."

---

40   Philippians 2:10-11 (KJV)

He stiffened, "One time I caught this joker inside a phone booth where I told him to call me from. I snuck around the corner and opened the door and stuck the gun right in his face and said, 'It's time to die *#^&$%!'

The guy yelled, 'Oh Jesus save me!' I shot five times in the phone booth with a snub-nose 38 at point blank range. Every bullet missed him. It broke the glass and the phone he was holding shattered, and he was still holding the top half. There is no way I could miss at that range, let alone in a phone booth. But he was standing there alive! Then I held the gun directly to his head with the last bullet and said, 'Time to die!' but he yelled out Jesus' Name again. When I pulled the trigger, my damn gun jammed!"

Jimmy continued, "But this ain't the only story. Two other times stuff like this happened. It got to the point when someone would call on Jesus I'd just shake my head and walk off, cuz I knew something would happen to save them! So I know from personal experience that the Name of Jesus has a power like no other name."[41]

He told me that when his old girlfriend started speaking in tongues and commanded that devil to come out in Jesus' Name, something happened to him. "I know something changed. It's like I get it now."

I asked, "Jimmy, would you like to accept Jesus into your heart and be forgiven all your sins, including the people you killed?"

He bowed his head, and then humbly got on his knees, surrendering his life to the all-powerful Name and person of Jesus. Jimmy came up fresh and cleaned, forgiven of his many sins, and suddenly looked 10 years younger. From that day forward he began reading a little pocket Gideon New Testament he found on top of a trash can. He grew in the Lord and was released a few months later to begin his new life in Christ on the outside. The 40-year cycle of bondage to the devil, money, heroin and the dangerous lifestyle that goes with that world was broken in an instant. Jimmy had finally met Jesus, the man behind the Name, who came to Earth to set the captives free.[42]

---

41   I was reminded of Acts 2:21 (NIV), **"And everyone who calls on the name of the Lord will be saved."**

42   Luke 4:18-19 (ESV), **"The Spirit of the Lord is upon me, because he has anointed me to proclaim good news to the poor. He has sent me to proclaim liberty to the captives and recovering of sight to the blind, to set at liberty those who are oppressed, to proclaim the year of the Lord's favor."**

Journey Insights

"All who call upon the Name of the Lord will be saved" (Acts 2:21). The inmate shared his story that each time he went to kill somebody and they called on the Name of Jesus, God saved them from being killed. No matter what we've done, when we cry out to Jesus and invite Him into our hearts, He doesn't say no. Have you invited Him into your heart yet?

33

THE RADIO PREACHER TEACHER

The year was 1992, I was standing by my bunk waiting for guards to arrive for the normal 4 p.m. stand-up count. I was surprised with the words that arose in my spirit, "Turn on your radio."

Where is it? I wondered. It had been months since I'd listened to my radio. I rummaged through my locker and grabbed it from the back corner, behind a bag of rice. "What station?" I asked the Lord.

"Turn it on," was all I heard. I was a little confused but I wanted to be obedient to what seemed like the Holy Spirit's voice. I turned the knob and heard two men talking. Before I could catch the name of the show, theme or subject matter, my spirit was instantly grieved. I'd never felt anything like this since becoming a Christian. The feeling was so intense that it reminded me of what I felt when the first girl I'd ever loved broke up with me. *What am I listening to that's causing this deep feeling of grief in me?*

It was a Christian radio show. The host and a caller were discussing a guest minister the caller had heard speak at a local church. He had questions about certain doctrinal issues and practices, and matters of the Holy Spirit. The caller was a growing Christian, who was genuinely trying to walk the plumbline of truth.

The host responded in a cavalier manner with what struck me as a know-it-all tone, "Well, send me the documents and any cassette recordings you can get ahold of and our team of apologetic[43] experts will investigate him and his ministry." He went on to state, "I can't tell you anything about him yet, and I don't want to slander a minister without cause, but I can tell you of several ministers who are false teachers, false apostles, and false prophets, posing as Christians in the Body of Christ."

He named a laundry list of men. I was shocked that I had read their books, enjoyed their ministries, and been nurtured by the Holy Spirit through their teachings. *How can you speak against these mighty men of God who are winning souls by the tens of thousands around the world?* He concluded his 60-second treatise with the words, "I'm The Radio Preacher Teacher, and we'll be back

---

43   Apologetics is the defense of the Christian faith.

131

after this two-minute commercial break!"

The Holy Spirit then spoke to me in the still small voice, "If you bite and devour one another, beware lest you be consumed by one another!" I stood dumbfounded. My feelings of grief intensified. I asked the Lord what this meant. I quickly looked up the word "bite" in the concordance and found three scriptures in the Old Testament and one in the New. The Old Testament verses each dealt with serpents biting the people of God. The New Testament passage warned Christian brethren not to bite and devour each other with their words.

As I read on, I discovered the *exact words* that the Holy Spirit spoke to me minutes earlier. The passage compares the proper Christian behavior of loving one another versus the forbidden behavior of biting and devouring each other. **"For you, brethren, have been called to liberty; only do not use liberty as an opportunity for the flesh, but through love serve one another. For all the law is fulfilled in one word, even in this: 'You shall love your neighbor as yourself.' But if you bite and devour one another, beware lest you be consumed by one another!"** (Galatians 5:13-15).

The grieving inside increased until the pain doubled me over. Holding my stomach, I asked "Lord what's happening? What are you trying to show me?" Then I begged him to deliver me from this horrible feeling. With a deeply hurt and saddened tone He said, "This is how I feel when my children bite and devour one another instead of loving and serving one another."

I felt the Holy Spirit's pain. For the first time in my life, I realized He could be grieved. Then the pain and grief lifted and I was able to stand up. I remembered the verse, **"And do not grieve the Holy Spirit of God, by whom you were sealed for the day of redemption. Let all bitterness, wrath, anger, clamor, and evil speaking be put away from you, with all malice. And be kind to one another, tenderhearted, forgiving one another, just as God in Christ forgave you."** (Ephesians 4:30-32) What followed over the next 18 months was one of the most difficult seasons in my walk with Jesus. Little did I know how important that verse would be.

The challenges didn't come from the guards, gang members, mafia dons or even prison life, but from six men who called themselves Christians. They attended Sunday service, weekly Bible studies and carried their Bibles on the compound. I later learned these men listened religiously to that radio show during the 4 p.m. count. They began a campaign to berate and verbally attack the ministers and ministries named on the radio show. Although they were willing to discuss any aspect of the Bible, and they were genuinely born again, the primary message of Jesus became secondary to their "newfound mission" to expose error and false teachers. In the process, these sincere men left their first love and began biting and devouring other Christians.

Many watched as the same arrogant and condescending tone replaced the love of God these men formerly carried when sharing the Gospel on the compound. They now preached an intellectual Gospel. They talked about love, but the light of Heaven's love grew dimmer. Like parrots, they repeated the talk show host's words they learned each day and became increasingly bold itinerant apologists.

Over a few months, they become eerily inseparable. They stood proudly mocking other Christians who weren't as knowledgeable about the Bible, or those who they didn't agree with doctrinally. They scorned the Holy Spirit's manifestations, calling them *emotionalism* or even *demonic*. Two worked for the chaplain, and the others volunteered for just about everything at the chapel and then took on leadership roles, worship, and Bible studies. They used their positions to warn other Christians about false doctrine, false ministers on TV, and then about me. They'd say things to other prisoners like, "Beware of David. He's a heretic! We only share these things because we care about you. We don't want you to be deceived by false teachers. We must teach sound doctrine and contend for the faith."

They would approach me on the compound, six against one, and try to argue with me doctrinally. When I pointed to the Scriptures, they responded by attacking TV preachers and what they taught. "This is what you teach and believe."

"No I don't, you've never heard me preach or teach these things." They ignored my response as if I hadn't even spoken. It was as if their minds couldn't even hear me. They continued attributing things they heard from the Radio Preacher-Teacher to me. These conversations became so egregious that my spirit felt the same grieving again. This feeling drove me to prayer for hours, which caused my relationship with the Lord to deepen.

Then things worsened. They began slandering me to everyone who would listen. Men who were either offended, grieved or hurt by their words about me reported back to me what they said, "David, you're being called a false teacher, false prophet, liar, heretic, manipulator, deceiver, deceived, the list is endless. These guys are even saying that you're not saved!" That one really hurt.

How can you guys do this? I wondered. *You're my Christian brothers who I love.* I remembered the times we fellowshipped together, and I prayed for their family members, early releases, marriages, and loved ones. It was hard to believe that they'd turned against me like this. "God," I cried out, "where is Your love in these men?" I felt the grieving of the Holy Spirit. The words from the Bible returned, "But if you bite and devour one another, beware lest you be consumed by one another!" (Galatians 5:15).

Before long these men claimed to be Greek and Hebrew experts, repeating what they had heard during the 4 p.m. count. The situation worsened. This same arrogant and condescending spirit infiltrated the church gatherings through these men. The joy of the Lord was being suffocated throughout the compound and eventually was replaced by a spirit of intellectualism posing as a love of the truth. The other brothers who loved Jesus were affected negatively and eventually they stopped attending Sunday services and Bible studies. Sunday services dwindled from over 100 to only 18 and six of these were the ones causing the division.

Our head chaplain, Loren VanGalder, had had enough. Chaplain Loren called me and a few others to speak with him privately in his office. He had a plan and he was serious. "I want you to tell the men who used to attend service to please come Sunday morning. I've got an announcement to make." He didn't tell us what it was, but we spread the word.

About 45 men attended. Chaplain Loren taught on love and the unity of the Brethren. He exposed a strategy of the enemy and a demon spirit he called "wrong-focus."

"This spirit is diabolical because it causes Christians to focus on the wrong thing. They begin to focus on what is wrong with everyone and everything instead of the right thing. Jesus is the right thing." The room was quiet.

"Let's agree on something, men. I'm asking you to agree to disagree agreeably on non-essentials of the faith, and to remain steadfast and immovable on the essentials." I looked around. The men were hanging on his words.

"We all agree on the essentials of the faith. I've spoken to each one of you, and you all believe in the Biblical Jesus, the virgin birth, his divinity, his bodily resurrection from the dead, etc." You are all genuinely born again Believers on your way to heaven. Then he boldly called everyone to come out of agreement with the spirit of wrong-focus and refocus on the main essential, Jesus. He invited us all to the communion table to make peace as we took the body and blood of Christ together. Everyone came forward *except for the six men* who protested by walking out.

They made their position clear, "We won't attend church anymore! We are the pillars, and without us the church will fail!" But, their negative speaking was no longer effective. The chaplain's words had prevailed and set the men free. Within a week, the church tripled in size. What's more, the joy of the Lord returned to the services. Men began loving and helping each other again. Then the men who had been so negative trickled in. By week six they were all back and one at a time they said they were wrong and they repented.

However, the repentance was false. Soon, they started the same divisive behavior again, in more subtle ways, and drove men away from fellowship. It became so intense that one of them, trying to provoke a fight in public, actually spit on me. He did this on the steps of the chapel and a flash of rage roared through me. My martial arts instincts rose up as I saw the three-piece knock out combo that would finish the job and leave him lying on his back, but the love of God prevailed, and I turned the other cheek.

He spat on this cheek as well! Fifty men watched. Would I be labeled a punk for allowing this or a man of God for enduring it? (In prison it doesn't normally bode well for you when you ignore such an obvious insult.) I can't explain it naturally, but the Holy Spirit on the inside constrained me. I held my composure as I wiped the spittle from my cheek and walked away.

An hour later three former drug dealers known on the streets for violent behavior came to me and said, "David, we heard what happened. We're ready to do whatever you tell us."

The thoughts came through my mind, *"Vengeance is mine sayeth the Lord."* Thoughts continued, *"Maybe these are God's avenging angels."* I knew this wasn't God, and I responded, "Whatever I say you'll do?"

"We've got shanks," said a stocky inmate with a smirk.

"Those six guys got it coming!" said another. They all nodded.

"Here's what we're going to do." They leaned forward for their marching orders. It was a moment of decision for me on how to govern spiritual influence and power with others. If I gave the order, these former drug dealers would gladly carry out the judgment. It's just the way things are in prison.

The Holy Spirit made the decision easy for me. Jesus words from the Cross came to remembrance, "...Father, forgive them, for they do not know what they do..." (Luke 23:34). I looked them in the eyes and said, "We're going to forgive them."

"Forgive them?" I saw confusion register on their faces. They looked at each other.

"Yes, forgive them, as Christ forgave us. Period."

"We're going to forgive them." Each repeated this phrase as the full implications sunk in. The atmosphere dramatically changed. They understood and one by one began to nod.

They smiled and said, "David, you are a better man than us, and a true Christian."

"Guys, you're true Christians as well." Joy returned to their faces as they smiled and nodded. We all prayed together and for the six men, that God would recover their minds out of the snare of the fowler and return them to their first love, Jesus. As they walked away, I stood amazed at the goodness of God. The Lord not only transformed these men's countenance in a matter of moments through the gift of forgiveness but in the process, it became clear that the spirit of anger, violence and potential murder that had tried to return to them had been broken instantly.

Later that night in my cell I prayed, *Lord, it's miraculous to me what I've witnessed. Men who would never pick up a knife or a gun or ever kill anyone, have had no problem slashing people to death with their tongues, and they made it appear that they were protecting Your people and doing it all in Your name. That's what the Pharisees did. And then Lord, these other men who just wanted to serve You but were being blocked by this Pharisee type spirit, picked up their swords like the zealots and were ready to do violence to defend their faith. The enemy almost won both groups, but God, You were victorious. I'm so grateful for Your wisdom and for your grace, without which I would never have been able to forgive. I would have been just like the zealots and felt fully justified in my sinful reaction.*

The impact of the the Holy Spirit's words spoken 18 months earlier had become stunningly profound, "If you bite and devour one another, beware lest you be consumed by one another!" I had assumed this Scripture referred to the importance of being unified but I had no idea it was also there to protect us from degenerating into our old ways. In prison, those ways often included violence that could lead to murder. It all begins with losing our focus from Jesus and His love for others.

I followed what happened to these six men when they were released and my heart broke. Four of them walked in serious failure, including arrests, drugs, murder threats, prostitutes, and self destruction.

A tree is known by its fruit. Jesus declared that the true litmus test for whether a person is a false teacher or a genuine Believer is by their fruit (Galatians 5:16-23) and the first fruit of the Spirit is love!

Journey Insights

When the six Christian Brothers became ensnared by pride and wrong focus, Chaplain Loren called everyone to a service. He talked to the congregation about walking in love, verses finding everything wrong in others and condemning them with a pointed finger. Their behavior caused grief, pain, strife and division in the body. Do you find yourself focused on the wrong thing in others, with pointed fingers or do you walk in love and Jesus' perspective?

34

THE 30-DAY CHALLENGE

FCI Englewood, Colorado (1990-94)

Again and again, the Lord brought to my mind what He said about fruit. Matthew 7:16 says, **"You can identify them by their fruit, that is, by the way they act..."** (NLTB). That Scripture is preceded by an admonishment to **"Beware of false prophets who come disguised as harmless sheep but are really vicious wolves."** My experiences with the diabolical enemy dividing and puffing up professed Believers on the compound, and seeing their ensuing actions, was deeply disturbing. Such foul behavior including witch-hunts where I was spit upon spoke volumes and drove me further into wanting to be nothing but a carrier of God's heart. Jesus, who is full of love, was the only way. I decided to seek an even deeper understanding of my King and all that He laid out for me to do in His Word.

Seeking God for the supernatural power in the life of Jesus and His disciples, in the four Gospels and the book of Acts, became an absolute priority in my life. My understanding became if God says it, we're to do it with His empowerment. Right from the start of my walk with Christ, I knew I wasn't to back down from believing God wants us to do what He says and to live as Jesus lived. I'd read in 1 John 2:6: "He who says he abides in Him ought himself also to walk just as He walked." I was behind bars, but my location or station in life didn't matter in God's perspective, just my obedience. I wanted the heart and mind of Christ.

I embarked deeper on my journey to trust the Holy Spirit as my Teacher. Psalm 32:8 says, "I will instruct you and teach you in the way which you should go; I will guide you with My eye." And Isaiah 28:26 assured me that, For He instructs him in right judgment, His God teaches him." So it came as no surprise to me when the Holy Spirit issued me what I heard as a "30-day challenge." Learning to hear His voice and being open to receive instruction from our Teacher undoubtedly led me to this powerful training experience.

The 30 days involved reading the first five books of the New Testament, Matthew, Mark, Luke, John and Acts, *three times*, and each time from a different perspective. I liked this idea, to focus specifically but I couldn't have imagined how doing so helped me understand at a much greater depth. I read the first time from an observer's perspective, the second time from the disciple's perspective, and finally from Jesus' perspective.

I was to mark what the Holy Spirit illuminated each time, using a different colored highlighter or ink pen. I didn't realize this would place me squarely in front of Jesus and the Holy Spirit's teaching power for two to three hours a day, requiring me to skip lunch several days a week. What occurred during the next 30 days was life-transforming.

The first reading was the observer's perspective, which was just getting a *general idea or interpretation* of Scripture. The Holy Spirit had me concentrate on Jesus Words, His teachings, His miracles, and the disciples' responses.

The second time I read was from the disciples' perspective, which was completely different. This time, I focused on how these men listened to Jesus, tried to apply His teaching, and responded to His demonstration of power, healings and miracles. The Holy Spirit helped me see the practical application of the Gospel. This helped prepare me for something even more amazing.

The last perspective I was to look through Jesus' eyes, how he saw and loved people, and how He released God's words and miracles into the earth by hearing the voice of the Father. Trying to receive the Holy Spirit's revelation of the heartbeat of Jesus provided a *prophetic implication* of the Gospel.

During this challenge, I came across John 5:19-20. It was here the Holy Spirit highlighted the main secret to releasing Heaven into the earth. I began to understand that it had to do with our identity in Him.

> **"Then Jesus answered and said to them, 'Most assuredly, I say to you, the Son can do nothing of Himself, but what He sees the Father do; for whatever He does, the Son also does in like manner. For the Father loves the Son, and shows Him all things that He Himself does; and He will show Him greater works than these, that you may marvel.'"**

Day after day I read intentionally with a laser focus, and I saw the Scriptures come alive, more and more. All three views were accurate and significant. My foundation and trust in God were being so seriously strengthened that I began sharing this teaching with others. Some got it, others didn't. But everyone who was willing to take the 30-day challenge said they were greatly impacted while reading through Matthew, Mark, Luke, John and the Book of Acts three times through in 30 days.

Taking this challenge also helped accelerate my understanding of how to be led by the Holy Spirit (Romans 8:14). My belief increased that I could move, speak and do what He directed, and my desire and focus was to do this and nothing else. Jesus taught that hearing and doing what Heaven is saying and doing are the primary keys to releasing Heaven into the earth (Matthew 6:10). The miraculous becomes the norm instead of the exception, and great fruit is the result of a life yielded to a miracle-working God.

Jesus said, **"My sheep hear My voice, and I know them, and they follow Me."** (John 10:27) Later He said, **"The same works that I do you will do also...."** (John 14:12-14). The key to releasing the miraculous is only two simple steps: (1) Hearing and (2) Obeying (doing).

Jesus' mother taught this by example at the wedding of Canaan, the first recorded miracle in the Bible: John 2:5 says, **"His mother said to the servants, 'Whatever He says to you, do it.'"** They heard the instruction from Jesus (fill the water pots) and did it (they filled the water pots) (John 2:7). Jesus then gave them a second instruction. **"And He said to them, 'Draw some out now, and take it to the master of the feast.' And they took it..."** (John 2:8). When they did what Jesus asked the second time, the miracle occurred, the water was turned into wine (John 2:9-11). This simple two-step pattern to release the miraculous is seen throughout the Bible — *hearing and doing.* James, the brother of Jesus, said in James 1:22, **"But be doers of the word, and not hearers only, deceiving yourselves."**

Whether in normal life conditions or buried deep in a prison cell, the 30-day challenge brings about faith where the impossible suddenly becomes logical. Faith comes by hearing (Romans 10:17). *God, thank You that you've made it clear to me that we are to hear You, and then do whatever You ask.* This understanding accelerated and intensified my journey into freedom, and has made me urge others to ask themselves, are you hearing? Are you doing what the Holy Spirit is saying? The miraculous will be released through you by obeying Jesus. Take the challenge!

Journey Insights

I was seeking God for the supernatural power that Jesus demonstrated. God told me to read Mathew, Mark, Luke, John and Acts as an observer, then to read them again as a disciple of Jesus, then to read them a third time through the eyes of Jesus talking to the disciples and people. It was astounding the insights I received. God wants all His children to operate in His supernatural power. Will you try the 30-day challenge and see what God shows you?

35

SPACE ALIENS AND 3,000 GODS

FCI Englewood, Colorado (1990-94)

Michael was 45-years-old and sure didn't seem like a criminal. When I met him in the prison law library he was doing time for marijuana and of course, like everyone behind bars, he had a story. Following his divorce, Michael had a mid-life crisis. Unfortunately, he began smoking pot with friends, and as often happens he began selling it, probably to finance his new recreational activity. Before he knew it, he had fifty pounds in his trunk and cash in his hand. It doesn't take long, living such a lifestyle before you get caught.

Michael took some comfort in knowing that he was a first-time offender, and the judge sentenced him to about 50 months if I remember correctly. In the prison world, we called anything less than five years a "drunk sentence," just enough time to sober up.

I felt prompted to ask Michael if he had any kind of spiritual beliefs. He replied enthusiastically, "Oh yeah, I probably pray more than anyone on this compound."

Surprised, I asked why I'd never seen him at the chapel. He said, "Oh, I do most of my praying in my cell, usually late at night."

I was curious, "Who do you pray to?"

"Lots of gods, about 3,000 of them, plus a few space aliens."

It sounded so ridiculous I started to laugh, but he looked at me with sincerity. I caught myself and responded with equal earnestness, "That's a lot of gods. How do you remember them all?"

"Well, it's not easy. I have a written list in case I forget any of them." At this point, the guards called the 4 p.m. count, and we returned to our cells.

The next day I saw Michael again in the law library. He was diligently working on a civil case. "What are you working on, Michael?"

"I fell in the dorm showers about a year ago, right after I got here. Landed on my back and hurt myself. See this lump on the back of my neck?" Sure enough, Michael had what looked like a tumor on the left side. He emphatically insisted, "I had to file on them to protect others." Again, he was very sincere. "They have since put safety strips on the shower floors," he said with a slight intonation of personal victory.

Seeing a real problem on his neck, I asked, "Would you mind if another Christian inmate and I come by and pray for you to be healed?" I told him the God of the Bible often releases healing when we invoke the Name of Jesus.

He replied rather nonchalantly, "Sure, one more god can't hurt. I can add Him to my list."

Later that night Robert and I visited Michael. I introduced them and asked if it would be okay to lay my hand on his neck. He nodded. Michael was about 6'3" and graciously leaned down to make it easier. I cursed the growth and commanded it to dry up in Jesus' Name. Suddenly my hand got hot, and the growth began to shrink right before our eyes. In a matter of about 15 seconds, it was completely gone!

Robert and I were amazed at God's love and power. I smiled broadly, "Michael it's gone. Jesus has healed you."

Michael's expression shocked us. A look of extreme fear contorted his face. "No, no, no, it can't be!" He reached with his left hand. "Where is it, no it can't be gone." And before our eyes, it reappeared in about seven seconds!

Michael heaved a sigh of relief and smiled, "I'm okay, now." Robert and I were shocked! How could God heal this man and he lose his healing just as quickly? It was like something out of a sci-fi movie. When we asked Michael if we could pray for him again, he replied, "Oh no, I'm fine." To say we were confounded would be an understatement.

He pointed to his shelf of about 100 thick green folders. "I have to continue my work."

All the more curious we asked, "What is all that? You must have thousands of pages."

"I've been working ever since I fell and I'm going to win my lawsuit. That's why I was scared when you said my growth had disappeared. I need the evidence of what they did to me!"

Robert and I were speechless. The Holy Spirit was showing us how people can choose to either receive or reject Heaven's healing power. Sometimes it is tied to people actually holding on to their sickness. I believe God wants to heal everyone, but many things can short circuit this. Some people honestly don't want to be healed. Many fear being healed from drug or alcohol addiction. They'd rather rot in prison between highs or DUI's than give up their pet sins. Jesus promises to deliver us from our enemies, but not "our buddies." In Michael's case, his buddy was the lawsuit. His buddy was the growth on his neck. He obviously didn't want to be healed. He wanted to win against the Feds. It gave him purpose.[44]

---

44   Jesus asked the man at the Pool of Bethesda, **"…Do you want to be made well?"** (John 5:6). Answering that he had no one to help him Jesus said, **"Rise, take up your bed and walk"** (John 5:8). The man was healed. Jesus is asking the same question today. Do we want to be well? If yes, we're to receive His healing power now.

A few days later Michael was looking tired. I asked him, "Are you sleeping well?" He admitted that he wasn't. "My neck's been hurting even more since you prayed for me, and I've been up going through my prayer list to my 3,000 gods."

"What if I could show you an easier way?"

"What do you mean?"

"Michael, what if I could show you how you could pray to just one God and He would take care of the rest?"

"Well, that would be great if it were possible." I opened my Bible and read, "For there is one God and one Mediator between God and men, the Man Christ Jesus, who gave Himself a ransom for all…" (1 Timothy 2:5-6). "What does that mean to you?"

He read it out loud a few times, "Well, it says that Jesus is the one true mediator between God and us."

"Do you believe it?" I asked. He responded that it would make things easier if it were true. I asked if he would like to receive Jesus as his personal Lord and Savior and let Jesus deal with the other 3,000 gods.

Without any hesitation, he said, "Sure!" I led him in a prayer of salvation, and he began reading the Bible and attending church. Later Michael was filled with the Holy Spirit and began to speak in other tongues. He was in church regularly after that.

Robert and I went to his room one day and asked him about the lawsuit.

"Reading the Bible has taken a lot of my time, and it's difficult to keep up with all the paperwork.

"You know Michael it may be that if you'll just toss all that in the trash that God will heal you again."

Michael said he would pray about it. More than a year of Michael's labor and hundreds of dollars in copy costs had gone into his legal work. The next day he asked us to come by his cell. He told us he was ready to throw out the paperwork and received his healing from Heaven, and that's exactly what happened!

Michael was shipped from the medium security facility in 1992 to the adjacent prison camp and then was released from prison a couple of years later. He pursued the one true God of the Bible and became active in his local church. Soon he was attending a Bible college and then took the retirement he had worked for in his early years and purchased a tiny island in the Philippines. He now runs an orphanage for the physically disabled, preaches evangelistic crusades, holds Bible studies, and brings Bibles into the prisons in Asia. Over 25 years after believing he was doing the right thing praying to aliens and 3,000 false gods, Michael whole-heartedly serves Christ Jesus and lives to make a positive difference in the lives of others.

Journey Insights

Jesus asked the man at the Pool of Bethesda, "Do you want to be healed?" (John 5:6 ESV). When the man answered that he had no one to help him Jesus simply said, "Get up, take up your bed, and walk" (v.8). Through Michael's experience, God taught us a lesson how people can choose to receive or reject Heaven's healing. "For there is one God and one Mediator between God and men, the Man Christ Jesus, who gave Himself a ransom for all…" (1 Timothy 2:5-6). Have you accepted or rejected Heaven's healing power? It's never too late to accept and receive it, if you ask.

36

CORNS AND FLOATERS

FCI Englewood, Colorado (1990-94)

Corns on the feet and floaters in eyes are two common physical problems among men in prisons. Neither falls into the category of a medical emergency, and the BOP won't even address them. I wondered, *Could this be the reason so many healings and miracles occur in prisons and in third world nations? People have nowhere to look but to Heaven.*

I arrived in prison with both, painful corns and distracting floaters. About a year into my new life with God I was reading a booklet by a minister who shared a simple revelation about the authority of every Believer. He wrote that the Holy Spirit revealed how to curse corns in the Name of Jesus. **"For assuredly, I say to you, whoever says to this mountain, 'Be removed and be cast into the sea,' and does not doubt in his heart, but believes that those things he says will be done, he will have whatever he says..."** (Mark 11-23). He said that corns are like little irritating mountains in our lives and can be removed easily by speaking directly to them, cursing them in the Name of Jesus, and then thanking God that it was already done, like the verse teaches.

He tried this the first time on himself, and he was corn free by the next morning. He went on to say that for more than 20 years, every time he cursed corns from the pulpit, people would report awakening to baby soft skin, and the evidence would be in their socks or their bed sheets. Many would shake these corns right out of their socks onto the floor. Most importantly they were free from the painful corns.

I was astounded by this possibility. *How perfect if that guy was actually here. I'd ask him to use his authority to curse my corns.* Then something so simple occurred that I almost didn't believe it. I felt the Holy Spirit nudging me to use my young Believer's authority and curse my irritating corns. So I pointed my finger at my feet and said, "Corns, you are not a blessing, you are a curse. Therefore, I use my Believer's authority and CURSE you in the Name of Jesus. I command you to dry up and die and fall off my feet now!"

My first thought was, *I wonder if it happened.* I didn't feel anything supernatural, and the same painful corns were still present as I moved my feet around. But, then I remembered part two of the above verse, **"...whatever things you ask when you pray, believe that you receive them, and you will have them"** (Mark 11:24).

So I blurted out the following words by faith (even though it seemed kind of foolish), "Jesus, I thank you that these corns are cursed, they are drying up, dying and falling off right now. Amen." A little faith rose up in me when I said these words in alignment with the Bible, so I repeated them about three times. Although nothing noticeable happened, I sensed I had been obedient to apply what the Bible taught about a Believer's authority.

That night I slept with my socks on by faith. The next morning, I'd forgotten about my prayer, yet when I pulled my socks off a bunch of little pieces of dried up skin flew across my bed and onto the floor! It surprised me because I didn't realize where these came from, or what they were. Then I remembered my prayer.

Could it be possible that these were my corns?

I grabbed my feet and discovered baby-soft skin where all the corns were! It had worked! The painful corns submitted to the Word of God coupled with faith. The Believer's authority was real, and I realized it was available for EVERY BELIEVER, regardless of their age in Christ.

It would be years before I tried this biblical principle with my eyes. "Floaters in my eyes, you are a hindrance and distraction from me reading my Bible and, therefore, you are not a blessing, but a curse. I use my authority now in the Name of Jesus, and I CURSE you and COMMAND you to dissolve IMMEDIATELY!" When I said these words the single floater in my left eye dissolved instantly and one of the three floaters in my right eye disappeared. I blinked a couple of times while thinking, *Am I imagining this, or did my floaters really go?*

I waited about 20 seconds because they float one direction and then float back. They were nowhere to be found. This was incredibly cool, but I wondered about the two that remained. I began to thank God for the two that were gone and then I realized Jesus prayed twice for a man born blind. After the first prayer, the man went from total blindness to fuzzy sight, it appeared, men looking like trees. The second time Jesus laid hands on him the man could see everyone clearly (see Mark 8:22-25).[45]

---

45   Mark 8:22-25, "Then He came to Bethsaida; and they brought a blind man to Him, and begged Him to touch him. So He took the blind man by the hand and led him out of the town. And when He had spit on his eyes and put His hands on him, He asked him if he saw anything. And he looked up and said, 'I see men like trees, walking.' Then He put His hands on his eyes again and made him look up. And he was

Jesus is our example so if He prayed twice, so could I! I spoke to the floaters again, this time with increased boldness, and said, "Floaters, I said DISSOLVE NOW IN JESUS NAME." One of the floaters dissolved completely in a matter of seconds, and the last one dissolved into a black dot. Tolerable, and certainly better than four good size distracting floaters. I thanked God and the thought came to me, *Jesus never told anyone to rise and limp.* So I cursed the black dot and said, "Be gone in Jesus mighty Name," and it disappeared. I was now free to read the Bible without hindrance or distraction.

I've learned that we have much more authority than we realize or utilize. But, whatever we tolerate, God will allow. Whatever we take authority over that is contrary to the will of God, Heaven will enforce. You can curse corns and floaters too, or whatever your ailment may be. I encourage (and respectfully nudge) you to use YOUR God-given authority now in Jesus' Name. And then after you curse it, begin to thank Jesus for having already done it.

Journey Insights

God began to teach me the power and authority we have in the Name of Christ. I started to learn to take authority over what was contrary to God's will. To my amazement, when I commanded the floaters to dissolve, they did in a matter of seconds. Have you ever prayed a prayer of healing? Ask God to give you the faith, boldness and courage to pray in that way. Try praying by saying, "In Jesus mighty Name I command _____ to be gone now!"

---

restored and saw everyone clearly."

37

TRANSFER MISERY AND MIRACLES

FCI Englewood, Colorado (1990-94)

It was March 1994, just over five years after my initial arrest, and four years since I'd been at FCI Englewood. I was taking my morning shower when I heard a page over the prison speaker system, calling me to Receiving and Discharge. Anticipating orders to give fresh fingerprints or an updated picture, I was caught off guard when the officer notified me that I needed to pack my belongings because I was going back to court.

"Court?" I was confused, but soon remembered a habeas corpus motion I had filed five months earlier appealing the 22-year sentence from the cocaine case. Maybe this is the answer to my prayers. I asked the guard, "Where am I going?"

"I can't tell you that."

I wanted to know if I was about to get back into court on my federal case in Missouri, so I said, "Come on, at least tell me if it's Kansas City."

He looked at the document and said, "Nope, not Missouri."

Stumped, I pressed further, "It's gotta' be Missouri; that's the only place where I have cases."

He looked at me with pity and said, "Not anymore. You're going south to a warmer climate!"

Just like that, I found out I was reassigned to Miami. When you live behind bars, control over your life is extremely limited. You quickly learn to mask your thoughts and feelings, and this was one of those times. These moves are usually a surprise and happen for a variety of reasons. It might be a permanent move with no explanation. Or, you could be heading to court appearances for new charges. The security levels may have decreased or increased at a facility. There might be administrative or discipline issues, or it could even be for medical reasons.

Regardless of relationships you've established, family or friends who visit you, attendance in prison chapel groups, education, or anything else you attempt to create to make life a bit more bearable, when it's announced you're leaving, usually with little notice, you're gone. It's no wonder that prisoners rarely develop long-lasting, meaningful friendships because you never know if you'll see a friend again.

Advance notice was non-existent from prison officials; however, God had prepared my heart in a miraculous way. Without knowing why, a year and a half earlier God had instructed me to relearn and expand my ability to speak Spanish. As an impressionable young child I'd had significant exposure to the Hispanic people, culture, and language; now I was to submerge fully in the task.

First, God led me to request a Spanish-speaking cellmate so I would be forced to learn. Pablo was the answer to that request. He was a kind man who sent every nickel he got back home to his wife and child. We agreed to teach each other our languages. As I began relearning Spanish from Pablo, who was nearly illiterate, I realized the Holy Spirit was teaching me about my pride. God had blessed me with Scripture memory and comprehension that amazed me, and also answered my prayers and worked healings through me. Relearning Spanish, the Lord showed me I was tempted at times to be high-minded (Romans 11:20) and inflated with pride (1 Corinthians 4:18). The Lord highlighted to me 1 Corinthians 8:1 (NIV), **"We know that we all possess knowledge. Knowledge puffs up, but love builds up."** The Lord led me back to the basics of the Gospel through the painstaking, methodical study of the Scriptures in Spanish.

Next, God showed me how to minister to Hispanic men and to Pablo. Even in the broken Spanish that I learned from Pablo, the Holy Spirit was knitting my heart to his. I found out much of the street Spanish I learned from him wasn't right at all, but it didn't matter because it was about obedience and not my ability to extrapolate "brilliantly" from the Scriptures. Finally, the Lord opened the door for me to minister using a Spanish Bible. I was thrilled when twelve Hispanic men were saved and introduced to the Holy Spirit with the evidence of praying in tongues, all through the power of the Holy Spirit, and my rudimentary sharing of the Gospel in Spanish.

God's done all this over the last year and a half, I thought. *Okay, God, I get it. After leading me to relearn Spanish, I'm headed to Miami. You never cease to amaze me!*

Leaving was often stressful, and travel was almost always miserable. The meager personal belongings you might accumulate, whether books, pictures, or a Bible, either never show up or arrive weeks or months later. To say you feel somewhat uncomfortable would be an understatement, but then, that's the way prison is most of the time. It isn't supposed to make you comfortable, and the psychological effects of constant scrutiny, no privacy, fear, loneliness, abandonment, violence, depression, bitterness, anger, and hopelessness— well, you get the picture—and without God to help you through it, it's not pretty.

I was still stunned by the abrupt announcement that I was going back to court, in Miami, and I was leaving immediately. The modes of U.S. Marshal transportation include car, bus, van and jet plane. I was to "fly the indicted skies on CON Airways, where you gotta' be indicted to be invited" (a typical referral by inmates to this miserable method of travel).

As to be expected, armed U.S. Marshals escorted us. Our plane was surrounded before and after takeoff by additional U.S. Marshals, heavily armed with shotguns and sidearms in case anyone tried to run. Running, however, would be a bit challenging since before transporting us to the plane they put us in leg shackles, handcuffs, and a belly chain.

The chain length between my shackles was just long enough so I could shuffle to and from the plane. Sometimes they add what is called a "black box" over the two handcuffs. This box, invented by an inmate and sold to law enforcement, forces the palms of your hands to face each other, and further limits movement. It makes an already uncomfortable situation, even more uncomfortable. If you cause any trouble, they might add some commercial grade nylon straps between the shackles further limiting the distance between your legs.

It is in these trappings inmates are flown, with little logic, crisscrossing the country, before arriving at their next destination. For example, you could start in Colorado on your way to Kansas. You'd be awakened at 3:30 a.m. for strip searches, given a T-shirt, and one-size-fits-all khaki pants, and then leg irons and cuffs for transport to the plane. Your first stop might be Utah, and then several stops in California, concluding the ride in Arizona for safe-keeping at a prison for the night, a 12-18 hour adventure. The next day the whole process starts again at around 3:30 a.m. for strip-searching and the stainless steel jewelry experience. Then back to crisscross the nation until arrival where U.S. Marshal vans and shotguns await you.

There were no friendly flight attendants offering coffee, tea, or soda on our CON Air flights. The U.S. Marshal *flight attendants*, sporting blackjacks and billy clubs, offered us lunch, which broke up the boredom a bit. This yummy meal consisted of a cheese sandwich on white bread and some Kool-Aid drink in a plastic container with an aluminum foil sealed top. Eating this Scooby snack while strapped into the plane seat, wearing handcuffs and restricted by a belly chain was, shall I say, challenging? Tilting my head down and forward to reach the drink container in hopes of extracting the liquid somehow at this angle, and then back into my mouth without a straw, was a downright art form!

Shortly after this 10-minute dining experience, a food film began forming on my teeth from the trifecta blend of white bread, cheese, and the sugary liquid. *No surprise,* I thought. *There aren't any dental hygiene breaks to rinse or brush.* This was just a little detail I noticed on my 13-hour trip that day and it was in this setting the Lord graciously answered an unusual prayer request.

We had just eaten our makeshift lunch, and that food film was on my teeth. While sitting on the tarmac watching the unloading and loading of inmates, these words came out of my inner man, "Father, it will be hours before I can brush my teeth. Would you be kind enough to brush them for me?"

As I pondered my prayer, I was astonished to feel something I can only describe as brushes scrubbing both sides of my upper teeth. It was accompanied by some flavorless micro bubble effect that felt a little like hydrogen peroxide. *What am I experiencing? Is this my imagination?*

I began to laugh as the joy of the Father's love for me filled my soul, and it was then I felt the scrubbing move to my bottom teeth. The experience lasted about 15-20 seconds, and it disappeared as quickly as it came. I was stunned. I ran my tongue across my teeth a couple of times to make sure I wasn't imagining all this and realized my teeth were cleaner than if I'd done the brushing. I thanked Jesus for His supernatural answer to prayer while seated handcuffed and shackled on a federal prisoner transport plane. It humbled me that, in this condition, God would choose to do a miracle for me. My mouth was fresh and clean and remained that way until we landed.

That night we had a layover in Phoenix. The U.S. Marshals offloaded us to prison guards who transported us by bus to a medium security prison for the night. Once inside the prison, the guards unlocked our cuffs, shackles, and chains, and then strip-searched us again. We were then given a hot meal and provided plenty to drink before guards directed about 100 of us to a room full of army cots for the three hours of sleep we'd get before being awakened to repeat the process.

Atop each cot was a small plastic bag with a disposable toothbrush with half a handle, toothpaste, and a flimsy plastic comb. These half-handled toothbrushes are difficult to use because some of your fingers have to reach into your mouth to brush your molars. The single bathroom sink had a line of men attempting to brush their teeth, wash their faces and smoke. (I didn't ask where they got the cigarettes. We'd already been through two strip searches!)

Looking at the line, I remembered the supernatural teeth-cleaning twelve hours earlier. "Lord, I'm exhausted. Will you please brush my teeth again?" The Holy Spirit immediately responded with a matter of fact tone, "Get up and brush your own teeth." I was shocked!

Have I done something wrong? He brushed my teeth on the plane, why not now?

Then He brought a Scripture to mind, **"And my God will meet all your needs according to the riches of his glory in Christ Jesus."** (Philippians 4:19 NIV). The Holy Spirit taught me the following principle: *God will graciously do for us what we cannot do for ourselves, but what He has already enabled us to do, He requires us to do to receive the benefit.*

In the wilderness, the Israelites were supernaturally given manna to eat and water from a rock to drink. When they asked for meat, God even sent them quail for a day. When they entered the Promised Land of Canaan, the supernatural supply suddenly stopped. They now had to gather their food that was waiting for them by God's *natural* form of provision.

My needs on the plane, cuffed and shackled, were beyond my ability, so God supplied supernatural teeth cleaning. The toothbrush at the prison had already been supplied through *natural* means. I thanked the Lord for the half handled toothbrush, stood in line and brushed my teeth. As I laid on my cot, preparing mentally for the remainder of days it might take to get to Miami, I pondered the variety of ways God meets our needs according to His riches in Christ Jesus. The misery of this trip had been trumped by the miraculous hand of a caring God Who accompanied me, cared for me, and met me in a small matter that mattered to me.

Journey Insights

Prison isn't supposed to make you comfortable, and the psychological effects of constant scrutiny, no privacy, fear, loneliness, abandonment, violence, depression, bitterness, anger and hopelessness can take its toll, but God will graciously do for us what we cannot do for ourselves. "And my God will meet all your needs according to the riches of his glory in Christ Jesus." (Philippians 4:19 NIV). What needs do you have today that you can ask Jesus about?

38

YOUR SINS WILL FIND YOU OUT

MCC FCI Miami, Florida (1994-95)

I was sent to Metropolitan Correctional Center (MCC) in Miami to go to court for my third case. My first case had been for stealing the Cessna jet. My second case was for payment in cocaine towards the jet. And the third case was for the stolen King Air 300 plane.

During the many hours of traveling to Miami, actually a two-week trip, the Lord reminded me of something that took place while still in Englewood. As often was the case, God had given me an understanding in advance of what was about to happen in that Miami courtroom. The day I received my transfer orders started out like any other. I was studying the Scriptures and flipped open to the following passage:

> **"Alexander the coppersmith did me much harm. May the Lord repay him according to his works. You also must beware of him, for he has greatly resisted our words. At my first defense, no one stood with me, but all forsook me. May it not be charged against them. But the Lord stood with me and strengthened me, so that the message might be preached fully through me, and that all the Gentiles might hear. And I was delivered out of the mouth of the lion."** (2 Timothy 4:14-17)

While reading, an immense compassion arose in me for the Apostle Paul. His brethren had turned against him, doing him "great evil." I began to pray for the Apostle Paul, even shedding some tears as I identified with his pain. In the midst of interceding, I realized Paul was already in Heaven, having been eternally "delivered out of the mouth of the lion."

Why is this passage grabbing me so powerfully? What are these tears about?

My identification with this verse was incredibly strong. *What is the application for me? God, are You preparing me for a similar experience?*

I rejected this thought, pleading with the Lord. "Oh Father, please don't ever let this happen to me. Don't allow my Christian brothers to turn against me and try to do me great harm." I resolved to go with Jesus regardless of where it led or who turned against me. Suddenly, the feeling of pain and hurt was displaced as God's peace and joy entered my soul. I was dumbfounded!

Later that day when informed I'd be heading back to court in Miami, I called Jackson Thomas, a criminal lawyer friend in Colorado. "Are there any indictments against me in South Florida, Jackson?" I explained about the stolen King Air 300 from December 1998 and told him that the five-year statute of limitations ran out a few months ago. I waited impatiently and then called an hour and a half later.

The answer came. "David, the Feds indicted you on the stolen King Air 300 twin turboprop."

"But, that makes no sense. The statute of limitations has run out. Has Vic been indicted as well?

He hesitated and cleared his throat. "Nope, just you, Alex, and some Colombian they can't find." The words of that Scripture again rose up in me, "but all forsook me."

The day after I arrived in Miami, I stood in the courtroom to face the music. My third and final indictment! I'd accepted Jesus four years earlier, been behind bars for nearly five, and genuinely repented of my sins, becoming fruitful for the Kingdom. Nevertheless, this case from my past surfaced; the King Air 300 theft in 1988 had come back to haunt me.

At the arraignment, I discovered that the Missouri prosecutor thought I was going to win my appeal on the 22-year sentence. As a result, he called the Florida prosecutor and encouraged him to indict us *three days before the 5 year statute of limitations ran out*. We were indicted four years, 11 months and 27 days after the theft. The government had sealed the indictment that day and then opened and announced it a few months after the statute of limitations ran out, all legal, according to federal law.

Are you kidding me? I couldn't believe it. My past transgression has returned like a boomerang thrown into the air and forgotten about only to return and knock me in the head!! The Old Testament verse concerning sins from the past lifted off the page **"…and you may be sure that your sin will find you out."** (Numbers 32:23 NIV).

As it turned out the government's key witness in the drug case was my helicopter pilot Bails. He was now being indicted for perjury charges based on his testimony against us five years earlier.

Maybe nobody else knows, but I do. Bails' motivation for testifying falsely was to conceal and keep the $200,000 he received in drug proceeds.

Bails had taken the majority of the money generated from sales of the two suitcases of cocaine paid to us from the King Air 300 theft, and turned in Vic and me for the crime. Bails lied to the government saying that I was the one who made all the money from the drugs. He claimed to only profit a total of $5,000 from the overall transaction.

Try the truth, Bails. The amount you profited is more like $200,000 from just the cocaine.

The truth didn't seem to matter. The prosecutor and the agent knew about this at the time of the indictment but *withheld the evidence* from our attorneys and the judge during the plea bargaining and sentencing. The prosecutor and agent also delayed indicting Bails until well after our direct appeals were denied. They used this strategy just in case they still needed Bails to testify against us, and they didn't want to discredit their principal witness. Bails' tailored testimony against me in 1989-90 resulted in my receiving nearly 12 more years in prison. Twelve!

If you'd told the truth, Bails, you would have had to give the money to the Feds as part of your immunity agreement. It didn't surprise me that he didn't let that happen; however, his sin of concealing the drug proceeds and burying me for an extra decade-plus in prison did find him out. That's the way sin is. It appears to be without cost at the time but comes with consequences later.

Upon arraignment, I discovered that Alex our pilot had made a deal with the government and was testifying against me. This was the same guy who just four years earlier told me never to snitch and always go to trial. But that was only the beginning. I also learned that Vic, my closest friend who helped lead me to the cross in 1990 for salvation, was now leading me to the cross a second time - for crucifixion! He was now the government's key witness against me. Like Paul, I felt betrayed.

I trusted you, Vic. It cut deep because he was my friend. It took some adjusting to the truth, but I didn't want to let it control me. I constantly saw prisoners consumed with bitterness and thoughts of vengeance in similar situations and I knew I needed to do what Jesus taught; forgive and my heavenly Father would forgive me.[46] It was just tough because of so much emotional turmoil.

After the arraignment, I had to wait a year before going to trial so I settled into prison life, Miami style. During this time, God showed me a great deal about forgiveness and grace. I realized Jesus Himself was betrayed by one of His closest friends, and yet He still called him friend. In spite of the immense pain, His eyes remained on the ministry yet to be accomplished.

I get it, Lord. You're inviting me to choose forgiveness over retaliation and bitterness.

46 Matthew 6:14-15, **"For if you forgive men their trespasses, your heavenly Father will also forgive you. But if you do not forgive men their trespasses, neither will your Father forgive your trespasses."**

Regardless of whether I ever receive an apology, You're telling me to overcome evil by focusing on good, and remaining obedient to forgive.

The journey to freedom had gotten real. It was a fierce fight in my mind and heart, but I began to truly trust God to handle injustice His way, and I turned my attention to His plans for this compound.

Journey Insights

Betrayal is painful. During this time I identified with the Apostle Paul when he was betrayed by Alexander the coppersmith. In the midst of the fire it is challenging to believe God is always for us and sometimes we just have to go through the fire. During this time frame God taught me an incredibly powerful lesson about forgiveness in the midst of utter betrayal, and then brought forth a blessing in disguise. Who do you need to forgive today?

39

RAT KINGDOM

MCC FCI Miami, Florida (1994-95)

A massive heaviness shrouded this place. Mistrust and betrayal permeated the pre-trial atmosphere at the Metropolitan Correctional Center (MCC) in Miami. Sure, trust is hard to come by in prison, but MCC was darker than anything I'd encountered. Inmates are often experts in crime, abuse, and deception, and the character of some prison officials doesn't engender trust. But, this compound was murkier than most, and for good reason.

People were being re-indicted, sentences were getting increased, and situations were worsening. It was not uncommon for an inmate who arrived here, already facing a potential five-year sentence, to get re-indicted or to have their sentence increased for what is called relevant drug conduct.

These people are being sentenced to 25 years or even life without parole! Why is this happening?

I didn't have to wonder long. It quickly became apparent what was going on. The atmosphere was poisoned with inmates informing on one another, much of which was fabricated. An inmate would see another prisoner on the compound and contact the prosecutor to snitch about real or imaginary crimes. It was a gold mine for both prosecutors and informers. Sentences could be enhanced, and the snitch would then be rewarded with a reduction of several years or even immediate release. Many here were highly motivated as they bought and sold the precious merchandise of men's souls.

There were several ways a snitch could benefit, not only once, but incredibly again and again. It began with inmate discovery files which contain the case the government has against you. Surveillance photos, interrogations, witness statements, admissions, debriefings, and depositions might all be in your file which made its value immense for a government snitch inside the prison. Gaining access to files became a business for many, so epidemic that some prisoners even sold their own criminal case files (once it became "safe" to do so) to one another for thousands of dollars.

I understood the game. A snitch first secured their own reduced sentence which limited any additional exposure. Once they'd made their deal, they were safe to sell their own file because it contained damning evidence about their co-defendants. The more information they had, the more they could work the system.

A snitch who'd never even met a defendant could get his discovery file and study the government's case against him as he was headed to trial. These informers were memorizing facts, dates, names, locations, cars driven, boats owned, names of girlfriends, house addresses, etc., until they became experts on someone the government was prosecuting. Then they would recruit another inmate who would agree to snitch. He would groom the new witness and then call the prosecutor and introduce him to another valuable cooperating "witness." Both snitches would receive greater reductions of sentences.

This almost seems like an acting school, with a script written by the government or their snitch. It's crazy! I thought, *Crazy, but happening.*

The worst part of this whole scenario was that at least one of the witnesses was lying, and sometimes both. Clearly there are honest and outstanding law-enforcing officers and attorneys for which we should all be grateful. Their job is difficult! I knew some agents that stood for truth and they were often castigated by the ones that would lie. But some prosecutors turned a deaf ear and blind eye to what was occurring at the rat infested MCC Miami. The disease of falsifying truth had become an epidemic where the end seemed to justify the means.

At least two of the South Florida agents were known to be dirty. Time and again they'd provide additional evidence to their cooperating witness which helped recruit others to enhance sentences. They'd also help convict defendants who they'd fabricated cases against or who they had weak cases against. This was often done through an attorney, providing a degree of separation between the secret paperwork and the snitches. The attorney would visit the inmate, hand off the paperwork, and then the prisoner would scour the compound to find, recruit and prep additional witnesses, often selling these discovery files for big money.

People continually felt threatened, and the intense wariness of inmates suspecting each other was more palpable than in regular prison, which is saying a lot. While an inmate would be in the visiting area or recreation, another prisoner would break into their personal locker, not to steal food or stamps or radios, but to steal the prisoner's discovery file. These were worth big money to them, or they could sell them to other prison rats who had no problem "bearing false witness on the stand."

On the prison yard, there was a makeshift group of professional power snitches that met each day. They would recruit, brief, educate and train new witnesses, and then call the agent to interview them for verification. If they passed, they'd graduate to the witness stand in federal court and then receive their sentence reduction. It was an ugly machine with a 99 percent conviction rate. Many of the inmates referred to MCC as "Miami Cheese Cage" filled to the brim with rats. They'd warn that if you weren't careful at MCC, it was just a matter of time before you had "More Charges Coming."

The five-year statute of limitations on my trifecta of cases had now actually run out. I had an alibi because I'd been in prison for more than five years, so none of these antics personally affected me. But the darkness that greeted me upon arrival in Miami was palpable and made me intensely grateful that I was on a journey to freedom with God. I knew I had to keep my eyes locked on His purposes, His ways, and His love to maneuver safely and bring forth His will on the compound.

Journey Insights

MCC was known as the "Miami Cheese Cage" filled with the rats of snitches and dirty agents. If you weren't careful it was only a matter of time before you had "More Charges Coming." I was all the more grateful for my journey to freedom with God. Where are you on the journey to freedom in the midst of darkness? Jesus wants to be your light: will you follow Him and not look back?

40

MIAMI OUTPOURING

FCI Miami, Florida (1994-95)

Hurricane Andrew tore through Miami two years before I arrived, causing catastrophic damage with its 165 miles an hour wind, knocking down prison fences. Inmates locked in their cells understandably panicked, without air, electricity, and even water. It's amazing that lives weren't lost in the prison. Animals from the nearby zoo were freed from their cages and made their way to the prison compound through the downed security fences as they sought food and water. A prison guard was even chased by a gorilla, barely escaping with his life.

The full recovery took time, and when I arrived, there was still no chapel. In most situations, no chapel meant no religious services, but the atheist captain unofficially allowed inmates to meet for religious studies on the recreation yard. This created an unusual opportunity for the Lord to move, which was especially stunning considering the murky atmosphere that permeated the grounds.

A Christian inmate named Maurice Madden taught me much about bringing joy to the Lord by demonstrating Jesus' command to **"Go therefore and make disciples of all the nations,"** (Matthew 28:19). I give him much credit, along with my mother, for standing on the truth that "if God said it, it was so." He was a genuine man of God with a true pastor's heart, and right away I joined with him. It was an honor to work alongside Maurice!

He was the unofficial inmate pastor who oversaw the nightly services. A great preacher, Maurice carried an unusually powerful healing and miracle anointing. He also heard the voice of the Lord accurately and delivered tremendous prophetic words. Maurice taught by example, believing what Jesus said in John 14:12 (HCSB), **"I assure you: The one who believes in Me will also do the works that I do. And he will do even greater works than these, because I am going to the Father."**

Every day, Maurice would meet with the men in the recreation yard for Bible study, going from 6:00 p.m. until the yard closed at 8:30 p.m. We only took Sundays off. On this day, we all attended a 90-minute church service with the prison chaplain. We met in an unfinished section of the education department that was being rebuilt. No walls. No podium. No speaker system or other amenities. It was just God with His children.

My continual thought was, *God, You can do far more with far less when the Holy Spirit shows up.* I was amazed to see Him move on the hearts of people.

His loving care was dramatically evident at this dark compound, and His presence began to take hold. The 800 pre-trial inmates on the compound, not yet knowing the outcome of their cases, made fertile ground for the Holy Spirit to do His work.

The higher truth is not signs and wonders but raising up others to know Jesus personally, and out of this relationship they will then go and do the same. It is called discipleship, as Matthew 28:18 teaches us, to go forth and make disciples of all nations. We were transparent about the many life-lessons we had learned by trial and error, and it was a joy to see that with mentoring, others would not have to make some of the same mistakes.

We mentored, trained, and discipled, trusting God that "our ceiling should be the floor" of those to whom we ministered. We hungered for them to rise to the next level and to go beyond us.[47] What a privilege it was to be a part of this discipleship training. We knew it glorified God, and it came forth by first introducing others to the One who can make a difference, the Holy Spirit. Once they met Him, they hungered to know Him more and more.

Each week Maurice would call a 24-hour fast, from 6 p.m. Thursday to 5 p.m. Friday. None of the 25-40 Christians who regularly attended our daily Bible study and nightly worship and equipping services entered the dining hall on Friday until the evening meal. Then we all met at a section in the dining hall, prayed silently at our four man tables and then broke our fast. This consistent weekly personal and corporate sacrifice helped create unity, friendship, discipline, fellowship and brotherly love among our group.

God would often call others within our fellowship to longer fasts. The Lord called me, in a dream, to a three and a half day fast. Maurice was called to a seven day fast. Another friend of ours, in a vision, while praying, was called to a 21-day fast. Men put down their forks and did "push-aways" from the food table and picked up their Bibles to dine from the spiritual banquet God provided us. Extreme accelerated growth was the result. Men who'd come to Christ just a few months earlier were set free from drug addictions, pornography, gang violence, witchcraft, sexual sin, anger issues, and even the love of money. It's amazing when anyone gets set free of habitual sins, but for a prisoner who has experienced so much negativity and hopelessness, it was monumental in their everyday living.

Men began to donate financially to the Christian locker ministry. This was an unofficial inmate-driven outreach where shower shoes, shampoo, and essentials are offered to those in need, no strings attached. We saw more

47   Just as Elijah had a single portion of the Holy Spirit and did many miracles, his protégé Elisha, received a double portion of the Holy Spirit and released twice as many miracles.

and more of those being discipled begin to shop for these items with the little funds they had to purchase their personal commissary items. When the Christian locker started overflowing with essentials, men started buying higher end items such as tennis shoes and radios to give anonymously through the Christian locker to the new inmates. Men from other religions were astonished to see the love of Jesus in action. As a result, they often came to our services where they saw brotherly love and the power of God.

Healings became common in this atmosphere, and the tangible Presence of God was so thick in one service when Maurice was prophesying that it looked like a white cloud. As I arrived and moved toward a picnic table on the recreation yard, it felt almost like walking through a pool of water. It became difficult to move. The sound of the men on the weight pile or basketball court on both sides of us seemed muted like we were in a sound booth with God.

God, this is holy ground and a holy time with You. Thank You, God, thank You! I could only describe it as life-changing and knew I'd remember it forever.

Several men in our discipleship group began having similar dreams where a fire from Heaven would fall on individuals and then spread to everyone in the service. Men not prone to emotionalism were rolling on the floor, and it appeared that God was burning out the old nature and destroying their strongholds. These dreams occurred in the new chapel that was about to open. We all wondered what God was about to do. None of us had ever seen in real life anything quite like what was being shown in these dreams.

A few weeks later the chapel opened. It was beautiful and had wonderful amenities such as microphones, speaker systems, padded chairs, etc. At the same time, God sent us a prison chaplain who was a mighty man of God by the name of Harold "One Love" Neville. Originally from the Bahamas, Chaplain One Love was filled to overflowing with the tender love of God. His being a carrier of this love had a profound and powerful effect on us all and really marked my ministry forever.

The power of love that I read about in the Bible came alive to me through Chaplain One Love. He not only celebrated Who God was, and what He was doing on the compound, but he was careful never to interrupt the move of the Holy Spirit. He truly valued and treasured the Holy Spirit. We easily and with joy submitted to his authority and enjoyed working with this vibrant, anointed and humble servant of God.

There was a point when God called us to a three-day corporate fast. On the final day, we were in the chapel and Maurice asked me if I had received a prophetic word for the congregation. I told him that I had. The Presence of

God was strong in the room, and I could tell something was about to happen. Standing at the pulpit in our beautiful new chapel, I opened my Bible and read Hosea 6:1-3 (NIV),

> **"Come, let us return to the LORD. He has torn us to pieces but he will heal us; he has injured us but he will bind up our wounds. After two days he will revive us; on the third day he will restore us, that we may live in his presence. Let us acknowledge the LORD; let us press on to acknowledge him. As surely as the sun rises, he will appear; he will come to us like the winter rains, like the spring rains that water the earth."**

After I had read these Scriptures, I closed my Bible. Everyone was waiting for what I would say next, but there was nothing else to say. I knew that the Word of God had spoken to us through this passage. It was the third day of the fast in the natural and also the third day spiritually. I quietly and quickly exited the pulpit and no sooner did I sit down when an inmate in the front row stood up and began to scream out, then cry, and then jump around. We were all reeling with astonishment as he fell to the floor and rolled on the ground. This man had never done anything like this before. Several of us got up to see what was wrong. The fire of God began hitting other men and knocking them to the floor, and it was then we remembered the dreams about the fire of God in the new chapel.

Maurice and I looked at each other, shrugging our shoulders as if to say, "What do we do now?" We knew not to get in God's way. Then the fire began falling on others. Men were getting set free from strongholds and delivered from hidden iniquity, rebellion and sin while rolling around on the carpet. God's Presence was thick. Eventually, it was lockdown time, and we had to close the service and return to our units.

Over the next two weeks, the power of God fell every single night. This genuine outpouring was like Heaven on Earth. It brought with it crowds, controversy, criticism, and conversions. So much is debated about "signs and wonders" being for today, but the *true test* of a real move of God is conversions that result in transformed lives, and many men surrendered their lives to Christ.

One night eight officers from the lieutenant's office came to the large windows just outside the chapel with a video camera. We thought they were going to shut down the service, but they didn't. They respectfully stood outside and watched while one of them videotaped the activities. God gave us favor and we honored those in authority. All the men in our Christian group treated the staff with the utmost respect, and it was wonderful to receive respect in return. I learned through this outpouring that God will show favor to prisoners who submit to authority (Romans 13:1-5, Luke 2:52).

The captain ruled security on the compound. What he said was law. Interestingly, he didn't believe in God but supported our Christian group. When asked by another staff member why he didn't shut us down he told them that although he didn't believe in God, he couldn't deny the changes in the men who attended the "unauthorized group that he authorized!" One staff member told me that he said, "It's simple math for me. I don't believe in God, but I can't deny the positive effect that group has on my security! And as much as the staff around here thinks these inmates are somehow using me, I'm using them for my benefit and the benefit of this facility."

He said he had been making deals with some of the unruly men in the disciplinary hole. They could get out of the hole under the condition that they attend our Christian group! He went on to tell the staff members that if the prisoners didn't attend, he would throw them back in the hole for breaking their word.

Within a couple of weeks of attending, these men started becoming more respectful. It was important to the captain to support whatever was stopping the fighting and helping the security problems. Because of this, we didn't have problems with staff members trying to shut us down by talking with the captain. God's grace was abounding. Men were growing rapidly in the Lord, and God's glory was radiant amidst the darkness I'd encountered upon arrival. It stunned me to see Him glorified, and burning brighter and brighter every day.

Journey Insights

God can do far more with far less when His Spirit shows up and moves on the hearts of people. Two things were evident to the observers that drew them to Christ...the brotherly love reflected in our behavior toward each other, and the power of God with incredible wonders. Are there any areas where you need to genuinely care about others? It begins with a decision to obey and then hearing God when He prompts us. They will know us by our fruit. What does your fruit say about you?

41

BIRTH OF A BIBLE MINISTRY

FCI Miami, Florida (1994-95)

Although my initial encounter in Miami was with the dark Rat Kingdom, the light of God's "Heaven on Earth Glorious Kingdom" triumphed in an extraordinary manner. Truly there were many miracles here resulting in dozens of men coming to Christ.

It was incredibly helpful that God had me relearn Spanish a year and a half earlier. In the 15 months, I was in Miami, I experienced salvations, healings, and deliverances that became commonplace, along with incredible legal victories God gave men through the work He anointed me to do on prisoner's cases. God was gracious to open the door and trust me to begin teaching in public prison settings. Gifts of the Holy Spirit became commonplace and it was in this setting that God did another marvelous work, the birth of a Bible ministry.

Here in the Rat Kingdom, God directed me to give away my first leather-bound Bible. Doing so resulted in what became a mighty ministry that continues today.[48] It was originally conceived four years earlier in Leavenworth just four months after I was saved, through a vision of the Lord called the "Tree of Books." The vision was clear and so shocking that it frightened me. I wrote it down then and shared it with a few people.

During what I can only describe as a virtual-reality type vision, my whole body shook as a giant tree of books sprang out of my right hand and reached unto the nations. Spiritual lumberjacks, one being a Satanist and the other a Christian, came to try and chop the tree down. Unbelievably, they were walking together, one in purpose.

Years later I would experience spiritual warfare combating the religious spirit, and would better understand how this spirit moves through Christians who are unaware that they are chopping down the work of God. Eventually, I would be moved by this to compile a draft copy of all the Scriptures in the New Testament that deal with this spirit of religion, opposing the work of the Holy Spirit.

Initially, I wanted nothing to do with the Tree of Books vision or its

---

48   To date Heart of America Prison Ministries has distributed nearly 10,000 individual study Bibles.

interpretation. I had no desire to read books, distribute books, or write books for the Lord. In fact, nothing seemed to interest me less. Before going to prison, I hadn't read a dozen books in my entire life. I sometimes cheated through school, never took notes, and relied on my recollection of what the teacher said in class. At test taking time my secret motto was, "When in doubt, look about." I intensely disliked reading. Over the years, the Lord radically changed my heart, attitude, and desire 180 degrees.

I also learned to respect dreams and visions and to write them down to pray and seek God's wisdom and understanding. Sometimes it may take years for a dream to be relevant but the Holy Spirit is faithful to bring things into remembrance as needed and a written record is important.

At the time of the vision, I was so sure that God had the wrong candidate that upon awaking, I said, "Lord, I don't want to be a writer. I don't even like to read!"

Immediately, the Holy Ghost spoke audibly, "Just as it was told to Joseph, it shall be done!"

Before I could digest the meaning of this, the Holy Spirit within me spoke back out of my mouth audibly, responding like an obedient soldier with two simple words, "Yes Lord!" This experience startled and scared me!

Thankfully I knew not to say anything else. Instead, sitting on my bed like a little child who was put in time-out seemed to be my best option. I may have been sitting down on the outside, but I was standing on the inside in defiance. *I have no intention of writing books.* God had much work to do with me, my understanding, and my heart.[49]

When I left Englewood, I wasn't allowed to take any of my property to Miami; not one item, and that included my Bible. I felt naked as my personal "sword" was locked in a property room 2,000 miles away. I called a childhood friend named Koren. Her brother Mark was one of my best friends in high school and continues to be to this day. During my time in prison, Koren and I enjoyed sharing our new found faith in Christ. She became like a second sister and was a supportive sister-in-Christ who visited annually and sometimes more.

Hebrews 3:13 says to encourage one another every day, and I've learned that Christian friends, like Koren, can deeply affect each other's spiritual walk. Such was the case during this time. When I didn't have my Bible, Koren supplied numerous Christian books, letters, and teachings that not only helped my studies and my progress in knowing the Lord but were part of the

---

49   Proverbs 16:9 (KJV) tells us, **"A man's heart plans his way: but the LORD directs his steps."**

materials I used to teach other inmates. She was a stalwart, trusted friend in the midst of many betrayals.

During this time, I asked Koren to order me a new Bible. She called a Bible publisher we trusted, made the purchase, and within a few days, I had another study Bible at mail call that included a concordance, study notes, Bible dictionary, geographical study maps, and that great smell of bonded leather. I felt complete again, like a soldier who is reissued his weapon.

Shortly after receiving this Bible the Holy Spirit spoke to me to give it away. Initially, I rebuked the devil, saying, "Devil, I will not give my Bible away. The Word says, 'If you have two, give one to the man who has none.' But I only have one, and I'm not giving it away!" Silence. Then the love of God filled my heart for a man who looked lost. The Lord pointed him out to me and said, "Him," then gave me a simple and brief message for him.

I walked over to the man and handed him my new Bible telling him this was a gift to him from the Lord. He gave me a strange look.

Then I said, "The Father wants you to know that He has forgiven you." At first, he just stared, and then suddenly the truth sank deep into his heart.

He began to sob. "I'm a backslidden Christian and I just got here. I've been praying for two days asking for forgiveness, but I didn't think it would happen. Now I know He has forgiven me."

Joy flooded his face. He thanked me, and we said a quick prayer, giving thanks to the Lord for the gift of His Son. He went to his room and read his new Bible for the rest of the afternoon and into the night. The last I saw of him was just before lockdown, 11:00 p.m. He was transferred unexpectedly in the middle of the night and he took his new Bible with him.

It was at this point I began to understand the Tree of Books vision. *God, You want to give Bibles to inmates who are ready to study Your Word,* I thought. *You know it's against prison rules, for a prisoner to run a business or ministry, but I believe You have a plan.*

God makes a way for His children and uses willing vessels to help carry out Heaven's assignments in holy teamwork. The birth of Heart of America Prison Ministries, helping change lives one Bible at a time, started with two friends, Koren, and Kent Hodges, and I was able to provide input. The Lord moved on Koren's heart, and she became instrumental in facilitating what would become the Bible ministry. We communicated on a regular basis, and she was willing to manage this little sapling of a ministry.

It was my Christian brother from Liberal, Kansas, Kent, who first sowed $100 into the work. I remembered that two years earlier, I'd watched Kent leave the medium security prison, and he told me, "I'll be in touch at the right time." I never really thought I'd hear from him again, as most people like to put prison behind them. Also, it's usually not allowed for ex-prisoners on parole to communicate with someone still incarcerated, so Kent maintained a safe degree of separation by sending money to Koren. He explained that the Lord told him to send me $100 every month for "whatever David wanted to do with it until he's released." That meant a lot to me. Kent was a different breed who did what he said.

The Lord told me to give, and more would be provided. I saw the $100 as the Lord's provision to buy four more leather-bound study Bibles. During the next few years, God began providing money in unexpected ways. People who had never sent me anything suddenly started dropping money orders to me in the mail, $25, $50 and $100 at a time. A Jewish chiropractor friend even sent me an unexpected gift of $1,000 that first year.

I used these to purchase more Bibles from a major publisher in Chattanooga, Tennessee. God gave me favor with one of their representatives named Janet Charrell. Simultaneously, God graced Janet with a heart for the prisoners. She and her husband were pastoring a Full Gospel congregation near Chattanooga, and when she spoke with Koren, they hit it off immediately.

We were given a special price for their leather-bound Greek/Hebrew Study Key Bible. These retailed for approximately $55-60 each at that time, but they provided them on an individual purchase basis, mailed to the prisoner direct at only $25, shipping and handling included. Janet followed the *detailed* mailroom rules in the federal system so the Bibles could get from the publisher to the prisoner.

Soon after we were led to create and send a newsletter to prisoners who were trying to turn their lives around and because of this had requested Bibles. We asked them their testimony which we often included in the newsletter, entitled "The Church Inside," along with teachings and expressions of appreciation for Bibles once they were received. The stories were awe-inspiring how God was working in their hearts.

God continued to raise up people to help get the Bibles and newsletters into the prisons and people who heard about the work began sending donations. It can be difficult for prisoners, without outside help, to truly accomplish a significant and lasting work, particularly when ministry begins expanding into other prisons. But God had a plan, and the ministry was up and running.

The initial scene of the Tree of Books vision the Lord gave me at Leavenworth five years earlier was beginning to take root and now began to sprout as a small sapling reaching its small branches up to the sun for growth.

Journey Insights

The Lord told me to give and more would be provided, so I bought leather-bound study Bibles with funds given to me and was amazed at the unexpected ways God began providing money. This was the birth of the Bible ministry. Is God putting something on your heart to do? Step out in obedience and watch how He will provide.

42

THE THIRD ARROW

FCI Miami, Florida (1994-95)

I had originally been brought to Miami for a third indictment, based primarily on the same evidence, and the same conduct, that I had already been convicted for in Kansas City nearly five years earlier. This third arrow shot at me by the Miami prosecutor was overkill. It reeked of vendetta and made no sense.

My attorney and I were perplexed. I was already serving 22 years. *How much more can they give me for a white collar crime? Five more years, maybe?* They thought it would have to be run concurrently, meaning I wouldn't have to do a day more, and it would be just another conviction against an already twice convicted felon for the same conduct. Most everyone agreed this would likely just become a waste of taxpayer dollars.

Then I learned the backstory: The Kansas City federal prosecutor who had authority in our first two cases was leaving office after 15 years. I had filed several motions that exposed him for prosecutorial misconduct, withholding evidence and using known perjury to enhance my sentences in the first two cases.

Bails, our helicopter pilot who was also the government's key witness against us in the drug case, was simultaneously under federal indictment for perjury charges. This was based on his 1989 tainted testimony against me in case number two. Based on these perjury charges it appeared my second case was now going to be overturned and my 22-year sentence would either be reduced, or I would possibly even go free. I really hoped God was going to turn everything around, and I would be released from prison since I'd already served more than five years, and clearly learned my lesson in life.

Just one year prior, in late 1993, the Kansas City prosecutor was having difficulty explaining to the sentencing judge why my 22 year sentence should not now be reduced. After all, his own key witness against me was being indicted for perjury. It now made little legal sense to the judge that my sentence had been increased by this testimony and the judge wanted answers.

Instead of asking for a hearing to hash this out in court, the Kansas City prosecutor wrote me a personal letter on U.S. Attorney letterhead and announced he was retiring. He said something to the effect of, "David, my reason for writing is to inform you that I'm resigning from office, not because of any of the allegations you've made against me in federal court, but on my own volition to pursue private practice." He then gave me the name of the new prosecutor who would be overseeing my case.

Strange communication from a federal prosecutor, I originally thought. *Why didn't he follow protocol and communicate with me through my attorney? Why didn't the new prosecutor write me a standard one paragraph letter informing me that he was taking over the case?* A few months later I learned that the person behind the scene who influenced the prosecutor in Miami to go to the grand jury to get the indictment against me was the same Kansas City prosecutor.

During the Florida hearings that came next on this third case, the original Kansas City Customs agent was cross-examined on the stand for the better part of the day by my attorney. This agent was caught in, well, let's just say several contradictions. As the hearings progressed, we learned that the agent was fed up with the snitch on my second case lying to him. He moved to have the snitch indicted for perjury based on his testimony against me. Instead of burning 10 kilos of cocaine to destroy it as he said, Bails sold it and kept more than $200,000.

The original prosecutor refused to indict the snitch. He had said in a hearing, "It's just not good business to indict your snitches." More and more new information spilled out as the hours passed in these hearings. Each day the perjured testimony that I'd claimed a few years earlier was finally coming to the surface. The more of this evidence that came forth, the more it potentially purged me from the second indictment and the 22-year sentence.

When the Florida judge realized that this indictment was generated by the Kansas City prosecutor, she wanted him in her courtroom to make him accountable. "I am ordering two more days of hearings and I want that retired Kansas City federal prosecutor in my courtroom to question him myself!" This would have taken place in the next couple of months. The Florida prosecutor paled as the judge spoke. He realized there was something sorely amiss and that nothing good was going to come out of this case for him.

Two weeks later I felt the Lord's prompting to call my Florida attorney. His voice swelled with pride, "I just got a fax that we won. The Florida charges are fully dismissed!"

What? I thought, incredulously. *That's terrible!*

"They can't do that," I blurted. "I need that case to uncover the evidence to overturn my 22-year sentence." Stunned silence was all I received from my attorney.

The government had just filed a Rule 48(a) dismissal of all charges against me in the third indictment, and the judge granted it. I learned that Rule 48(a) federal rules of criminal procedure can be filed by the government at any time, *dismissing this third indictment* without giving any reasons. If two more days of hearing had occurred, the former Kansas City prosecutor would have been grilled which would have brought forth evidence that could have overturned my 22-year sentence in my second case!

I was shocked as I thought of all this meant. *He circumvented allowing himself to be caught which closes the door for any further evidence coming out that could reduce or overturn my sentence! Instead, any more fighting I do on my case will have to be conducted without the benefit of the additional truth.*

I wanted those extra days of the hearing, and I was livid. *How can it be that I've helped other people get out of prison that were second, third, and fourth-time offenders, and as a first-time offender I've been indicted three times on the same evidence?* No matter my questions, a sickening feeling settled in: I was stuck. *I've missed my opportunity to finally uncover the corruption that would overturn or reduce my 22-year sentence.* The window to make something happen had been shut down by the prosecutor's strategic move.

God was gracious to reveal His purposes in later years, but at the time, I couldn't see it. Disillusionment and despair over this were almost a constant battle. These didn't prevail because of God's inner strengthening and through His answering the prayers of others. (I cannot stress enough the value and critical importance of people praying for others going through trials of any kind.) I was able to stay focused that God was good and that He works all things together for good according to Romans 8:28.

This Miami injustice was not the winner. Years later I understood the positive effects from it: it allowed me to become seasoned in teaching in public settings. It developed much-needed character and maturity in me, including showing me more of my pride, lack of love, showmanship, approval addiction, and being puffed up with knowledge. I was trained up in how to disciple others. The Lord began to develop in me the writing gift. I learned how to operate in the gifts of the Spirit in a group setting. I learned the importance of submitting to authority, and the impact of brotherly love, biblical unity, and the power of weekly fasting. He even began to anoint me for legal work to help other prisoners battling injustice. God is incredibly gracious to deliver and heal us in our weak areas, and faithful to shape and train us in our calling and destiny.

Leaving Miami affected me significantly. I had been sent there for a third indictment, we won the case, but walked away from evidence that could have reduced or eliminated my 22-year sentence. I was immediately shipped out of Miami, still stunned by the courtroom procedures, coming to grips with my lengthy sentence remaining unchanged, but profoundly grateful for the remarkable outpouring of God's Spirit.

I first went back to Englewood. Shortly after that, my custody level dropped due to having less than 15 years remaining on my sentence coupled with good behavior. Because of this, I was transferred to Springfield, Missouri, which was a blessing as it was a mere three and a half hours from my family. Regular contact with the outside world helps keep a prisoner sane and also insulates them from becoming institutionalized.[50] *God, being closer to my family and friends means regular visits. Thank You. I immensely value and appreciate this blessing.*

Journey Insights

How is it possible that I had been indicted three times on the same evidence and given 22 years as a first time offender? Especially when God was using me to help third time offenders get out. I was utterly disillusioned, but God, answering the prayers of others, helped keep me sane. Years later I'd see the character development and maturity that God was perfecting in me. Is a friend going through a tough time? Pray for them. Are you in a place of total disillusionment? I pray Romans 8:28 which says that God will work out all things together for good.

---

50 Wikipedia: Institutionalization or institutional syndrome refers to deficits or disabilities in social and life skills, which develop after a person has spent a long period living in mental hospitals, prisons, or other remote institutions. In other words, individuals in institutions may be deprived (whether unintentionally or not) of independence and of responsibility, to the point that once they return to "outside life" they are often unable to manage many of its demands; it has also been argued that institutionalized individuals become psychologically more prone to mental health problems.

43

MEDICAL CENTER WAR ZONE

MCFP Springfield, Missouri (1995-98)

Prison takes getting used to for an endless number of reasons. I'd been behind bars for nearly seven years between Leavenworth, Englewood, and Miami, and with my new Springfield "home," I'd seen a full spectrum of behaviors. No matter where they sent me I learned some prisoners try to turn their life around, and, of course, others sink further into degradation.

Lord, I thought I'd seen it all in Leavenworth and the Rat Kingdom, but this place...

My thoughts swirled as I assessed the environment. *I haven't seen anything even close to the devastation that's apparent here on many faces.* In prison, you become hardened to a lot of things and a tough exterior is almost a requirement, but inside I was truly concerned for the well-being of a number of inmates I encountered.

MCFP was one of five federal facilities at that time providing medical services and treatment, both mental and physical, to inmates. Many of these men were extremely sick, and it was common seeing heart failure, kidney dialysis, diabetes, amputations, cancer, tumors, HIV-AIDs, and more. A few were in comas on what we referred to as "the death ward." Some had arrived on life flights after a penitentiary bludgeoning on the weight pile, or a stabbing, usually over a gambling or drug debt, or a gang related turf war, or over cutting in line at the washing machines. A good number of these death ward prisoners were holding on by a thread, and most appeared to be utterly hopeless.

This place reminds me of a war zone! I was acutely aware of my new home, taking it all in. When you're doing your best to follow hard after God, you keep your eyes and ears open wherever you are, because God cares and uses those who desire to be used. I noticed many of the staff were surprisingly caring and genuinely tried to help extend or save lives, even though some of these men had committed terrible crimes. One guard I spoke with told me something powerful.

"David, we're here to house prisoners not to judge you. Your sentences are your judgment; your consciences are your judges, daily. Being locked away from family, friends, loved ones, or freedom is the judgment. Ultimately, God is your judge, not us." There were guards, however, who took just the opposite position, and made prison life even more unbearable whenever possible, treating prisoners like vermin.

As I walked the compound, some men from Building Ten, the psyche ward, rambled around with glazed eyes. Most were injected, against the prisoner's will, with psychotropic drugs such as Thorazine, Prolixin, and Haldol, usually after a court order from a judge or BOP physiatrist recommendation. *What are these "P Numbers" I'm hearing about?* I didn't have to wonder long.

I discovered the letter P stands for the word Permanent, meaning these men would never be released. This P Number issuance was accomplished under a particular statute on the federal books that allows a psychiatrist to deem the individual too dangerous to the public, and to be held until a review hearing, or indefinitely. Some prisoners with a P Number will never be released from prison, even if their prison sentence expires. In certain situations, a P Number can be issued if they have never even been charged with or convicted of a crime.

Springfield had a variety of prisoners, representing almost every type of crime, from white collar to serial killers. Therefore, security levels ranged from campers (level 1) to super max (level 6). Once I witnessed something I am certain I was not supposed to see. I knew it was a problem because guards immediately reacted when they noticed I was seeing what was happening. When I came around the corner into the hall way, I saw guards I'd never seen before, who shouted at me, "Get back, get back. You're not supposed to be here."

What I witnessed was a prisoner being transported with escorts of five guards in black suits and night sticks. The prisoner was clothed in a full face mask and straight-jacket and strapped to a chair with wheels. I learned these "special moves" only occurred when the compound was on a temporary lockdown while the other inmates were confined to their units and unable to witness this. I was in that part of the facility only because of my job. The only way I can describe what I saw during the prisoner transport was like something from the 1991 Serial Killer movie *Silence of the Lambs*.

Sobering, I thought. *Just about anything could occur here.* I decided that especially in this facility it was wiser to remain on the right side of the staff because although not probable, it was possible to be temporarily or permanently placed in Building Ten, and "juiced up" with psychotropic drugs. No one wanted to end up with a P Number and be in prison the rest of their life, especially when you still had an out date, and some semblance of hope.

One day I discovered that Springfield had its own federal courtroom located on the ground floor. This courtroom was used for "special hearings" that included determining a prisoners' sanity and for the issuance of P Numbers. I learned this truth when being called to a legal deposition by phone for a civil case. Two years earlier I helped an inmate file a suit to defend himself from a false assault claim by a staff member who lost his presence of mind. He attacked a Jamaican prisoner for no apparent reason in front of me at Miami. The prisoner could have quickly whipped the out of shape staff member, but just told him to stop hitting him.

The inmate was willing to let things go, but when the officer came to himself, he realized he'd been so out of line, with many witnesses, that he could lose his job. Out of fear and desperation he falsified documents to charge the inmate with assaulting him, and the prisoner was taken to the hole by guards. Another guard who witnessed the whole thing, and eventually pulled the staff member off the inmate, later said, "I didn't see anything."

Two years later an attorney for the FBOP wanted to depose me by phone. The only location for a legal phone call that day turned out to be inside this empty courtroom. A guard escorted me into that eerie looking room. It had a large mahogany looking conference table with about twelve seats, with a judge's bench facing it. I was taken behind the judge's bench and handed the phone. The FBOP attorney asked me questions that only confirmed his beliefs, the staff member was completely out of line and lying on his statements and the inmate was telling the truth. The 15-minute call ended and I couldn't wait to get out of that room and back to more "normal" prison life.

I knew I needed to be very, very careful. My mom told me of a warning dream she'd had. She was shown that there was a Jezebel spirit in operation here and its plan was to get me locked away in the psych ward in Building 10. At the same time, I also had an ominous feeling about these P numbers. I was clear of the increasing importance to hear the wisdom of God and the strategies of Heaven so this Jezebel spirit didn't use a staff member to get me locked away in the psych ward in Building 10. I didn't want to end up in the hidden courtroom with a P number.

Before this day, I had no idea this courtroom even existed. I later talked with a few Building 10 inmates who had been judged incompetent for society or psychotic and unsafe in this very courtroom. They all told me similar accounts. They were given the same public defender, the same psychiatrist, the same prosecutor, and they were in front of the same judge. Very creepy. It was a triple-braided cord that could not be easily broken once caught within this noose and the court entered the order. From what I was told the judge pounded the gavel with some class of P Number every time.

Each of these prisoners reported being "juiced up" before the hearing. The ones I talked with had similar experiences, saying "David, I could hardly speak, let alone defend myself. It was like a bad dream, and all I could do was drool down my chin while I watched my attorney agree with the psychiatrist and prosecutor. Of course, they were told they had an attorney to represent them making these hearings legal and binding. By the time the drugs wore off it was 7-10 days later, and I'd been locked in a solitary cell in Building 10. This whole thing is like a blur!"

Some of these men were clearly dangerous and had done some terrible crimes to which they'd admitted. Others appeared very sane and said they'd never even been convicted of a crime. Only God knows the real stories behind each situation, and I'm confident the Judge of Heaven and Earth will handle rewards and punishments righteously on the given day. Moreover, I believe it is important to remember that we all make mistakes and even misuse our power and authority. God in His mercy gives each of us time to reflect, repent and be forgiven. This process and opportunity occurs in various ways throughout our lives, and what is most important is not what happens to us, but who we become through it.

For many, Springfield was a crossroads where a man is finally brought to the end of himself, what you might call the end of the line. Approximately 100 inmates died at this facility each year, which represented about 25% of the medical prisoner population. I was housed in the non-medical, work cadre buildings with approximately 450 inmates who were sent there as manpower for food service, sanitation, laundry, nurse attendants, etc. We heard about and sometimes witnessed inmate patients die every week. These deaths occurred in various places, including the Hospice units, the recreation yard, walking down the hall, or often during or after surgery.

Eternity became intensely real for many men in Springfield. My thoughts were focused on what God wanted to do. *This is the perfect powder keg for God's power to blow away the enemy's plans for their lives by performing miracles and bringing them to Christ.* And this He did. What happened next was amazing!

Journey Insights

Some of these men were clearly dangerous and had done some terrible crimes to which they'd admitted. Others guilt seemed in question, and a few seemed innocent, but for all of us, only God knows the real stories behind each of our situations. Do you feel like you're at the end of the line yet? Do you need to do business with God? Don't wait until you get to a "medical center war zone." You can approach God now and receive His mercy. He gives each of us time to reflect, repent and be forgiven.

44

SETTING THE CAPTIVES FREE

MCFP Springfield, Missouri (1995-98)

God desires to set the captives free. He began anointing my ink pen in the law library starting with pre-trial defendants in Miami and continuing to more complex, post-trial appeals at the institutions that followed. As a result, God reduced or reversed sentences of men, and some received immediate release, in ways that could only be considered miraculous.

Sentencing judges began granting these motions much to the shock of the attorneys and prosecutors. Their attorneys made statements like, "That motion will never work. You're wasting your time." The attorneys sometimes even arrogantly fought against the filings of these motions, denouncing them on transcript in federal court. God, however, had different plans.[51] He took the simple things and confounded the wise, catching them in their own craftiness.

It was at this time the Holy Spirit illumined the passage from Proverbs 21:1 (NLT), "The king's heart is like a stream of water directed by the LORD; he turns it wherever he pleases." The Lord not only granted these prisoners favor with the judges, but they also began rebuking the lawyers for their failures to properly research the federal sentencing guidelines or recent case law on their client's behalf. Prisoners were receiving greatly reduced sentences on technicalities and new provisions in the guidelines and law that the attorneys refused to present for mitigation.

In early 1996, a few months after being transferred to the MCFP Springfield, the anointing to write legal briefs increased. God's wisdom and favor through this avenue of writing, resulted in winning 11 legal briefs that year. Christ's compassion shown in this unique way led several men to Christ. Jesus, their Advocate, was defending them in the Courtroom after their attorneys had forsaken them.

However, not everything during this era was coming up roses. After God had delivered a couple of men with immediate release orders from the judges, I came under scrutiny by the Special Investigating Supervisor (SIS) of the

---

51   **"You do not have because you do not ask."** (James 4:2 NASB). Simply by asking, God was granting through the judges, who are His representatives on Earth in these matters (Romans 13:1-5). **"The lot is cast into the lap, but its every decision is from the Lord."** (Proverbs 16:33).

prison. I was called to the SIS office and harassed for winning prisoner's legal cases. The SIS officer threatened to throw me in the hole, a common punishment for jailhouse lawyers that win, unless I stopped helping inmates with their legal work.

"Hairabedian, sit down." I obeyed, wondering what this was about. Was it about the Bibles? Maybe about praying for the sick in the hallways? Perhaps unauthorized casting out of demons out of psych ward inmates? I never knew.

"We know you're the best jailhouse lawyer on the compound." I was confused why he brought this up because it obviously was not a compliment.

"Well sir, with all due respect, I didn't know I was in competition with anyone."

"Don't get smart with me. I can have you locked in solitary or put on diesel therapy for months.[52] Watch it."

I remained quiet. There didn't seem to be anything to say, so I just waited.

"We know you're the one who's behind winning all these inmate's legal cases." I'd heard that I was called "the lethal pen." Although the legal work I was doing was definitely legal, and not an actual prison rule violation, the prison officials had great latitude in the way they interpreted various rules. A prisoner, in effect, can be locked in solitary confinement for any number of reasons, be it for an investigation, a safety and security concern, someone dropping a snitch note on him, whether genuine or false, possessing another inmate's legal materials outside the law library, etc. An inmate working on other inmate's cases often bothered authorities, especially those who skirted the rules themselves.

"Look, we don't want you filing any civil cases on us over questionable medical treatment of our prisoners."

"Sir, I don't do civil cases; I only do criminal."

"Well then, we have an understanding, correct? Civil cases are off limits. Criminal cases are fair game. You stay out of our business, and we'll stay out of yours. If I find out different, you'll be back in my office. Now get out of here."

As this season of walking on eggshells continued, I asked the Lord for protection and He provided it. He gave me favor with the investigating officers for the next several months. During this timeframe, the Lord impressed me to take a correspondence course, providing the necessary finances through

---

52   Diesel therapy is where you're constantly being transported from one facility to another, be it train, bus, plane, or car, and never arriving at a designated facility for more than one night. Your property never catches up with you, you don't get mail, phone calls, or commissary notes. No benefits. Nothing!

my family. In 1998, I completed my paralegal degree.

In the process of my learning, God also miraculously reduced several inmates' sentences and others received immediate release. Two of these men's cases were thrown out and they are no longer convicted felons. Some of these would give money in appreciation and Koren would purchase more Bibles.

I later found out the SIS's department's main concern with me was not so much my assisting inmates with their criminal cases, but their fear of me writing civil cases against the institution for medical treatment violations. Some of the medical treatment at Springfield was so poor during this time that lawsuits were flying right and left and several inmates died! In a facility of only 850 prisoners, about 100 inmates a year died during this timeframe. The Holy Spirit impressed me to write to an internationally known ministry and ask for a donation of their 15-hour *How to Heal the Sick* video series. They quickly sent the videos which were placed in the recreation media area for checkout. From this seed, God birthed a wonderful healing revival and we witnessed a score of healing miracles.

A great deal of individual and corporate prayer and fasting occurred during this marvelous season. In a dream, the Lord instructed me to fast for 21 days. I needed to build up my spiritual fasting stamina. I first tried three days and then bailed out. A week later I was on my fourth day and Hamburger Day in the cafeteria called my name.

Then a man of God, a pastor, and prophet by the name of Terry Dante,[53] had a prophetic word for the Believers to go on a corporate fast. "Some of you will be called to fast only one day, others two days, and others three. Several of you will be called to fast seven days, and a couple of us will be called to go longer. At the end of this fast a great number of miracles, signs and wonders will be released from Heaven onto this compound."

The men responded in mass and about 65 men fasted. Fifteen brothers fasted seven days to release God's power. By day seven I knew this was the time God appointed for me to complete the full 21 days, and He supernaturally supplied the grace. The Lord directed Terry to fast for a full 40 days. I later learned this was Terry's 30th, 40-day fast during his 40 years of ministry.

At the close of this corporate fasting time, incredible healing miracles broke out on the yard, chapel, units, and hallways. It was like the Miami outpouring. Demons were coming out of the Psyche Ward inmates, and healings were breaking forth on the hospital floors. It was a wonderful time

---

53 Terry Dante, was in prison on a very controversial case. He had ordained more than 2500 pastors under his ministry, and at one point was in the Guinness Book of World records for preaching the longest amount of time without stopping. More than 500 people came to Christ as he taught the 66 books of the Bible from the roof of his church, one hour for each book. Even though he had won millions of souls to Christ on several continents he was the most humble and anointed man of God I'd ever met. The Lord used him in many ways to teach me about the person of the Holy Spirit, the authority of the Believer, how to accurately operate in the prophetic gifts, and the hidden power and importance of Biblical fasting.

in the Lord. Many miracles and salvations occurred during the Tuesday night chapel services.

Henry and Chris Grant from New Hope Fellowship Full Gospel Church in Springfield ministered on Tuesday nights. Senior Pastor Nathan Deal preached about once a year in the prison and when he arrived, Brother Terry Dante was at the piano. Pastor Deal walked up to him and said, "Prophet Dante, is that you?"

Terry didn't recognize him. He asked, "Who are you?"

Nathan told him that he ordained him 26 years ago. "You also preached a revival at my church that lasted eight weeks. We haven't had miracles like that since!"

The atmosphere was pregnant with faith in these services and God used this environment for supernatural manifestations of his grace, love and power. God placed Brother Terry at the piano for worship, breaking up the heavenlies above and the fallow hearts of the men beneath.

The Grants asked me to help do some of the altar calls and notable miracles occurred through them as they invoked the Name of Jesus. Cancers disappeared, inoperable heart conditions were healed instantly and two men came up out of their wheelchairs and walked. Many were filled with the Holy Spirit. Most importantly, lives were being transformed by Jesus' love and the person of the Holy Spirit.

It was like the days of Heaven on Earth yet each day I returned to my prison cell and combatted the cold reality that I still had twelve more years remaining on my prison sentence. *Surely, God, You will intervene and do a miracle, won't You? You won't allow Your servant to stay in prison all these years, will You?* Self-righteous thoughts ran through my mind. *Look at my works. Look at the fruit. Who else is doing this? Everybody is getting out through my ink pen but me.*

By this time Bibles were coming in regularly. This caused opposition from the enemy in many ways. While God was moving powerfully on one front, the enemy was making a strategic counter move. The prison administration stopped their investigation against me for the law work and for the next two years constantly began harassing me over the small but growing Bible ministry to the prisoners.

Journey Insights

God took the simple things and confounded the wise, catching them in their own craftiness. There may be seasons where God increases His anointing, wisdom, favor, miracles, revival and at the same time warfare (opposition) may also increase. It is important to trust Him instead of trusting the opinions of man. Are you willing to really trust God regardless of what things look like?

45

THE VISITING ROOM

MCFP Springfield, Missouri (1995-98)

Regardless of facilities, when you're on the inside, contact with the outside world is incredibly important to almost everyone. Communication of any kind, be it a letter or a phone call, was often a ray of hope, but an actual visit was immensely better. Why?

First, there is experiencing physical touch with another human being. Brief hugs or handshakes are often allowed, usually at the beginning or end of each visit.

Next, prisoners get to have a face-to-face conversation with someone from the outside world, without being on a monitored and recorded telephone call.

Finally, prisoners have access to vending machine food that is not otherwise available.

Each prison visiting room was different, and depending on the guard or guards who oversaw the visiting room, visits could be relaxing and refreshing or miserable and confining. The guards can legally make it tough for a visitor, scrutinizing pre-approved visiting authorizations, intentionally losing paperwork, or making it challenging to get through security. The guards have been known to turn up the sensitivity of the metal detectors or drug sensors, so that no one can pass. They've degraded visitors with pat-searches like TSA at the airport, and even made a woman rotate publicly so the guards can assess whether she is dressed appropriately for the visiting room. The bottom line is the guards wield a great deal of discretionary power in these situations and visitors just have the choice to either suck it up or be turned away from the visit after a long drive to see their loved one.

In these settings, it can almost be like getting out of prison for the day, if you can mentally overcome and ignore the guards, video cameras, security gates, and other prisoners all dressed in the same color. It was disheartening to notice how many inmates had few visitors, or mail for that matter. As prison security levels increased, and sentences lengthened, visits tended to be rare to non-existent.

The world behind bars is all these guys know, and what an education it is! People are disassociated with real-life to the point their view of life is distorted, shaped only by fellow-criminals, most of whom are not reformed in any way. This is tragic, Lord. The loneliness and slanted mindsets seem to make people worse than when they arrived.

Sadly, at times I witnessed visits become status symbols. An excitement swirled around visits, like a person returning from vacation to the other side of the world and then sharing it with their co-worker. In the same way, prisoners often hung on to every detail of their cell mate's time in the visiting room. Inmates would vicariously re-live the conversations that prisoners were willing to share. They eagerly listened to jokes, news, and fads taking place in the world. Relationship issues were intriguing. *Okay, this is amazing,* I thought. *Above everything else, I can't believe how these guys almost "feast" on hearing details of the vending machines!* Those machines were highly coveted!

I was fortunate over the years to have a lot of visits wherever the BOP sent me. *If I didn't have visits, I'd probably be "feasting" on vending machine details too!* God seemed to release a grace on me in this way, and I was very grateful. It was always uplifting to see supportive family, get hugs, and talk face-to-face. These visits helped keep me grounded, sane, and helped insulate me from becoming institutionalized.[54]

There were other varied reasons I was grateful for visits. I appreciated having an opportunity to share with my family and friends about the exciting work God was doing with the men behind bars, including the fruit of the Bible ministry. My visitors treated me with respect and seemed encouraged, amazed, and even grateful, for the miraculous to the mundane evidence of God's hand at work behind bars. We'd pray and share what God was speaking to us individually, as a family, etc. We were also able to agree on strategies to more effectively navigate through the often challenging waters of prison ministry with Heart of America Prison Ministries, which was now in quite a few facilities.

The importance, and even the drama, of a prison visit, is something I could not have fully imagined without experiencing it. It was in Springfield when I had an unbelievably shocking visit. Most visits occurred during the weekend or holidays when civilians were off work, and the prison population had little to do. One Tuesday afternoon I was called to an unexpected visit. "Inmate Hairabedian, #27530-004, report to visiting."

---

54 This phenomenon commonly develops after a person has spent a long period living in mental hospitals, prisons, state or private institutions. Individuals in such institutions may be deprived (whether unintentionally or not) of independence and responsibility, to the point that once released they are often unable to manage social and life skills." Having visitors and receiving letters can help protect against this.

Hmmm, who could this be, I wondered? *The family usually comes on weekends. I've no planned visits. Hope nothing's wrong.* I moved quickly, questioning who it could be to no avail. On the outside, we all take for granted keeping in touch with others. Inside, it's a privilege, and it's sporadic at best, so an unexpected visit could stir up wild imaginings. You just never knew when someone on the outside might be in trouble or had possibly died, as it could be challenging getting messages through prison authorities.

I walked in the visiting room to see my mother sitting alone. She had her authorized "clear plastic prison purse" filled with $20 in quarters for the vending machines along with what looked like a newspaper article. My heart started racing. When we hugged, she exhibited unusually stoic posture. One learns quickly in prison not to overreact to new information. I sat down across from her, a small table between us, and asked, "Is everything okay?"

"Yes." She rummaged in her plastic purse. "I have something, but before you read it, I want to tell you what happened last night as I was about to doze off watching the evening news."

She had my full attention. "The TV stations in Kansas City are airing 'John TV,' including the names of the men who are arrested and charged with soliciting prostitutes. I heard the names of those who were charged this week and then I heard a name that made me wonder if I was dreaming or if I imagined it."

Her gaze intensified as she finished. "I thought I heard the name of your federal prosecutor being charged with offering money to an undercover police officer posing as a prostitute."

Shaking my head, I surmised internally, *No way. This must have been a dream.*

With my thoughts spinning, Mom handed me the paper. "This was in USA Today." I opened the small article and read the headline, "Former Federal Prosecutor Arrested for Soliciting a Prostitute in Kansas City."

I was dumbfounded! *The man who facilitated three indictments against me, used perjured testimony to enhance my sentence upward by many years, and then withheld the actual evidence on appeal that would enable the judge to reduce my 22-year sentence, was arrested? He was exposed for sexual indiscretions that made national news?* Trying to wrap my thoughts around his arrest was mindboggling.

I've learned that God has a way of exposing our hidden sin publicly when we won't repent with Him in private. Still taken aback, I felt like I was dreaming. I grabbed some quarters and went to the vending machine to clear my thoughts. I looked again at the article in my hand as I shoved some quarters in the slot. The machine began dispensing the soda, and I was startled by a beeping sound I'd never heard before. My quarters were being shot back out to me, and bright blue LED letters flashed the words, "WINNER, WINNER, WINNER."

What's going on? God, is Your hand of judgment finally coming down? It's about time!

I later learned that this vending machine gave a free soda to every 100th customer. This unique experience happened as I held the USA Today article in hand. Simultaneously, the Holy Spirit reminded me of a verse: "Do not rejoice when your enemy falls, And do not let your heart be glad when he stumbles; Lest the LORD see it, and it displease Him, And He turn away His wrath from him." (Proverbs 24:17-18).

I've heard of visiting room drama, God, but never dreamed I'd experience it myself. Surely You'll now use this character revelation about the former prosecutor to help reduce my 22-year sentence, and I will be released early. I've been incarcerated nearly eight years! How much more time, God, how much more time?

Journey Insights

My visiting room drama shocked me to the core. My prosecutor had been arrested for soliciting sexual favors from an undercover prostitute! God has a way of exposing our sin publicly when we won't repent of hidden issues privately. Do you have a secret sin? If so… it's time to get free and get right.

46

GETTING A FIX

My original attitude when the judge sentenced me and slammed the gavel down was the same as every other prisoner's attitude: "It's not my fault it was the _____" (fill in the blank) snitch, prosecutor, judge, incompetent lawyer, idiot lawmakers. "I'm the victim!" I proclaimed. I took everything except responsibility.

Most drug addicts are looking for what they call "a fix," a drug that will temporarily fix their pain, give them a high or help escape reality. In a similar way, most prisoners —and really people in general—are looking for a fix, or fix-It lawyer, to get them out of their situation. Few want to get fixed in the process.

Over the years, I learned (the hard way) that God had a plan to help me mature. Every time I solved a problem *through my own efforts,* He just allowed a worse fix to come along. Then the Lord showed me this Scripture, **"When I was a child, I talked like a child, I thought like a child, I reasoned like a child. When I became a man, I put childish ways behind me."** (1 Corinthians 13:11 NIV) Although an adult, I still thought like a child. This started me on a long process of growing up and learning to take responsibility.

Of the criminal cases I worked in Springfield, God allowed me to help deliver 11 men with my ink pen. Unfortunately, only a few of them grew from children to men in the process. Most ended up in another fix within a few years and were back in prison, or dead.

Doug was a man in his early 50's. He was raised in a Christian home but left his moral upbringing and became a drinker and womanizer with an affinity for pornography. To help fund his club lifestyle, he also got into the drug business. This led to a small level of power and what he referred to as "free money."

Four years earlier Doug had arrived in prison on a small crack cocaine case. Instead of growing up, putting away childish ways, and returning to the faith of his mother who he loved, Doug gravitated toward a religion known as The Moor Science Temple of America[55]

---

55 The Moors believe the teachings of Noble Drew Ali, who reported that during his travels, he met with a

One day I heard Doug verbally abusing a woman over the phone. I asked him about this and he had no qualms about how he treated females. He said, "God put women on Earth for my pleasure."

I asked him if he felt this way about all women. He emphatically said, "Yes! And you should too!"

I leaned forward and asked, "What if I spoke to your mother like you just spoke to that woman?" I could see his blood start to boil.

"That's different! I love my mother!" Realizing his hypocrisy, he abruptly ended our conversation. I knew it wasn't the time to pursue this but went to prayer for Doug.

A few months later he sheepishly asked if I'd work on his legal case based on a new law that had been made retroactive. He said, "I don't know what you charge, but I don't have much money. I work in the kitchen. The guards let me have two sandwiches. I can bring you one and I'll sell the other."

"I'll do it for free if you come to church every week."

"I attend the Moor Science Temple of America," he sputtered.

"Then have one of your Moor brothers help you."

"My mom's a Christian; she's praying for me. I don't want her to die before I get out. I know God helps you to win. Please help me." After praying alone, the Holy Spirit prompted me to help because of his mother prayers.

As Doug's case slowly progressed toward victory, I pleaded with him to return to Jesus and his Christian morals. I told him that if he wanted to see his mother after she died, he would need to accept Jesus, and they could spend eternity together in Heaven. During our conversations, he was sometimes convicted of his sin and often waffled. He knew the truth, he just wouldn't allow this truth to set him free. He even acted spiritual when he needed me to file another motion or respond to the prosecutor's argument. He would use the Name of Jesus to his benefit, but never re-committed his heart to Jesus as Lord. He wasn't finished with his old lifestyle, childish thinking, and ways. He was still just a kid in an adult body, looking for a quick fix for his problem.

During this nine-month process, his mother was fervently praying him out of prison. While typing his motions in the law library, I could literally feel the pull of Heaven to release him. A few months later the good news came

high priest of Egyptian magic. In one version of Drew's biography, the high priest considered Drew a reincarnation of Jesus, the Buddha, Muhammad and other religious prophets and he trained Drew in mysticism and gave him a "lost section" of the Quran, known as the Holy Koran of the Moorish Science Temple of America (which is not to be confused with the Islamic Quran).

that his sentencing judge reversed a portion of his case. This placed Doug in a lower guideline range and he was now positioned for immediate release.

Within a few hours of receiving this news, instead of praising and thanking God for his miracle, he couldn't wait to get out to start womanizing and misusing women again. I went to his cell and begged him to give his heart to Jesus so that a worse thing didn't happen to him. He laughed at me and said, "I'll never sell drugs again, but I'm not giving up women. They were put here for my pleasure!" The next day Doug walked out of Springfield a free man.

Forty-five days later another inmate brought me a Chicago newspaper and just shook his head. In the Metropolitan section, there was an article about Doug. As it turned out Doug's ex-wife had shot him in the chest and face five times with a 38 special at point blank range, while he sat in a barber's chair getting ready for a date. The article read that Doug had been recently released from federal prison and had been harassing his ex-wife. She warned him that if he didn't leave her alone, he would regret it. She told other people, "Doug will never hurt me and beat me again!"

Doug's Christian mother's prayers had been answered for his early release. He got to see her before she died, and she got to see him one last time before he died. God mercifully got Doug out of the prison fix he was in, but Doug didn't get fixed, and now he was in a worse fix, for eternity.

Another man named Bill was released eight years early through a motion I filed and God opened the prison doors for him. I pleaded with Bill to fully surrender his life to Jesus. He said, "I believe in Jesus."

"Bill, you listen to the same music, you watch the same TV, and you read the same books as the world. You are *playing* Christian." My words were falling on deaf ears, but I continued. "The Bible says that a good tree can't bear bad fruit and a bad tree can't bear good fruit. Good root, good fruit. Bad root, bad fruit. You don't have good fruit." He shrugged it off and was released from prison through an appeal I'd written.

Two years later a guy said to me, "Remember Bill? You helped get him out early?"

"Said he was going to send money to help buy Bibles, but I never heard from him."

"He's back in prison and he's blaming you!" I was doubly shocked.

"Uh, blaming me? I'm the one that helped get him out."

"I thought maybe he was going to say some crazy story like you snitched on him, but that's not it. Bill looked me squarely in the eyes in and said, 'If David hadn't gotten me out of prison early, I'd be released in just five more years, but because of David I was released early. And because I was released early I caught this new case and a fresh 30 years! It's all his fault!'"

I was speechless.

The other inmate continued. "I got mad and told him not to spread this crap. I wanted to hit him in the mouth, but I'm a Christian now so I just walked away and asked God to correct him. Well get this, about 15 minutes ago Bill got into an argument with another guy and that guy hit him in the mouth, several times. They're both in solitary."

My fault? What's wrong with people? You just can't make this stuff up, I thought. I remembered a funny statement I'd once heard *"De-nial* is not a river in Egypt!" It was then I heard the still small voice of the Holy Spirit.

"There were numerous times I got you out of a fix, *but you didn't allow Me to fix you* in the process."

Every time that happened, Lord, I'd end up in another fix. Thank You for showing me, for warning me, with this guy who just got 30 more years. The truth of this whole revelation landed on me like a ton of bricks. I knew that others who God places in our paths can either be great role models or horrible warnings. Bill was a horrible warning. I got down on my knees right then and there.

God, fix me from the inside out so I'd never have to see the inside of another prison to get fixed again. Help me with my hidden sin, whatever it might be, so that nothing has dominion over me. Help me, God, not hold on to anything that doesn't honor You.

King David came to mind. He'd committed adultery and conspiratorial murder, while in office as one of God's anointed Kings. His prayer echoed within me, **"Who can understand his errors? Cleanse me from secret faults. Keep back Your servant also from presumptuous sins; Let them not have dominion over me. Then I shall be blameless, and I shall be innocent of great transgression."** (Psalm 19:12-13)

Before I arose from my knees, I prayed this same prayer from my heart. I was grateful because I knew that God was doing a deep work as He directed me to put away yet a few more childish things. He showed me things that were holding me back from growing up into the man of God He wanted me to become.

Journey Insights

The Holy Spirit reminded me of a number of times that God had gotten me out of a fix, but I didn't allow God to fix me in the process, and therefore I ended up in a worse fix. I blamed everyone else but me. The same thing happened with the other inmate. He blamed me for getting back into prison and couldn't take responsibility for the crimes he committed that got him back in prison. Where do you need to take responsibility and stop blaming everyone and everything else?

47

GOD'S HEALING POWER ON THE DEATH WARD

MCFP Springfield, Missouri (1995-98)

I wanted to pray at the death ward, but I couldn't get in unless I had a Hospice Helper badge. Since the staff knew that I performed paralegal work for other inmates and because the medical treatment wasn't always administered with MAYO Clinic standards, I could never get one. There was concern that I would help an inmate file a civil complaint against the facility for medical violations. So for me to be on the death ward, without expressed permission, could mean a trip to the hole.

When the Holy Spirit spoke to me, "Go to Building 3-2 today and administer My healing power," I seriously counted the cost. Building 3, floor 2 was the hospital's death ward. I remembered how Peter and John had healed a man at the Gate Beautiful and ended up in prison (Acts chapters 3-4). While still pondering this, a prisoner named Geoff came up to me. The week before he had been miraculously healed when Terry Dante and I prayed for him.

Geoff said, "Hey, do you ever go to building 3-2 to pray?" I looked back at him, stunned. He continued, "The Lord healed me. Why can't we release healing for them? You lay hands on 'em and I'll back you up. I want to learn how to do it."

I said, "The Holy Spirit just told me to go and the Bible says for us to go out in two's (Mark 6:7) so this is confirmation. Let's talk to the guard."

We approached with firm confidence knowing God's favor had gone before us. I peered through the glass and knocked. The guard was entertaining three nurses with crass jokes and wasn't happy to be interrupted. "What the hell are you doing here without permission?"

In a respectful tone, I replied, "We aren't here without permission, Sir. We came directly to you to get permission before we entered."

"Well the way I see it," he smirked, "you're already here without my permission. You're both going to the SHU! (Segregated Housing Unit)" He glanced at the nurses to see if they were impressed with his authority and wit.

"Okay, we don't have a problem going to the SHU, but could we first please pray for the sick?"

The atmosphere changed as if the oxygen had just been sucked out of the room. The three nurses looked at the guard, then us, then each other. The guard muttered, "What?"

I repeated myself, adding that these inmates weren't allowed off the floor to attend church for healing prayer so we thought we'd bring it to them. I ended with the words, "It is Sunday, you know?"

He thought for a minute and replied in a matter of fact tone, "You're both still going to the SHU, but if it's okay with the nurses...."

The head nurse shrugged her shoulders and said, "Prayer can't hurt these guys! Let 'em pray!"

The guard said, "Okay, go and pray, but report back to me after you're done and prepare to go to the SHU. And the first room you're going to is there!" He pointed to a special needs type hospital room. The nurses nodded and smiled.

I didn't know what we'd discover behind that wall. I pushed open the door to see three comatose men. The first was lying on his back, loosely restrained, wearing only boxer shorts. The bed was encased in a rectangular blue framed box with white mesh-netting. In a strange sort of way it reminded me of a casket displayed at a funeral. I later discovered this was to keep him from rolling out of bed. He had been hit on his head from behind, with a metal bar, while lifting weights at a penitentiary in California. Three months earlier his unconscious body was delivered here. He hadn't even opened his eyes.

We raised our hands to Heaven and then stretched them toward him and prayed, "Lord Jesus, we ask for Your healing Presence to enter this room. You said, 'if we lay hands on the sick they will recover.'" We waited on the Lord for about 30 seconds. Nothing happened. My mind raced. "Holy Spirit, You told me to come here and we're going to be tossed into the SHU for obeying. The guard ordered us to the room of someone in an impossible situation. There's not enough anointing here to lay hands on him and heal him (Mark 16:18)."

I looked at Geoff, "What do you think?"

He shrugged, "I'm new at this; I'm following you."

Shaking my head I asked, "Holy Spirit, what do we do now?"

Two words came to mind, *"Trust Me."* I thanked the Lord as these words gave me peace, and encouraged me to wait on Him with outstretched hands. About two minutes later the atmosphere changed. God's love and power entered like a tsunami over this man's bed. Geoff and I wept. The patient suddenly moved. With wrists strapped to the bed, he sat up, arched his back, opened his eyes, and stared directly at us!

If the eyes are the windows to the soul, this man's soul was in the torments of hell! I immediately took authority over demons in Jesus' Name, commanding them to depart. The look in his eyes became personal, defiant, and murderous, as if entities from another realm wanted to kill us for disturbing their work. With increased resolve and purpose, I repeated the commands, speaking directly to the demons just as Jesus did many time when He was healing the sick.

"In the Name of Jesus, leave this man now!" I ordered. After a short struggle, the tormenting entities seemed to depart and the look in his eyes changed from terror and torment to relief and peace. The arch in his back disappeared and he relaxed onto the bed as if he passed out into a deep sleep.

Geoff looked at me, astonished. I said, "God is moving; let's follow His lead!" For the next 90 minutes, we went from room to room as the power of God touched and healed people. We prayed for men with the devastating disease of AIDS. Some were touched instantly and strength was restored to their bodies. One man who was lame in both legs from three bullets, still lodged in his back and confined to a wheel chair for life, received feeling in both legs. Within two weeks, he was walking.

On the way out we returned to the first room, raised our hands toward the man, and said under the anointing, "Holy Spirit, come!" Immediately God's tangible Presence returned and within seconds, he opened his eyes, sat up, and looked at us with great appreciation.

But he still looked lost. I asked if he wanted to accept Jesus as his Lord and Savior. He couldn't speak, but looked at us with great interest. I briefly shared the Gospel. He nodded, more with his eyes than his head. I said a prayer to accept Jesus. He looked at us in agreement and suddenly the lost look transformed into a look of inner knowing and peace. It was as if, for a moment, he was seeing the divine Presence that we knew was there. He smiled and then lay down and slept.

Our work was done. Jesus, the Prince of Life, had showed Himself marvelously on the death ward that Sunday. We reported to the guard to go to SHU. The guard and nurses were laughing and talking about God. The nurses said, "You can't throw these guys in the SHU for asking to pray. They're the real deal. Let 'em go back to their units for God's sake. It's Sunday!"

The guard acquiesced and we were overjoyed at what he said next, "Okay, but only if you pray for me. The nurses all say that I need it!" He escorted us to the elevator, we prayed God's blessing on him and went back to our unit.

We learned later that only nine minutes after we left, the man in the coma died and went to be with Jesus.

Journey Insights

When I asked, "Holy Spirit, what do we do now?" two words came into my mind: "Trust Me." These words gave me peace and so we waited on God with our hands stretched out toward the man. About two minutes went by and God's Presence entered the room like a tsunami over this man's bed. The man in the coma suddenly began moving. When the Holy Spirit instructs you to lay hands on the sick, will you do so?

48

TIME WITH THE MAFIA DONS

MCFP Springfield, Missouri (1995-98)

During my three years at Springfield, housed in the work cadre unit at MCFP, I did time with some of the nation's most notorious "wise guys," also known as Mafia Dons. Years earlier, when I arrived in the system in Oklahoma I was put in the cell with a Mafia Don. This guy was doing life plus 20 and had had five million in cash confiscated from him upon arrest. He'd just recently picked up another 15 years for ordering a murder for hire from behind bars. Because I was a friend of another Italian he knew in Kansas City, he made a quick phone call and determined I was okay. He then told me he'd introduce me to his friends, "the Dons."

Maybe they're father and son — Don Sr. and Don Jr, I thought.

On the day I was introduced I shook the first man's hand and he said, "I'm Tony."

The other Don said, "You can call me Frank." I wondered why I'd do that if their names were Don. Thank goodness I didn't open my mouth and show my ignorance. I later learned from a guy who wasn't even Italian that the word "Don" refers to a mob boss, crime lord, or kingpin in charge of a criminal organization.

A lot of the incarcerated mob bosses were housed in one of the nation's five maximum security penitentiaries or at the five medical facilities, based mainly on their age, or declining health. Few were kept in prison camps. Most of these Dons didn't cause much trouble with the guards or other inmates, and at times, they actually helped the place run a little smoother.

Many were in for racketeering, gambling, extortion, tax evasion, or murder. A few were in for large scale heroin operations. Most seemed like nice guys, which was, of course, only the side I saw of them. The Lord gave me great favor with many of these Dons for what I would later discover as His divine purpose, and several even came to salvation.

One time, I was asked to set up a meeting between two of the five crime bosses out of New York for peace-making purposes. One Mafia Don was transferred for oral surgery from a Super Max facility. He was being housed in an off-limits hospital floor room. Another Mafia Don asked me if I could arrange a meeting between the two of them. I said, "How can I possibly set up a meeting? He's in an off-limits room on a hospital floor."

He replied, "He's got to go to the dentist in the next few days. Find out when he's going and have the inmate transporting him in the wheelchair roll past the dental office by accident. I'll be waiting at the recreation yard locked gate. All I need is 15-20 seconds. This will mean a lot to my family and me, and help bring peace between our groups."

I met with the inmate that would be escorting the Mafia Don and told him what I needed. He said, "I could be thrown in SHU and lose my job."

"It's important and I'm asking as a favor." On the appointed day, everything went perfectly and that's saying something because these were two mob bosses who'd both been accused of ordering several gangland-style murders of one another's members. I was there to witness it, helping to block the conversation with my laundry cart outside of camera range and long enough for them to talk eye-to-eye.

The one Mafia boss told me later that this helped establish a peace treaty between two of the five crime families out of New York and stopped any further unnecessary bloodshed between them. Jesus said, **"Blessed are the peacemakers..."** (Matthew 5:9). The difference between a peacemaker and a peacekeeper is this: A peacekeeper keeps peace using a weapon, like a gun. The peace-maker, on the other hand, makes peace by simply using words. That day the Peacemaker, Jesus, may have done more to make peace among two of New York's notorious crime families in 15-20 seconds than the entire FBI had done to keep peace among them in the previous 15-20 years.

The same Sunday Geoff and I went to Building 3-2 (the death ward) to pray for the sick. The Lord had healed Geoff of an incurable disease a few months earlier. We entered and found ourselves locking eyes with one of the highest level New York crime bosses, Vito "the Chin" Binnetti. I'd seen him several times on 60 Minutes. He was allegedly crazy, but today he was just sitting on his bed watching TV.[56]

I couldn't help but stare. *You've got to be kidding, this is Vito the Chin? He looks like death warmed over.* He stared back at me for a second and in a gruff tone said, "What do *you* want?"

Smiling, I kept looking in his eyes and politely said, "We're going room to room and offering prayer for healing."

---

56   Later, out of curiosity, I reviewed his case in the law library. He was charged with, among other things, conspiracy to murder eight men. He was also later acquitted of the failed attempt to assassinate another infamous mob boss.

He looked at me in utter disbelief, "Kid, *you* want ta' pray for *me?*" Then he repeated it a second time in a cynical, irritated manner.

Unmoved, I continued smiling and waited. Vito turned to his Italian roommate, reportedly a lieutenant in the mob, and said, "Hey Frankie, get a load of this, this kid wants ta' pray for me!" They both laughed. Then Frankie said, "You get the hell outta' here!"

"I'll leave if you want," I told Vito, and I also looked directly at Frankie. "But you guys are both in pretty bad shape and prayer in your situation sure can't hurt."

They both stared incredulously at me, and then each other. Then this hardened mob boss said, "You got balls, kid. I think I kinda' like you!" He then added, "You wanna' pray for me? Go ahead and pray."

Geoff and I moved to his bed. "Do you believe in God?" I asked.

He grabbed my wrist, with surprising strength, stared at me eye to eye, with unexpected passion, and said, "Kid, He's *all* we've got left!" Those poignant words struck a chord within me.

Here we all were in prison for some sort of crime. Away from our families, stripped of most of our dignity, being told when to get up, when to lie down, when we could eat, when we could make a phone call, when we could go outside, and when we could return. We didn't control much of anything. Vito was on 3-2, the death ward, ready to pass into eternity. Earthly money and power were, for the most part, useless at this point. Vito spoke truth from his soul. God really was all we had left.

I prayed the prayer of faith. God's power became tangible for a moment. Vito thanked me and said, "Kid, if you ever need anything, just ask." I later discovered what "anything" included when he said it.

Within two days, Vito, along with several others we'd prayed for, were miraculously released from the death ward and moved to a lesser level hospital floor. I spotted him walking around the rec yard in the afternoon sunshine. He approached me and said, with his hand away from his mouth, "Kid, remember me?" He stood erect with his hands in the air as if on display before His God, angels, and mankind, and awaited my response.

I burst into a smile, "Of course, you look great!"

He said, "I FEEL great! I'll never forget what you did for me."

"I didn't do it, God did it for you."

He grinned and said, "But you had the balls to obey Him!"

Vito the Chin Binnetti lived 12 more years before finally dying in prison.

Journey Insights

The peace-maker makes peace by simply using words. That day Jesus may have done more to make peace among two of New York's notorious crime families in 15-20 seconds than the entire FBI had done in the previous 15-20 years. It took courage and obedience to pray for the Dons. Do you need to ask God for courage and obedience? God wants to change your destiny and use you to help change someone else's.

49

ENCOUNTERING JEZEBEL

MCFP Springfield, Missouri (1995-98)

After two years of what seemed like a continuous revival, a new chaplain named Larissa Lester arrived from Oklahoma. She was from a conservative denominational background. We appreciated the additional staff chaplaincy position and welcomed her with open arms.

The first time Chaplain Lester preached, the message was right on, but she offered no altar call. The second time, the same thing happened. I didn't think much of it, knowing that everyone has different ministry styles. The third time she preached, however, the Holy Spirit spoke to me.

"She's about to divide this congregation down the middle and take disciples after herself." I didn't want to believe it. I did, however, remember my mother's warning dream she'd had, that there was a Jezebel spirit here with a plan to get me locked away in the psych ward in Building 10. Caution and wisdom were needed and when I told the Holy Spirit I didn't believe she would divide the Church, I heard these words:

"Watch and see!"

That day her message changed. She subtly bashed anything to do with miracles, present day charismatic gifting, and manifestations of the Spirit's power.

I spoke privately with the Head Chaplain, Monty Reynolds, an Assemblies' of God pastor. Because the services were videotaped, I encouraged Chaplain Monty to listen to the sermon. He did, and saw the subtleties, but didn't know how to address them. We prayed about the situation.

The following week she began removing every Christian program she could where the Spirit seemed to be moving. She accomplished this by pointing to the policy that no inmate services can occur without staff supervision. She used the regional chaplain's authority to execute these changes. She also refused to supervise the gatherings that occurred during Chaplain Monty's days off.

She called me into her office. "Now don't kill the messenger; it's not my doing," she said with a smirk. "This is from Chaplain Monty. Your Saturday service is canceled until further notice." The Saturday service was a two-hour Bible study and prayer time. I knew she was going to dismantle the program because of what the Holy Spirit had told me so I wasn't surprised. I stood to leave.

She stiffened, "Aren't you upset?"

"No, seasons come and seasons go. God obviously has something better." When I failed to react, she became visibly angry. I left and notified the 35 regulars that the meeting was canceled until further notice. We prayed in the yard seeking God's wisdom.

Chaplain Lester and Father Jamison, a Charismatic Catholic priest, locked horns next. She began writing him up to the regional chaplain for alleged policy violations. Father Jamison asked us to pray for him, saying he'd never met a chaplain quite like this. We began to fast and pray. About 15 of us entered spiritual warfare asking God to cleanse the chaplaincy office of all evil.

A few days later we heard the chapel was closed for a week. We were told that the water sprayers on the fire alarm systems went off at midnight, but the alarms never sounded. Hundreds of gallons of water destroyed the computers in the chaplain's office and all the paper copies of the volunteer profiles were saturated. Nearly everything had to be regenerated from scratch.

A few months later, Father Jamison had had enough and transferred to another prison, but not before writing a three-page complaint letter against her to the head chaplain in Washington.

Chaplain Lester then focused in on Chaplain Monty and me! She wanted me transferred and she wanted Chaplain Monty's job! The next several months were ugly. God's Spirit continued to move and the warfare increased.

During this time, God's favor was upon my life in a special way with staff and inmates. Several warned me of Chaplain Lester's strategies to get me locked up. Nothing would stop her. She wrote internal memos to the SIS trying to stop the Bible ministry. The head of SIS, the SIA (Cross-sworn Special Investigating Agent for the FBI), a devout atheist, asked every inmate who came into his office for information about me. He got the same basic response, "He's into Jesus. He'll invite you to church, pray for you for healing, and get you a free Bible. He's not into any of the illegal stuff."

Over time, the SIA watched these same trouble-makers become Christians. He also saw us walking on the track together and saw their lives being changed. God eventually used this atheist's witness to protect me from Chaplain Lester's allegations. At Miami, God gave us protection and favor through the most unlikely in authority, the atheist Captain. Here history was repeating itself, yet with one twist. On the other side was Chaplain Lester, a Christian, who appeared to become the devil's emissary. She had written all kinds of memorandums to get me placed under investigation, locked up and shipped out. However, since the SIA had already performed his own investigation, he ignored the security memorandums she wrote to him, the captain, warden, and lieutenant's office. This made her even angrier.

Next, she tried to get inmates in her Bible study to *beat me up!* The situation seemed surreal. The inmates were stunned as they came to tell me of her suggestions. Attendance at her classes dwindled. God opened the door via correction officers allowing us to pray for the sick on the hospital floors during these same class times. Prisoners started getting healed and showing up at church. I learned through this that where the devil closes a door God always opens a window, if we're patient, choose to remain unoffended, and are willing to search for it. His anointing continued increasing through these times of trials.

One afternoon I was called to SIS. A new captain had arrived the month prior. The SIA was sitting with him. The captain asked me to empty my pockets -- notepad, pocket bible, phone list, etc. He looked through my belongings then reached into a file folder and removed a copy of a teaching from a book entitled *Combating the Jezebel Spirit*. He asked, "You familiar with this?"

"Sure, it's from a book called *The Three Battlegrounds*. It deals with a commonly taught subject in Charismatic settings called 'the spirit of Jezebel.'"

"Have you been distributing it?"

"I've shared this on three compounds since I found it five years ago, and several other teachings on various topics."

"I've got a memo here from Lester that says other inmates have told her that you referred to her as having a Jezebel spirit, and you're distributing this teaching. She says that since Jezebel was murdered in the Bible, as long as you're here, her life is in danger because of your influence with other inmates. I have to lock you up and ship you."

"Okay, but would you do me one favor?" I asked politely.

"What?"

"Would you read the teaching, because one of Jezebel's tools is to use a man's position of authority to accomplish her private agenda without the use of physical force? If you read that, you'll know how this spirit has just used you to accomplish its agenda. I say this so your authority won't be manipulated in the future." The captain glared at me, threw my belongings on the desk and walked out.

The SIA said he couldn't find anything negative on me and that he'd ignored Chaplain Lester's memos because he'd heard she was out to get me. He heaved a sigh and said, "I don't even believe in God, but I'd rather have Chaplain Lester shipped and keep you here."

We both smiled.

He continued, "She went behind my back to the new captain, and before I could stop him he put in the transfer order. I'm sorry about this but mark my words, she hasn't gotten away with it. She'll have hell to pay from me over this whole deal. Now I've gotta' lock you up."

Off to solitary confinement in lockdown I went, handcuffed and shackled. A five-man hold was placed on me. Whenever I went to the shower, I was black boxed, cuffed, shackled and belly chained with five guards escorting me holding riot batons. It was August of 1998.

Journey Insights

Throughout the attacks from the Chaplain, God's favor was upon my life in a special way with both staff and the inmates. Even though the devil tried to make me bow down, I refused and it caused me to get solitary confinement. Yet God always opened another door and multiplied His Kingdom fruits through these times of trials and tests. Are you willing to stand up for God regardless of the cost?

50

THE SPIRIT OF GOD IN LOCKDOWN

MCFP Springfield, Missouri (1995-98)

There comes a time when you can feel God calling you to an undistracted, much-needed period of rest and refreshing in His Presence. I had been involved in ministry endeavors, spiritual warfare, and answering legal questions for nearly three years, without a break. The Jezebel incident led me to be "sequestered to the hole," yet I felt the Spirit of God and His glory resting upon me.

Grateful and eventually delighted, solitary confinement provided me with few distractions and interruptions, a rarity in prison. The first four days I sought the Lord and His counsel. I prayed, read most of the Old Testament, and meditated on His wonderful Word, which came alive to me in that "quiet alone time" with Him. I was able to pray in tongues unhindered for several hours a day. I also fasted, making sure to flush my food down the toilet so the guards wouldn't think I was a religious nut on some sort of hunger strike.

God's peace is in this place of man's punishment, I acknowledged. You're here, God. Just us. I'm truly thankful.

The Holy Spirit illumined a verse from 1 Peter that seemed to fit my present situation:

"Dear friends, don't be bewildered or surprised when you go through the fiery trials ahead, for this is no strange, unusual thing that is going to happen to you. Instead, be really glad--because these trials will make you partners with Christ in his suffering, and afterwards you will have the wonderful joy of sharing his glory in that coming day when it will be displayed. Be happy if you are cursed and insulted for being a Christian, for when that happens the Spirit of God will come upon you with great glory." (1 Peter 4:12-15 LVB)

These words greatly encouraged me and I felt the tangible Presence of the Lord. Locked in solitary, several cells away from the other inmates, it became increasingly like a spiritual prayer retreat alone with God on the mountaintop. Suddenly the Holy Spirit spoke to me, "I'm sending you to Waseca."

"Waseca, *Minnesota?* What for?"

In a still small voice, I heard, "I have need of you there." I felt the Lord's peace and confirmation that I was in His perfect will.

Shortly after God's revelation about this impending move, Chaplain Monty came to see me, peeking at me through the small window. He had heard that I wasn't coming back to the compound, but was slated for immediate transfer.

"How's it going, David?" His tone was one of concern.

"Great!" My answer came across in a buoyant manner for I truly felt filled to overflowing with God's love.

Chaplain Monty didn't acknowledge my answer, instead he seemed unusually contemplative. He waited a moment, then gently said, "I'm sorry about what's happened; there's nothing I can do. It took Chaplain Lester nearly a year, but she finally got you."

"Chaplain, she didn't get me. She got herself. I'm in God's perfect will." Chaplain Monty agreed that I was in God's will, but he was concerned about my transfer and chose that moment to tell me.

"David, you're getting shipped out tomorrow, away from your family, to Sandstone, Minnesota." The surprise and disappointment he expected from me didn't come; instead, I responded with confidence.

"Not Sandstone, Chaplain, Waseca."

"I've seen the paperwork. Who told you Waseca?" When I told him it was the Holy Spirit, he looked at me and said, "Well, I saw Sandstone and that's most likely where you're going."

"I think I heard correctly. If not, I'm okay with wherever God sends me."

Chaplain Monty confided, "David, it's terrible at church. The whole compound is divided over the conflict between you and Chaplain Lester, both staff and inmates. Half are siding with you, half are siding with her. I've never seen anything like it." He gave a big sigh. "Staff never sides with the inmate in situations like this, and many are saying that she needs to be shipped instead of you. Half the congregation is boycotting Sunday services. They say they won't return until she apologizes and gets you out."

I remembered 11 months earlier when the Holy Spirit told me that she was about to divide the congregation down the middle and take disciples after herself. As I reminded Chaplain Monty of the Holy Spirit's warning, his eyes widened.

"That's exactly what's happening, David."

"Chaplain, please tell the congregation that our battle is not against flesh and blood, but against the unseen realm, and if they boycott Sunday service because of this, then the devil has won."

Moving closer to the door, I said, "Tell them I said to go back to church and act as if nothing has happened. This will stymie the devil and his plans. And tell them to love her as Jesus loves her."

Chaplain Monty just stared at me, which prompted me to ask him if I could pray for him. He put his hands through the food slot and I asked for God to strengthen him to stand and contend for the faith.

The following morning at 4:00 a.m. the guard woke me, "Hairabedian, pack your stuff. You're being transferred."

I told him I didn't have any stuff. "The last I saw of my property was in my regular living unit." He just shook his head and said, "I'll track down your property and make sure it makes it to your next institution."

Thirty minutes later I was cuffed, shackled with a belly chain and black boxed again. The guards escorted me to Receiving and Discharge. I was placed in a cell with half a dozen others who were only wearing handcuffs.

A lieutenant who had been on vacation the week prior saw me through the bars. He said, "Hairabedian, they're transferring you?"

I'd gotten used to things not making much sense. I responded, "I guess so."

He seemed stunned. "What the hell for?"

All I knew to say was, "Chaplain Lester requested it."

He shook his head, "That's crazy. No one likes her; she's a trouble maker." He thought for a moment and then said, "Hey, can I ask you a favor? I need someone I can trust on the bus as the orderly. Will you do it?"

Not much startled me, but that did. *I'm standing here with shackles, cuffs, chains, and black box, and now I'm the bus orderly? I was amazed. In thirty seconds, I've gone from being a maximum-security prisoner to an honor inmate. Don't they know I've still got 11 years?* He ordered the guards to take me out of the cell and remove all the hardware. What a switch from all the other times I'd traveled while incarcerated.

On the bus, I was free to roam the cabin serving the inmates drinks and meals, and I made the most of it. "More coffee?" They were cuffed and shackled, definitely uncomfortable. I may have been flabbergasted at my freedom, but I was thankful for the chance to serve these guys. It was especially delightful when God gave me opportunity to pray with a couple of the Psyche Ward inmates. One came to Christ and I was able to cast demons out of the other.

God, You amaze me. Talk about parting the Red Sea! It was a humbling yet thrilling time being used by God, and it continued as several others *asked me* to pray with them during that unexpected morning trip.

I was bound again at the next facility, but all I could do was stand in amazement from the fruit of the Lord's Presence on that bus ride. Over the years, I learned not to allow my soul – my mind, emotions, and will – be in charge, but rather to stand on His Word and walk in the Spirit. Leaving Springfield behind and heading to Waseca, I realized once again that I have the Spirit of Christ, the hope of glory within me (Colossians 1:27). I absolutely could always live in hope. Not some random wishful thinking, but Biblical hope which I'd learned is the confident expectation of God's goodness.

Being notified by the Lord of my transfer, and the kindness of experiencing a taste of freedom on the bus ride reminded me I could trust and believe in God's goodness despite my circumstances. The Holy Spirit taught me the undeniable message from 2 Timothy 2:9 (ESV), that although the prisoners may be bound, **"the word of God is not bound!"**

Journey Insights

God makes a way. It seemed like the Jezebel Chaplain had won by manipulating the system to land me in solitary confinement, but in serving God with my whole heart, I learned to expect the unexpected. In one moment I went from being shackled with a black box to unshackled as a bus orderly, serving the inmates. Do you need a reminder of the power of hoping in God's goodness? I pray He intervenes with the unexpected now in Jesus' Name.

51

SPIRITUAL GROUND SWELL

FCI Waseca, Minnesota (1998-2001)

I heard that spiritually there was very little taking place at FCI Waseca. Yet, it quickly became clear why God moved me here. I was met with very little expectation of God's miracles, but because of what I'd been taught in Miami and Springfield, I was able to release the Lord's power. Within a week, God moved mightily and swiftly. The name Waseca is a Dakota word meaning fertile, and I was encouraged by how extraordinarily fertile the spiritual ground was here. Several men were filled with the Holy Ghost instantaneously and many others received healing. It wasn't unusual that this happened, but it happened in *the first week* and it all took place *outside the chapel!*

Many citizens in the outside community were praying over this new facility. I believe this made a big difference in the groundswell of God's power and Presence. I learned the important lesson that God will send a person with spiritual gifts, in answer to another's prayers. Those prayers accomplish great things, creating a hunger for God in hurting and unfulfilled people.[57]

The chaplain, Michael Longanecker, was on annual leave during this time. When he returned there was an e-mail from Chaplain Lester. Before praying about it, Chaplain Longanecker tracked me down at my new job in the law library. He escorted me outside, to a private place behind a building, and asked in an accusatory manner, "Are you David Hairabedian, #27530-004?"

Somewhat puzzled I replied, "Yes."

He looked sternly in my eyes and demanded, "Well then why don't you tell me why every prison compound you go to, you end up causing problems for the chaplains and wreaking havoc in the body of Christ?"

Shocked, I answered, "Excuse me?"

He repeated his statement and wagged his finger at me, "If you don't tell me the truth, I'll have you shipped to an FCI at Sheridan, Oregon, 1,200 miles from your family."

I was absolutely stunned. "Where'd you get your info?"

---

57   James 5:16 (AMP) tells us, "The earnest (heartfelt, continued) prayer of a righteous man makes tremendous power available [dynamic in its working]."

His eyes narrowed, "That's none of your business."

I said, "What you've described is simply not true." Then I respectfully asked, "Can I give you the names of the head chaplains at every facility I've been at during the last nine years so you can investigate this accusation yourself?" Before he could answer I began naming the different chaplains: "Chaplain Loren, FCI Englewood, Chaplain 'One Love,' FCI Miami, Chaplain Reynolds, USMCFP Springfield--"

He interrupted, "I just heard about you from the chaplain at Springfield."

As kindly as I could I countered, "You didn't hear this from the head chaplain. You heard this from Chaplain Larissa Lester. She's the only chaplain I've ever had problems with in nine years. If you'll contact Chaplain Reynolds, and the other head chaplains I've named, I believe you'll discover that I've always submitted to their authority and been fruitful."

The Holy Spirit then came upon me in boldness and prompted me to say, "Chaplain, with all due respect, since I've been here the last two weeks, several inmates have told me that you don't serve G.O.D., but BOP (Bureau of Prisons). Each time, I've told them I didn't want to hear their negative comments about the chaplain God placed in authority over us. I told them that as far as I'm concerned, Chaplain Longanecker is a man of God until he proves otherwise." This seemed to stop him in his tracks.

He cleared his throat and finally spoke, "I agree with that." His face softened and he said, "In fact, I agree wholeheartedly, and as far as I'm concerned, you also are a man of God until you prove otherwise."

I looked at him with appreciation and said, "If one of us isn't a man of God, it won't take long before we'll both know it. A tree is clearly known by its fruit." We sized each other up for just a moment, then shook hands. Chaplain Longanecker turned and walked off and I returned to my unit to pray about this. Although the enemy often tries to create division, that turned out to be an honest encounter between two Believers.

This Jezebel-spirited Chaplain Lester was "hunting me in the system." I remembered when I was nine and having my God-dreams, Terese had it out for me and nothing I could do would change her mind. But this was a much bigger problem. I was angry at the enemy for trying to stop the Holy Spirit move of God on this compound.

My first thoughts, before seeking the Lord's counsel, involved taking care of this problem with Chaplain Lester through legal filings. (How easily we slip back into the soulish realm!) God had been increasing the legal anointing on my life. I had become a paralegal and God had given me the understanding and capability to file lawsuits effectively against BOP Officials who liked harassing inmates.

Filing a civil action against her to "place a formal lien on her personal assets" seemed like the appropriate measure. The words, "skin for skin" came to mind. I wanted to know what she'd written about me. She probably muddied up my file to turn other staff members against me wherever I go in the prison system. An FIOA (Freedom of Information Act) request would provide the evidence I need to get even. I decided to begin the lengthy paperwork process. This would be my first mission at Waseca!

I clenched my fists, anticipating the first step. Then the Holy Spirit prompted me to humble myself and get down on my knees and pray. I don't want to pray. It's time for war. The Holy Spirit prompted me a second time. I heaved a sigh and reluctantly obeyed, falling prostrate before the Lord. After a few minutes of prayer, I jumped up and headed down the hall to start the paperwork. Halfway down the hallway, the Holy Spirit turned me around and sent me back for more prayer. This scenario occurred two more times.

Finally, I "died to self" on this issue, telling God, "I choose not to vindicate myself. If you choose to vindicate me, so be it. I fully lay this situation on the altar before You." God's peace flooded my soul.

Crucifying the flesh so the nature of Christ can come forth was a very difficult test. More of my old nature was being removed to make room for more of His nature in my life.[58] This is often a painful and arduous process as His Spirit changes us more into the image of His Son.

In retrospect, I honestly believe that if I'd chosen to file legal paperwork, I would have miserably failed this test and had to repeat it in a different scenario. Moreover, I believe I would have missed the blessing of what God was soon to do at FCI Waseca.

Three hours later Chaplain Longanecker saw me standing in line in the commissary. He said, "I prayed and the Lord convicted me. I should have prayed before confronting you. Will you forgive me?"

I was stunned and waited briefly for the other shoe to drop. When I realized he was really speaking from his heart, I said, "I absolutely forgive you. We all make mistakes and I've made some real bad ones myself."

Chaplain Longanecker smiled, and then said, "Well then, let's win this compound to Christ!"

Joy suddenly filled my heart. I was glad I didn't try to vindicate myself. God

58   John 3:30, **"He must increase, but I must decrease."**

was already at work doing a much better job than I ever could.

Chaplain Longanecker asked, "What are your ministry gifts?"

"Well, I can do almost anything. Wherever you need me, I'll serve."

"What about leading worship?"

I gulped. "Worship is the area I'm least gifted in. In fact, I may not have any gifting in this area, but there's a seasoned Christian named Ned, who just arrived a couple of weeks ago." Ned began leading worship on his guitar and the services took on a whole new dynamic. The Spirit started moving and Chaplain Longanecker (or Chaplain Mike as I began calling him) started prophesying during the Sunday morning worship services. Everyone's gifts soon began operating in this refreshing worship atmosphere.

A couple of months later, Chaplain Mike hired Ned and me to work at the chapel full time. Chaplain Mike and I began praying and God revealed His plans for evangelism and discipleship programs. Men who earlier spoke negatively about the chaplain started noticing a change. The congregation tripled in size within a few weeks' time. Chaplain Mike started demonstrating his pastor's heart by implementing an "open door policy" in his office.

The Lord directed me to begin laying hands on the men for the infilling of the Holy Spirit, and many instantly received their prayer language. The Lord filled about a dozen men with the Spirit in all and several healings occurred. Monday night prayer circle increased from two of us to twenty-two.

One evening, 30 minutes before the Wednesday service, I walked into Chaplain Mike's office. He was wearing ecclesiastical robes. My eyebrows shot up, "What's with the robes?" He told me that he felt like the Lord wanted him to conduct an Ash Wednesday service. I didn't understand. "You're not Catholic. You're not even Lutheran. In fact, you're Pentecostal. You're the only Four-Square Gospel chaplain in the entire BOP."

He nodded, "I know, but I feel led to do this."

He opened a small film container and showed me its contents. "The ashes are to anoint people's foreheads at the close of the service."

I took the canister and looked at it. "Mike, I've got to be honest, this is outside my denominational paradigm, but I believe you when you say God's in it."

He put the container on the desk between us. We joined hands and asked the Lord for an outpouring of His Holy Spirit. After a couple of minutes, the tangible anointing of the Holy Spirit came down on the film container between our hands and it began to vibrate. We looked at each other and then back at the canister. We prayed with increased fervency. God's Presence increased. The Master was in our midst and we knew in our hearts that God was about to do something special.

Chaplain Mike chose not to announce the service, "God will bring those He's drawing." As men returned from recreation during the 8:30 p.m. inmate move, I stood outside the chapel and simply invited them to attend our first ever Ash Wednesday service. Much to my surprise, they filed in one by one like sheep.

Candles shone through the darkness. Chaplain Mike explained the meaning of Ash Wednesday and then lit incense liturgical style and walked around the room swinging the metal cantor. The Ash Wednesday Service lasted about 20 minutes then he preached the death, burial and resurrection of Jesus Christ, offering men forgiveness of sins and salvation. This portion of the message lasted less than three minutes. Seven men responded. Chaplain Mike was dumbfounded. This was more coming to Christ in one service than in the entire eight years of his ministry behind bars.

Similar moves of God began to occur in almost every meeting. The chapel services went from bare to packed. In the next 45 days, I had the privilege of leading 65 men to Christ. This began happening all over the compound. It was a sovereign move of God.

I remembered the Holy Spirit's words while I was being kicked out of Springfield, "I have need of you there!" I learned that God takes "what the devil means for harm and turns it around for good," if we'll just have patience, forgive, and keep our eyes on Jesus. God turned Chaplain Lester's efforts to cause division between Chaplain Mike and me into a powerful alliance to win the compound to Christ. We both thanked God for this Holy Spirit's conviction that drove us both to prayer for wisdom after our initial confrontational meeting.

As the move of God continued some of the Muslims began coming into our "Holy Ghost services," just to check things out. God miraculously healed two of them. They gave their lives to Christ as they realized that God loves them and sent His Son to die for their sins. God demonstrated the "…goodness of God leads you to repentance" (Romans 2:4). Some of the Native Americans also received instant healings and a couple of them received salvation. The Muslim and Native American faith communities then persecuted these new converts, calling them traitors. Before all was said and done, the chapel was too small and God sovereignly moved it to the larger auditorium.

The BOP also added an assistant chaplain, Nate Fairchild, who was truly a man with a pastoral heart. All the inmates seemed to love him. As part of the discipleship strategy from the Lord, Chaplains Nate and Mike authorized chapel funds to purchase 10 new TV/VCRs for the expanding media room and several CD and audio tape players. Now we needed videos. After a letter writing campaign at the typewriter, during the next two years approximately 500 Christian videotapes were donated from 50 different television and radio ministries. The TV/VCR's, CD's and audio players were in constant use. Men were growing in the Lord. The chapel became the most happening place on the entire compound.

Much to the surprise of Chaplain Mike, the chapel was awarded "Department of the Year" in 1999. The news even spread to the local community. Chaplain Mike started receiving calls from churches on the outside wanting to participate. When he asked them what ministry they wanted to bring in, many replied, "We don't want to bring in our ministry, we've heard there's a genuine revival and we want permission to get some too!"

Journey Insights

The citizens in the outside community were praying over this new facility. It made a big difference in the groundswell of God's power and Presence. I learned that God will send a person with spiritual gifts in answer to another's prayers. Those prayers accomplish great things. Are you a praying person? If not, is this a good time to start lighting up the heavens?

52

BURNOUT

Nine years into my walk with God something happened that put me on the sidelines. It happened right in the midst of a great move of God. If I'd recognized the signs, this could have been avoided. But I didn't. During a three-week period, the Holy Spirit orchestrated one-on-one divine appointments that resulted in 65 men coming to Christ. Gang members, white collar criminals, child molesters, bank robbers, tax cheats and more were all the usual suspects in need of a Savior.

No one truly expected the revival that hit the compound. We had no real discipleship program in place. There were only a handful of other mature Christians, and few were willing to disciple others. We were unprepared for the great catch of fish from the Lord, and they were overloading and almost sinking our boat (Luke 5:4-6). The challenge that resulted was dozens of newborn Christians now looking to me, the man who introduced them to Jesus, for spiritual guidance and discipleship. I was their spiritual father, of sorts, regardless of their age.

Three men in one day received notification that their wives were filing for divorce. Each time the weight of their pain hit me. Instead of going to my prayer closet to pass the burden to the Lord, who alone can carry such things, or bringing in another person to help bear this burden, I foolishly took the weight on myself. Instead of ministering to them out of the overflow of the Holy Spirit's life and wisdom in me, I was ministering out of my human spirit and wisdom. This was good for neither of us.

By the time the third man arrived holding divorce papers in hand, it was as if I'd hit a spiritual barrier. I respectfully told the distraught man that only God had answers and handed him off to a Christian brother. Shoulders down and defeated I walked back to my room -- this was the beginning of another life-lesson.

After praying in the Spirit for about an hour, I felt a little revived. But the minute someone asked spiritual advice, my battery plunged to near zero again. The only place I could feel God's Presence was alone with Him in prayer and the minute I stood up, His Presence lifted. There was no anointing for me to minister to others. It was as if God's power for ministry had evaporated overnight.

God, what's wrong? Have I sinned? I had far more questions than answers.

One night volunteers Don and Kathryn Smith came in with a group to the chapel. Don approached, looked directly into my eyes and then asked if I was doing okay.

I replied, "I'm fine." Don looked at me again and I realized this was a Holy Spirit inquiry. Sheepishly, I replied, "Not really." I told him what was happening and embarrassedly said, "I don't know what I did wrong, Don. If I sinned, or what…."

Don looked at me, then raised his eyes to God and inquired, "Lord, what's the answer?" He nodded as he received instructions, and then said, "David, I give you permission from the Lord not to come to church for a month, not to minister to anyone, and not to feel responsibility for anyone." When Don said this, it felt as if I'd been released from a burdensome military post and sent on leave to another country.

Nothing had really changed in the natural, but something had shifted spiritually. Then Don announced, "Men of God in this room, let's gather around David and pray for him." He and Kathryn prayed and the men and other volunteers agreed. Then he charged them not to seek me for any spiritual advice for 30 days and not to be concerned that I had in any way backslidden when I didn't show up for church. Don further instructed them to tell others the same thing.

"David's suffering from spiritual burnout. He needs to be refreshed and restored by the Lord, in his cell, alone."

He then whispered in my ear, "Go play chess, son. Play basketball or handball with a non-Believer or lukewarm Christian." I could hardly believe what I was hearing, but Don continued, "Don't witness to them. Just get your mind off ministry and people."

Then as an afterthought, he added, "Oh, and pray in tongues, a lot. David, always remember, God is Father, Son, and Holy Spirit. He's a Trinity, not a quartet. There's no room for a Holy Ghost junior. The church will be fine without you for a season."

The church will be fine without you for a season. I repeated in my head as he hugged me with the Father's love. Those words rang in my head and still do.

Smiling warmly, Don kicked me out of church for 30 days! It was exactly what I needed. For the next 30 days, I played chess, basketball, and handball.

God restored my spirit as I relaxed in His love.

After a wonderful month of being regenerated spiritually, I returned to the chapel, ready to go! Chaplain Mike gave me permission to set up a couple of discipleship programs under his authority. He seemed glad to put me to work as he was busy administrating his chaplaincy duties over 22 different religions, and what a difference it now was to be refreshed and eager to help.

I dove into creating and teaching new discipleship programs. One was a 12-week Hearing God course I'd written. Men learned how to hear and identify the voice of the Holy Spirit. At the end of the 12 weeks a 70-year-old missionary, who was incarcerated for a 120-day sentence for civil disobedience, protesting in front of a military training site, said something stunning about the class.

"David, I've got more than 30 years' experience in the mission field. I've pastored congregations for 15 years. I have a Master's degree and a Doctorate in Theology and nearly 50 years' experience in ministry. I believe I've learned more about how to hear God's voice in 12 weeks of this class than in all my years in seminary and ministry combined!" That blessed me and confirmed that the time of refreshing and restoration had been tremendously valuable.

We were amazed at how the Lord was training up the men in these discipleship programs. Water baptisms came next. Someone donated a portable baptismal font. Our chaplain water baptized about 25 prisoners during the first baptismal service. The church continued to grow and flourish. The chapel became the place to be on the prison compound. Now it was properly centered on Jesus and His love for His church, instead of a single minister, ministry gift, or personality.

I vowed never to allow the gifts and ministry of God to get in the way of my relationship with God again. The Holy Spirit showed me that it was necessary to always keep things in this order: God first, wife and family second, ministry third. From this divine order, everything else would flow into the Earth and Heaven's purposes would be accomplished.

Journey Insights

Instead of ministering out of the overflow of the Holy Spirit's life and wisdom in me, I was ministering out of my human spirit and wisdom. This didn't work for anyone and I became spiritually burnt out. The chaplain told me to take a break from church and ministry and have fun. I learned how important it is to relax in His love. He also showed me God first, wife and family second, ministry third. What are your priorities and do you need to learn to relax in His love?

53

A TASTE OF FREEDOM

FCI Waseca, Minnesota (1998-2001)

One day the Assistant Chaplain, Nate Fairchild, walked by me in the front lobby of the prison. I had been granted a reduced custody level and was working on a special project for an inspection ordered by the warden. Nate operated out of a genuine pastoral heart, filled with the Father's love for the men on the compound. When you were in the room with Nate, you could sense the tangible love of God emanating from him. Most of the men appreciated and respected him, even those from other faiths.

He said, "David, come see me at my office after lunch; I need you for the afternoon."

"I can stop by, but I have to get back and finish this job for the warden. It's mandated that we finish this by this afternoon."

He replied very uncharacteristically and in a matter of fact tone, "This afternoon, you're helping me and not the warden. I have the authority!"

Stunned by his words and tone, I thought, *how can the assistant chaplain have more authority on this day than the warden?*

Upon arriving at the Chaplain's office, Nate handed me a document and said, "Read these papers and then sign them." His demeanor remained the same.

I looked at the paperwork. It was something I'd never seen before entitled, "Furlough Authorization." I had served 11 years of my 22-year sentence. Furloughs were only allowed when you had two years or less remaining on your sentence, or when someone died and you received the rarely granted permission to attend a funeral accompanied by guards, at your expense.

I read the papers. Was this a joke he was playing on me? If so, he'd got me. If not, what in Heaven was going on? He said, "You and I are going on a day trip 45 minutes from here to pick up some new rocks for the Native American Sweat Lodge. No cuffs, shackles or chains. It's just you and me in a pickup truck for the afternoon in Minnesota."

Am I dreaming? My thoughts were racing as I read the paperwork, signed by the warden's office. This is where Nate got the authority, the warden signed off on it. Nate was asked to go pick up some rocks for the chapel department needs and they were short on staff. Someone in the warden's office suggested he take an inmate with him that had dropped in custody and was getting ready to get transferred to a camp.

Nate said, "Can I take Hairabedian?"

"Sure," they told him. I'll get the papers signed." The papers were sitting in front of me for the signing. We'd be leaving immediately. I felt the Father's love, trusting me for a day of freedom, smack dab at the halfway point of a 22-year prison bit. I picked up the pen and signed and dated the Furlough Authorization document and we walked to the rear gate and got in an unmarked Federal Bureau of Prisons truck.

He looked directly into my eyes and simply said, "Put your seat belt on, David."

"Oh yeah, haven't done that in more than a decade." My heart was racing.

Nate handed the guard the furlough paperwork, and after asking me a few security questions, he opened the gate. As we were driving on the perimeter road, I peered through the windshield. Everything was moving fast; shrubs, plants, and trees were flying by us.

Seeing a stop sign ahead, I said, "Nate, stop sign coming up!" He said, "Yeah, I see it, and he kept driving the same speed!" Alarmed he was going to slide through it, I asked, "How fast are you going?"

"About 25 miles an hour." My response, in retrospect, surprised me. He could clearly hear the anxiety in my voice. "Well SLOW DOWN!" Nate gently took his foot off the pedal and allowed the vehicle to coast to the stop sign.

Assessing the speed, time, and space differences of a car driving versus a man walking on foot—which I'd been on foot for the last 11 years—had thrown my car travel speed orientation completely off base. Sitting at the stop sign, Nate slowly looked over at me and said, "Are you going to be okay with this?"

"Yeah, yeah, everything's going to be fine. I just haven't been in a car for a long time. Keep driving. Uh, just start off slow. I need to adapt."

He smiled and pulled out slowly, monitoring my reaction. Within a few minutes, he began to add speed. Before long we were traveling on the highway at 45 miles an hour, with cars passing us. I put my hand out the passenger side window like a little kid. The next thing I knew I was surfing the wind coming at us, up and down, up and down. It was fun! Fresh air in my face, I stuck my head out of the window, sun shining down from Heaven. This taste of freedom was a remarkable gift of grace from God.

Later I discovered that right before that outing, my mother had felt led to ask

God to make a way for me to get a taste of freedom. She was concerned and wanted God to help insulate me from getting institutionalized.

We picked up a several hundred pounds of rocks at the quarry, tossed them in the back of the truck and headed back to the prison. Nate was gracious to take the scenic route back, through towns and neighborhoods. As we drove around, I was fascinated seeing people do everyday things: working in their yards, walking, bicycling; I even enjoyed watching a postal worker deliver mail.

This is beautiful! I thought. *I could easily live in one of these houses and work in the community as a productive citizen. I'd take walks, talk to neighbors, and attend church…"* How quickly my thoughts wrapped around a normal vision for the future. After I learned how my mom prayed and I appreciated this powerful experience helping me think on the outside while remaining years behind bars.

When we hit the highway to return the final leg to the prison, I told Nate with a smile, "Take er' all the way up to 55 miles an hour. I'm back to normal!"

Journey Insights

I found out later that my mother had prayed, asking God to make a way for me to get a taste of freedom, so that I wouldn't become institutionalized. The next thing I knew I was in a car for the first time after 11 years, the wind blowing my hair and the sun on my face. This moment helped me remain thinking on the outside while still having to serve 11 more years. Do you need a moment of freedom? I pray God gives you what you need right now in Jesus' Name.

54

WHO WANTS A PRESIDENTIAL PARDON?

FCI Waseca, Minnesota (1998-2001)

Chaplain Mike announced that a guest speaker was coming to our chapel. He'd done hard time as a car thief, bank robber, and drug dealer. He'd fought with the cops on numerous occasions, and had a laundry list of other crimes. The man had more than 20 convictions but had somehow been granted a presidential pardon. He even had his gun rights back! *How could this be possible?* I wondered.

There were flyers put up in every unit that said, *Come find out how to get a presidential pardon!* Men from all walks of life, criminal backgrounds, and religious affiliations turned up on this Tuesday night in the middle of winter.

The chapel was packed with men who rarely, if ever, attended. These men were primarily unrepentant pimps, drug dealers, gang-bangers, gambling bookies and a few mafia guys. The majority of them were still involved in the same lifestyle on the inside, or running something on the outside, in one form or another. The only time one of these guys showed their faces at the chapel was during free greeting card night, and then they were gone again.

In secure facilities, prisoners are allowed to move from one location to another five minutes before to five minutes after the hour in a "controlled movement." If you go to the recreation yard, gym, law library, education department, etc. guards lock the doors and you're stuck there for at least 50 minutes. Anyone caught moving any other time is questioned by a hall guard. If the inmate doesn't have authorization or a written pass, they're immediately taken to the lieutenant's office and then usually tossed in the hole for breaking the rules. So, after arriving at this unique service, they were essentially a captive audience for almost an hour.

Chaplain Mike called me into his office during the service and said, "David, the guest speaker isn't coming."

Alarmed, I asked, "What do you mean 'he's not coming'? We have a chapel full of the worst sinners on the compound who'd otherwise never set foot in here."

He replied, "Black ice. Winter weather in Minnesota. He can't get here."

My stomach contracted into a knot. "Chaplain, you have to preach to these guys, we don't want to lose this once in a lifetime opportunity to share Jesus with them!"

He put his hand on my shoulder and calmly replied, "No, David, I think you should preach to them. Go in there and just do it."

Thankfully I had learned to consult the Holy Spirit. As I walked into the packed house with my heart fluttering, I asked, "Holy Spirit, what would you have me to say? Do you want me to preach about the Prodigal Son who came home?"[59] No response came from the Lord, so I inquired again, "What about the straight road that leads to everlasting life (Matthew 7:13-14)?"[60] Still no response. "Lord, I need a message and quick!"

Then God spoke to me in the still, small voice. His words shook me to the core. He said, "Visiting the iniquity of the fathers upon the children unto the third and fourth generation of them that hate me." I was stunned. My palms grew clammy as I approached the pulpit to face the congregation of hardened criminals. With no time to prepare, I simply turned to Exodus ready to read the passage that led into the Ten Commandments. It went something like this....

"Due to inclement weather our guest speaker who received a presidential pardon has to come another night. However, due to controlled movements, we're here for at least another 30 minutes. The chaplain asked me to say a few words as long as we're all gathered." Most of the men crossed their arms in disgust and mumbled to themselves or their neighbors.

"Gentlemen," I began, over the confusion, "each of you claims to love your children. In fact, many of you wear a lanyard around your neck with your prisoner ID card on one side and a picture or pictures of your children on the other. Some of you have even showed me these pictures and told me how much you love and care for your kids. Tonight I want to read a passage from the Ten Commandments with which many of us are familiar. In fact, almost everyone in this room has broken at least nine of these, some, all ten."

This was a tough atmosphere to be sharing the truth, and from the looks on their faces, I was glad to be looking only to the Holy Spirit as I spoke. "The Bible is very clear about what it means to really love our children and what it means to not love them. If I asked anyone in this room if they wanted their children to be in prison, for a week, let alone a decade, 20 years, or life without parole, each and every one of you would say 'no.' Most of you would

---

59   Luke 15:11-32

60   Matthew 7:13-14

say, 'hell no.'"

The silence in the room seemed deafening, yet I sensed a tenderness coming forth at the mention of children. "Did you know that the statistical likelihood of your child going to prison because you are currently here increases by 300%? In other words, men, it's three times more likely that your children will come to prison because you're here. You could have heard a pin drop as I asked, "How do we break this cycle and set your children free? What can you do while you're in prison to reverse this curse? If you really love your children you want to see them succeed and prison is not success. Let's find out what the Bible says about it."

Arms were uncrossed and many were leaning forward, engaged, ready to hear more. "This comes from the Book of Exodus. Many of you have seen the movie, *The Ten Commandments*. Moses came down from Mount Sinai and said these famous words,"

"You shall have no other gods before Me. You shall not make for yourself a carved image—any likeness of anything that is in heaven above, or that is in the earth beneath, or that is in the water under the earth; you shall not bow down to them nor serve them. For I, the Lord your God, am a jealous God, visiting the iniquity of the fathers upon the children to the third and fourth generations of those who hate Me, but showing mercy to thousands, to those who love Me and keep My commandments" (Exodus 20:3-6).

"God will show mercy to thousands of those who love Him and keep His commandments. But, to those who reject His ways and commandments, He will visit the sins and iniquities of the fathers - that's you and me - upon our children, those wonderful kids in the pictures in the lanyards around your neck.

"Tonight, you have an opportunity. If you really love your children, you will serve the Lord. You'll put down your idols of drug trafficking, drug use, pimping, pornography, gambling, mafia control, gang-banging, sleeping with anyone who isn't your wife, and murder. If, however, you aren't willing to serve the Lord, then the Bible indicates that you really don't love your children, but rather you love your own sin and your wicked ways more than them."

"Tonight, you've been assembled here by Divine appointment to hear this message and receive the opportunity to turn from your old ways, to serve the Lord, and to release a blessing on your children. Or you have the choice to walk out knowing the truth and allow the curse to continue in your kid's lives. You can even donate into the Christian locker in advance so we'll have some extra shower shoes and shampoo waiting for them. But why should you allow the curse of prison to continue? I implore you tonight to repent and serve the Lord!"

This whole thing had only taken five minutes and it was still 25 minutes before the move. But the Holy Spirit spoke in the still small voice with urgency, "Make an altar call now." I opened the altar and invited men to come, for their children's sake and their own sake. Five minutes later as music was playing in the background and men were crying at the altar, an emergency move time was called by the lieutenant's office. Everyone was to return to their units immediately, due to the snowstorm. A prison guard vehicle had slipped off the perimeter road on black ice and ran into the outside fence setting off an alarm. An emergency count was ordered to make certain no one had escaped.

There are always dramatic responses to genuine moves of God and I saw both.[61] Several men came to Christ that night and received a full pardon for their sins from the *President of the Universe!* These had escaped hell and would enter Heaven, fully forgiven for all their past acts. Their children were now in a much better situation. The curse was broken spiritually. They demonstrated their love for God and their children.

Other men rejected this pardon and curse-breaking gift from God; they walked out the same way they'd walked in. I asked God to send others to help intervene in their lives with clear instructions of how to reverse the generational curse of willful rebellion, iniquity, and sin by simply humbling themselves and submitting their lives to God once and for all. I also prayed that God would reach their children with the good news of the Gospel so they wouldn't have to experience the iniquities of their fathers.

In the days that followed, some of these men who repented became instant friends. Those who didn't, looked at me with anger in their eyes, and then just looked away. Others reported that I had accused them of hating their children publicly. A couple of men even threatened me. I just ignored them. We were in revival and God was "adding to the church" daily.

---

61 People may respond to the Gospel and be saved, loving God and receiving those who preached the message, or people reject the Gospel, remain unsaved, hate God and reject those who preached the message. Stephen was full of the Holy Ghost and preached the Gospel. Many received the message and were radically transformed. Acts 6:7-9 says, **"Then the word of God spread, and the number of the disciples multiplied greatly in Jerusalem, and a great many of the priests were obedient to the faith. And Stephen, full of faith and power, did great wonders and signs among the people."** In Acts 7:57-58 we see just the opposite reaction: **"Then they cried out with a loud voice, stopped their ears, and ran at him {Stephen} with one accord; and they cast him out of the city and stoned him…"** The greater the power, the greater the fruit, the increase of souls saved, and revival; and also the greater the opposition and persecution from those who reject Jesus and the free gift of salvation.

Journey Insights

Generational curses left unbroken can go from one generation to the next. Some of the men rejected the opportunity to repent; they walked out the same way they'd walked in. I asked God to intervene and prayed that God would reach their children, so they wouldn't have to experience the iniquities of their fathers. Are you willing to repent, humble yourself, and ask God to break generational curses off you and your children?

55

MARRIAGE AND DIVORCE

FCI Waseca, Minnesota (1998-2001)

I'd never been married. I wasn't even asking God about marriage when He spoke to me in the still, small voice: "David, the wife will only submit to the husband when the husband is submitted to the Lord, Ephesians chapter five." Surprised by this statement, I opened to Ephesians to "test the spirits" of what I'd just heard. These words lifted off the page:

Ephesians 5:22-33 **"Wives, submit to your own husbands, as to the Lord. For the husband is head of the wife, as also Christ is head of the church; and He is the Savior of the body. Therefore, just as the church is subject to Christ, so let the wives be to their own husbands in everything. Husbands, love your wives, just as Christ also loved the church and gave Himself for her, that He might sanctify and cleanse her with the washing of water by the word, that He might present her to Himself a glorious church, not having spot or wrinkle or any such thing, but that she should be holy and without blemish.**

"So husbands ought to love their own wives as their own bodies; he who loves his wife loves himself. For no one ever hated his own flesh, but nourishes and cherishes it, just as the Lord does the church. For we are members of His body, of His flesh and of His bones. For this reason a man shall leave his father and mother and be joined to his wife, and the two shall become one flesh.

"This is a great mystery, but I speak concerning Christ and the church. Nevertheless let each one of you in particular so love his own wife as himself, and let the wife see that she respects her husband."

As I read this passage the Holy Spirit highlighted these four verses:

Verse 23: "Wives, submit to your own husbands, as to the Lord."

Verse 25: "Husbands, love your wives, just as Christ also loved the church and gave Himself for her."

Verse 28: "So husbands ought to love their own wives as their own bodies; he who loves his wife loves himself."

Verse 33: "Let each one of you in particular so love his own wife as himself, and let the wife see that she respects her husband."

I realized that the wife is called to submit to the Lord Jesus *in* her husband, who loves her and gave Himself for her. She's designed to respond and submit to God's love for her flowing through the man who is submitted to the Lord. She was never designed to submit to the devil in a man.

When the man is genuinely submitted to the Lord, there are few marriage problems that can't be worked out. In fact, the woman rejoices and loves her husband more and more as the years go on. She has little difficulty submitting, honoring, and respecting her husband when he is acting Christ-like.

Sadly, most prisoners were submitted to the devil when they arrived in prison, myself included. God never directed me to sell cocaine and steal jets. That was suggested by the enemy and I willingly took the bait! This doesn't mean a prisoner can't change powerfully while incarcerated, and also become a wonderful husband, father and genuine man of God. But until this happens the divorce rate for prisoners will most likely remain at around 90%. Why? Because God never called a woman to submit to the devil, but rather to submit to God. In fact, we are actually called to resist the devil (James 4:7).

Shortly after this revelation, married men started coming to me for counsel. They would quote Ephesians 5:23 about wives needing to submit. I would respond lovingly, "Have you read the passage in context?" Then we would read the whole passage together.

At first, they couldn't see it. But when I shared what the Holy Spirit had showed me, it began to sink in. They realized they were still acting like the devil in a lot of ways; even after professing Christ. They still had fits of rage, were manipulative and intimidating, occasionally used pornography, or they were still in contact with another girl on the side, etc. The list is endless.

When I asked them, "If your daughter's boyfriend or husband treated your daughter like you treated your wife, and he asked you to make her come back, would you force your daughter to return to that same situation?" Nearly every time the man would reply, not only *"no,"* but *"hell no!"*

Then I'd say, "Why should we expect God, her Father, to force her to return to you unless you change?"

The man would get it, and say, "God would be doing her a disservice if he forced her to come back. I know what's still in me."

At this point, I'd ask, "What if we ask God to change you into a biblical husband, and then return your wife to submit to the love of Christ in you?"

Sometimes they'd say, "Yes, pray with me." Other times they would say, "I'm not going to change; she's better off without me. I'm going to call her and set her free!" Either way, the truth went forth. The man was either reconciled to Christ, and then often to his wife, or the man no longer blamed God for his failed marriage. He realized it was his submission to the devil's ways that caused the woman to leave.

I believe an unwillingness to change is the primary reason that 86 percent of men return to prison while only 14 percent remain free. The journey to freedom begins when a person truly desires to change, and this change begins by submitting to Christ and His ways.

Journey Insights

The wife is called to submit to Jesus in her husband, who loves her and gave Himself for her. She is not called to submit to the devil manifesting in her husband. When the man is genuinely submitted to the Lord, there are few problems in a marriage that can't be easily worked out. Is the root of your marriage problem your failure to submit to the Lord or is it possible that you're submitting to the devil and his ways?

56

ELECTRONIC ROBOT PRINCIPALITY DREAM

FCI Waseca, Minnesota (1998-2001)

My dream opened in brilliant color. It was a sunny day and I was filled with the joy of the Lord. All of a sudden the atmosphere changed. In the near distance, I heard huge footsteps crushing the ground. Looking up, I saw a giant electronic, metallic robot towering 40-feet tall. The fists were oversized, its eyes were locked on me, and it was definitely in the hunt and destroy mode.

I stood boldly and rebuked it in the Name of Jesus. Unlike other dream experiences this beast was unmoved by my words. I lacked the necessary authority, and the spiritual weapons I wielded were insufficient to defeat this type of creature. It moved slowly, but each huge stride covered great distances and destroyed everything in its path. Once in range, this machine began to swat at me like a human would swat at a fly, barely missing me each time.

Fight or flight instincts took over and I sprinted into a nearby three-story building. I could hear the giant's steps right behind me. I watched in horror as he tore the roof off and spotted me again, swatted and barely missed. I slid under a large, wooden conference table. With one fist he slapped the heavy table away, with the other, he swung, trying to crush me.

Before I could get out of the way, he slapped me and I flew 20 feet into the air. I crashed against the wall near the tall ceiling and then ricocheted forward, landing on the ground. I assessed the damage -- my skin was only slightly scraped and lightly bruised.

The beast temporarily lost track of me. I darted into the next room where I discovered my parents peacefully asleep in bed, dreaming about the fruitfulness of Heart of America Prison Ministries, which at this time they were running. They were sleeping so peacefully they hadn't heard any of the destruction around them. I tried to shake them awake to warn them.

I sat up in the darkness; my heart was racing. Realizing this was a dream, I gathered my bearings and then sought the Lord. "Why was this attack allowed?"

The Holy Spirit responded instantly, "Because you lack intercessors!" I reflected on the dream. The giant electronic principality didn't respond to the authority in my words when I wielded the Name of Jesus. This was the first time in a dream this had happened. The Holy Spirit illuminated the Scriptures from 1 Corinthians chapter 12 regarding the diversity of gifts and spiritual weapons that He has given. My gifts were mainly for evangelism, teaching, preaching, healing and casting out devils -- primarily ground level warfare.

The Scripture came to mind, **"We wrestle not against flesh and blood, but principalities, powers, rulers of darkness and spiritual wickedness in high places"** (Ephesians 6:12). The Holy Spirit caused me to understand that devils come out with the Name of Jesus, at ground-level warfare. Principalities, powers, and spiritual wickedness in high places are defeated through intercessory prayer.

It was 5:00 a.m. when I wrote down the dream.[62] Guards came by and counted the sleeping inmates. At 5:30 a.m. count was cleared, allowing people to move around the unit. I was prompted to go to one of the inmate television rooms to watch a Christian TV program before others arrived. The host was an international healing evangelist who had just returned from a very fruitful international crusade.

He began, "God opened an incredible door to India. Nearly one million people showed up and hundreds of thousands were saved. Upon returning, our ministry came under horrible scrutiny, false accusation, attack, slander, and financial problems. I asked the Lord why this was happening. He immediately responded, 'Because you lack intercessors!'"

I sat stunned in front of the television. The evangelist then said, "God told me to raise up an army of intercessors, an army marching on their knees." He went on to explain that the Holy Spirit showed him from Scripture that when you go into new territory and win souls, the principalities, powers, rulers of darkness and spiritual wickedness in high places don't just willingly bow down and leave the area because Christians arrived. Rather, the war moves to a new level and intensity. Men's souls hang in the balance.

In 1 Corinthians 16:9 (NLT) the apostle Paul said, **"There is a wide-open door for a great work here, although many oppose me."** He ran into spiritual warfare at Ephesus that got him locked up when a principality referred to as Diana stirred up the people against him.[63] Paul could cast out

---

62   Habakkuk 2:2-3, "Then the Lord answered me and said: 'Write the vision and make it plain on tablets, that he may run who reads it. For the vision is yet for an appointed time; but at the end it will speak, and it will not lie. Though it tarries, wait for it; because it will surely come, it will not tarry.'"

63   The whole city was in an uproar and Paul didn't even know why hundreds of them had gathered against

devils using Jesus' Name, but a principality was a whole different story. This second heaven principality almost got him killed. Paul literally had to leave the city with very little success and then went to Macedonia where things were very fruitful.

Our Bible ministry to prisoners had tripled in size recently, expanding into more than 700 prisons. We had just completed our largest single Bible mailing sending in more than 1,000 leather-bound study Bibles to individual prisoners. The enemy was being displaced and wanted to stop lives being transformed.

The Holy Spirit reminded me of Matthew 26:31: **"I will strike the Shepherd, and the sheep of the flock will be scattered."** The dream indicated the adversary was targeting me as the shepherd/visionary for the ministry. I realized the potential severity of my situation. I wrote a letter to our ministry and asked them to raise up a small army of intercessors. Our ministry volunteer staff read my letter at the monthly meeting, prayed over it, and then shelved it, seeing no need for immediate action since I was safely tucked away behind bars. In effect, they were sleeping peacefully and couldn't hear or discern the destruction taking place around them.

I also shared the dream with Chaplain Mike who recognized something was afoot in the spirit realm. He graciously prayed over me and said, "Lord, protect David from this principality You showed him in the dream and raise up intercessors." Ten days later I was called into the lieutenant's office.

Upon arrival, I saw a lieutenant with whom I'd never even had a conversation. He was very angry with me, for reasons I can only attribute to spiritual warfare. He was breathing heavily, his balding forehead was sweating, and it looked like his head was going to blow off his shoulders. He pounded the table and said, "We've got you Hairabedian and we've got you good!"

"Sir, I have no idea what you're talking about.

He shot back, "You know what you've done!" and then handed me an incident report, a disciplinary action. The charge read, "Tampering with a locking or blocking device, Code 267." I was clueless. I hadn't tampered with any locks.

Reading on, the explanation was that my telephone number to my parent's home in Missouri was a local Waseca, Minnesota number that automatically transferred to my parent's home. This enabled me to make a local phone call that rang at my parent's house for 50 cents instead of $3.25. This wasn't

---

him chanting for hours. Acts 19:28-29, 32 (KJV): **"They were full of wrath, and cried out, saying, 'Great is Diana of the Ephesians' and the whole city was filled with confusion...they rushed with one accord into the theatre. 32 Some therefore cried one thing, and some another: for the assembly was confused; and the more part knew not wherefore they were come together."**

against the rules like call-forwarding or a three-way call. It was, in fact, advertised in publications in the law library and, therefore, something our family utilized for years. As it turned out, however, the rules were amended with an umbrella statement a few months prior, using the language, "and any other type."

These amended rules were supposed to be published and made available for inmate access in the law library, but our prison library never received them. I was never notified, or given the opportunity to simply remove the number. In fact, I was the ONLY inmate to be charged with this unique telephone based offense in the entire Federal Bureau of Prisons at that time. As the captain, who was head of security, explained to me as an encouragement, "David, all you were trying to do was save your parents money. Plus, quoting from the BOP guidelines, you were simply 'building family relationships'."

At that time, inmates were losing 90-365 days of phone privileges for making just one three-way phone call, or call-forwarding to a number that wasn't on their approved list. I was charged with 1,165 phone calls over a three-year period and locked up immediately. While in the hole, I asked the Lord, "How long will I be here?"

He replied in the still, small voice, "Just as Jonah was three days in the heart of the earth so you will be three days in the heart of this prison."

Chaplain Mike showed up the next day. "This is just like your dream of the electronic principality coming after you. You're locked up on an obscure electronics-based charge."

I thought about it and said, "Yeah, but in the dream I wasn't really hurt. I'm going to be fine."

Chaplain Mel asked, "Has the Lord told you how long you'll be here?"

"Three days." He just looked at me. I said, "Chaplain Mike, what do you know that I don't?"

He said, "The entire compound was locked down this morning while we had a staff meeting. You were one of the main topics. The majority of the staff who liked and trusted you feel like you betrayed their trust." He reservedly added, "And, the uh, FBI may be brought in on this."

This was seriously bizarre and I said so. "All I was doing was talking to my family. It has never been against the rules before."

Chaplain Mike said, "Well, they're talking about keeping you here for a minimum of six months, maybe a year, and then shipping you to make you an example."

"I'll be out of here within three days to teach the final session of Hearing God. If I'm not, then enroll me as a student in the next class!"

On the third day, a lieutenant came in and said, "What is Hairabedian doing in here?" They showed him the incident report. He said, "This is ridiculous! Get him out of here and back on the compound!"

I showed up at Chaplain Mike's office wearing a big smile. He was surprised and very pleased to see me. That night I administered the final class and the graduation of the students enrolled in 12-week "Hearing God," curriculum.

In January 2001, my custody level dropped, making me "camp eligible." Shortly after that, I was transferred.

Journey Insights

In the dream God showed me that the technology principality ignored my authority because I lacked intercessors to pray and intercede for me and the ministry. Are you gifted in prayer and not using your gift? Maybe it's time to start praying because someone else needs your prayers. Are you in ministry and not covered by enough prayer coverage? Then I pray that God raises up people to pray for you in Jesus' Name!

57

FEAR TOLERATED IS FAITH CONTAMINATED

USP Terra Haute, Indiana (7 days in 2003)

Leaving Waseca Minnesota was bittersweet. Sweet because my custody level had miraculously been reduced from a level 2-3 secure facility to a level 1 honor camp which would bring more freedom and privileges. Bitter because I was leaving behind a group of really good brothers, and it was tough saying goodbye to meaningful friends.

I'm gonna' miss our solid chapel plus the remarkable leadership of our chaplain, I thought. I'd learned by now to appreciate good chaplains. *Most important, I'll miss the Lord's Presence that has been here continuously during chapel services and fellowship all over the compound.*

Since my custody level had dropped to camp status, I was allowed to be transported by prison bus. The anticipation of more freedom was palpable. *I'm free! Man, it feels good! I checked myself a bit. Well, free from normal security restraints anyway. No handcuffs, shackles or belly chains. So, this is what the prison "honor system" feels like.*

Our one week stop-over location was at the infamous maximum-security penitentiary in Terra Haute, Indiana. The place was filled with dangerous criminals serving 20, 30, 40, and 50 years, and about 20 percent lifers without the possibility of parole. In fact, it was established as a facility to carry out federal death sentences, and this added to the oppressive, death-like atmosphere. This environment was ripe for unexpected violence, so both inmates and guards were on edge. Prisoners, no matter where they are, battle sporadic feelings of anger, rage, bitterness, depression, hopelessness, suicide and despair, but those negative emotions were often amplified in Terra Haute.

The day we arrived I noticed breathing seemed difficult at first. I did a quick health check finding nothing wrong and then I attributed this to the obvious oppression and dark spiritual clouds at the penitentiary. I prayed and was able to breathe more easily, but continued to sense the oppressive spirit that loomed over this place. Although campers, we were still processed inside the level 5-6 max facility.

Some things never change, I thought. *Being processed! It's demeaning being reduced to a number, but hey, it is what it is.*

The standard rules for campers in transit is they are safely housed away from the penitentiary population in lock down in the SHU (solitary housing unit, aka, the hole) until the next bus arrives. Campers aren't allowed on the compound because many penitentiary prisoners have a disdain toward campers and are highly motivated to harm them. On more than one occasion, a camper had been attacked and even killed while in transit by a penitentiary convict serving a long sentence.

Acutely aware of the prisoner's worldly hopelessness, I prayed. *Lord, without divine intervention, the people here have a miserably long journey to freedom in the natural. Some will die here. I ask You to help them. I ask you to help the campers as well.*

God had taught me over the years that true biblical hope was critical, and that I was to be confident that He'd show up with His goodness. Plus, I knew faith was the substance of things hoped for, and that meant taking action. I wasn't about to attempt anything here without hearing from God, but I was genuinely concerned about those trying to live in this place. I wanted to be hopeful but I have to admit I had no real expectation of God doing anything in the short seven days I'd be here. I should have known better. I was wrong.

We campers were headed to the safety of lockdown in the penitentiary when something unusual happened. The SHU was overcrowded due to a prison fight earlier that day. *Okay, this helps explain the increased spiritual cloud of darkness here,* I thought. Instead of having to stay in solitary, suddenly about a dozen of us were redirected to be housed in the adjacent honor camp until our bus to Colorado arrived. The next thing I knew we were being escorted to the rear gate for release to the camp.

The guards in the towers 25 feet above had rifles drawn on us as one by one we gave our name and prison ID number and answered a security question. Walking through the main penitentiary gates that led to two additional security entrances offered an eerie sensation. We were still near the main penitentiary and you could feel it in the air.

God, thank You that You are the Life and You live in me. Your light shines in the darkness, and the darkness can never extinguish it. Encourage people to pray for inmates suffering in the depths of darkness and despair. Lift the hearts of my brothers in Christ who are here, both in the max pen and in the honor camp. Stir the hearts of those yet to know You. Bring hope to this place, in Jesus' Name. And, just like that, I found myself in the new experience of being in an honor camp.

I quickly learned that as a camper, I needed to shift my mindset accordingly, or risk ending up back in the penitentiary. *It's a whole different world here,*

David, I told myself, *with entirely different rules for survival. Adjust quickly!* It was tricky but important to understand. Campers think differently than penitentiary inmates, primarily because of the length of sentences and the crimes in which they've been convicted. It's as different as night and day, or another way to say it would be as different as MMA fighting compared to flag football. Regardless, trouble could still come if you didn't handle situations correctly.

Disrespect in a penitentiary can cost you your life. You learn quickly to be smart and tough which gets you respected and thereby helps keep you safe. In camp, on the other hand, acting too tough was often seen as a threat and could cost you. Many campers who would routinely disrespect you, once you threatened back they'd snitch on you to the guards. I had to remind myself of my priorities. *You're a Christian first, David, then you're a convict on assignment from Heaven! Choose to overlook the self-serving and privileged mentalities.* I consistently encountered a condescending, arrogant attitude from many inmates.

God, I prayed, *after serving all these years, You know I've got issues with many of these campers! Their entitlement-spirit mentalities are ridiculous and my prison habit, along with my flesh, says fight fire with fire. That's not what You say and I trust You to lead me. Thank You for helping me, God.* I knew I had to overlook or ignore the issues that they had if I had any hope of fitting in and seeing God at work.

What God had for us during the next seven days would prove to be remarkable.

After being directed to my temporary living quarters and given a cot to sleep on, my first thoughts were, *where's the chapel?* Once I found it, I had one thing on my mind. *Is the 130 hour video curriculum donated from our prison ministry here?* I wanted to ensure they had been released into the chapel library for inmate use and not stuck in a closet or tossed in the trash. I spotted them on the shelf near the VHS and DVD players. This confirmation helped me know that we were making an impact across the Federal Bureau of Prisons.

I saw two inmates praying in a side room and asking God for a revival. A third inmate joined them. One of the two praying inmates began prophesying urging the third inmate to move from lukewarm Christianity to being on fire for God. He was offended at first, but as the Presence of God increased, the Holy Spirit moved him from offended to convicted. He began to weep. He then made a deeper commitment to Christ.

I joined these men in the process and we all rejoiced. At the close of our prayer time, we introduced ourselves. This small unit of three committed

Terra Haute campers and a camper in transit were who God would use during the next seven days to establish an impacting visitation of the Lord at this Indiana honor camp.

The Holy Spirit called us to a three-day fast and we all accepted. Instead of going to the dining hall during meals we met in the chapel for spiritual food and prayer. Each time we gathered, God's Presence became stronger. God began supernaturally drawing men into the chapel. Something was brewing and we could all sense it.

On the second night, a weekly Bible study was scheduled in the chapel. The topic was whether the Baptism in the Holy Spirit with the outward evidence of speaking in tongues was for today, or just for the first-century apostles and those on whom they laid hands. I sat silently as the men discussed their theological positions on what I'd come to learn was unnecessarily and, unfortunately, a controversial subject.

Men on both sides clearly loved Jesus and were committed Christians, but it quickly moved from discussion to harsh words and then labeling. I stood up to intervene. "Men of God, my name is David and I'm just passing through. I don't personally have a horse in this race, but I do believe the Holy Spirit is doing something special on this compound. Would you mind if I share a teaching on this subject tomorrow night?" I suggested everyone fast for 24 hours and we meet in the chapel asking God to reveal His truth.

The following night the chairs were arranged in a circle and about 25-30 men were present. The Lord prompted me to share a few specific verses on the baptism in the Holy Spirit. I pointed out the difference between a public use of tongues with an interpreter that edifies and strengthens the Body of Christ[64] (1 Corinthians 14:27) which is clearly distinguished from a private prayer language in tongues that edifies and strengthens the individual (1 Corinthians 14:4). [65]

I pointed out that the latter type of tongue is available for every Believer. Then the Holy Spirit prompted me to invite the men who wanted to receive this personal prayer language to stand up. One by one the men stood up in front of their chairs and we all began praying in unity in our English language.

The Holy Spirit prompted me to lay my hand on a specific man. He had his eyes closed and was asking God for this gift. When my hand got about eight inches from his forehead the power of God hit him and he flew backward over

---

64 1 Corinthians 14:27, **"If anyone speaks in a tongue, let there be two or at the most three, each in turn, and let one interpret."**

65 1 Corinthians 14:4, **"He who speaks in a tongue edifies himself, but he who prophesies edifies the church."**

his chair landing on several empty chairs about 10 feet away. I was shocked and looked at my hand in disbelief. Within about five seconds the man on the ground was speaking in tongues.

The Presence of God descended on many others and they received this gift as well. The next several days at Terra Haute included physical healing in the units, several men rededicating their lives to Christ and a great stirring of prayer and newfound hunger for the Word of God. Fasting followed and the services filled up as God poured out His Holy Spirit, all within the week!

I later learned that one man had been praying daily for three years that a move of God would come to Terra Haute camp. I believe it was primarily his prayers that created the ripe spiritual atmosphere for what happened. No real move of God happens without prayer, intercession, and fasting. These three things are the keys to unlocking Heaven over Earth.

On the eighth day, I was transferred from Terra Haute to the Honor Camp at Florence, Colorado.

Journey Insight

I knew I had to ignore the issues of the other campers that had self-serving entitlement mentalities, if I had any hope of fitting in and seeing God at work here. When I prayed, God helped me remember I was a Christian first and a convict second. More importantly, He reminded me that I was on assignment from Heaven. He wanted to touch these men and fill them with the power of the Holy Spirit, giving them their private prayer language. Are you ready to receive your prayer language?

58

RELIGIOUS SPIRIT STRATEGIES

When I first entered the system 11½ years earlier, my case manager leaned over his desk and said with a smirk, "Hairabedian, the only way you'll ever see a camp is when you get out after 20 years and drive by one in your car!" He was wrong. By the grace of God, I was transferred to the minimum-security camp at Florence, Colorado, and that was good news.

Florence is nestled in the high-desert Colorado foothills. It's a four-facility complex that includes a minimum-security camp, all the way to the infamous supermax facility, ADX Florence (known as the Alcatraz of the Rockies) for inmates with violent behavior in other prisons. The latter is the nation's highest-security prison, housing the worst of the worst such as terrorists involved in the 1993 bombing and later the 2011 attacks on the World Trade Center, as well as the Atlanta Olympics and Boston Marathon bombings. Also landing in this forbidding fortress have been the Unabomber, the Oklahoma City Bomber, Cartel Kingpins, and inmates who attempted to murder federal judges, etc.

What a difference camp was compared to the rest of the Florence facility, the dark Terre Haute prison, and all of my previous prison "homes". When incarcerated, every small freedom is good news, big and noticed immediately, whether it is relaxed housing, lower staff to inmate ratios, more food choices, better mail and phone privileges, and increased opportunities for educational and physical activities.

More good news followed in that I quickly ran into Cari Noonan, an education instructor I'd met at FCI Englewood. She was now the Camp Education Coordinator. She offered me a job in Education as her head clerk. I took the position.

Cari encouraged me to enroll in college correspondence courses and finish my degree. She said my credits from college years before incarceration would transfer. I didn't have any desire to go back to college and told her so. She burst into a confident smile and said, "Well then, why don't you just pray about it Mr. Hairabedian?" I prayed, heard back from Heaven, and enrolled through a college in New York the following week. My goal was to get a bachelor's degree in international business.

I was encouraged.

The not-as-good news was this compound was spiritually dead.

Shortly after arriving I discovered that the chapel had been closed for two years; that's a long time when you're incarcerated. One of the primary cable networks where inmates often received a variety of Bible teaching was Trinity Broadcasting Network (TBN) and it was filtered off. This atmosphere was completely opposite of FCI Waseca where the Spirit of God pulsated through the Believers. There was work to do here.

I met my old friend from FCI Englewood, a Christian named William. We had roomed together for about 20 months eight years earlier. Assessing the situation and praying together, William and I decided to start a couple of prayer groups in our two-man cells. Each unit housed about 250 men.

Over the next several weeks, this nightly prayer group grew from two and three to 12 to 15. We decided to begin meeting under the stars, between the two housing units from 9:00-9:30 each night. The numbers grew from 20 to as many as 40. Prisoners from all different denominations, races, creeds and cultural backgrounds gathered in the Name of Jesus. Several non-Believers came for prayer and left with Jesus in their hearts.

For nine months, we continued meeting through rain, snow, and in blistering summer heat with the blood-sucking bull gnats biting us. Nevertheless, what a joy it was to witness God's grace in diverse ways. Sometimes a staff member would join us in prayer, holding hands with the inmates in the circle. God began slowly breaking the hardened barriers between inmates and staff. The enemy was losing his grip on Florence Camp, one soul at a time.

During this time, we continued to ask God to re-open the chapel. The only time it was open was during the weekly one-hour Sunday church service with the FCI chaplains, Chaplain Roger Lunce, and Chaplain Mori.

Chaplain Mori also came to the camp for a 90-minute Tuesday Bible study during the day for the 20 to 25 inmates who were able to take off work. Later Chaplain Mori offered a New Testament Greek Course. I attended for approximately four months and learned the basics of the Koiné Greek language in which the New Testament was written. This later helped me with more in-depth teaching, preaching, and doctrinally balanced exposition of the Word.

As winter approached, we asked if the chaplains would use their influence to re-open the chapel from 9:00 to 9:30 p.m. so the men didn't have to pray outside in the snow each night. They told us there was nothing they could do, their hands were tied, and we'd "just have to continue to pray."

I responded, "We've prayed seven nights a week for almost a year. Faith without works is dead." They agreed and encouraged me to write to the warden across the street at the FCI, who oversaw both prisons.

Then they told us the history of the chapel being closed. "A few years ago a guard found some pornographic videos in one of the living units, so the camp administrator closed the chapel, and it's been closed ever since. The camp administrator refuses to even refer to the building as a chapel. Instead, he calls it an *assembly room*."

I discovered that everyone, including the staff, disliked this administrator. He never left his office, was unapproachable, unsocial, and drove an old pickup truck to work. I asked a staff member, "Does he drive that old pick-up to keep the inmates from vandalizing his car?"

She laughed, "No, he drives it to keep *staff members* from vandalizing his car!"

During another conversation with the chaplains, I asked them, "What do porn videos found in a housing unit three years ago have to do with closing the chapel?"

They just shook their heads and said, "Well, the camp administrator says you can play the porn tapes on the two TV/VCR's in the chapel."

I replied, "You can do the same thing at the Education Department, but it isn't closed." It was at this point I realized the chapel closing had nothing to do with the righteous trying to keep porn videos out of Florence Camp. It had everything to do with the devil trying to close God and his Gospel out of Florence Camp.

Slowly, but surely the Lord began opening my eyes to *the various strategies of the religious spirit* working outside the body and within the body of Christ. Things were about to get better, but first a giant had to be felled. Little did I know that instead of making me into a David against Goliath, God was going to send me as the rock out of his sling.

Right after 9/11, President Bush had requested prayer for our country from U.S. citizens. At the direction of the Lord, William and I drafted a very careful filing on the chapel issue to the warden, tying in President Bush's national request for prayer.

William said, "Although it shouldn't be, it's very dangerous to file on staff at *this* facility. They hand out all kinds of retribution to campers who file on them."

I'd heard the stories. Certain Florence staff at the ADX and USP referred to as "the cowboys" were charged with severely beating several of the inmates. One inmate had dysentery so badly he almost died. When the doctors checked his stool, they discovered dog feces in it. The only way dog feces could get into a maximum-security inmate's system is if a guard put it in his food. A couple of other inmates were found dead in their cells. One autopsy revealed the inmate had been dead for three days before it was reported. Record logs reveal that the guards claim this guy was standing up at the 4:00 p.m. count each day and that he'd been to recreation twice. No other inmate interviewed remembers seeing him during this time.

God only knows everything these guards were doing to the inmates during that treacherous season. I told William, "We know the risks. One of us has to be on the front lines. The other can be behind the scenes praying." He agreed. We prayed over the carefully worded document, I signed my name, and we mailed it across the street to the warden.

The chaplains met with us the following Sunday and said, "The warden sent your filing over for our input. He doesn't see any reason why the chapel shouldn't be open. We're telling him we wholeheartedly agree. Things are looking good." This encouraged us. We shared this breakthrough with the rest of the group, encouraging them to keep on praying. This was the last week of October, 2001.

Journey Insights

I realized the chapel closing had nothing to do with the righteous trying to keep porn videos out of Florence Camp. It had everything to do with the devil trying to keep God and the Gospel out of the Camp. The Lord began opening my eyes to the various strategies of the religious spirit working outside and within the body of Christ to keep the Gospel out. Things were about to get better, but first a giant had to be felled. What are the giants in your life that need to be felled?

59

I SAID, "YOU CAN'T PRAY!"

It is often said that truth is stranger than fiction. When it comes to spiritual matters, I believe this is almost always the case. On Halloween of 2001, nine months after arriving in Florence, I was ordered to the camp administrator's office. He, the head counselor, and the unit manager were waiting. The administrator was holding my request to the warden to re-open the chapel. He didn't look pleased.

He immediately accused me of "going above his head" and "not following protocol." In reality, I had spoken about the chapel with all three of these men on different occasions, to no avail. I had followed protocol, submitted to chaplain authority on the matter, and spent nine months in daily prayer with nearly 10 percent of the compound.

The camp administrator then berated me and attempted to get me to respond with something incriminating so he could lock me up. He hissed, "I've got you on paper in your own handwriting admitting to being the self-proclaimed ringleader of an unauthorized gathering of men." He was referring to our peaceful prayer circle. He continued, "Who do you think you are bringing trouble to my camp?" Then he ordered me to disband the prayer group or suffer the consequences.[66] As these accusations were flying, a supernatural peace came over me.

After silently asking for God's wisdom, I politely told him that I wasn't the leader of the prayer group.

His brow wrinkled, "Who is then?"

"The Holy Spirit. He gathers the men each night." The veins on his forehead pulsed, "I'm ordering you to tell those men not to gather for prayer anymore. They're only allowed to pray during authorized services in the assembly hall when the chaplain is present."

I couldn't believe what I was hearing. Was I still in the land of freedom of

---

66 I was reminded of the story from the Book of Acts where Peter is told not to preach or speak any longer in the Name of Jesus. **"But so that it spreads no further among the people, let us severely threaten them, that from now on they speak to no man in this name. So they called them and commanded them not to speak at all nor teach in the name of Jesus. But Peter and John answered and said to them, "Whether it is right in the sight of God to listen to you more than to God, you judge"** (Acts 4:17-19).

religion? Or was America becoming the land of freedom *from* religion? I politely responded, 'Well sir, why don't we just re-open the chapel for the men to pray each night and the officer in charge can monitor us. We don't need any musical equipment, TV's, radios, VCR's or even song books, just a place to pray."

He jumped to his feet and leaned over his desk, "As long as I'm camp administrator that chapel will never be open! Do you understand me?"

I remained silent and the Holy Spirit's peace caused me to smile inside. I knew from past experience that when a person in authority makes such a challenge against God, it means God is about to step in and change things. When I didn't respond, he became enraged and shook two fingers an inch from my face, "I don't even want you praying with another inmate, not even in your cell, or I'll personally have you locked up. Do you understand me? Do you?!"

When I respectfully responded, "Yes Sir," he seemed to calm down. After a minute, I continued, "Maybe you can help me understand. I've obviously committed some sort of horrible sin in your eyes."

Blood surged to his face. He pointed at the door and yelled, "Get out! Get out! Get out!"

The head counselor and unit manager immediately ushered me outside to wait for my fate. Several inmates had heard the ruckus, "David, what's going on in there?"

I heaved a sigh and shook my head, "I'm about to get thrown in the hole for praying."

"What?"

"I'll explain later. Please grab my personal belongings so the officers don't throw them away." Two of these inmates sped off toward my room.

Five minutes later I was called back inside. The head counselor notified me that they were "locking me up."

"Do you mind if I ask what for?"

He replied, "We haven't quite figured that out yet, but believe me, we'll think of something."

Then the head counselor cuffed me and walked me across the street to the medium security FCI. I was stripped, given a pair of boxers, a T-shirt, a pair of slip on shoes and placed in solitary. A couple of hours later a lieutenant presented me with an incident report for "insolence." He started reading in an intimidating, authoritative manner but the further he read, the less intense he became.

He read the last line and looked up at me, "They told you not to pray?" His eyes widened, "And then wrote you up for insolence? What religion are you?"

"I'm a Christian, sir."

He just shook his head and said, "There's got to be more to it than this." He handed me the report and left.

I was stumped when I saw that the head counselor, not the camp administrator, had written it. And they actually admitted on paper that they ordered me not to pray anywhere outside the chapel. The paralegal in me immediately thought *I can have a heyday with this one in federal court.*

Then the Holy Spirit brought to my mind, "our battle is not against flesh and blood..."

While I was in the hole, the head counselor came and admitted that the camp administrator ordered him to write me up. He told me that he didn't want to and agreed that the chapel should be reopened. He added, "During the last five years, I've seen him angry with inmates, but never like this. I actually thought his head was going to explode!" We shared a laugh and he continued, "I wrote the incident report, including the prayer issue, in such a way that you should be able to win on appeal. And if you don't, well, hell, that's just what the Bureau of Prisons has come to." The following day, two members of the camp unit team found me guilty. They sanctioned me to loss of commissary privileges for 15 days and ordered me back to the camp.

When I asked them what they thought about my constitutional right to prayer, one of them sputtered, "Well, you lose certain constitutional rights when you come to prison -- the right to vote, carry a weapon, uh, and a few others. Um, I guess prayer is also one of them." I just shook my head and realized these were not the two people with whom to address my issue. I later found out they both were ordered by the camp administrator to find me guilty.

I spent four total days in solitary. During this time I fasted, prayed, caught up on Bible reading and my personal prayer time with the Lord. Upon returning to the camp, the head counselor used his authority to restore my job in Education Department as the head clerk and placed me back into the honor wing of the camp housing unit. God provided favor through this storm and, although I continued to battle religious spirits and the intellectual reasoning of prideful men, God moved on many men on the compound.

Journey Insights

The camp administrator was enraged, pointing two fingers in my face, screaming at me, and he forbid me to pray in my cell or for any other inmate. Then he had me thrown in the hole for requesting the chapel be reopened. It reminded me of Peter's story in the Book of Acts, where he's told not to preach or speak in the Name of Jesus. Our battle isn't against flesh and blood... Do you know how to discern between spiritual forces of evil and the person they are using? Ask God for the strategies of Heaven to win these spiritual battles.

60

BLESSING TURNS INTO A CURSE

FPC Florence, Colorado (2001-2003)

Two months later God answered our prayer in another way. Father Jamison had retired, and a new chaplain was sent to our facility, a Southern Baptist named Miranda Jones. Seriously? I thought. Another female chaplain? Visions of Chaplain Lester danced in my head. I prayed, "God, I don't know if I can live through this again."

The news was positive. Chaplain Miranda proved to be just the opposite of Chaplain Lester, who had tried to stop so much of what the Holy Spirit was doing. We praised God for Chaplain Miranda. God was graciously changing things in response to our prayers, even beyond our requests.

The chapel was reopened seven days a week, from 6:00 a.m. to 10:00 p.m. We were authorized to hold inmate led Bible Studies. Volunteer programs started coming in and the TV/VCRs were accessible for the first time in over three years which meant we could watch Christian programming. There was a power outage at the prison. When the power came back on the filter on the cable station was removed and Christian TV was restored. Our chapel became full of activities where men developed their walk with Christ. The chaplain had asked me to preach the Father's Day message, which was the first time an inmate was allowed to preach at a Sunday Service in many years.

The Lord warns us to be aware of the enemy's schemes so the next attack shouldn't have been a surprise. When the enemy had locked us out of the physical church building, he kept many from fellowshipping for three years. When the doors opened, he switched strategies. He found a way inside and then wreaked havoc from within the Body through other Believers.

As I sought the Lord, the Holy Spirit prepared me for what occurred next. I knew it was critical to follow His exact instructions. The month before this division coming to a head, I was directed to once again read through Matthew, Mark, Luke, John, and Acts, three times in 30 days. Ten years earlier the Holy Spirit had directed me to do this. Each time the Lord illumined something different about healing and deliverance. After those 30 days had been completed, a small healing revival broke out at FCI Englewood as I applied the principles I'd learned. I thought, this time, would be a similar teaching about healing and casting out demons.

But this 30 days He would teach me about the strategies of the religious spirit. The third time through these five books, the Holy Spirit directed me to write down every Scripture where the religious spirit (human, demonic or a religious mindset that opposed Jesus, the Apostles or the moving of the Holy Spirit) operated and then compile these into an appendix for a book.

William hadn't been speaking much to me for the last month. The day after I completed the reading portion of this assignment, William saw me outside the chapel and asked me to come into the chaplain's office. Without my knowledge, he'd asked Miranda Jones to mediate. To my surprise, William accused me of being a false teacher, a false prophet, a liar, a deceiver, and a manipulator. As my friend's words came like arrows toward my heart, the Holy Spirit began bringing to remembrance the many darts of accusation that came against Jesus and the Apostles.

I heard every word, but somehow they didn't have a deep impact. God's peace caused me to sit calmly while William continued assailing me. I silently asked God what I was to say or do. He spoke to me in the still small voice saying, "Affirm him in his calling as a Christian and tell him you love him."

When the opportunity presented itself, I told William that I respected him as a Christian, a brother in the Lord, and then affirmed him in his calling as a wise leader in the body of Christ. All these things were true regardless of the current attack I was enduring. I also looked William directly in his eyes and told him from my heart that I loved him. This seemed to disarm him.[67] William paused in partial disbelief and then responded, "David, I also affirm you in your calling as a Christian and as a powerful soul-winner." This took me by surprise.

William went from fully accusing me of being a false teacher and false prophet to affirming me as a powerful soul-winner? I had to ask the next question. As gently as I could I asked, "How can both of these extremes be true about me?" William shook his head, "One thing has nothing to do with the other David!" His facial expression appeared confused by the words coming from his own mouth.

He continued, "David, during these last 13 years in prison I've only seen one other person who could consistently win souls to Christ like you and that's Charles Martin. You two have the gift of evangelism like no one else I've met. My problem with you is that you think God also called you to perform miracles, see visions, and prophesy. God never called you to pray for the sick.

---

67   **"…Against such there is no law"** (Galatians 5:23).

You have no healing virtue in your hands. No one has ever been healed when you've laid hands and prayed for them."

He looked at Chaplain Jones and then back at me. "You're deceived in your calling. You need to get back to soul winning and leave all this other weird stuff alone. You've watched too much Dominic Hinst TV. No one's ever been healed in his ministry either, it's documented that he's a fraud and a false prophet. And the way he blows on people and they fall down, that's just total nonsense. God doesn't work that way!"

Chaplain Miranda intervened and asked William if he believed the Holy Spirit could touch someone through a minister, other than Dominic Hinst, by blowing on him.

William stiffened, "No, not through Hinst, or anyone else for that matter. God just won't work that way, it's not His nature."

Chaplain Miranda said, "William, as your chaplain I have to tell you that when you begin to say God can't work a certain way, you're standing on shaky ground. I'm not a Charismatic, but I've been slain in the Spirit when a minister laid hands on me. I wasn't expecting to fall under the power, but I did. It was a wonderful experience in the Lord. You may not like certain TV Ministers, and that's okay, but to say that God can't or won't work through someone in this manner is to limit God. As your chaplain, I have to warn you not to go down this path."

I sensed a holy fear of God enter the room as she repeated, "Again I say, William, you're on shaky ground, be very careful." With this, I suggested we all pray together. William and I prayed for Chaplain Miranda, who'd sat through 90 minutes of this and was looking frazzled.

William and I genuinely hugged and we walked out the door together and went our separate ways. I returned to my unit to pray. I realized that my spirit was barely even affected by this hour and a half session of accusation. Normally this would have destroyed me for weeks. God, by his grace, had mercifully prepared me for this confrontation by illuminating the spiritual strategies of the religious spirit from the 30-day reading assignment. I thanked God, praising Him for being faithful not to put us through more than we are able to bear.

The next day during the worship portion of the Father's Day service Chaplain Miranda handed me a post-it note. It simply said, "I hope you're okay. I've been praying for you all night."

This encouraged me. I went to the pulpit and preached a message the Lord gave me, "Are you hiding in God or from God?" I shared that Moses hid in God, with the Psalm 91 promise, whereas Adam hid from God amongst the trees of the garden of life. I called men to stop hiding from God but instead to enter into the sanctuary of God's Presence and hide in God. An altar call followed and many men stepped away from their worldly ways and into their God-given purpose and calling.

Journey Insights

A new chaplain was in town and authorized the chapel to be reopened after being closed for three years. This was a great win for the Kingdom. The Lord warns us to be aware of the enemy's schemes so that when the next attack comes, it's not a surprise. The next attack came through my friend and brother in Christ. He accused me of being deceived and said no one had been healed through my prayers. God had prepared me and filled me with peace so that the arrows couldn't pierce my heart. Through this came the message: Are you hiding from God or hiding in God? Which one are you doing?

61

THE ATTACKS GET WORSE

A couple of weeks later, Robert Sanchez, a pastor/prophet from California, flew in to preach at the prison with his psalmist wife. William and his entourage were present. At the close of the first service, several men gave their hearts to Christ. During the second service, Minister Sanchez began flowing in the office of prophet and the service was extended. William and his group observed with noticeable skepticism.

Inmates were called out, and it was as if their personal mail was being read. They were incredibly encouraged in the Lord, receiving poignant and meaningful messages, in great detail. It was beautiful. Grown men were weeping as he was speaking over their lives, confirming their callings and true identities and purposes.

He was able to identify both natural and spiritual gifts with razor-sharp accuracy. For example, he told one man, "The Lord shows me you're a carpenter by trade, and your favorite wood to work with is poplar. Is that accurate?"

The man shook his head, yes. Then Minister Sanchez gave a more detailed word to him regarding his true purpose and how God wanted to use his carpentry gift for the Kingdom..

He pointed to another man and said, "I see an image of you holding a number two pencil. You're an instructor, a teacher, and the Lord shows me you teach other inmates how to read, write, and do math. Is that accurate?"

"Yes," he responded. "I teach G.E.D. classes and I was a teacher on the street."

"The Lord wants you to know you're also called to the office of teacher in the body of Christ, to teach, train, and disciple others in the things of God." The Presence of God was rich in the room and all in all, he spoke to over 25 men personally, each with detailed accuracy.

Suddenly, Minister Sanchez pointed at me and asked me to stand. He didn't know me but began prophesying while giving details of an open vision he was experiencing. He saw me with a scribe's pen authoring several books. He went on to name the specific gifts God's Spirit had given me for the edification of the body of Christ, including healing, miracles, words of wisdom, words of knowledge, prophecy, and a strong anointing to cast out demons and set the captives free. He said that God gave me an unusual anointing that would be misunderstood. He continued, "At times you've suffered persecution and rejection from those who you call your friends because of these gifts and callings. Be encouraged, God is developing character in you through this pruning and purging process."

Then he said, "God tells me that you are like Joseph in the prison house. The day is coming when God will call for you to be released and then you'll be given great authority, just like it was done unto Joseph so shall it be done unto you." This was the second time I'd heard these words. The first time was 1990 when God graced me with the Tree of Books vision. This prophetic word during this 2002 service both humbled and encouraged me.

After the service had ended, we discovered that several of the men were deeply touched by the Lord. Family reconciliations occurred over the next few days by phone. Others were delivered from drugs and alcohol or freed from sexual battles, such as pornography and adultery. God moved powerfully during those two days.

Instead of the attacks ending, things became worse. After Prophet Sanchez' visit, William and two other Christian inmates began verbally assailing his ministry and the people over whom he'd prophesied. People took sides. Hindsight is 20/20, but during that season, we forgot that Paul admonished Christians not to follow him or Apollos or Cephas, but only Christ Jesus (see 1 Corinthians 1).

Now that the chapel was open seven days a week, inmate led Bible studies were occurring three nights a week. William and the entourage attended faithfully, not to hear the Word, but rather to debate it. Instead of celebrating our diversity and staying in unity, the men began to bite and devour one another on non-essentials of the faith (a very old scheme of the enemy). The church splintered into several small "us four and no more" groups. Men began majoring on the minors (non-essentials of worship style, preference of baptism, manifestations of the Spirit, etc.) and minoring on the majors (evangelism, Jesus' love for us, loving one another, and preaching the death, burial and bodily resurrection of Jesus).

The spirit of division continued to lay hold. Slander, false accusations, and doctrinal strife increased. The body was divided and nearly conquered during this era. Young Believers who were wounded withdrew from fellowship, and even went to other faith communities where more unity and love was demonstrated. Regardless of how much we prayed and fasted, this spirit gained a stronger hold. It was as if some of the men invited it into the congregation. They actually seemed to enjoy the conflict. When confronted on this, they bristled and then claimed their actions were in line with what Jesus would do. They replied, "We're contending for the faith." One even claimed, "What I'm doing is by the anointing of the Holy Spirit."

During this time I learned to follow the advice of the Moravians of the 1700's, "In the essentials, unity, in non-essentials, liberty, in all things, charity." I also learned to never compromise with the religious spirit and never shrink back from my calling. I continued to stand firm sharing the Gospel, winning souls, praying for the sick and casting out devils whenever the Lord opened the door. At the same time, I respected other Christian's beliefs and nurtured an environment for unity when possible. Hebrews 12:14 (ESV) says, **"Strive for peace with everyone, and for the holiness without which no one will see the Lord."**

A fresh anointing to write fell upon me and the Lord graced me with several teachings from these experiences. One of the teachings entitled, "No Divisions among You" was about biblical unity. God has since made way for this teaching to be placed in the hands of more than 5,000 prisoners in nearly 1,300 prisons across the United States. God is using this teaching to help nurture biblical unity behind bars among Christians from diverse backgrounds. What appeared to be a curse from the devil turned into a blessing from God. He redeemed the time from the days of evil.

Journey Insights

Instead of celebrating diversity and staying in unity, the men started to devour one another in non-essentials of the faith (a very old scheme of the enemy). They forgot about focusing on the love of Jesus for us, loving one another, and His resurrection. Instead they slandered others, hurled false accusations, and doctrinal strife increased. Believers were wounded and withdrew. Have you been wounded by another Believer and walked away from God because of it? That wasn't Jesus. I pray for His love to wash over you and heal those broken places. He's calling you back to Himself.

62

DEMONS AND DELIVERANCE

FPC Florence, Colorado (2001-2003)

One day while reflecting on the nearly 20 years behind bars the Holy Spirit brought to remembrance several men He transformed overnight by delivering them from a demon or a demonic influence. Their lives literally changed from night to day, from bondage to freedom, from darkness to light. Once set free, they were able to choose for themselves whether they now wanted to continue to live for Christ. They were free from the voice and influence of the devil that had been oppressing them and drove them to bad behavior.

I had searched the Scriptures to learn about this subject and found that Jesus often cast out evil spirits, so it didn't surprise me to see the need for this in prison. Jesus spoke directly to Satan himself, telling him it is written, you shall worship the Lord your God, and serve Him only. He cast out a demon, and a mute man spoke. We're told many who were demon-possessed were brought to Him, and He cast out those spirits with a word and then healed all who were ill.

Mark 1:39 says, **"And He was preaching in their synagogues throughout all Galilee, and casting out demons."** Jesus would say, **"Come out of the man, unclean spirit!"** (Mark 5:8). Scriptures speak of a demon driving a man into the desert. Often when I read about Jesus healing many diseases, He cast out demons, not permitting them to speak. Luke 4:41 teaches that demons recognized Jesus, shouting, **"You are the Christ, the Son of God!"** Jesus told them to come out and not come back again. Even Mary Magdalene had seven demons cast out of her.

There was a man at Florence Camp, who once had been a Satanist. His name was Jose and he was from El Paso, Texas. After landing in prison for drug charges, Jose had time to reflect on his life and now wanted to be free. He had even once called on Jesus but the devil wouldn't let him go. He didn't know how to break the covenant he'd made with the devil. So, for a couple more years, he remained in bondage.

One night Jose had a dream that he was taken to hell and was burning alive. He woke from the dream, glad to still be living for the dream seemed like reality. He was just about to dismiss the episode as his mind playing tricks on him when he discovered two unexplained burn marks on his neck. This cemented the seriousness of the moment. In his heart, he knew he was going to hell. He wanted to be free, but how? He'd already committed his life to Satan. Would God forgive him? Would Jesus, or could Jesus, set him free from Satan?

In his bed, Jose cried out to God. Nothing happened. He went back to sleep terrified that he would have another dream about hell. Instead, he dreamt of an inmate, with a group of men, who broke Satan's power over his life using the authority of Jesus' Name. Several demons were being expelled. When he awoke, he began to ponder the meaning of the dream. Could he really be free? Was he supposed to find this inmate and ask him to pray for him? He had seen the prisoner on the compound but had never spoken to him.

Later that day during chow call I was talking with an inmate named Rocky. I often played racquetball with him and he lived only a few cells down the hall from Jose. We mistakenly believed everyone had left the dorm since the unit became silent. The Holy Spirit compelled me to tell Rocky about the time the devil appeared to me in a dream and tried to kill me as a young Christian at Leavenworth.

I shared how real the dream felt and when I awakened my bed was vibrating. A demon was floating above my bed and staring me right in the face, and all the while I was wide awake! A blanket of overwhelming helplessness and fear enveloped me. I could hardly speak. But when I called out to Jesus, His Presence and power came, removing the demon. Jesus saved and delivered me in an instant. My relationship with the Lord developed rapidly after this. Little did we know God had prepared this moment in time for Jose to hear a powerful story of hope.

As I headed for the dorm exit Jose stopped me and said, "Excuse me, could I speak with you?"

"Sure," I replied.

Reluctantly he said, "I didn't mean to eavesdrop on your conversation, but, uh, well, I've had a similar experience, and I believe you're to cast the demon out of me." He then told me the back story and his history with Satan. I invited him to give his life to Jesus, and we set up a time to cast the devils out of him at the chapel. We asked the Lutheran chaplain to participate along with a couple of willing Christian inmates, Anthony and Scott, who believed Jose's story.

The chaplain said, "I don't have a lot of experience doing this kind of stuff, none actually, but let's see what God does." Chaplain proceeded to ask Jose to sit in a chair and then got behind him to pray a blessing over him. A couple of minutes went by. Nothing seemed to be happening. Jose looked at me a little perplexed as if to say, "What next?"

The chaplain finished his prayer and said, "Where do we go from here?"

I sensed permission from the Holy Spirit to step forward and do what He had taught me through previous deliverance and demon casting situations. I spoke boldly and directly to the devils hiding in Jose, "In the Name of Jesus Christ of Nazareth, the Son of the living God, Whom I serve, and by the power of the Holy Spirit, I command you devils to come out of Jose now!"

The atmosphere in the room changed instantly, and the spiritual fireworks began. The previously calm and polite Jose turned into a man whose arms began to flail uncontrollably. His eyes rolled back in his head and his body slid from the chair to the floor while the sound of a guttural voice began to speak from his mouth. And then, as we often said in prison, "It's was on like Donkey Kong!" Everyone could feel God's Presence in the room and the anointing of the Holy Spirit (God's power) on us to combat the evil.

Spiritual warfare between good and evil was manifesting before our eyes. Jose was caught in the middle. The Holy Spirit began giving Anthony and me words of knowledge about the names of the devils. As we commanded these by name to come out of Jose in Jesus' Name, they left one at a time. Jose was suddenly bathed in the love of God and filled with the Holy Spirit. Joy and peace filled his countenance. Then he began to speak and pray fluently and beautifully in tongues as he praised God. During this encounter, Scott also received the baptism in the Holy Spirit. (Scott and I discussed this later. He felt he most likely received the baptism in the Spirit more out of immediate need than theological desire at the time.)

A few things were noticeably different after this 10-minute encounter. Jose's countenance went from darkness to light. He was filled with the Holy Spirit and had a new prayer language. He no longer heard voices in his head. He had peace, overflowing with joy because he was free for the first time since he'd make a covenant with Satan. One more thing was different. The wonderful Lutheran chaplain, who we all appreciated and knew truly cared and loved the inmates, had just witnessed first-hand what he had previously only read about during his six years of theological training and ten years of ministry. We all hugged and returned to our units for the night. Jose slept like a baby for the first time in years.

The next day I saw the chaplain about the event. He said, "David, all I can say is, they don't teach this stuff at the seminary. I can't deny what I saw and experienced and it's caused me to adjust my theology." We smiled at each other, giving God the glory for Jose's deliverance, and discussed the power that can be released when inmates and chaplaincy staff are willing to work together to see God's sheep set free. His pastoral side then kicked in, and he lovingly and curiously inquired, "How is Jose doing today?"

"Great," I replied, "want to see him?"

He smiled and sighed with relief. "Yes, please bring him to the chapel." Jose and I returned a few minutes later with the chaplain. He talked about the fruit of his deliverance, comparing the before and after, and discussing the fruit. The chaplain was elated to hear about the stark differences. But, this was only the beginning of Jose's transformation.

Five days later Jose took me to his cell and said, "David, I gotta' show you something." He opened his locker and said, "Look at this!" He was pointing to a carton of cigarettes, a full bag of coffee and a six-pack of unopened Snicker's bars."

Confused I said, "Uh, I don't get it."

"David, it's been five days since you guys cast the demons out of me. I haven't smoked a cigarette, drank a cup of coffee, or eaten a single chocolate bar!"

Still a little miffed I said, "Well, this is good, isn't it?"

"Yes, but you don't understand. Before the deliverance I smoked two to three packs of cigarettes a day, I drank twelve extra-large cups of coffee a day, and I ate, at least, two candy bars a day. But for the last five days, I forgot to do any of this. No one told me to stop. I didn't try to stop. I just forgot to do any of it! Then, I also realized I don't cuss anymore."

Puzzled by his lack of addictive behavior, he said, "Holy Spirit what is happening to me?" Simultaneously, we both realized when Jesus delivered him from the demons, in Jose's case, the addictions left with them! I then remembered the verse where Jesus declared, **"...Every plant which My heavenly Father has not planted will be uprooted"** (Matthew 15:13).

We rejoiced that God didn't plant nicotine, caffeine, or sugar addictions in Jose, but took these out, by their roots, with the demons. Jose was a new man in Christ. The former things had passed away, and all things had become new.[68] God also gave Jose a new tongue, one that spoke words of blessings instead of cursing.

We thanked God for his mercy and then I challenged Jose to a one-on-one

---

68   2 Corinthians 5:17, **"Therefore, if anyone is in Christ, he is a new creation; old things have passed away; behold, all things have become new."**

basketball game. (Time to get into shape!) That's when I asked Jose if I could have a Snicker's bar. He laughed and said, "I'm throwing away the cigarettes and coffee, and I'm glad God delivered me from cursing, but I don't think I'm going to give up an occasional Snicker's bar."

The next day Jose emerged from the phone room from a call with his family. He was sporting a joyous and yet surreal look on his face like he was dreaming. "David, pinch me, I want to make sure I'm not dreaming." I did, and he said, "Oow!"

"Jose, what's going on? Is everything okay?"

His eyes were wide open. "God is sooo amazing! He just enabled me to lead my father, mother and brother to Christ on the phone!"

"In fifteen minutes you were able to accomplish all that?"

"Yes, it's amazing! I first spoke with my brother and shared what Jesus did for me. You don't know this, but he's in a wheelchair. He also was in the drug business but was shot and left to die, but he lived. I told him about what God did for me. He said he wanted to be free from the devil too and wanted Jesus. I led him in a prayer repenting of his sins and receiving Jesus. When he accepted Christ, my mother and father wanted Jesus too!"

Over the next two weeks, Jose brought Latino men to my cell, for prayer to be healed, and to receive Jesus. God healed every one of them! One man had a metal rod in his forearm. He'd had an accident at age seven. Twelve surgeries followed, and his arm was always in pain and immovable from the elbow down. The Holy Spirit directed me to command the metal to bend into place. I had never done this before. In front of our eyes his muscles began twitching and he was suddenly able to move his forearm for the first time in more than 20 years. He wept. The next day he was able to lift weights for the first time and play handball, totally healed. Then, a small group of Latino Christians and many ex-gang members began forming on the compound. They were following Jesus because of Jose's testimony and dramatic transformation.

At every facility, God delivered men from demons who were hungry for freedom. The list of spirits that were cast out seemed endless, e.g. spirits of rage, murder, drug addiction, alcoholism, rejection, bitterness and rebellion, resentment, self-will, self-rejection, hatred, stubbornness, self-hatred, unforgiveness, disobedience, violence, temper, anger, retaliation, and murder. It was a joy to see the accompanying behavior leave as well!

I've learned that the two primary reasons Jesus came to Earth were to set the captives free and to destroy the works of the devil.[69] This work is just the

---

69 1 John 3:8, **"He who sins is of the devil, for the devil has sinned from the beginning. For this purpose**

norm for Jesus. I believe this can be the standard for you and me when we call on Jesus and use his authority to set others free in His mighty Name!

Journey Insights

God miraculously delivered Jose from the demons by giving the people praying for him words of knowledge. God had given him a dream that we was in hell and he woke up with unexplainable burn marks. God not only delivered Jose from demons, but also delivered countless other men who were hungry for Him. They were delivered from spirits of rage, bitterness, murder, unforgiveness, etc. Is fear blocking you from being set free from demonic bondage? Are there thoughts in your head that say that's not really true? Step out in faith and ask God to reveal any demonic bondage so that you can be set free today!

---

the Son of God was manifested, that He might destroy the works of the devil."

63

HALLOWEEN WARFARE AND A MIRACLE LAYOVER

FPC Florence, Colorado (2001-2003)

By now I was getting very close to being transferred closer to my family and friends in Kansas City. Here at Florence, they had to drive 12 hours to see me. The Lord had shown me in a dream that my next destination would be Leavenworth Camp, less than one hour from home.

The entire time I was incarcerated I experienced unusually strong spiritual warfare and attacks during the last two weeks of October through the first week of November. Every year! During this timeframe, I learned to ask my intercessors to pray. As Halloween approached, I sensed the warfare increase over my life. I could feel it tangibly at times, but more importantly, I felt God protecting me from the enemy's plans, foiling them each time he launched an attack.

The first week of November I said to Chaplain Miranda, "I don't understand it. I've been sensing incredible warfare from the enemy, but haven't seen any evidence of it in the natural."

"I forgot to tell you, David," looking a bit sheepish. "Last week I received an e-mail from the head chaplain in Washington, D.C. She attached a three-page e-mail from Chaplain Lester."

My breath caught in my throat. "Chaplain Lester isn't even at Springfield anymore and I'm two institutions removed from her. It's been more than five years. What's she still after me for?"

"She claims you're writing unauthorized teachings from prison to other prisoners through the Heart Ministries Newsletters under the pen name Caleb. She also alleged that your parents were involved in all this."

I cringed knowing how close I was to the transfer to Leavenworth. This could mess everything up in an instant. "What did the head chaplain in D.C. say?"

"She asked if I knew you and was aware of any of this."

"And you said…?" My heart was pounding as I looked at Chaplain Miranda, anxious to hear her answer.

"I said that I knew you and had read your teachings. I also said the authorities here had already addressed the issue last year and they were fine with it as long as you wrote under a pen name, and that I didn't have any problems with you. I closed my e-mail asking her what she wanted me to do."

I held my breath and waited for the other shoe to drop. Chaplain Miranda continued. "She wrote back just one word in response, 'Nothing.' So, you're in the clear this year David!"

That was an amazing moment. Exhaling slowly, it dawned on me I'd been saved from Jezebel's schemes. "Chaplain Miranda, I'm grateful you were the one to receive that e-mail. I've been too many places where BOP officials tend to lock up inmates first and ask questions later." She simply smiled.

"David, I wish you and your family the best with the prison ministry. Getting Bibles into the hands of prisoners changes things around here." God had made a way, and I was in the clear for transfer.

On December 18, 2003, I began the relocation process to Leavenworth, Kansas. Shocked would be too mild of a sentiment to describe my emotions. I was finally going closer to home. No more 12-hour drives for my aging parents who would spend two nights in a hotel room for a three-day weekend visit. Leavenworth placed me less than an hour's drive from my family who'd supported and believed in me for the entire time I'd been in prison.

The Florence prison authorities handed me a bus ticket. No CON Air travel this time but an actual public bus ticket! They also gave me $25 in cash, then dropped me off at the public bus station in Pueblo, Colorado and told me I had 30 hours to report to Leavenworth Prison. *Were they serious or was this some sort of joke?* First it looked like Monopoly money. The heads on the two tens and the five dollar bill had grown considerably! I held it up and looked at the prison official. "Is this spendable?"

He laughed and asked, "How long's it been since you've been out?"

"Fourteen and a half years."

"A lot has changed. Enjoy your bus trip!"

Another inmate named Benito Angeli was being transferred to Leavenworth for the Spanish drug program. Benito was not yet saved, but God would do a quick work.

A chaplain friend, by the name of Linda Greenlee, and her son met us at the bus station in Denver. Jeff Gay, my boss from my high school job at Quik Trip, also met us. After giving his life back to Christ six years earlier, Jeff had been faithful and God opened the door for him to become Director of Operations at Heart of America Prison Ministries. I was still stunned as the five of us took a cab to a Brazilian Grill about a mile away on the 16th Street

Mall.

For the first time in nearly a decade and a half, I had real food on real plates, with real glasses, on a real table with a real tablecloth! Oh, and real metal flatware. After eating with a plastic "spork" for years, I almost broke my tooth with the first bite!

Suffice it to say that having 35 different types of roasted and grilled meats on skewers brought to our table by waiters in white outfits left me almost, but not quite, speechless. They shaved the meat with knives onto our plates, seemingly non-stop, until we finally groaned, "no more!" Funny how I remember every detail of that miraculous time! Even dessert was wonderful. We shared delicious flan and chocolate cake and ice cream between the five of us.

During the meal, Linda's cell phone rang. It was for me. Cell phones had downsized considerably from my eight and a half pound clunker to four and a half ounces and the clarity was phenomenal. I was able to speak and pray with a Christian friend I hadn't spoken to in years.

After dinner, we found a private place and for the next hour and a half, we thanked God for all He'd done. We also entered into intercession together. Benito was raised Catholic and this was all new to him. He was so touched by the Presence of the Holy Spirit that he asked how he could give his life to Christ. God marvelously saved this wonderful Hispanic man on his way from one prison to the next! Our bus for departure from Denver to Kansas City was called, and Benito and I were off to prison again.

After 29 and a half hours of freedom, Benito and I re-surrendered to Leavenworth Penitentiary to complete service on our sentences. This was where my prison experience began nearly a decade and a half earlier. I still had five years and three months left on my 22-year sentence. This time, however, instead of being housed in the penitentiary, I was designated to the honor camp outside.

Journey Insights

The miracle breakthrough happened and I began the relocation process to Leavenworth Camp, Kansas. No words could describe the feeling of finally being closer to home. No more hotels and 12-hour drives for my aging parents. I would now be less than an hour away from my family and friends. In route to the camp I was allowed to go to dinner for the first time in nearly 15 years. Do you need a miracle breakthrough? Don't give up. I pray for the heavens to open and the hand of God to move on your behalf in Jesus' Name!

64

OUTSIDE THE BELLY OF THE BEAST

USP Leavenworth, Kansas (2003-2008)

It was no more than 15 minutes back inside the infamous Leavenworth Penitentiary, when I heard a staff radio blaring, "Stabbing in B Unit, stabbing in B Unit, lock down B Unit." A sick feeling flooded my stomach. *Yeah, I'm back at Leavenworth. Some things never change.* A convicted child molester disrespected another inmate and was subsequently stabbed. He ended up losing an eye and part of a lung, but he lived. The penitentiary was on lockdown status for the next four days.

An hour later I was placed in population at the satellite camp. They gave me a set of bed sheets, a pillow, and a cot. Just as I lay down for some much-needed sleep, I heard my name called followed by "report immediately to the kitchen." I groaned and rolled out of my cot.

Upon arrival, the food service foreman ordered me to the sandwich crew, making 4,000 bologna sandwiches for 1,750 inmates. This took four long, arduous 12 hour days.

After the siege had been concluded, the unit manager and camp administrator offered me the warden's orderly position. The catch? I'd be working at the Big House which is the actual penitentiary. This job could entail just about anything as the warden supervised the entire prison operation. It also could be precarious, especially because inmates often don't trust someone working near the warden. Worst of all, I'd finally reached the point where I didn't have to spend my days inside a rough prison, but if I accepted, back I'd go.

The position offer came with a two-man room *outside* of the Big House, in the honor wing no less. I'd sleep on an actual single sized bed with a thick mattress instead of that cot. *It's been a long, long time,* I thought. The honor wing would give me a quiet place to sleep. *What would that finally be like?* No smoking allowed there? *Seriously amazing.*[70] As much as I didn't want to go back inside Leavenworth Penitentiary, these tradeoffs seemed worth it. I also sensed this was God's leading.

My first day reporting, I approached those 42 steps leading to the penitentiary. I looked around. *Even after nearly 15 years in prison and eight federal*

---

70   Smoking was allowed inside prisons until 2005-06.

penitentiaries, everything about this place is still a little intimidating. I focused on where I was. *The belly of the beast. Five manned and armed guard towers, maximum-security cameras, two sliding metal security doors, all in and around those 44-foot tall, six-foot thick, infamous Leavenworth walls. Good thing I've learned never to be intimidated because of God's Psalm 91 promise of protection.*

Although unafraid or intimidated, the place was daunting and prompted a conversation with God. *I need answers, God, about my time here at Leavenworth.* Confident that He wanted me to inquire of Him whenever I was uncertain, I asked, *Lord, what am I here for this time?*

"To bind Pharaoh's princes at your pleasure; and teach his senators wisdom," was the immediate and crystal clear response that came in my spirit.

I knew this passage came from Psalm 105:22 and chronicled the life of Joseph. *Once again the Joseph theme pertaining to my life!* He'd been a showboat in his youth, trafficked into slavery by his brothers, spent 13 years in captivity, then Pharaoh made Joseph lord of his house and ruler of all his substance. He was productive and trusted. Pharaoh wanted Joseph **"To bind his princes at his pleasure; and teach his senators wisdom"** (Psalm 105:22). The anticipation of what God would do here and how He'd use me was paramount to me. I knew to start with what was taking place in the spiritual realm before I looked to the natural.

Throughout my journey, I'd been tested. I'd grown into a place of maturity and trust in the Lord. No longer was the cry of my heart for God to get me out, even though I was serving additional years that were unjustly added to my sentence. I'd learned to be about my Heavenly Father's business, so this mandate that referenced Joseph's life was no surprise. It spoke to me of the authority bestowed upon me as a Believer in Christ, to bind and loose, and to teach God's divine wisdom, all according to His Word. Planning to keep this verse uppermost in my mind, I set about settling in to my new temporary home.

It was December, 2003 and I'd been locked up since July 1989. That's a lot of time and I wasn't finished; I still had 5 more years. *I could be moved again, but I don't think I will be. I believe I'll fulfill my sentence at this infamous facility.* Similar to moving to a new city in the outside world, I set about discovering the lay of the land. The Education Department was shut down at Leavenworth Camp. No staff members were willing to administer the exams. This placed my international business degree on hold with seven classes remaining; however, I trusted the Lord as He orchestrated my focus. The Religious Services Department offered a quarterly class through the local church of an accredited Bible College, and I embarked on this part of my education.

The professors taught mainline evangelical doctrine and stuck to the essentials of the faith. On all non-essentials, they maintained liberty, which was important as I had experienced those who expected absolute agreement with their perspective or division occurred. Not here! I was able to take five quarterly classes which greatly anchored me in my faith, and brought balance to some areas, without limiting me in areas of the supernatural.

Lord, thank You for allowing me to be "seminary free" for the first 15 years of my Christian walk. And, thank You now for progress in my formal education and licensing to follow before my release.

The job I'd accepted at the Big House gave me access to the warden and camp administrator in various ways. I cleaned their offices, along with the executive staff areas, and God opened divinely appointed conversations there. These helped bring significant and positive changes to the camp, such as new washing machines, a commercial driver's license program for approved inmates being initiated, a couple of inmates receiving rare emergency furloughs to see a dying parent or attend a funeral, etc. I was trusted to an extent and seemed to have uncommon influence.

These benefits, however, were sometimes short-lived because of the rogue behavior of some of the inmates. *How disappointing to see the few ruining it for the many,* I thought. It's called the "two percent rule" in prison. Two percent of the prisoners cause 98 percent of the problems. At Leavenworth Camp, it was more like 20 percent.

Many of these camp inmates still thought they were living on the streets and brought with them street habits. Because many of them worked in the community up to eight hours a day at Fort Leavenworth, it was easy for them to smuggle in contraband. They got creative. Sometimes they would cut open a plastic football and fill it with contraband and simply throw it over the fence into the recreation yard for a waiting inmate. It was nearly impossible for the staff to effectively police the facility.

Contraband was everywhere which created a very challenging atmosphere for both inmates and staff. A lot of the inmates were rebels. To combat the contraband, the staff just made up the rules as they went, and they broke a few others. There was anarchy, unlike anything I'd ever witnessed at a federal prison, in both the inmates and staff.

To put things in perspective, it wasn't uncommon for the staff to do a random shake-down of the camp and find a dozen illegal cell phones, several half gallons of alcohol, ounces of marijuana, unused syringes, steroids and unauthorized weight lifting supplements. At one point, I walked into the rec yard with a couple of brothers talking about Jesus and nearly a third of the inmates were smoking marijuana like it was legal. They were just taking hits and passing to the next person. Leavenworth Camp was, in prison terms, "wide open." I tried to steer clear of the train wrecks waiting to happen that were all around me. And they wrecked, often.

It was in this environment a few of us began to pray mightily for a move of God. A former meth chef named Dusty was one of the key intercessors with whom I prayed. Dusty had an evangelism gift and was a tremendous worship leader. The Jacksons, two brothers who loved the Lord, also came along side of us in prayer, plus a wonderful spiritual father who had previously pastored a sizable congregation in Wichita, Kansas.

Leavenworth became a powerful season of worshipping, praying, sharing God's Word, and seeking His hand. My heart was at peace as I kept the words ever present in my mind that He'd spoken to me upon arrival. This became a season of teaching and declaring what was on His mind, whether it be doctrinally or in natural matters, and expressing His love. I continued to see how His love captivated hearts and the truth about Jesus set free the souls of many who'd been subject to bondages, other than prison, all of their lives.

In the Big House by day amidst the most hardened criminals, working as the warden's orderly. Outside of Leavenworth by night, living in the honor camp, sleeping on a real bunk bed. A move of God once again igniting hearts to receive God's love. *God, regardless of circumstances, You never change and Your love knows no bounds! Thank You for opening doors to set the captives free.*

Journey Insight

I was back inside the ominous, maximum-security 44-foot tall, six-foot thick, oppressive walls of Leavenworth, where it all started 15 years prior. Memories I'd care not to remember came flooding back and now I was in transition of serving the last 5 years of my sentence. I wasn't intimidated or afraid, yet needed answers from God as to why I was back here. No longer was the primary cry of my heart to get out for serving years that had been unjustly added. I was at peace because I trusted God. I trusted Him to orchestrate my steps in these last years in this dark place. Are you in a situation where you are facing a choice? Is it time to trust God and know that He's still in control instead of being fearful, bitter, angry or wanting revenge?

65

THE BITTERNESS WAS GONE

The warden's office was located strategically just outside a secure hallway tunnel entrance that led through two steel gates into the penitentiary prison population. One day I stepped out of the warden's complex and had an unexpected encounter. I was across the hall from the visitor area that heads through two locked gates into the prison visiting room. A man filling out paperwork to visit an inmate caught my eye. He looked familiar.

This was a compromising situation that I had to avoid. In these circumstances I'd have to act as if I didn't know the person, or I could lose my job as warden's orderly.[71] The man looked at me and I looked at him. *Who was he?* I wondered. Then it hit me. I hadn't seen him in more than 15 years. *That's my prosecutor, the one behind all three of my cases!* Something happened next that I never expected in a million years. I found myself tipping my hat to him with a look of honor and respect.

What just happened? I wondered. All the anger and bitterness inside my heart toward this man, this arch-enemy and personal courtroom nemesis, had vanished. Where'd it go? It's gone! As I left the area, I became angry at first, because I didn't have any anger. Then it hit me, God had delivered me!

All the years of bitterness, frustration and anger vanished. Joy filled my heart as I recognized God had graciously set me free. I felt nothing negative! The words of Jesus came to me, **"But I say to you, love your enemies, bless those who curse you, do good to those who hate you, and pray for those who spitefully use you and persecute you, that you may be sons of your Father in heaven…"** (Matthew 5:44-45).

The former prosecutor, now a defense lawyer, had gone into the visiting room to see a client. The staff member overseeing visiting called me over. "Do you know that man?" She expected me to lie to keep my job. I replied in a matter

---

71 Because I was the only inmate who had direct access to the warden I could theoretically take him hostage. Of course, what inmate who was at a camp and about to get out would do such a thing? Nevertheless, if a visitor wanted to pressure a family member of yours on the outside and take them hostage, this could possibly motivate you to take the warden hostage in a prisoner exchange. In reality, the instant a staff member is taken hostage, prison policy dictates that they lose all decision making authority. This renders them powerless to order the opening or closing of any doors.

of fact tone, "Yes, I know him."

"When was the last time you saw him?"

"About 15 years ago."

"Where?"

"In the courtroom. He was my prosecutor."

She knew a little about my case because I'd been in Leavenworth 15 years earlier. She said, "I saw you look at him like you two were friends."

I said, "No, we're not friends, but he's not my enemy either. Not anymore anyway. Just, someone I met in life under very bad circumstances."

She said, "Tell me a little more about your case."

I started talking. The more I said the angrier she became at the former prosecutor. This was not my intent, but it was as if she was pre-disposed to a certain outcome.

"I don't like this guy." Staring at me, it was obvious she was irritated. "The minute you left he swelled up and began bragging about being a former federal prosecutor for 15 years. Then he started boasting about being a full bird colonel. He's extremely arrogant. I don't know how you can just act like this guy doesn't bother you."

"Honestly, it's a mystery; I actually believe it's supernatural." She was listening so I continued. "God has apparently washed all the hatred for this man out of my soul." I shook my head in wonder, feeling somewhat introspective. "I'm actually kind of dumbfounded. It's really a miracle." She shook her head, as if she couldn't quite believe me, yet she was hanging on to every word.

"You know, God has a way of exposing people who do wrong. You may not believe this but about a decade ago he was arrested for soliciting sexual favors from an undercover prostitute in Kansas City."

She scoffed, "You don't expect me to believe that do you?"

"Actually I do, because he made John TV locally, and USA Today nationally."

Realizing I was actually telling the truth, something happened that I can only describe as righteous anger. This was the catalyst that caused her to take action. She was clearly disgusted. "Well you may have forgiven him, but I'm not going to let him get away with this." She picked up the phone. I didn't know what she was about to do, but it wasn't my business, so I returned to the warden's office to complete my work.

Two hours later this visiting room officer caught me in the hallway and said, "Your former prosecutor is banned from Leavenworth Penitentiary," as she beamed with accomplishment.

Confused, I asked, "What do you mean? Uh, how?"

"I called the SIS Lieutenant and had him check the arrest records. You were right, David. I don't think they actually convicted him for the sex thing. I think he pled to some lesser offense, but it's enough to ban him from Leavenworth for a while. Also, he was handing a prisoner his business card without permission. He's still doing solicitation in my book!"

"You know what else?" I was surprised at how worked up she was. "His wife called here twice to make sure he's actually here. What wife calls a federal prison to see if her attorney husband is actually visiting a prisoner? She doesn't even trust him! He's probably still up to his old ways." She chuckled somewhat deviously as she added, "I muddied up his file pretty good. From now on he can send another lawyer or paralegal to visit his clients or run his practice from his office, but he's not coming in here anymore!"

I stood astonished. I didn't try to get this man banned from Leavenworth. I wondered if he had simply tipped his hat back, or even made a gesture of peace, would God have seen his heart and this never would have happened to him. Forgiveness evidently only went one direction that day.

God, I'm in prison, but free. He's free, but apparently still in prison.

Fascinated, although actually feeling sorry for him, I was learning how unforgiveness is an ugly burden to carry through life. *This kind of load should be dropped at the foot of the Cross, God, at the first available moment.*

There was also another lesson, even more powerful that I see as I reflect back on my life. To send a much-needed fatal blow to my pride, arrogance, self-reliance, and being a self-made man, God strategically sent someone into my life *similar to me that helped drive my three indictments.*

I now realize, 25 years after my arrest, that all the pain, anger, frustration, and bitterness I had towards this man was misdirected. It should have been directed at resolving *my root issues* which until resolved, opened the door to many of the troubles I suffered at his hand.

Jonah was instructed to go to Nineveh.[72] His pride and arrogance caused him to buy a ticket to Tarshish instead and he eventually ended up in the belly of the beast, which has interesting similarities to prison. Jonah wasn't spit out onto the beach *until he repented.*

Better late than never, I thought. I'm now grateful for whatever God allowed that brought me to the end of myself. God can do far more with us when we

---

72 Jonah 1-3

yield to Him.

Journey Insights

In utter shock I stared at my nemesis, the prosecutor, who stood in front of me in the waiting room. I looked him in the eye, tipped my hat out of respect, and when he recognized who I was, his face twisted in disgust. What was more shocking is all the bitterness, hatred, anger that I had toward him was completely gone. I was free and he was still locked in the prison of his heart. Is there a private prison in which you've been living? God wants to heal you and set you free.

66

THE FAVOR OF JOSEPH

After working nearly a year for the warden, the new camp administrator asked me what I'd like to do. He had me stumped so I asked, "What do you mean?"

"You've done an excellent job and I believe people should be rewarded for good work." I was shocked. Receiving a commendation for anything was rare and he had my attention. "Do you like working here or do you want a different job? I can get you any job at the camp."

I gathered my thoughts quickly. How I answered could affect my life dramatically. "Well, Sir, there is a job I'd like to have, but I need community custody. It's at the military base at Fort Leavenworth. It's the clerk position at the Roads and Grounds Department."

He said with confidence, "For you, I can have the assistant warden do a favor." The next thing I knew I was approved for community custody, and sent to work during the weekdays amongst the public *in a community* of 10,000 people, just a couple of miles from the prison. This community included playgrounds, restaurants, swimming pools, adults, children, families playing together, and so much more of just real life.

All those years inside prison walls, I mused. *How extraordinarily enjoyable it is seeing families walk and laugh together, pushing their kids on swing sets.* It seemed a lifetime ago when I had experienced those normal little things, and actually, I'd not appreciated them before. This was an ideal transition back into normal living, five days a week from 7:00 a.m. to 3:00 p.m. *It's so odd, as if I'm living in two worlds, but I'll take it.* During those days, I developed an appreciation for the ordinary instead of the adrenaline highs I used to seek. Night times were back to the absolute control of authority every moment.

God, it's as if You are transitioning me back into society, step-by-step, and helping me appreciate the life You died to give me.

During my time working at Roads and Grounds, helping take care of the six square miles at Fort Leavenworth, I learned how to drive heavy equipment, and was able to get my commercial driver's license (CDL). Civilians were all around me as I drove a 36,000-pound dump truck with air brakes through family neighborhoods and down the highway. Again and again, I asked God, *Are You preparing me for release? Thank You for restoring my soul. Thank You for helping me appreciate 'normal living.' Thank You for leading and guiding me, preparing me for the days to come.*

Way back at the beginning of my sentence, prison authorities had informed me that because of the severity of my crime, I'd never see a camp while incarcerated. Yet against all odds, God's favor opened the door for me to be granted camp custody. Now with the authorizing signature of the warden, I was experiencing community custody on a zero-turn-radius riding lawn mower in the sunshine, and eating civilian food for lunch.

Two weeks after arriving at this new day job in the Ft. Leavenworth community, my civilian mowing crew supervisor sent me on a special lawn-mowing mission. Location: Ft. Leavenworth Airport! *Airport?! Did you say, airport?* To say I was shocked was an understatement.

After doing a double-take, I carefully and respectfully asked, "Are you sure you want *me* to go inside the security fence by the airplanes?"

"They called for us to send someone. I'm sending you." My civilian supervisor didn't know what my crime was. I swallowed hard. *Oh God, this must be a setup! If the prosecutor gets wind of this, he'll try to use it against me.*

The airport was the last place I wanted to be on this cloudy morning! I knew the enemy of my soul could easily try to falsely accuse me of tampering with or stealing another jet. To top it off, this was post 9/11 on a military installation which could result in some sort of terrorism charge. Heart pounding, I spotted my supervisor arrive in his pickup truck. He unlocked the security gate and directed me to drive my mower onto the airfield tarmac. My mind was anything but peaceful.

He said, "Hairabedian, tell the guy inside to let you out when you're done." He pointed at the grassy areas on both sides of the landing strip and told me to mow around the landing lights. "This should only take about an hour; see you back at the shop," and off he went in his truck.

My last experience on an airport tarmac that wasn't CON Air was in 1989 when I was arrested with a stolen Cessna Citation jet. I looked around and saw only small propeller type planes. This raised my comfort level a smidgen.

I prayed in tongues as I mowed. Years earlier the Holy Spirit had taught me to do this when I was on a push mower crew in Colorado. Rarely could anyone hear because of the noise, so it made a perfect private time with God and it was building up my faith. I mowed and prayed. Not a single plane took off or landed.

Five minutes before finishing I heard the familiar sound of an incoming jet. *No, it's not possible, I thought, I'm almost finished.* But here it came, a Cessna Citation Jet, the General's plane no less! It landed less than 200 feet from me. The pilot exited and entered the control center, which left the jet and me. Sitting on my mower in the sunshine, I noticed it was 9:05 a.m., the exact same time my jet ride to hell came to a crashing halt, on the tarmac in Florida, leading to my incarceration.

My thoughts and emotions were all over the place as I drove my mower right past the plane to get to the exit gate. I actually had to duck my head while going under the plane's right wing. Suddenly, the sun peaked out from behind a cloud, first shining on my face, and then enlarged over the entire scene. The unmanned Cessna Jet, shining in the morning sun, had its door wide open and its steps down as if it was inviting me inside! I shook my head in disbelief. How did I slip through the cracks of security on this one?

As I drove by the plane, the Holy Spirit said, "I trust you!" A warm peace flowed over my soul as I experienced the Father's love. *God, You washed me clean from my past. It no longer matters what others think or say, because Your Word says, "If any man be in Christ he is a new creation, the former things have passed away and ALL THINGS become new"* (2 Corinthians 5:17). How grateful I was at that moment, that God would communicate with me, that I would recognize His voice above my apprehension, and that I could receive His comfort.

On the way back to the shop the main civilian supervisor asked, "Where are you coming from?"

"The airport."

"Yeah right," he chuckled.

"No seriously, they called and needed someone to mow around the lights."

He shook his head in disbelief, "Who did that?"

I told him it was the landscape crew supervisor. "David, I'll talk with him. Don't EVER go back there again for your own protection!"

The favor of the Lord continued to increase in my life.[73] The Lord opened the door for me to take over the head clerk's position. I was given a key to my own office, with offline computers, and military communications radios. Six months after being on the landscape crew I realized I had been praying in the

---

73 Jesus, our example, "**...increased in wisdom and stature, and in favor with God and men**" (Luke 2:52).

spirit over 500 hours and God's favor continued to increase in my life.

I was serious about praying in the spirit because of the encouraging words of the Apostle Paul. First Corinthians 14:18 and 14 say, **"I thank my God I speak with tongues more than you all…"** and **"For if I pray in a tongue, my spirit prays, but my understanding is unfruitful."** I purposefully did not limit my prayers to my reasoning and finite understanding, nor my emotions; instead, I allowed my spirit to pray in harmony with the Holy Spirit. I sensed God was preparing me for the next part of my journey and He knew precisely how to pray what I did not!

God, Your Spirit knows exactly how to pray for me, and through me, for my life. I'm uncertain what my future holds, but You're not, and I trust You. Thank You that I never have to be overwhelmed because You're not. You know what I need. You say in Ephesians 6:18 through the Apostle Paul that I should pray "always with ALL prayer and supplication in the Spirit" and that's what I'm trying to do.

For the next two and a half years working at the Fort, I discovered the kind of favor Joseph experienced during his years in the prison under Pharaoh.[74] My job as clerk included dispatch over 25 vehicles, check out and return, the entire tool room, clerical accounting, inmate payroll, as well as ordering and dispensing lunches to all the inmates each day. I had the virtual freedom to drive any of the vehicles over six square miles at Ft. Leavenworth. My duties included executing assignments for the garrison commander, the second most powerful man next to the general. Approximately 20 civilians came to my window throughout the day as well as 30 inmates. The guards from the penitentiary and the camp were not allowed into my office without permission. They lacked jurisdiction to enter the premises without authorization from the military police or my head supervisor.

During the winter, I helped run the emergency snow crews including the midnight shifts. My supervisor asked me to ghostwrite award and recommendation letters for the general to sign on behalf of the snow crew inmates, acknowledging the hundreds of thousands of dollars the program was saving the military each year.

During the weekdays from 7 a.m. to 3 p.m., I was treated with respect and given vast liberty, responsibility, and authority. When arriving back at the camp during the afternoon, I was treated with dishonor and impugned by many of the staff members. These were the best of times and the worst of

---

74 Genesis 39:21-23 explains further what I was feeling: **"But the LORD was with Joseph and showed him mercy, and He gave him favor in the sight of the keeper of the prison. And the keeper of the prison committed to Joseph's hand all the prisoners who were in the prison; whatever they did there, it was his doing. The keeper of the prison did not look into anything that was under Joseph's authority, because the LORD was with him; and whatever he did, the LORD made it prosper."**

times.

The civilians had zero problems with my unique position. I even helped some of them with their spiritual issues and a little legal advice from time to time. Some of the inmates, on the other hand, didn't necessarily like the fact that they had to report in to me, and the truth was, it was fairly awkward. Little did they know that behind the scenes, I was using my position of favor to help create programs for them to get certifications for heavy equipment, forklift, skid loaders, and expand the commercial driver's license program. These programs would enable them to have bona fide skills and documented work experience, on an OSHEA installation, that they could use upon release to join the workforce and become productive citizens in society. I would even write a resume for them, along with a letter of recommendation, on my computer to be signed by the head civilian on their behalf. With these two solid documents in hand, many were hired on the spot after release, and landed good-paying jobs, never to return to prison again.

Journey Insights

The favor of God on my life was unbelievable. I realized that when God washes you clean from your past it doesn't matter what others think or say. "Therefore, if anyone is in Christ, he is a new creation; old things have passed away; behold, all things have become new" (2 Corinthians 5:17). What are the stains of your past? Regardless of what they are, Jesus is prepared to cleanse you if you will ask Him.

67

A RAY OF HOPE

USP Leavenworth, Kansas (2003-2008)

There was a lower-level drug dealer, a friend of mine from Kansas City, named Lee Lawson. Lee was not part of the jet thefts, but he later became a co-defendant on our drug case. In addition to cash, when Bails, Vic, and I stole the plane, we received cocaine as partial payment. Lee sold the cocaine for Bails who was to share the proceeds equally with Vic and me. That never happened. Bails kept our portion and turned us in for the crime. He falsely testified that he only got $5000, and that Vic and I got over $200,000. Years later it was proven he kept the lion's share. Before that information ever came out, Bails became the government's key witness.

In anyone's world, Bails was considered dirty. In his former days as a deputy sheriff who flew a helicopter scanning marijuana fields for the DEA, he stole cocaine from the police evidence room. I knew of two of these incidences because Bails brought the stolen cocaine to me for resale. He played both sides of the law, whichever suited him at the time.

Lee's drug involvement with Bails had caused him to become a co-defendant. Lee had been released ten years earlier, receiving a *reduction* of sentence for his testimony against Bails for perjury. My sentence, on the other hand, was *doubled (adding 12 years!)* for Bails' version of the story.

Lee was in perfect position to tell all. He had been on the run for about a year while we were all out on bond and when we went to trial for the first two cases. The rest of us had been sentenced the same week that Lee was picked up by the Feds. I was the only one who knew Lee other than Bails. There was no way I could testify against Lee knowing it would result in a sentence of life without parole. He was a third-time offender, but was no Cartel connected drug kingpin. Bails provided him kilos of cocaine on credit and the more Lee sold the more he used.

Lee's first two arrests earlier in life were for small amounts of cocaine as a user. He had never even done time. So in 1991, when Lee's attorney came to speak with me at FCI Englewood he was shocked to learn that I had no intention of testifying against his client to get my 22-year sentence reduced.

"David, everyone testifies nowadays. It's just the way the system is set up."

"Let me give you the backstory about Bails," I told him. "Including the fact that he used to work for the sheriff's department and turned dirty." Filling him in on the details, he was stunned.

"The Feds haven't told me any of this stuff, David." I was quiet as he continued processing out loud. "It's not in the discovery file." His response made me laugh and then explain it further.

"They call the courtroom a truth-seeking process, but somehow they have a tendency to withhold truth that could hinder their prosecution. Might I suggest something? Why don't you consider having Lee make a deal with the government? Let them know you discovered a few things that weren't in the discovery file about Bails. Tell them Hairabedian isn't testifying. Bails is their only witness. It's Lee's word against his. A drug addict versus a dirty ex-cop, turned drug dealer and jet thief, who has been re-immunized and caught lying on major issues three times, including walking off with $200,000 in drug money."

I had his full attention and so continued with my suggestions. "Tell them Lee is willing to plead guilty for, say, five years. This gives them a win on the conviction and getting Lee off the streets. Tell Lee I encourage him at this point to debrief and testify against Bails for perjury. After the fact, maybe they can reduce Lee's sentence for his cooperation. Lee can get into a much-needed drug and alcohol program and then transition out as a productive citizen in society instead of serving life without the possibility of parole for being a drug addict. You know, Lee is a really good guy deep down who has lost his way and needs to reboot and get back on the right path."

He cocked his head and said, "What about you? You're serving 22 years as a first-time offender."

I sat back in my chair and thought about the reality of serving nearly 20 years before being released instead of trading Lee's freedom for my own. "It's risky, but if Bails goes to prison for perjury based on his testimony against us, this should result in our sentences being overturned or at least reduced. The lead customs agent knows that Bails has repeatedly lied about his real involvement in this case. The prosecutor hasn't wanted to know the truth and repeatedly and intentionally has turned a blind eye, and even buried evidence."

He responded, "David, are you sure about all of this?"

I didn't hesitate. "Yes I'm sure. My parents hired a private investigator to go to Bails' town and uncover the dirt on him. I'll have him mail you the documents. The facts are clear. They have continually allowed Bails to change his story, withheld evidence and re-immunized Bails. With Lee's testimony about what happened, things I don't even know about, and the fact that Lee sold about $180-220,000 in cocaine for Bails this will be the third time Bails is caught lying. And at this point, with all of us convicted, the agent no longer needs Bails. He will likely turn against him and prosecute him for multiple violations of his immunity agreement and squirrelling away the drug profits.[75]

The attorney agreed to talk to Lee and make a deal with the Feds. Fast forward to 2006. Lee had been out for 10 years. God graced and put his life back together. He was now married with a child. He and his new wife adopted two more children. They built a mortgage company that specializes in helping credit-challenged people get back on the right track and then qualify to purchase their home. His company quickly expanded to locations in three states and employed a number of people. He was drug-free and a productive member of society.

Lee heard the BOP transferred me to Leavenworth near my family. He contacted my mother and said, "Susan, I've gotta help David get out of prison! Bails only did one day in prison, and I could have served life. David pled guilty, told the truth and is serving 22 years, partially based on Bails' lies. I feel like I have to do something. I'm going to call the lead agent and then meet him in person. Pray for me. Let's see what I can do to help out."

The meeting between Lee and the lead customs agent went surprisingly well. Lee reported to my mother that the agent acknowledged things weren't right in this case, that Bails was dirty and went free, and I was never supposed to get that much time. He said that everyone else was out, and sometimes things just don't make sense. Lee asked the agent that if my attorney wrote a letter with supporting documents to the new prosecutor, would he in turn go to bat for me behind the scenes to get my sentence reduced?

The agent waffled for a second. Lee continued, saying the attorney could write things in such a way that no one has any egg on their face. Lee told my mother his exact words, "Agent, it's been nearly 16 years! David's family just wants him home. What's right is right, so let's make this right." The agent paused and then nodded in agreement. My Florida attorney went to work immediately. A ray of hope appeared. My release should be just around the corner now...

Then *two years* of paperwork went back and forth. My Florida attorney who

---

75   As it turned out, Bails then cooperated with the Government in trade for immunity from all his crimes, including trafficking in 17 kilos of cocaine and his spearheading the theft of our first plane in December 1988, the 3.2 million dollar King Aire 300 in Ft. Lauderdale. Bails served one day. Lee was a third-time offender and served about five years before his release. I was a first-time offender and had already served 15 years with 5 more to go.

represented me in my third indictment flew to Kansas City to meet with the lead agent and new prosecutor. Following the meeting, he came directly to the prison to give me the news.

"David, the agent says he is too close to retirement and doesn't want to mess up his record. The prosecutor says without support from the agent; he can't do anything for you.

In disbelief I sputtered, "What? What exactly does this mean?"

He spoke softly, "It appears that you have to finish your prison sentence. I'm sorry." This news was the final blow that allowed *Hope Deferred* to set in...

Journey Insight

Life isn't always fair. The agent was too close to retirement and didn't want to mess up his record. As a result, I'd have to finish out my entire prison sentence. Fairness was not prevailing. When hope deferred sets in, there is still hope at the end of the tunnel. Even though the agent did the wrong thing, I did the right thing and that's what counts. Do you have hope deferred over a situation right now? I break it off you in the name of Jesus and pray God's hand to turn around your situation. You did the right thing by doing the right thing! God promises to work out all things together for our good.

68

HOPE DEFERRED

My final years at Leavenworth, I experienced great favor and yet, I also encountered a higher level of spiritual warfare that warred against my mind. This was far more strategic, subtle, and diabolical than anything I'd endured in previous years. I was now eighteen years into my prison sentence. Three years earlier something began to shadow me. The only way I can describe it was "greyish" in nature and very subtle.

I'd dealt with demon spirits before, but this one was different and difficult to identify. It was not like other spirits, those that attempt to impose their will on you, like lust, rage, hatred, racism, suicide, murder, or the other demon spirits that are common in the prison system. Those kind roam the hallways looking for willing vessels to partner with them so they can express their nature in the earth. This was different. It went from shadowing me to gradually approaching and resting on my back on the left side at various times, usually while reading my Bible in bed.

Is my mind playing tricks on me? Am I just not feeling well? Is this a physical sickness? WHAT'S GOING ON? As I thought about it, I realized I was even having difficulty concentrating, praying, and sometimes reading my Bible. No matter, I focused on my Bible reading and ignored the unseen spiritual force. I'd been taught that the Bible will keep either me from Satan or Satan will keep me from the Bible, so I just kept reading, but this didn't seem to work. In fact, while I read the faith-filled stories from the Scriptures a sudden feeling of utter hopelessness would descend upon me.

How could this be? I thought. The Bible is God's Word and faith comes by hearing the Word of God (Romans 10:17). The enemy's voice would subtly speak opposing thoughts into my mind, "Where is the promise of his coming? He delivered others from prison, but you're still here. Look around you, metal bars and cement walls. You serve God faithfully, and this is your reward! You aren't even guilty for the extra time you're serving now…but God allows you to sit here and rot! He doesn't even love you or He would have already delivered you."

The circumstances seemingly matched many of the words spoken, but I knew these were lies from the evil one. I immediately fought back by quoting the promises of the Bible. **"And we know that all things work together for good to those who love God, to those who are the called according to His purpose"** (Romans 8:28). "God will give me double for my trouble (Isaiah 61:7) as I stay single minded on Him and His purposes." **"The devil, who deceived them, was cast into the lake of fire and brimstone where the beast and the false prophet are. And they will be tormented day and night forever and ever"** (Revelation 20:10).

The enemy would retort back with more thoughts, "Ha! You can write winning appeals for others, they're out, and you're still in! They don't even write to say thanks or send money to help support the Bible ministry. No one cares about you, and you will do EVERY DAY OF YOUR SENTENCE. You are a laughing stock to those around you!" I would press on, reading the Scriptures out loud, quoting Revelation 18:2-6 until faith would breakthrough in my heart and the greyish shadow would depart for a few hours.

"...Babylon the great is fallen, is fallen, and has become a dwelling place of demons, a prison for every foul spirit, and a cage for every unclean and hated bird! For all the nations have drunk of the wine of the wrath of her fornication, the kings of the earth have committed fornication with her, and the merchants of the earth have become rich through the abundance of her luxury.

"And I heard another voice from heaven saying, "Come out of her, my people, lest you share in her sins, and lest you receive of her plagues. For her sins have reached to heaven, and God has remembered her iniquities. Render to her just as she rendered to you, and repay her double according to her works; in the cup which she has mixed, mix double for her."

This spiritual battle lasted off and on for *three arduous years,* and I was starting to lose traction against it. It was a strange time for I also was experiencing great favor in the natural with my jobs working with the warden, then in the community, and as a clerk at Fort Leavenworth with my own office. But spiritually, during the prior six months, I could hardly read my Bible because of the thoughts that came from the greyish shadowing presence.

Now the words were compounded by sharp physical pain in the left side of my back that was increasing daily. It felt like I had some sort of cancer. I told no one but stood against the pain and the thoughts of this horrible disease.

"Pain, in the name of Jesus, I command you to depart." The pain remained.

"I plead the blood of Jesus Christ over you." Some relief would come and the pain would reduce from sharp to dull in nature, however, within 30 minutes the pain had returned.

God, I will pray in tongues until Your presence descends, I told Him. Again and again, with hands raised I'd pray and eventually more relief would come. Then I'd teach a Bible study, or share Jesus on the prison compound. I was determined, but evidently this spirit was too.

The battle became daily and was increasing. Slowly, I started to succumb to the thoughts that pounded my head and even found myself repeating some of these from time to time in my mind and then out loud.

"Where is the promise of your coming God? You delivered others, but I'm still here. I preach YOUR Gospel, lead staff and inmates to Christ, teach Bible study, heal the sick, cast out devils, and run a Bible ministry to prisoners for you that reach into 700 facilities from behind bars. What is my reward?"

My tirades increased. "God, I've been persecuted by prison chaplains, other inmates, and staff for my labor. And what about my pen that you anoint to write winning appeals for others, yet you allow my appeals to fall on deaf ears in the court? The government's key witness is convicted for perjury based on his false testimony against me. Everyone knows it and I still can't get released!"

My words were more accusatory than inquisitive, settling on, "You're not being fair, God." Ever so slowly, without being consciously aware, my words began to mirror and sound like the enemy's words. I'd preach and teach, telling others of the love of Jesus, yet my heart wasn't in it. They'd get saved, or grow in faith while my trust withered. The pain in my side *always* deepened when I spoke words in agreement with the enemy, but my focus on disappointment kept me from connecting the two.

"Diabolos" is one of the names the New Testament uses to describe the devil, his nature, and strategy against mankind. It's the same word used to describe the devil during the three temptations of Christ in the wilderness while Jesus was fasting for forty days (see Matthew 4:1-11). If the devil could speak to Jesus in detail during the time Jesus should have been the most spiritual, we shouldn't be surprised when we face such opposition while living the Gospel and seeking God.

This word, dee-ab'-ol-os literally means, "Prone to slander, slanderous, accusing falsely, *one who comes to pound on the mind until finding access inside.*" This same word is also used to describe man, "who by opposing the cause of God, may be said to act the part of the devil, or to side with him."[76] The Bible says that **"lest Satan should take advantage of us; for we are not ignorant of his devices."** (2 Corinthians 2:11). Solomon, the wisest man in the Old

---

76   Strong's NT Greek, Diabolos #1228

Testament, said, **"...there is nothing new under the sun. Is there anything of which it may be said, "See, this is new"? It has already been in ancient times before us."** (Ecclesiastes 1:9-10)

More than two and a half years after I'd first began struggling with this spirit, things reached a crescendo. I'd been a committed Christian for more than 17 years now, and had made it my habit right from the start, to study, worship, pray, and act out my faith. "Help me, God!" I cried out, seemingly to no avail, for simultaneously I fell prey to the pounding thoughts of "diabolos" and "acting the part of the devil." I did this by inadvertently siding with him every time I repeated his words against God and adding a few of my own.

Confusion and despair were taking root, and I knew enough to finally call for help! *Who should I trust, God?* I thought about how in times past when higher level spiritual warfare was occurring, I'd made mistakes. When I'd asked an inmate to pray who was committed to the Lord and full of godly zeal, but lacked maturity, there would always be issues. They'd get walloped by the spirit attacking me and within minutes of their praying for me, or "standing in the gap,"[77] they'd become physically sick for weeks.

If I asked a more mature Christian inmate to pray, someone who knew the Word, but didn't carry the same type of mantle or gift mix as me, he'd often fall prey to a spirit of competition or jealousy. This would show up as the accuser of the brethren. Either way, the results were disastrous. I'd have to combat two fronts; (1) combatting the original strategy and attack from the enemy on me, and (2) the secondary attack of false accusation operating through Christians who have sided with diabolos and are now, "acting the part of the devil."

I'm glad I asked God where to turn because He responded. Two people I trusted for higher level prayer situations outside of prison were Lee and Doris Harms, directors of the christian Healing Rooms in Missouri. The Lord had moved upon them a couple of years earlier to come visit me at Leavenworth, with subsequent visits on a few occasions. They'd trained hundreds of people in healing and warfare prayer, and also planted healing rooms in other nations.

The Holy Spirit prompted me to call. Dialing their home it rang a few times and Doris answered. I asked for Lee. "He's out running errands, David. Anything I can help with?"

"Doris, I've been going through an increasingly difficult time spiritually, emotionally, and physically. I haven't voiced this to anyone, but it's been a tremendously challenging and long period of time. Would you be willing to pray for pain throughout the left side of my back?"

---

77 Ezekiel 22:30-31 (emphasis added), **"So I sought for a man among them who would make a wall, and stand in the gap before Me on behalf of the land, that I should not destroy it; but I found no one. Therefore I have poured out My indignation on them; I have consumed them with the fire of My wrath; and I have recompensed their deeds on their own heads," says the Lord God."**

Doris began to pray and suddenly stopped in mid-sentence. "Oh my, you're suffering from deferred hope."

What is deferred hope? What in the world? She had me stumped.

Calmly, yet with noticeable authority, she spoke directly to the problem. "Deferred hope, in the Name of Jesus Christ, I break you off my brother's life right now, and order you not to return to him again."

Instantly, I was delivered! The pain in the left side of my back departed simultaneously. I was incredibly grateful for this miracle. The only way I can describe what occurred is to say that all the chronic pain in my back, neck, and shoulders that had been increasing in intensity for the last six months snapped off me like a tightly stretched rubber band being cut with a knife. I was free! Then in the same gentle voice of authority, she said, "I now replace these areas in your life with *God's desire fulfilled,* which the Bible says is a *tree of life.*"

The next miracle took place as she spoke those words. My mind, which had been saturated with frustration and tormented with stress and chronic disappointment, was suddenly purged with the in-flooding mind of Christ. My faith level spiked instantaneously and my spiritual vision was renewed like an eagle.

"It's as if my viewpoint and understanding of my life, and its seemingly arduous circumstances, has suddenly changed!" I explained to Doris. She was delighted but I was thrilled! "I feel like God is showing me Heaven's perspective – His aerial point of view – on the life issues with which I've been struggling." As I thought about it, I realized my heart was filled with new anticipation and godly optimism of what the Lord was about to do for me, as well as through my life, for others. In a word, hope was restored!

As I stood amazed and praised God for this mighty deliverance, a renewed vigor and strength to finish the course set before me filled my soul. I then realized God had just supernaturally delivered me from malicious unseen spiritual forces. They'd been hindering my life, oppressing my mind, and tormenting my body. *Lord, I now see these have been increasing against me for almost three years.* It all crystallized instantly and, as Doris and I hung up the phone, I was finally able to praise God unhindered by disturbing emotions. My mind was free!

Wow! I thought as I laid on my bed that night. These forces of darkness have been subtle. *Although I've been unaware, they increasingly hindered and oppressed my mind and body and even begun to vex my spirit.* After this powerful prayer encounter, the Holy Spirit began to reveal to me how subtle yet devastating deferred hope can be. I meditated on Proverbs 13:12, **"Hope deferred makes the heart sick..."**

I knew many Christians suffer from hope deferred at some time in their lives, especially those behind bars. Parole denials, appeal denials, loss of good time, lack of family relationships, delays in favorable law changes, and a plethora of other things delay hope. The worst part is most aren't aware of it but their life begins to suffer. Satan then compounds the issue by sending a spirit of discouragement.

God, if the body of Christ isn't careful, or if they're ignorant of the enemy's strategies, this can catapult them into a spiritual tailspin and eventual crash. I immediately thanked him again for intervening through giving Doris Harms the wisdom. *If it hadn't been for her availability and her wisdom and experience with this spirit, deferred hope could have easily prevailed against me, derailing my walk with You. I could have become shipwrecked in my faith, God! Thank You for caring about me through every aspect of my walk with You. I know You'll use this experience for good.*[78]

Journey Insights

Deferred hope is one of the strategic weapons the enemy employs against Christians. This weapon, if not recognized and properly guarded against, can cause our hearts to become sick. **"Hope deferred makes the heart sick..."** *(Proverbs 13:12). This is why Solomon admonishes,* **"Keep your heart with all diligence, for out of it spring the issues of life"** *(Proverbs 4:23). Other areas will suffer as well including our attitude, spiritual vision, physical and mental health, and our love relationships with Jesus and others. The Prophet Hosea said,* **"My people are destroyed for lack of knowledge..."** *(Hosea 4:6), and the Apostle Paul admonished,* **"lest Satan should take advantage of us; for we are not ignorant of his devices"** *(2 Corinthians 2:11). Has the Devil been able to keep you defeated by deferred hope? Trust me. It is God's desire to deliver you. (See prayer for deliverance from deferred hope in the appendix.)*

---

78   Hope Deferred teaching, https://store.virtualchurchmedia.com

69

AN OUNCE OF PREVENTION

The dream that morning began and ended with the words, an ounce of prevention is better than a pound of cure. Upon awaking a Latino Christian inmate named Santiago arrived at my cell offering fresh-baked supersized cinnamon rolls. Behind bars, choices are usually quite limited. These prison-made Cinnabons were aromatic, baked to perfection, and top-dressed with a trifecta of butter, cinnamon, and white icing.

Santiago said, "David, I have a friend who works in the bakery and the Lord has been blessing me the last few years with this treat several times a week. I usually share with my Latino brothers, but wanted to bless you today since you're my true brother in Christ." He offered me two.

As I was salivating, the words of John the Baptist came to mind, **"He who has two coats, let him give to him who has none. He who has food, let him do likewise"** (Luke 3:11 WEB). I thought of another person to share with, but while snarfing the first one, it tasted so delicious I couldn't seem to stop. The second one tasted just as good! The Holy Spirit reminded me of the dream and its message, *an ounce of prevention is better than a pound of cure*. He emphasized the words, better than. I wasn't yet sure to what it referred.

As the morning progressed, I felt a little sluggish. Reflecting on my bedside breakfast, I realized I'd started my day with white flour, white sugar, and zero protein. Not the wisest choice, but very tasty, and besides, I rationalized, doctors say that cinnamon is very healthy for the heart. By lunch, I was ready for a 30-minute nap, but instead, went to the dining hall because it was hamburger day. In federal prison, every Tuesday or Wednesday is usually hamburger day. My 20-year sentence from the Feds provided for a thousand hamburger days and I didn't want to miss too many of these.

The French fries that day were genuine Burger King. These raw fries came from an 18 wheeler that had been stolen and recovered by the Feds. Our facility scored the load from the insurance company as a write-off. I couldn't pass up these delicious fries. My friend working on the line doubled dosed my tray. The Lord's favor was upon me! These were hot out of the grease and everyone was enjoying this special treat. It was also soda pop day, all you could drink. I had two big cold glasses.

I left the chow hall and within 15 minutes felt like I needed a nap, but I had to go to work. Someone offered me a "Jailhouse Jamaican" (hot chocolate mixed with coffee), to help perk me up. I rarely drank coffee but needed some type of caffeine boost. The words, *an ounce of prevention is better than a pound of cure*, came again. I began to contemplate my day and realized that if the Lord was speaking, this was a teachable moment. I later learned that I'd been divinely set up through my own choices for for a personal object lesson I would never forget. (There's an old saying, "The burnt hand learns quickly".)

Later that afternoon Santiago came to me wearing a worried look and asked for prayer. He said, "David, I just came back from the doctor and was diagnosed as a diabetic. Please pray for me. I need healing."

We prayed and the words came up in my spirit again, *an ounce of prevention is better than a pound of cure*. I stopped and shared my dream and its message.

Santiago dropped his head sheepishly and remorsefully confessed, "I've been eating two or three cinnamon rolls a couple days a week for the last three years. I thought these were a blessing from the Lord but now realize what appeared to be a blessing was actually a curse."

It never failed to amaze me how God taught me everyday life lessons in prison, like this one about wisdom and self-control. I learned that no matter where I am in life, God will tell me the truth if I humble myself, care about His heart, and choose to listen. Santiago and I talked about the children of Israel asking for meat instead of manna. God may have provided, but the Bible says, **"But while the meat was still between their teeth, before it was chewed, the wrath of the Lord was aroused against the people, and the Lord struck the people with a very great plague."** (Numbers 11:33)

We discussed how the Bible teaches us in 1 Corinthians 9:25 that we are to exercise self-control in ALL things, and he said, "David, I've lived in cinnamon bun excess, gained 30 pounds and now I'm reaping the reward in my flesh with diabetes." The Bible says, **"Do not be deceived: God cannot be mocked. A man reaps what he sows."**[79](Galatians 6:7 NIV)

"Santiago, God is merciful. When we repent he is faithful and just to forgive us and to cleanse and heal us."

His response showed me his heart. "David, let's pray about the root of the problem, not just the symptoms. The problem is ME and my desire for unhealthy food! Will you help me pray that God changes my lustful nature

---

79   1 John 1:9, **"If we confess our sins, He is faithful and just to forgive us our sins and to cleanse us from all unrighteousness."**

from the inside out?"

Santiago looked chagrined but continued telling me what he wanted to ask God. "Pray he changes me from a TV watching couch-potato Christian into a healthy, productive, well-balanced man of God."

The two of us collaborated in prayer. Santiago prayed, "Jesus, I need deliverance from the root that causes me to reach out to these false comforters. Just like you cursed the fig tree that didn't bear any real fruit, and it withered up overnight (Matthew 21:18-22), I now give you permission to curse this thing that is unhealthy in me and will shorten my lifespan. I choose to live and want to declare Your good works. God, I thank you for supernaturally gracing me with a new desire on the inside for healthy and wholesome foods, so that I might live out all my days. In Jesus' Name. Amen."

After we had prayed for both of us that day, we watched God answer over the next 90 days. Santiago lost 30 pounds! He became energetic, his health was restored, and diabetes disappeared. We talked about how many Christians come to the healing line with caffeine and sugar addictions, poor diets, poor sleep, and exercise habits.

"They ask for the healing of their bodies instead of addressing the real cause," Santiago said. "My testimony now is to help others know this higher truth; to ask for God's healing power to go directly to the root, and the symptoms will then fix themselves. We all have an old nature and wounded soul that God wants to heal."

While I prayed and was listening for the Lord to speak, a verse came to mind, **"Beloved, I pray that you may prosper in all things and be in health, just as your soul prospers."** (3 John 1:2) How marvelous that God cares about delivering us from all our addictions, whether it is food, caffeine, sugar, tobacco, alcohol, drugs, or lust! We can simply ask God to go to the root and set us free by also bringing healing to our souls.

It was at this point I thought about what would happen to me when my release day finally arrives. I didn't struggle with any of those issues while in prison, and I praised God for it. Then I asked, *God, what will happen once I'm out in regard to women? I want to remain pure.* This used to be an issue for me on the outside, but all the time I'd been in prison, God had guarded my heart. *One day soon I'll be faced with women of all kinds, in ministry, business, in church, and everyday life situations. Will I remain pure, God?* I asked Him to continue guarding my heart in this area.

Thinking of the crippled man at the pool of Bethesda, I remembered that

Jesus asked him, "Do you want to get well?"[80] That's a question we all must wrestle with if we're going to ask God to help us. If we want, God will lovingly sit back and allow us to reap the eventual consequences of our behavior. But, as Santiago learned when he told God that He wanted to get well, Jesus was willing to uproot the iniquity inside that drove him to his unhealthy behavior. An ounce of prevention was not only possible, but it was also God's highest and best plan. Santiago and I learned first-hand through this experience that *an ounce of prevention is better than a pound of cure!*

Journey Insights

An ounce of prevention is better than a pound of cure. Many people seek healing, yet continue with tobacco, caffeine and sugar addictions, poor diets, lack of sleep, and inadequate exercise, instead of seeking to uncover the real (root) cause in their wounded souls. "Beloved, I pray that you may prosper in all things and be in health, just as your soul prospers" (3 John 1:2). What unhealthy choices are you making for your body? God is ready and waiting to set you free at the root.

---

80   John 5:6, **"When Jesus saw him lying there, and knew that he already had been in that condition a long time, He said to him, 'Do you want to be made well?'"**

70

SHORTITIS AND RELEASE

The Journey Continues

Shortitis is a term often used for prisoners who are near the end of their sentence. They are "short to the door" and often agitated. Prisoners count days not only in prison but how long until they're out. When someone is getting close to release they're often referred to as a "time-midget": triple digit midget has 100 days left on his sentence, double-digit has 99 days or less, and single-digit is in the final 9-day countdown for release.

Chaotic thoughts and erratic behavior often accompany shortitis, attributed to the anxiety and fear of freedom. An inmate may pick a fight with another inmate to lose good-time and delay his release to the halfway house. Inside he believes he's not ready for the outside yet. He may suffer from being institutionalized and no longer knows how to live on the outside.

Psalm 90:12 says, **"So teach us to number our days, that we may gain a heart of wisdom."** As is the case with all people, and definitely with prisoners, if our eyes aren't on God and we're not moving with Him, it's easy to get into a comfort zone and not make much progress on our journeys.

Shortitis was on my mind as my time to leave prison approached. *If I'm not progressing with God, I'm regressing. There is no middle ground. When it comes to my walk with Christ, remaining stagnant isn't an option. God's always drawing each of us forward and He simply asks us to follow Him. The enemy, on the other hand, loves to lull us to sleep and offers us many excuses to distract us from following God.* As I thought about what I would soon be facing on the outside I was clear that this massive change in my life would work best with God leading the way.

Many other inmates getting out would talk about what new crimes they'd commit or I'd hear them planning to return to drugs, loose women, and the ways of the world. They often begin to show their true colors. For example, a prisoner approaching release may gravitate toward criminals who are still actively connected from the inside, getting a fresh hookup for the outside. He may reconnect with an old drug buddy or girlfriend, or get a visit from someone their past, inviting them back into the game. For prisoners with shortitis it can be a tumultuous time, filled with temptation and a gamut of emotions, for those with shortitis, and challenging for those who have to live near them.

In the 20 years incarcerated I had, at least, a dozen cellmates and several dozen friends who were released. I was always happy as they walked out the door. Others were jealous, or bitter, lamenting, "when am I going to see freedom?" We usually threw the short ones a party, with Ramen noodles, nachos, soda and ice cream, the best of what we could buy from the commissary. The time had finally arrived when the party was for me.

A few guys brought the usual food items and we had a small gathering in my cell. They were all genuinely happy for me. No one was jealous or bitter because I'd served two to five times the amount most of them had on their sentences. In prison terms, I'd earned my release day.

Surprisingly, the only difficulty I had sleeping was from a little too much food. For what I can only attribute to the grace of God I didn't experience shortitis and I never became institutionalized. Everything was just another mile down the road on the journey to freedom. Reflecting on my journey, knowing I'd be walking out of Leavenworth in the morning, who would have guessed I'd just be feeling grateful?

What am I thankful for? I thought.

I've spent 19 years, 6 months, a week, and a day behind bars and my walk with the Lord would perhaps not even exist if I wasn't here. God has trained me well, teaching me to wait patiently, to have absolute trust in Him, and to be about His business. He's given me a love for His Word. He's refined me and allowed me to partner with Him wherever I landed, in spite of challenging circumstances. He's taught me forgiveness, first for myself and the mountain of mistakes I made, and then for the injustices done to me, and that He can use it all to accomplish His sovereign will. I'm not bitter, I'm better, knowing God is always good and He loves me unconditionally.

My thoughts moved back and forth into prayer. *God, You loved me where I was at, but You loved me too much to leave me in that condition. You loved me when my character was marginal at best and when I misquoted and misunderstood certain Scriptures. Early on I was wrong—focused on getting out instead of realizing You were getting out of me what caused me to get here in the first place. You loved me that much! Thank You. Just thank You. I'm grateful this is available to every single prisoner (inside or outside of prison)! Your hand is outstretched to us all.* Somewhere amidst my prayers and thoughts, I drifted off to sleep, one last time in my prison bunk bed.

September 12, 2008, the prison doors finally swung open. I'd served 1000 hamburger days! I would immediately head to a halfway house to prepare for five months of home confinement, and then five years of supervised release, but, I was finally free!

As I awoke, it seemed like I should have been jumping for joy, after all, I was walking away from 20 years in prison! But somehow, as I took my first steps of freedom, prison immediately seemed surreal and what I was doing seemed normal. As dramatic as that moment should have been, it wasn't. As I thought about it, I realized that somehow I'd never become institutionalized.

God, You did this. You made it possible for me, at this moment, to feel like I never was in prison. I'm not bitter, I'm not blaming anyone, and I don't feel like an ex-con. You preserved me, God, and I'm incredibly thankful.

Now more than ever before I understood the 2 Corinthians 5:17 (NLT) verse, **"This means that anyone who belongs to Christ has become a new person. The old life is gone; a new life has begun!"**

My steadfast parents, along with my sage-wise sister, Carron, all who'd encouraged me *for two decades behind bars*, met me in the Leavenworth camp foyer. I knew I was embarking on a new journey as I opened the door, stepping out into the world as a free man. Rain hit my face on that dreary, overcast day. It was actually refreshing. The sunlight seemed to be missing, but inside my heart and soul, the light was brilliant. I placed my meager belongings into their vehicle and got in the back seat. My mother turned and said, "It's too bad the sun isn't shining on such a momentous day." The words came from my mouth without thinking, "God allowed it to rain today because he wanted to tell us the devil's crying." We all laughed together.

As my father drove, my mother looked through the rear window at the prison, and something supernatural occurred in her. She told us what was happening.

"In this instant, God has washed all the pain and anguish of those 20 years out of my soul. All the bitterness I had, as your mother, over denied appeals, dashed hopes, a spiteful prosecutor, and lost time together as a family, has suddenly been cleansed. David, it's as if it never happened."

She couldn't believe she was healed in a moment of all the grief and pain. Mom reflected on her relatives who had survived the nightmare of Hitler and the Holocaust. They'd written about similar miracles where they were healed in a moment, as if it had never happened.

"What kind of amazing God is this who allows the pain and suffering that we experienced, and then supernaturally delivers and heals in the twinkling of an eye? Why? How?"[81] She was literally stunned as she explained what

---

81   Isaiah 61:1-3, **"The Spirit of the Lord God is upon Me, because the Lord has anointed Me to preach good tidings to the poor; He has sent Me to heal the brokenhearted, to proclaim liberty to the captives, and the opening of the prison to those who are bound; to proclaim the acceptable year of the Lord, and**

was happening to her.

I thought how interesting that both my mother and I almost simultaneously were experiencing nearly the same thing from God. We were both set free in a moment from 20 years of prison as if it had never happened.

There's an old prison saying, "What doesn't kill you makes you stronger." God could easily have delivered me from prison at any time, supernaturally, or changed a law through the court system. There were also enough reversible issues to overturn or reduce my sentence at any juncture. The government's key witness had been indicted and convicted of perjury five years into my sentence. The prosecutor had been arrested for soliciting sexual favors from an undercover prostitute while I was on appeal eight years into my sentence. A national newspaper article chronicling the prosecutorial misconduct had even been published by a well-respected investigative journalist.

Why 20 years? Thought came to my mind as we rode in the car, and God brought to my mind Moses and Joseph. The same question could be asked by Moses regarding his 40 years on the backside of the mountain. Or with Joseph's 13-year journey from the slave-house, through the prison-house, and then overnight into the palace as prime minister. God knows how to develop character in his servants. He did it with me. He knows exactly how much time this takes for each person and how much they can endure. Upon completion, He can then trust us to carry the glory of His Presence and represent Him to the others.

Let's do this God. I believe I'm ready.

In response, He brought to mind Isaiah 48:10-11. **"Behold, I have refined you, but not as silver; I have tested you in the furnace of affliction. For My own sake, for My own sake, I will do it; For how should My name be profaned? And I will not give My glory to another..."**

---

the day of vengeance of our God; to comfort all who mourn, to console those who mourn in Zion, to give them beauty for ashes, the oil of joy for mourning, the garment of praise for the spirit of heaviness; that they may be called trees of righteousness, the planting of the Lord, that He may be glorified."

Journey Insights

In an instant my mother was healed of all the years of pain and bitterness from denied appeals, deferred hope, and lost time as a family. Isaiah 61:1-3 (NIV): "The Spirit of the LORD God is upon me...to proclaim the year of the LORD's favor...to comfort all who mourn, and provide for those who grieve in Zion-- to bestow on them a crown of beauty instead of ashes, the oil of gladness instead of mourning, and a garment of praise instead of a spirit of despair." What years of pain and deferred hope have you experienced? God can take the years of pain and heal it. He can turn it from ashes to beauty.

71

TESTING CONTINUES

The Journey Continues

Forty minutes later my parents dropped me at the halfway house in downtown Kansas City, Missouri. I was scheduled to serve five months and then go live with my parents and begin five more years of supervised release.

At the halfway house, I had my own cell phone. I could call anyone, unmonitored by the Bureau of Prisons staff for the first time in 20 years. The Scripture, **"For you, brethren, have been called to liberty; only do not use liberty as an opportunity for the flesh, but through love serve one another,"** resonated in my spirit (Galatians 5:13). As I listened to men talking on their cell phones, it was evident the majority of them were back into their old ways: womanizing, conniving, and looking for a quick money score.

Others seemed lost without a compass. They had no real direction and some were filled with fear: fear of failure, fear of returning to prison, or fear of people. They were all over the map in their emotions. Very few prison church goers were interested in going to church now that they were free again. "Born again until they're out again" rang true.

A few, however, were still seeking God and the staff could immediately tell the difference. During the three weeks I was housed there, I watched how God opened doors of opportunity and favor for those whose hearts were fully toward Him. God was faithful to honor His Word as these few men sought His Kingdom. God provided jobs, clothing, housing, transportation, and truly whatever else they needed. He even restored family relationships. I thought of Luke 12:31 (NLT): **"Seek the Kingdom of God above all else, and he will give you everything you need."**

One day a staff member called me into his office, "Well Hairabedian, we're sending you to home confinement this week."

I was taken aback, "Doesn't that take *at least* a couple of months?"

"Usually. Some people do their entire halfway house time here. A lot of guys mess up here and go directly back to prison, but you're different. We're setting a new precedent because of you. You're the fastest release from a halfway house to home confinement in the history of our program."

The next morning couldn't come fast enough. I was heading home! Okay, it was home confinement with an ankle bracelet on my leg, but it was still home! At 45-years-old, I arrived at my parent's house for the first time since I was 19.

This is incredibly odd, I mused, noticing my confused feelings. *Odd yet wonderful!*

At 19 years old as I was accelerating into sin, I couldn't wait to get out of my parent's home, and away from their authority. At 45-years-old, now walking in obedience to God, I couldn't wait to get home. Their house was a safe haven, provided by the Lord through my family, to reintegrate back into society, transition into fulltime ministry, and be a blessing to our family as we enjoyed each other's company.

It was fascinating to me that God gave me a covering of sorts by being in my parent's home. Although I no longer had any interest in drug trafficking or illegal activities, I was concerned about keeping myself pure with the opposite sex. I was glad to be in my parent's home because when I was in prison, I'd heard many stories from backslidden men of God. They would fall into the trap of ministering—helping a woman in some way—and it would end up in sin. I knew I would soon be actively involved in preaching and teaching. I wanted the accountability, and God blessed me with this covering.

Although I'd been set free from many strongholds through the years, it would be five years after I was released before I realized that I had *permission to feel* again. Behind bars you're rarely given permission to feel; instead, you're expected to react and you're sporadically goaded, whether by prisoners or officials. You learn quickly that feelings are seen as a weakness, as is fear. I praise God that I didn't walk in worry and fear while in prison; instead, God helped me discover His intense affection and holy emotions. As an image-bearer of Jesus Christ, I'm learning the important part of life that godly emotions play, whether it be love, compassion, joy, delight or even sadness.

Upon arriving home, I noticed a box on the doorstep addressed to me from a prisoner named Pauly who I'd known 17 years earlier at Leavenworth. I was excited to open it, and thrilled to see it contained a state of the art laptop. God had used me to help him avoid a 30-years-to-life sentence with information unknown to his own attorney about new case law. All these years later God moved on his heart to send the computer as a "coming out" gift. God can cause people to remember you as He did for His servant Mordecai with

King Xerxes in the Old Testament.[82]

That laptop became a powerful instrument for the Bible ministry and business for the next several years. The Lord rewarded this man for his obedience and began to prosper his business shortly after that. A few years later the Lord gave me the knowledge to help this same man quickly prevail on a business legal matter.

Another former prisoner named Jerry, who had heard me preach at a local fellowship, saw that my clothing was in need of an upgrade. After the service, he said, "Go to the shop where you used to buy your suits and pick out the one you want; it's on me."

Upon arriving the owner said, "David, it's really good to see you. Jerry said he wanted to buy you a suit. I've got just the one for you." I put on the conservative yet classy Italian black suit, and it fit like a glove. He gave me a white shirt and a tie to go along with it.

What fun it was to see God adding things unto me, sometimes even before I realized I had a need. A 10-year-old car came next. I got an entry level sales job before leaving the halfway house. The economy had just crashed the month I was released, September, 2008. People began losing their homes, and cars were getting repossessed. Churches were closing due to lack of tithing revenues. God birthed me out of prison during a financial famine in the land. I really had to rely on Him. Things were not always easy, but God always made a way.

Then my boss told me, "David if you cash that check it will bounce. I'm working on some funding. Just stay with us." I felt fear try to grip me. I had to give the halfway house 25% of the face value of my check that week or return there. Borrowing the money embarrassed me, but it was my only option while on home confinement. There weren't a lot of jobs available for ex-felons who had just been released from a 20-year sentence for drugs and stolen jets. My bills were stacking up, and I was seeking God's face for His provision. Inside my spirit, I had total peace, but on the outside and in my head and emotions, frustration and anger were trying to get a foothold.

On top of the mounting bills, the Lord directed me to take the money I received when preaching and sow it sacrificially into another ministry. Years earlier God had spoken a very clear verse to me about what he wanted me to

---

82   God had strategically positioned Mordecai with information to save the King's life years earlier (Esther 6:1-5). Later God caused the King to remember and reward Mordecai for his act. It's important to remember that we work unto the Lord and not to man. Man will disappoint us, but God will always reward or repay us for everything we do (Galatians 6:7-10).

do upon my release. Genesis 26:12 says, **"Then Isaac sowed in that land, and reaped in the same year a hundredfold; and the Lord blessed him."** The Holy Spirit had spoken by the internal audible voice during this experience saying, "Test me in this!" America was in a financial famine the month I was released from prison, and God was directing me to "sow, sow, and sow!"[83]

Journey Insights

God taught me about sowing finances, allowing myself to feel again, and not to lose heart. "So do not throw away your confidence; it will be richly rewarded. You need to persevere so that when you have done the will of God, you will receive what he has promised" (Hebrews 10:35-36 NIV). It took five years after I was released from prison before I realized that I had permission to feel again. Behind bars you are rarely given permission to feel. What invisible bars exist in your life that are not allowing you to feel or express your true feelings?

---

83 The only time in Scripture God commands us to test him is with tithes and offerings (**"…Test me in this…"** Malachi 3:10 NIV). He promises to throw open the floodgates of Heaven and pour down a blessing in such abundance that we won't have room to contain it. I was being tested by obeying the Lord's directive to test him! The context of Isaac receiving a hundred fold harvest "on all that he planted" that same year is found in Genesis 26:1: **"There was a famine in the land…"**

72

HEART BIBLE MINISTRY AND MY FAMILY

The Journey Continues

When I was released, it was a great joy to see in person all that God continued to do with Heart of America Prison Ministries (HEART). To say there is a need for ministry to prisoners is a vast understatement. It is certainly the heart of the Lord. Matthew 25:43-45 records Jesus words:

"I was a stranger and you did not take Me in, naked and you did not clothe Me, sick and in prison and you did not visit Me." The people answered Jesus saying, "'Lord, when did we see You hungry or thirsty or a stranger or naked or sick or in prison, and did not minister to You?' Then He will answer them, saying, 'Assuredly, I say to you, inasmuch as you did not do it to one of the least of these, you did not do it to Me.'"

Prisons are a huge fertile field of people in need of the Gospel. The United States alone has over two million incarcerated adults and another four million are on probation or parole. In total over six million adults are under correctional supervision. There is little rehabilitation of the incarcerated, and upon release, they're often worse than when they went in which is one reason that 68% are re-arrested for a new crime.

Prisoners are often isolated from loved ones and surrounded by manipulative, violent people. They're forced to look for fellowship within the criminal community. It's easy to understand why being incarcerated often perpetuates bad behavior. Lives are often filled with shame, trauma, and discouragement or denial, and when a prisoner gets out, the recidivism rate within five years of release is over 75%. Crime takes a high toll not only on the inmate and society but also on the children of inmates who suffer much trauma, stigma, and blame towards their incarcerated parents.

Is transformation possible? When I was incarcerated in Miami, I obeyed the Lord's leading to give away a leather-bound study Bible. Not a cheap paperback that becomes dog-eared right away and won't hold up for the many years an inmate endures, but a quality Bible that those on the outside sometimes take for granted. A leather-bound study Bible is the nicest "book" many inmates have ever owned. After I had given my Bible away, I received another one. Wanting to keep that one, again I felt directed to give it away, and thus a Bible distribution ministry was birthed.

The ministry grew over the years. Thousands of Bibles were sent out to inmates who were making an effort to turn their lives around. But can a prisoner's heart truly be transformed? The answer is yes. We've seen it happen again and again, with the Word of God being a critical agent for change.

How is change possible? The challenge is, most prisoners have no idea that God truly is there to help. Due to their surroundings, it's especially difficult to believe for and live any type of a hopeful, positive life. But when God shows up and draws the inmate to His love, salvation is the answer. It is sustained by the Word of God and that's when the true change takes place.

HEART began with a vision and giving away my personal study Bibles. It took root with Koren initially facilitating the ministry with funds received from Kent and others. Once my parents, Susan and Tom Hairabedian, got involved, they were both given a heart to expand the ministry, and they worked tirelessly to get Bibles to prisoners. This came as no surprise because Mom and Dad saw firsthand the effect that my salvation and Bible study had on my life and how the change in me affected others behind bars.

My sister and brother consistently demonstrated love to me as well as my parents, although I wasn't always aware of their sacrifices. Many of the things they did for me I didn't learn about until 25 years later. Carron was an incredible encouragement to me, writing to me weekly and visiting me, plus handling legal work, and her sacrifices and commitment were endless. Cary sacrificed much to pay many of my legal fees, and he supported my parents, purchasing them a new home for their retirement years. My parents, in turn, utilized their finished basement as headquarters for HEART.

Prisoners often don't understand that when they go to prison, a part of their family goes to prison with them. Sometimes, as in my case, there is a good relationship and the family sacrificially ends up having to make prison part of their life through prison visits. Others have burned their relationships, leaving spouses and former friends, and their family has been negatively affected. Sadly, many inmates never receive a visit from those on the outside. I am profoundly grateful first to God and then to my family for the way they support me. My entire family has become closer together through this overall experience and many lives, both behind and outside of prison bars, have been positively affected. **"You intended to harm me, but God intended it for good to accomplish what is now being done, the saving of many lives..."** (Genesis 50:20 NIV).

My parents took the helm of HEART in 1997 about a year before my arrival at FCI Waseca. Then, with a $500 donation from a Christian businessman, they contacted a Christian lawyer to officially incorporate HEART as a 501(c)(3) not-for-profit organization in 1998. When the lawyer heard what the Lord was doing behind bars through the ministry of Bibles to prisoners, he offered to incorporate HEART for free, and for the next few years became its corporate lawyer pro bono. All positions at HEART have been volunteer and unpaid. In 2006, my parents retired from HEART, passing their mantles to Jeff Gay (President) and others who have served in various offices and positions over the years. HEART currently has approximately 10,000 prisoners on its discipleship newsletter mailing list and an average of at least 2,000 waiting for leather-bound Bibles.

Many people have been sacrificially and tirelessly involved over the last 20 years. There have been many helpers who shipped Bibles, attended meetings, wrote newsletters, ran the database, responded to prisoner letters and requests, served as board members, and worked in countless ways under the leadership of those God raised up to lead the ministry. God has seen every effort on behalf of the prisoner.

Hundreds of people have donated financially, whether it has been out of their abundance or lack, whether free or still behind bars. Today, God has expanded HEART to reach into more than 1300 prisons with hundreds of leather-bound study Bibles. We've distributed teaching materials and a yearly campaign to send personally written Christmas cards to inmates who are on our mailing list.

The Lord's hand has been manifesting the initial two scenes in the Tree of Books vision received all the way back in 1990. The next scene He showed me involves a great multiplication of the above outreaches. So we continue because God is sending more people to remember the prisoners as if bound with them. Hebrews 13:3 (NLT) says, **"Remember those in prison, as if you were there yourself. Remember also those being mistreated, as if you felt their pain in your own bodies."**

Amazing testimonies, like the ones following, have poured in over the years from inmates deeply grateful for the help they've received from Heart Ministries:

After receiving Bibles from HEART Ministries: *In the 15 years I've spent in prison, Heart of America Ministries is the most worthwhile ministry I've found.... You have no idea how meaningful, or what an impact that a study Bible is to an inmate and the version you give of the Disciples Bible – was truly created for people like us, who so often have no one worthy or wise to turn for guidance. (Years ago, the Bible that my husband gave me was lost when I was transferred. I felt the loss of that Bible so deeply – it had become a part of me, it was like losing a best friend.) Right now I can only offer 10 stamps, but I will send whatever I can during the next two years. Once I'm released, I know I can do much more to support your organization. Thank you for your faithfulness to His service. Sincerely in Christ, Barbara, California*

Thank you for your teachings and correspondence through this past five years. I and many others whose lives you have reached out and touched with love, affection, and direction of our Lord's Word, feel so much love for you. I received my beautiful Bible today. No matter what obstacles I may face, I know I can handle all, with the help and guidance from you and, first and foremost, our Lord. Larry, Florida

I wanted to write you a note and express my deep gratitude for the awesome study Bible that I received from you. I spent the rest of the day immersed in the articles and am pleased that this Bible is both accessible and comprehensive (and I appreciate that it's durable). In fact, several of the articles address issues I had not been able to find a Biblical perspective on anywhere else (UFO's, gambling, yoga, etc.). May you continue to touch the lives of those behind bars, as you sow good seed for the Kingdom. Jeremy, Florida

My friend here in prison lost his Bible in transfer and he only had a small, tattered paperback to replace it. I remembered David's kind help, so through your ministry he received a leather-bound Study Key Bible. He was elated. I also received my own Bible, which now, three years later, is well worn and full of notes. Since I left prison, my life has changed dramatically for the better. I am attending church regularly and working in our videotape ministry. Something that began three years ago in prison with those teaching tapes now continues and is bearing fruit unto others in the free world. Praise God! I'm living proof that God can change us. Ryan, Ohio

I would like the privilege of contributing to your ministry. I cannot imagine a more worthwhile effort because I have seen the incredible joy on inmate's faces who received a Bible from you. Thank you for thinking of some of God's children who are frequently forgotten. Scott, Colorado

After receiving a personally written Christmas card, one inmate wrote: *That night when all was quiet, I put my head under my blankets and wept. I was feeling so unloved. Thank you all so much for caring for the undesirables. It's been 30 years since I cried. What a release it brought.*

Yet another one says: *I would like to take this opportunity to thank you for the Christmas card. Your gesture helped me realize what Christmas stands for.*

Christmas is about people joining in a family – the Lord's family. It isn't about gifts under a tree or dinner at Grandma's. It is a card to a prisoner, a Christmas greeting to a homeless person, giving a gift so some child might have a Christmas. It is a time for others, not me. It is a time for giving and sharing in the manner in which Jesus gave us an example. Your card reminded me of that example; for that I thank you. John, Minnesota

On the verge of suicide, one inmate wrote: *I want to thank you for the Christmas card you sent me. I have been a Believer for 30 years. But since I've been incarcerated, the enemy has done everything to keep me from spreading the love and Word of God. I'm writing to you because you were obedient to God's Word and saved my life. I was placed in Segregation (the hole) for no reason. And I was tired of the abuse by staff in the system. I had lost all hope. Well, on 12-14-09, the night I had received your card, I had made a rope and was just minutes from hanging myself. I got up on the chair and had the rope around my neck. And for some reason, known only to God, I had the card in my hand. I opened the card and read the words and the Holy Spirit said, "You see, there is somebody that cares about you." Then I saw the Scripture you wrote from Matthew 19:26 about Jesus looking at them and telling them with man this is impossible, but with God all things are possible. Tears rolled off of my face and the love of God from you came into my heart and I had new hope. So I took the rope off of my neck and got off the chair to praise the Lord. And I thanked Him for using you to save my life. Your words changed my life. Thank you and may the Lord bless you. Much love, in Christ Jesus, Tony*

Jesus Christ can change the worst person completely around. I know. I will soon be leaving this establishment as a better and new man. I will never forget you people for being there when I was in need. Thank you for encouraging me. May our wonderful Lord and Savior have His loving hands around your ministry. Ron, Minnesota

Please don't give up on prisoners. We get here through wrong living… but with help, one by one we begin to see the light. Anthony, Alabama

Journey Insights

The prisoner had received a Christmas card from HEART, and was just minutes from hanging himself. Something made him stop and read the Scripture in the card. His testimony was that a simple word of encouragement in that personally-written Christmas card stopped him from killing himself. Hebrews 13:3 (NLT) says "Remember those in prison, as if you were there yourself. Remember also those being mistreated, as if you felt their pain in your own bodies." Is God speaking to you to bless a prisoner with a Bible? If so, just do it and be someone's light in a dark place! (http://heartprisonministries.org/Prisons)

73

THE BIRTH OF A FELLOWSHIP

The Journey Continues

While on home confinement my parents' home phone rang and my Dad answered.

"Yes. Who is this? Okay, I'll get him." The next thing I knew Dad was informing me that I had a phone call.

Strange, I thought, *I'm just out of prison and someone is calling me on my parent's home phone. No one should have this number. Might as well check it out.*

"This is David."

"This is Ray." He gave me his last name and my mind raced through nine facilities and 20 years of prison to mentally connect a name with the voice. Nothing matched.

He continued, "I understand you've written a booklet?"

I paused and then responded, "I've written several booklets, Ray. Which one are you talking about?"

"Well, it's got something in it about the Holy Spirit."

My immediate response was, "*All* my booklets have something in them about the Holy Spirit. Did you hear me speak at a church?"

"Well, no."

I realized this conversation was going nowhere fast which furthered my curiosity. "Did someone give you a copy of one of my booklets?"

"No they didn't."

At this point, the thought came to me, *David, you just survived 20 years in prison only to come out to a stalker!* I pointedly said, "Where exactly did you hear about my book, Ray?"

He replied, "Well, my wife was at the UPS Store where you were getting copies made and she spotted the booklet. She looked at the back cover and saw your name and the ministry address was here in Independence. I looked up your last name in the phone book and it was listed, so I called."

Now we're getting somewhere, I thought, noticing my spirit had calmed down.

The day before we had just made another 100 copies of two of my booklets, *Hearing God 25 Different Biblical Ways*, and *What the Bible Really says on the Subject of Tongues*. "Great. I currently have two books that teach about the Holy Spirit."

"Then, if available, I'd like to buy them."

"Okay. They're five dollars each." Ray seemed to be a man of few words, but he knew what he wanted. I had a Bible distribution meeting scheduled later with one of our ministry volunteers at a local pizza place, so I invited Ray to pick up the books there.

At the restaurant, I was a bit lost in thought tasting quality pizza. *It's been 20 years since I've tasted pizza this good. Delicious!* So many simple things I was doing these days mesmerized me, including eating good pizza.

Ray arrived at our table. He handed me 10 dollars, and I handed him two booklets. Just like that he was gone and I was back to my tantalizing pizza. Two days later I received another call from Ray.

"David, I'd like to get 10 copies of each book. We have a Friday night Bible study group at my home, and I want everyone there to read one."

I asked a little bit about his background and discovered he was a reputable business owner, a family man, and we had some common friends.

"Stop by my parent's home, Ray, and the booklets would be there."

Upon arriving home, Ray had already been there to pick up the booklets. His envelope contained a 10 dollar bill. *This guy is serious about getting these booklets, I thought. He's already come and gone. But, this is strange, he only paid us 50 cents per copy for the booklets instead of five dollars each.*

Immediately I made a decision not to be offended, but rather rejoice that the Gospel message about my friend the Holy Spirit was about to be released in a local Bible study. The Holy Spirit brought to mind Psalm 119:165 (KJV), **"Great peace have they which love thy law: and nothing shall offend them."** I thanked the Lord for helping me make a conscious decision not to allow offense to settle in, remembering that doing so often prevents the receipt of a blessing down the road.

The next call from Ray was an invitation to share my testimony at his house church on a Friday night. How delightful it was not to be dealing with offense from the booklet issue, and instead to be grateful for the speaking invitation. I contacted the halfway house to receive permission to be away from my home confinement monitoring box for the evening.

"You've got three hours, Hairabedian. If you're not back home by 9 p.m., you're in in violation." At every turn I found opportunities to be humbled and wearing this monitoring device basically being tracked, was just another in the long list. *God, I'm going to thank You, every time I notice these choices to be irritated and inconvenienced, or to be grateful and trusting that You're leading the way. Please help me with every decision.* To help make light of the situation we referred to the monitor as my friendship bracelet from the Feds.

So, I agreed to be back on time and on Friday night, I arrived, with expectancy, at a rural house in Independence, Missouri, located off the GPS grid. *Here we go, Lord. Ministry to a few or many, behind bars or at a home church, I'm Yours to command. May Your Kingdom come this night.*

Ray warmly greeted me. He then introduced me to his delightfully gracious wife, Pam, who had spotted the booklet at the UPS Store. The house was full of about 35 people, ready to hear what the former convict had to say about "his Friend," the Holy Spirit.

A couple named Jim and Barbie came to me and Jim asked, "You don't mind if I record this, do you?"

"Not at all," I said, smiling. "I always want to be accountable for what I say from the pulpit." Jim smiled at me and nodded.

This little congregation was birthed primarily from a group of local church people who were dissatisfied with the denomination in which they had been raised. They wanted more of the Holy Spirit. For the next 90 minutes, I preached on the power of the Holy Spirit from the Book of Acts, and in the process, gave my testimony.

We then moved into what I refer to as "laboratory time," because people need a safe environment to practice doing what Jesus did and demonstrated. I invited the congregation to do what they read about in Scripture, teaching how to lay hands on the sick in Jesus' Name, expecting the power of the Holy Spirit to come with immediate results. The first woman had a frozen shoulder. I directed her husband to lay hands on her and command the shoulder to be released, healed, and restored in Jesus' Name. Instantly the power of God went into her shoulder and she was able to raise it up about 50% of the way. She began to cry with a measure of relief. The pain had also diminished by half.

We rejoiced, and I said, "This is good, but Jesus never said, 'Rise up and limp.'" They thought about it and agreed. Then I directed the woman to lay her own hand on her shoulder and make the same command again. This time, the power of God hit her deeper and she was fully restored. She began to weep with tears of joy. The power of the Lord was present to heal (Luke

5:16 NIV), and many started receiving a healing touch from the Holy Spirit.

I looked at my watch and realized it was yellow warning time to get my ankle bracelet back to my home-confinement monitor, or be in violation. I told the people I had to go! The Holy Spirit directed me to call out words of knowledge of sicknesses and diseases that Jesus wanted to heal them from as they stood in front of their chairs. Eczema, knee problems, breast cancer, spirits of fear, and numerous other things were addressed in the Name of Jesus, and God touched His children with his healing and delivering power in a matter of two minutes time. I jumped in my car and was home five minutes before the monitor would have sent the alarm signal.

As I reflected on the evening, I was consumed with God's goodness and faithfulness to His promises. It didn't take long to enter a wondrous time of prayer, there in my basement bedroom in my parent's home.

God, You are faithful. Here I am, just barely on the outside, and You've already brought forth a group of Believers with whom I can worship. They're hungry to know of You, God, and I'm grateful. My five years of parole hasn't even begun and You're already putting me to work. Thank You, God. Thank You.

Journey Insights

This little congregation was birthed primarily from a group of local church people who wanted more of the Holy Spirit. They knew there had to be something more to their walk with God than what they had. For the next 90 minutes I preached on the power of the Holy Spirit from the Book of Acts and God showed up to touch this little church group with His love, healing, and miracles. Are you hungry for more of the Holy Spirit? He's waiting for you to cry out to Him!

74

THE BLOW BEFORE THE BREAKTHROUGH

The Journey Continues

One morning a week before Easter I received a phone call from a former prisoner from Texas. He'd been faithfully supporting our Bible ministry for several years, beginning behind bars, and then increasingly after his release. He spoke in a very sober and direct tone.

"David, the Lord told me to write you a letter of a personal nature." He paused long and then said, "Can you please give me your address? This letter is between you and me only."

After getting off the phone, my heart sank. Heart Prison Ministries was moving forward and the small fellowship connection had opened a ministry outlet. All of that was good, but the lack of funds to operate in my personal life brought with it a constant tension and temptation to bemoan my circumstances. It took tremendous diligence and focus meditating in the Word to remain hopeful. I'd remind myself that biblical hope is expecting God's goodness in everyday life, and faith is built upon that hope, yet when I heard his very serious tone, my thoughts raced, heading in a less-than-hopeful direction.

What else could go wrong? He's probably sending a prophetic word of rebuke. Are we now also losing the ministry's number one supporter? Is this my own personal black Monday?

I collapsed on my face before God and cried out, "Lord Jesus, help me pass this test. Again, if I'm somehow deceived, just tell me. I'll quit the ministry and get a regular job. I'll serve you in whatever capacity you require, just speak and I'll obey!"

The everyday stress of seemingly not having enough regardless of my efforts was mounting. I was involved in a less than secure business endeavor with another former prisoner who I'd discipled in Christ 10 years earlier. He had offered me what seemed like a solid business opportunity using my laptop computer online. Our agreement was that he would send me 50% of the profits. This would offset the uncashable checks on which I had to pay 25%. With my help, this online business in his name was now making $1,000/week. The $500 he said he'd sent was delayed and I desperately needed it. I called again and asked where the money was. He finally confessed.

"Uh, David, I don't know how to tell you this, so I'll just say it. I spent it on drugs." My blood boiled. *He'd returned to drug use and spent it!*

I was silent and furious, and just spoke to God in my mind. *He's back on drugs, God! He took what was mine and blew it!*

The Holy Spirit said, "Forgive him."

Lord, I'm broke. The U.S. economy is in a shambles. I'm sitting on three thousand dollars of rubber checks! Pastors are stealing my offerings to help pay their own bills, and now this Christian just snorted the income from the business I helped build!

Psalm 20:7 (NIV) rose in my spirit. "Some trust in chariots and some in horses, but we trust in the name of the LORD our God," followed by the same prompting, "Forgive him."

This backslidden businessman who I'd trusted hadn't spoken a word since his confession. The silence was deafening until I obeyed the Holy Spirit. Quietly and slowly I uttered words that were confusing, even to me. "I forgive and release you."

This was Good Friday of 2009, and forgiving did not *feel* good. We were still speaking as I walked into my bedroom and discovered a letter. It was from the former prisoner from Texas, the man who'd been faithfully supporting the ministry who'd called one week before Easter, the man whose serious tone had me imagining bad news. Hanging up from one difficult call, I read the letter, written in Spanish, as a check fell out.

Translating his words, I was stunned. *David, the enclosed check is from God the Boss, for you. It's not for the Bible ministry, but to be used for YOUR personal needs as God's servant. God told me to send it directly to you. God Bless.*

Overjoyed, it dawned on me that it was larger than any personal donation or offering I'd ever received. I opened my electronic phone book to call and thank him and my mind went blank. For the life of me, I couldn't remember his name. *How can this be?* I wondered as I never seemed to have trouble with recall.

Suddenly the Holy Spirit said, "Why don't you first thank God your Boss?" Immediately, I fell to my knees in gratitude praising God, *my Boss*, for His provision. God, my Boss, had spoken to a man in Texas about my need amidst my doubt and discouragement. His Presence washed over me, as I asked Him to forgive me for my discouragement. He is always the answer and He always has answers. I realigned my heart then and there to keep my eyes on "my good and perfect Boss", regardless of my circumstances. After several minutes of worship, He opened my mind to remember the donor's name. I called, thanking him for being the extended hand of the Lord's miracle provision, and we rejoiced together at the goodness of the Lord.

Lord, thank You for this reminder. There are many serving You faithfully. Bless them with knowing what You've reminded me, that it does not matter if people reward us for our labor of love unto You. We're not to lose our confidence. You want us to stand firm, trusting You, knowing that You always take care of us after we do what You want us to do (Hebrews 10:35-36).[84]

The first thing I did with the money was tithe and give an offering to the Lord from this unexpected bountiful harvest. The Holy Spirit directed me to give to two fruitful, soul-winning, TV ministries that had blessed me through their broadcasts and with free ministry materials, during the years I'd been incarcerated. I then brought my bills current and paid back the personal loans. I was debt free overnight!

Now my college tuition was current and I was also able to complete the final two courses for a bachelor's degree in Theology from the Bible College in Florida. This college had been gracious enough to grant me a scholarship for all the classes completed while incarcerated, but upon release, the school rightly required me to pay for the final three classes. After completing these courses, my supervised release officer approved my request to travel to Florida for graduation.

I used the remaining funds to pay for plane tickets and hotel rooms for my parents and me. As we flew I couldn't help but remember all of the atrocious, arduous flights I'd taken, bound in chains, when moving from prison to prison. Sometimes what would have been an afternoon flight took a week or even two to reach our destination. This time, I enjoyed the simplicity of flying directly to our location, with the gracious assistance of real flight attendants, generously offering coffee, water, and soda pop.

This is the first time I've been in Florida as a free man since my arrest, 22 years ago! I'd been preaching and teaching the Gospel for more than 20 years, but as the dean of the Bible College handed me a diploma, he informed me with a smile that I was now officially licensed "to marry and bury!" God had privately credentialed me in a prison cell more than two decades earlier, and now He had publicly credentialed me a second time before men. I knew He had a purpose for all of this and was confident new doors would soon open to share the love of God with others.

---

84 Hebrews 10:35-36, **"Therefore do not cast away your confidence, which has great reward. For you have need of endurance, so that after you have done the will of God, you may receive the promise."**

Journey Insights

God told me to forgive the man that robbed me of hard-earned money and the pastors that named the Name of Christ yet withheld the offerings designated to me. I forgave them and decided to trust God for my provision. The next day a check was mailed to me for an amount that more than took care of all my needs and helped me become debt free. Do you have unforgiveness toward someone or people that have hurt or betrayed you? Ask God now to help you let go and break the cords.

75

FROM HOUSE CHURCH TO THE NATIONS

The Journey Continues

The house church met every other Friday night. After being released from five months of home confinement, we began to meet weekly while I served five years of supervised release. There were numerous people who helped behind the scenes with filming, audio, hospitality, printing, etc.

The Holy Spirit directed me to bring the dozens of ministry books I'd received in prison from Koren, and share these resources with the group. In that moment, I saw what was like a movie of those nearly 20 years, with inmates growing in the faith because people on the outside had invested their personal resources into our lives. Someone blessed me with a Bible. I gave it away at the Holy Spirit's direction and someone else blessed me with another Bible. I saw the flow of Bibles and resources as nourishment being fed to the hungry, locked in prison.

God, thank You for touching the hearts of people to invest in the lives of people like me behind bars. Thank You for all of the materials, and especially Bibles, that have been sent to the prisons. I'm amazed how some of the same materials that You used to help me grow in the faith behind bars, are now being used with civilians on the outside!

The congregation now began learning what I'd learned behind bars. Many of the people were hungry for the deeper walk with the Holy Spirit. One man named Mike, who had been a pastor in several congregations over a 30-year period, boldly prayed for and saw many healings in his church. The good news? People were receiving healing. The other news? Church leadership instructed him to leave his denomination. He later stated, "David, this was the best thing that could happen to me. My wife and I now freely serve Jesus first, instead of focusing primarily on our denomination."

The fire was catching, and it all started with a housewife spotting a booklet about the Holy Spirit sitting on a copy machine at a UPS Store. A few years later I joked with Ray about the $10 for the 20 booklets.

"What are you talking about?" he asked. As it turned out, Ray had been having vision problems during that season and actually thought he'd placed a $100 bill in the envelope for the 20 $5 booklets. Embarrassed, he immediately offered to pay for them.

"That's not necessary, Ray. Look what the Lord has done over the last 36 months!" I laughed. "Boy, I'm sure glad the Holy Spirit teaches us not to be offended or we might have missed a genuine move of God."

It was 2010 and we'd been meeting at the house for a little over a year when we began to sense it was time to move. Our time there had been incredibly intimate with the Lord, and the gracious and sacrificial hospitality of Ray and Pam was nothing like I'd ever experienced. The Lord was calling us to expand into a larger location. We moved the gathering to a room at a hotel for many months, and then we eventually shared a lease on a building with another fellowship. We called the gathering Eagle Heart Fellowship. Each week videos were recorded of the service with a $100 pocket camera on a tripod. A friend taught me how to upload these onto YouTube for others to access. Those who couldn't attend service would watch later in the week online. *A virtual church was forming.*

People from around the world began watching online and subscribing to our YouTube Channel. Audio CD's were recorded during these services and eventually 25 different teaching series were created and offered on our website. Unbeknownst to me, the Holy Spirit was orchestrating something much, much bigger! Each week the Presence of God seemed to be increasing. Healings and miracles were occurring in almost every service.

Testimonies were coming forth. One woman who had titanium metal in her back from surgery, was still in great pain and had limited mobility. I remembered what God taught me about His ability to bend surgical metal in prison. That day she was completely healed by Jesus. Pain meds were no longer needed their pain meds and returned to work. Their doctor was flabbergasted when new x-rays showed the metal had either bent into a different direction to allow for mobility, or completely disappeared.

Invitations to speak at churches around the country were coming in online. I was still limited on travel because of the five years of federal supervised release. I petitioned the court for early release from parole but my request was denied. Invitations from Taiwan and Indonesia were coming in. I requested permission for international travel to Taiwan. My supervised release officer verbally approved it.

One morning I was walking from my bedroom to my bathroom when suddenly I had a vision in the large mirror that covered the wall over the sink area. It was the same evil Asian prince dressed in ancient military garb that had manifested in my Leavenworth prison cell 22 years earlier. The first time my co-defendant was present and we were experiencing a powerful prayer time in my cell. I'd been speaking in tongues with interpretation as a young Christian when this evil spirit manifested. This time instead of fear, a supernatural feeling of authority and power came upon me. With unusual boldness, I pointed directly in the face of the demonic Asian Prince and said, "I'm coming for you!" The spirit just glared back at me defiantly, and then turned and walked off into the distance of the mirror, as if to say, 'I'll be waiting…'"

Just before we purchased tickets to Taiwan, I was informed by my supervised release officer that the Court would *not* grant my travel request for ministry. The reason was that the U.S. didn't yet have an extradition treaty with Taiwan. What a rollercoaster. I felt like the carpet was repeatedly being pulled out from under me. *What was God doing?* Shortly after that, an unexplained sickness came upon me which lasted weeks. My energy was zapped. I continued to preach on Friday nights and upload videos each weekend.

Finally, a minister friend prayed over me and said, "The Holy Spirit tells me to break off Asian witchcraft that has been sent against you." He prayed in the authority of Jesus' Name and instantly the sickness left my body and strength returned.

Witchcraft is real. Few people in the United States realize the battle that rages in the heavenlies over souls. The Apostle Paul was very familiar with spiritual warfare and evangelism. He said, in 1 Corinthians 16:9, before entering another nation to preach the Gospel, **"For a great and effective door has opened to me, and there are many adversaries."** He learned there is a spiritual and often a physical price to pay for winning souls to Christ.

Paul was repeatedly beaten, whipped, thrown in prison, stoned, etc. A further study of Taiwan revealed that at the time, only 2% of the nation was Christian. It was legal in some parts of Indonesia to kill Christians. God was indeed opening a door, but the adversarial spiritual forces over that nation didn't plan to roll out the red carpet nor give up the souls that were captive under its control. While waiting out my remaining supervised release I had the privilege of helping facilitate three ministers to preach 21-day tours in Taiwan over the next three years through these wonderful Taiwanese Christian contacts. The opposition was simply a confirmation that God was moving us from house church to the nations. What came next would astound us.

Journey Insights

"Great peace have those who love Your law, and nothing causes them to stumble" (Psalm 119:165). This Scripture became poignant to me as I was assimilating back into society and God was expanding my ministry. It looked as if my friend had shorted me the money and I could have assumed the worst, but in reality he couldn't see well and thought he'd paid $100 instead of $10. Being offended is a choice. Are you easily offended, harboring an offense against others, and possibly losing out on a bigger blessing?

76

BROTHER, CAN YOU SPARE A DIME?

The Journey Continues

The Lord introduced me to a minister in Nigeria, West Africa, through a friend who was a pastor in the United States. They'd preached in Nigeria together. This Nigerian-born, Igbo speaking evangelist had won several million people to Christ during his 35 years of service to the Lord. He'd ministered throughout the U.S. in churches, on Christian television, and in two of my friend's churches.

When the U.S. economy tanked, the Nigerian evangelist lost funding support, literally crippling his ministry. He eventually lost his housing and $150,000 in crusade equipment that was inside the house. Reduced to living on the street with his wife and children, after serving the Lord faithfully in radio, TV, crusade, and church ministry for three decades was a terribly difficult time for this family. There's an old saying, "When America sneezes the third world countries catch a cold." This maxim was true in this servant's case.

The Holy Spirit told me to personally sow into his ministry. When I did, it came as no surprise that the Lord directed someone to refill my personal coffers *the next day*. I knew the Lord was preparing to do something significant through this relationship despite his circumstances or mine. During that trying time, the Lord called the evangelist and his small ministry team to a 30-day fast. They also stepped out in faith to prepare for a miracle crusade in a rural area of West Africa, even though they had no money and were homeless themselves.

The Holy Spirit instructed me to share the vision to help raise funds for the upcoming crusade. As I prayed and meditated on God's Word, the Lord gave me a message entitled, "Brother, Can You Spare a Dime?" In a vision, I'd been shown to lay a dime on each chair before the people walked into Eagle Heart Fellowship. On the night of our service, each person picked up the dime and sat in their chairs.

"This is a roll of 50 dimes," I told them while holding up the object lesson. "It's a mere five dollars. Our congregation has been given the opportunity, a divine opportunity, to literally fund the spread of the Gospel in Nigeria for only 10 cents per soul."

Everyone in the congregation seemed riveted as I went on to explain this situation taking place across the world, 6,500 miles away. "The rural area the Nigerian ministry team is going into has no electricity or running water. The average income is $300-500/year, yet gasoline sells for six dollars a gallon." I thought of Christ's instruction immediately before He ascended and took His place at the right hand of the Father. He said, **"...Go into all the world and preach the gospel to every creature"** (Mark 16:15).

"We've been given an opportunity to send the Gospel to a place filled with Muslims, Hindus, Sheiks and witch doctors, the latter of which control people through fear, spells, incantations, hexes, voodoo and black magic."

When God wants something to happen in the earth, He first calls people to prayer. Heaven then responds with the provision. God also graciously sent Pastors Dan and Patricia Jensen from Independence, Missouri, to partner with us. They stepped up sacrificially to fully support this opportunity with their congregation in prayer, finances, and fasting. To this day, we all share a wonderful fellowship that was forged during this initial partnering in the harvest.

The funds came in through our two small congregations for the evangelist to rent K-27 generators, crusade lights, and a sound system in Nigeria. The crusade was beginning to take shape! They also needed generator fuel, bottled water for the workers, rice and beans for food, and batteries for flashlights to help safely usher tens of thousands of people. We were thrilled as a body of Believers when all the money came in, and we learned their crusade team was incredibly encouraged.

The Lord allowed for a supernatural power encounter a week before the crusade was to start. Two witch doctors, whose family-generations had controlled the people for 60 years in this city, vehemently opposed the crusade. They mocked the evangelist and his team, threatening them with black magic and sudden death if they didn't leave the city of 260,000 people by nightfall.

"God has sent my team and me into this city to preach the Gospel," he responded. "I warn you not to get in the way of what God is doing, or you may reap what you intend for us." He quoted Psalm 7:14-16, **"Behold, the wicked brings forth iniquity; Yes, he conceives trouble and brings forth falsehood. He made a pit and dug it out, And has fallen into the ditch which he made. His trouble shall return upon his own head, And his violent dealing shall come down on his own crown."**

Ignoring the threats, the evangelism team continued to walk and pray for several hours. Upon arriving in one area of the city, they discovered many people gathered around two large stones.

"What is this area?" He asked with authority, given him by the Lord.

"These are the *speaking stones*," they answered, with great reverence. The evangelist knew they were associated with witchcraft, the speaking stones were a demonic tool used to deceive the people. The two witch doctors were making money and controlling the people. The evangelist understood what the Bible says, **"Our battle is not against flesh and blood, but the unseen powers of darkness"** (Ephesians 6:12). The witch doctors were sleeping in their makeshift houses at the time.

"These stones speak only by the power of demons," the evangelist said. "They are lying spirits! Jesus is the way, the truth, and the life. He wants you to know the truth. Do you want to know the truth that brings freedom? Jesus is the Son of God and He has ALL power! Do you want to be set free?"

"Yes, we want to be free!" The crowd that had gathered around this prayer team had become emboldened, that in Jesus' Name, they could come against the witchcraft control they were under. They roared in unison, enthusiastically responding to the evangelist's question.

He then took authority over the spirits that enabled the stones to speak. "In the Name of Jesus I command you demon spirits to leave the stones and the area NOW!" When he said this, the stones began to shake and a horrible scream came from *inside the stones*. These evil spirits manifested, flying 30 feet into the air, hovering above the people briefly, and disappearing as the Presence of God descended upon the place. Those who'd witnessed this accepted Jesus as the one true God right then and there! They willingly and joyously renounced all witchcraft in response to the evangelist's teaching and prayer. (How important it is to be willing and prepared to lead people to Christ when the opportunity avails itself!)

While he continued to teach them about Jesus, two men came from the city shouting breathlessly, "Minutes ago the two head witch doctors *died in their sleep!* We are free from their witchcraft!" The people began rejoicing with all their hearts right there in the area where the stones remained. It was with this anointing that the next seven nights of crusades resulted in *35,000* souls coming to Christ. Crusade pictures, testimonies, and video footage, captured on an old VHS Recorder, were sent back to Eagle Heart Fellowship. We were thrilled.

Five months later our fellowship raised about $15,000 and funded the second crusade. This time 170,000 souls came to Christ in 21 days. The Scriptures promise, **"For nothing restrains the Lord from saving by many or by few"**

(1 Samuel 14:6).

During the crusade, God was setting the people free from fear and tormenting spirits that had harassed their families in this village for more than 60 years. The witch doctors were making their living from the people's pain and suffering. In the night, they'd perform incantations, spells, hexes and send curses against the sleeping people. Demons would then go out and torment, attack, sexually molest, and physically assault the people. Demonic spirits are real and incredibly evil! The villagers would commonly yell and scream with fear throughout the night in their native Igbo tongue, *"Metromacha! Metromacha!"* This translates, "He touched me! He touched me!" The person was reacting to being attacked, tormented, molested, or physically assaulted by an evil spirit they couldn't see.

The victims would then to come to the witch doctor to remove the curse and restore their peace. The price for this service varied. They'd have to bring what they could afford whether it was a bag of vegetables or a live chicken. They were required to pay to be protected! The witch doctor would either take the vegetables and pray a curse-breaking spell or incantation over them, or cut off the chicken's head, sprinkle blood on the person's face and chest, accompanied by a prayer, and send them on their way. The witch doctor would, of course, keep the rest of the chicken for themselves. It's like spiritual search engine marketing. Sending out emails until you get a response. In this case, the emails are demons!

During the crusade one night, the evangelist called me from the mountainside where he could get a cell phone signal from the large city of Lagos many miles away. He told me, "David, we are out of generator fuel. It costs about $300/ night."

"Why aren't you at the crusade?" I asked.

"There is no reason for me to be there. This is night 14 of a 10-day crusade. The Holy Spirit has taken over the services. The people show up and I don't even preach anymore. They start to worship God and the miracles begin as they call on Jesus. I just watch." His joy and excitement were tangible and all I could do was rejoice with him.

"Right now they are singing 'Hallelujah' in the dark, in unison. They've been singing this song for over three hours. Jesus is appearing to them individually and tumors are falling off their bodies. Blind eyes are opening. Deaf ears are popping open. And for the first time in their lives they are using the word, 'Metromacha' in a positive sense. They are yelling out, 'Jesus, Metromacha, Jesus Metromacha! Jesus, *He* touched me, Jesus, He touched me!' And David, they are being made whole!"

The following day the evangelist called me on his little flip phone with pre-paid minutes and said, "David, is it REALLY you?"

I said, "Yes Brother, it's really me. Why do you ask?"

"It's a miracle!"

"What's a miracle?"

"That I'm actually talking to you from here!"

I laughed and said, "No, this is not a miracle, it's called a cell phone. And we've talked by cell phone dozens of times."

"Brother David, you do not understand. I'm in the rural area of Nigeria, the witch doctors are the only ones who can sometimes get a cell phone signal from the mountain. God always gives me a cell phone signal when I need to talk to you from the mountain. This frustrates the witch doctors. But I am not calling you from the mountain. I'm calling you from the crusade grounds! No one has EVER had a cell phone signal from the flatlands! This is a miracle!" His enthusiasm was contagious as he continued sharing the what God was doing.

"The Holy Spirit told me to call you from here and I argued with him. But now I am talking with you. He has a divine purpose for this! I will call you back in a few hours when the crusade is going on! There will be about 45,000 people present!" He hung up and I pondered the significance of what just occurred.

A few hours later on the highway while driving my car using the modern day miracle of cruise control and listening to worship music and praying in the Holy Spirit, I heard a call in my ear. This, of course, came through the modern day miracle of a bluetooth device.

"This is David," I said, answering through my earpiece.

A voice filled with authority responded back, "Pastor David Hairabedian, this is evangelist so and so from Nigeria, West Africa. The crusade is in full swing here and Jesus is Lord! I have you on speaker phone. Please say hello to the people!"

Not fully understanding the scene I simply said, "Hello." To my amazement, the roar of the crowd responded back, *"HELLOOOOO!"* This sent a Holy Spirit shiver up my spine. I then said enthusiastically, "Hallelujah!" The crowd responded back, "Hallelujah!" I said, "Glory to God!" The crowd responded, "Gloorrryy to God!"

The Holy Spirit then prompted me to speak in the Igbo language the words, *"Jesus Metromacha, Jesus Metromacha!"* There was no response on their end. *Did we lose the phone signal? Did I offend them as a white man speaking Igbo?* Suddenly I heard the first voice in the crowd shout with joy and adulation, and then the entire crowd roared for about 30 seconds. I heard the evangelist's laughter.

While the huge crowd was still shouting individual praises to God, the evangelist took me off speaker phone and said, "Pastor David, you have no idea what just happened. When you said 'Hello,' the people heard it through the speaker system and responded. The same thing occurred when you said, 'Hallelujah' and 'Glory to God.' But when you spoke to them in their native Igbo tongue, two miracles occurred. First, the Holy Spirit guided your tongue with a perfect Igbo accent, which they have never before heard spoken by a white man. Second, the words 'Jesus Metromacha' didn't come just through the speaker system. We heard these words from around the crusade grounds, and it reverberated throughout our bodies!"

He finished the astounding conversation, telling me, "I will call you tomorrow!" And hung up. A world away, I smiled, giving thanks to Jesus, thinking of that simple request, *brother, can you spare a dime?*

Journey Insights

When God wants something to happen in the earth He first calls people to prayer. Heaven then responds with provision. "For nothing restrains the Lord from saving by many or by few" (1 Samuel 14:6). The witch doctors put very real witchcraft curses onto the people in the village. "Our battle is not against flesh and blood, but the unseen powers of darkness" (Ephesians 6:12). Do you have curses operating in your life? God wants to deliver you and break those bondages.

77

THE MIRACLE OF THE TWINS

The Journey Continues

About a year after being released from prison, a friend asked if I would come look at an investment opportunity involving a start-up he was considering. Another contact of mine was also in town who was looking for technology investment opportunities, so we attended the meeting together. The conference table was attended by several "over 40" businessmen. During the 90 minute meeting a final piece of technology was displayed for us on the presentation screen. Up until this point, we were not interested in anything they offered. This technology, however, was a potential game-changer.

I earnestly responded, "We're very interested in this piece of technology. If you can prove its authenticity and document that you have exclusivity, then I believe we can do business. Otherwise, respectfully, we are not interested in the other items you have."

The principles in the company looked at one another and then one nodded and stood up. "Wait here," he instructed. "I'll be back in a few minutes." He returned with two young men who looked about 18 years old. Later we discovered they were actually 23. We also discovered something that would prove to be life-altering.

Wearing high end monogrammed dress shirts with jeans, they were introduced. "Gentlemen, I want to introduce you to Austin and Zach, who, by the way, are twins." Austin began to explain the technology and as he spoke, we were both amazed at the clear teaching and presentation gift he had. The words flowed effortlessly from his mouth. When his twin brother Zach took over and finished the presentation, with the same type of articulate flow, I thought, *both of them have a remarkable level of communication.*

Jokingly I whispered to my friend, "In some ways they remind me of myself at their age, only they're smarter and they're legal!" He didn't laugh. Instead, he looked at them and then looked at me, twice. I bumped his arm and laughed, and he responded briefly with a small smile. Then he looked at them, and then peered into my eyes briefly and then looked back at them again. *He's acting strange,* I thought.

The twins gave us their business card and we exchanged phone numbers.

We met a few days later with their older business partner. We had follow-up meetings on two more occasions in person, and then three times by conference call with a subject matter expert on our side to properly vet the technology. We got to know them on a personal level. They shared they were adopted at birth and raised in a Leawood, Kansas home by Jewish parents.

Their parents required them to read several books a week in addition to their homework. Bedtime was 8:30 p.m. and inside their room they discovered a new e-commerce company called eBay. *At age 11,* they applied for an account and launched a business! *These guys are astonishing,* I thought, totally engrossed in their story. They attended Jewish youth group at the local synagogue, at age 13 they had a Jewish bar mitzvah, and also achieved super-seller status on eBay.

Everyone was quiet while learning more about the twins. At age 15 they learned web design and development when the web was still just on dial-up speed. They sold websites to the parents of their high school students, giving an affiliate fee to the student for the introduction. They were building websites for half the price and doing a better job than the professional companies. The parents were saving money, the students were making cash for the introduction, and the twins were striking it rich for high school students and all parties were happy. By age 17 the twins were designing graphics and websites for Fortune 500 companies.

Their senior year Austin received a text message while sitting in class. It was from an attorney representing a company that was interested in buying their web-hosting company. The twins earlier had researched the industry and determined that the vast majority of people who purchased a hosting account never put up a website. With this statistic, they ran the additional numbers and determined they could offer unlimited hosting at half the price larger companies were offering for a single website. After marketing their company online people started piling on to their platform, and just as the twins had projected, only about 17 percent of the people actually put up a website. Somehow the business model they created while still in high school had grabbed the attention of a larger hosting company.

Austin stepped out of class to respond to the call. He sold their company for a sizeable sum in his high school hallway. With their newfound capital gains "problem", they could either use it or lose it to taxes. They decided to purchase enough private chartered jet hours, complete with a private pilot and stand-by limousine, for the next year! They did all of this while still in high school. These two young men were fascinating.

The current piece of technology my friend wanted to invest in took us about 90 days to complete the vetting process. Then I received the phone call that became one of my life-changing, defining moments.

It was the Monday morning before Thanksgiving. The twins' older partner called me. "David, how are you this morning?"

I replied with a silly cliché, "If it got any better for me, I'd have to be twins just to contain the joy!"

He laughed, a little harder than usual, and spoke somewhat slowly, "Well... speaking of the twins, I told you they were adopted." I pointed out that it was truly an amazing story. Abruptly he seemed to change the subject as he nonchalantly asked, "By the way, did you ever date a girl by the name of Angelique?"

Surprised by the direction to the conversation, I thought back and jarred my memory. "Wow, that's a name from the past. Yeah, it was a short term relationship. I think she was a runway model I met in a bar. It only lasted a few weeks."

He persisted in his questioning. "How old were you?"

The oddity of the conversation intrigued me. "About 21 I guess."

Strangely, he said, "Uh huh. How old are you now?"

I kept answering his questions but had no idea where he was headed. I replied, "45" and that seemed to send him into deep thought. He had paused for a time, took a breath, and said, "Uh-huh, yeah, that's about right."

"David, the twins are heading to Canada on business. They needed their birth certificates, so they stopped by their adoptive parent's house. Evidently they've never known the names of their biological mother or father." I already knew this as they'd told me so in one of our meetings.

He went on, "Inside their legal box they discovered a 1986 one page adoption decree folded up in an envelope they'd never seen before. The names of their biological parents were on the decree."

I liked these young men and was genuinely happy for them. I said, "Wow, that's wonderful! I'm so happy for them."

"David, the name of the biological mother is Angelique, adding her full name."

I thought for a moment and then explained, "Angelique had gone by different names, but it's possible this is her. No one ever saw her pregnant. She disappeared for about eight months and then reappeared on the scene, looking just the same. She never mentioned this to anyone. God bless her for not aborting them!"

"David, the biological father was also named."

I thought for a moment. *I'm guessing the twins want me to call a cyberspace contact I know who can probably track down the father for the reunion.* A small swelling of pride rose up in me. *Fresh out of prison I'll be able to help locate the father for these astute young men.* I was excited, looking forward to helping these 'kids' that I respected and liked.

Jarring me out of my thoughts, his next words spoken slowly to me rocked my world. "The name of the biological father on the birth certificate is *David C. Hairabeeian.* The spelling is close to yours. It could be a typo, 'd' versus an 'e'. By the way, what's your middle name?"

Stunned, I answered, "My middle name is Caleb, spelled with a 'C.' It's *me!*"

Surprised at how quickly I responded, he questioned, "How do you know?"

"This is all a confirmation of a vivid dream I had when they were 11 years old." I'd learned years ago that God spoke to me through dreams, and I respected and remembered this particular incredibly unusual dream. "I was speaking to a congregation in the United States. After the service, I left the pulpit area to mingle with and continue ministering to any remaining people. A young man approached me who appeared to be about 11 years of age. I knelt down on one knee and said, 'How can I pray for you, young man?'

"He said, 'I didn't come for prayer.' I then asked him what he came for and he told me that he was my biological son! Pointing backward to another young man about the same age he told me that he was his twin brother. *What kind of game is this kid playing and who put him up to it?* I thought in my dream. I first rejected this possibility, sliding backward on one knee, but looking at him and his twin brother in the distance, my whole being moved forward to embrace them.

"In the dream I broke out in tears from the depths of my spirit while saying the words, 'I'm so sorry!' I then awakened and discovered myself in tears with the Presence of the Holy Spirit covering my bed area like a canopy. I continued to cry for several minutes, which was not my normal nature. I remember wondering, *How could this be, and if so, what do I do with the information? I'm in prison! How do I test the spirits on this dream? Who would I contact? Where is the mother? What are their names?*

"The Lord gave me no more information. Yet from time to time people would ask me if I had children and I'd reply jokingly with this dream in mind, 'Not that I know of...' On a few occasions over the next 10 years, I shared privately with another prisoner, and one time with a chaplain, about the dream of being the father of twins. Each time we would pray for my possible sons, asking God to bless, guide, protect, and give them supernatural wisdom, and to keep them from making any of the mistakes and poor life choices I made that landed me in prison."

When I finished telling the dream. I was utterly still, dazed as the truth was confirmed in my head. My heart was pounding but I had no more words. I knew. I've never believed in coincidences, and it was astounding that I had been doing business with the twins.

He too was silent as he processed all I'd told him. Then came the critical question, "David, do you want to be in their life?"

My heart leaped as my spirit immediately embraced them. I wanted to shout, "Yes!" Instead I felt wisdom and respect overflowing for the twins and carefully said, "I want whatever they want. Whatever they are comfortable with, I'm comfortable with."

"Okay then. Do you want them to call you, or do you want to call them?"

"Give me about 45 minutes to process all this and pray." I took a shower, prayed, and the same Presence I'd experienced in the dream 12 years earlier returned. To me, this was a final confirmation from the Lord. I dried off and then the phone rang. It was Austin (who also had approached me in the dream). Zach was listening in the background. I told Austin what little I knew about Angelique, confirming we'd had a short term relationship that could easily have resulted in their conception. I also shared the time frame she and I were together and the detailed dream from years earlier.

Austin asked me if I had ever seen a particular movie. I said, "No, I haven't. What was it about?"

"Well, it was about a kid that didn't meet his biological father until later in life. And when the father met him he learned that the son was very successful. The father then chose to become friends with the son only because he wanted to get some of the son's money."

"That sounds like a sick movie to me." He paused, and then I realized where he was going with the conversation. I said, "Austin, just so you know, I like to make my own money!"

He laughed and said, "Yeah, us too. It's probably a DNA thing." We all laughed together. Austin then asked if we should get together.

"Absolutely," I said. "Come over to the house for dinner tonight and meet your biological grandparents for the first time. My mother, uh, your grandmother is a full-blooded Jew. My dad and your grandfather is full-blooded Armenian." I explained this made Zach and him 50 percent "Jew-manian!" We laughed again. I said, "Your biological mom is part Thai, and I believe Dutch. This may give you a better idea of your lineage. See you tonight for dinner." We hung up.

Incredibly humbled, I thought, *Wow! I serve 20 years in prison, am not in a position to be married and procreate, then suddenly am a father of 23-year-old twins in a day! God, You're such a redeemer of lost time! By now I shouldn't be surprised at Your miracles, but I am, God, and I am more grateful than I know how to put in words.*

My musings continued. *What a blessing they didn't know me the first part of their lives. I may have negatively influenced them. Now, with the changes God has made in my life, I can be a good influence.*

While I was still shaking my head at the whole thing my Dad walked by my computer desk and said, "Anything new?" That made me smile.

"Uh, yeah, a little something." For some reason I kept it somewhat nonchalant, handing him a picture of the twins I'd just printed off the Internet. "Dad, these are your two grandsons."

Dad looked at the picture, as if to say, "Yeah right!" He handed it back a bit annoyed. What made me do that? I wondered, but couldn't help smiling, knowing the truth would soon be revealed and his world be would rocked as well as mine!

I walked upstairs. My mother was getting ready to go out to an early lunch with several friends. Three of them were standing in the living room preparing to go out the door when I arrived. She said, "How are you doing? Anything new today?" In our world, this was a common question because so many God-incidents happened on a regular basis.

I handed her the picture and said, "Do these two kids look familiar?" I wanted to see if she recognized a family resemblance.

She looked at the picture, shook her head, and said, "No. Are they the Jackson brothers you used to play sports with when you were in Leavenworth?"

"No."

"Well then, they don't look familiar to me. Who are they?"

I took a deep breath, looked into her eyes, and answered. "These are your two biological grandsons."

Startled, with her friends looking on, she asked, "David, what are you talking about?"

I shared the story with her in brief. "Mom, my name is on their birth certificate dated June 1986."

She looked at the picture, and looked at me, flabbergasted, and her face filled with a bright hope. It wasn't often she was at a loss for words! Meanwhile, Dad came in, overhearing the truth, and he was visibly moved, tears welling up in his eyes. How beautiful it was for our family as we stood there astounded, each of us contemplating what this meant.

Later that evening we had a small family reunion at my parents' Missouri home. My parents, older sister, Carron, and I all had a wonderful evening of dinner and conversation with the twins. Over the next few hours, we got to know one another, asking questions, and sharing stories. We loved the conversation, taking turns laughing, talking, listening, and being stunned.

With every unusual story and life incident growing up that I shared, the twins had a similar one and vice versa. Sports, high school, business, the entrepreneurial spirit, etc. DNA can run strong in a bloodline. They left for the evening and flew to Canada on business. A couple of weeks later they were in Southern California for business and my sister set up a meeting with our older brother Cary. The twins met their uncle for the first time. Lunch turned into a thirteen-hour conversation. The twins now had the gift of discovering their biological relatives. Missing gaps in their understanding of where they came from, why they acted the way they did, thought the way they thought, etc., were answered. It was like a puzzle finally coming together.

The following month was Christmas, 2009. The twins, along with their adoptive parents, Victor and Diana, my parents (Tom and Susan Hairabedian), Cary, Carron, her son Djavan, who was the same age as the twins, all gathered at my parent's home in Missouri to spend the day together. An unusual oversized snowfall dumped on Kansas City in a matter of hours. The city was overwhelmed and businesses were shut down. The twins' sports car had low profile tires that couldn't move on a flat surface of snow, let alone up and down a hill leading to and from our home. They parked at a convenience store and we picked them up as the snow continued to fall, more than 10 inches in all.

It took three days for the city to return to normal transit. During what became a divine delay we all had time to bond as we got to know each other on a personal and deeper level as a family. We discovered things during conversation such as, the twins had hernia operations when they were kids.

My brother said, "I had a hernia operation when I was a kid."

My dad said, "I had a hernia operation too."

Djavan said, "I have a hernia now."

Everyone looked at me and said, "What about you?"

"At age eight, I had a double hernia operation!" What were the odds of every male member of the bloodline in our family having had hernias? We discovered other similarities, each one revealing itself as what we began referring to as "a DNA thing." Hairlines, the way our pants hung the same on our waist, tastes in clothing, natural bents toward technology, similar stories growing up in high school, and, of course, an early age affinity for jet airplanes!

Over the next few months, all family members on each side developed a deep respect, appreciation, and admiration for one another. There was no division, pride, competition, or anything of the sort. Rather, we all rejoiced for one another's individual investment into the twin's lives. It was, and continues to be, an amazing journey.

About six months later I answered a phone call from Austin. "David, we need a favor."

I said, "What kind?"

"We need a high-level contact at a technology company in Taiwan, and we know you have the contact who can introduce us."

He shared the name of the company. Coincidentally, I had met a wonderful Taiwanese family through our ministry. The wife was a powerful international evangelist who happened to be personal friends with the owners of the company. *What were the odds?* My response was simply, "Let me pray about it." The Lord prompted me to call the evangelist and request she pray about it. Her response was a simple, "Let me pray about it and then make a call."

The green light was given and 10 days later the twins were warmly greeted in Taiwan by the evangelist and her family, and they were on their business adventure. The twins were later told the red carpet was rolled out for them because they were, "the twin sons of Pastor David from the United States." I was greatly humbled for this Taiwanese family modeled the highest levels of integrity, humility, and respect as ministers. What an honor and privilege to introduce them to this God-given Kingdom contact. It was and is an even greater honor that the Lord redeemed my time behind bars, miraculously restoring a non-existent awareness and relationship with my two biological sons.

Journey Insights

I came out after serving 20 years in prison and in one moment found out I was the father of 23-year-old twins. Only God! Now, at this point time, I could be a positive influence to my twin sons instead of a negative one. God is not a respecter of people. He redeemed something that appeared to be impossible. Is there something you don't think can be redeemed in your life? What He did for one person, He will do for another.

78

HE WHO FINDS A WIFE FINDS A GOOD THING

The Journey Continues

A good friend, Jolene, called me and said, "David, I want you to send a friend request to a friend of mine named Joanna. She's on Facebook. We went to the same Supernatural School of Ministry together. I think you'd really like each other."

My response was immediate. "I'm not interested in dating anyone."

"No, no, no, that's not why I'm introducing you two. I think you would be great ministry friends. You'll really like her." I sent the Facebook request and didn't think about it again.

Two weeks later Jolene called me to see if Joanna had accepted the request. I looked on the computer. "Uh, no she didn't."

"Okay. I'll follow up with her." The subject wasn't discussed again, until...

A year later I was speaking in San Diego, about 90 minutes from my brother's home in Orange County. I needed a few days of rest and relaxation and I really wanted to connect with Cary and his wife. That afternoon I called Jolene and asked her if she'd like to come to eat dinner with the three of us and catch up.

"Sure, can I bring my friend, Joanna?"

"No problem, the more, the merrier."

We all went to dinner and had a lot of fun. Later that evening, Joanna, Jolene and I fellowshipped and prayed together. It was a wonderful time in the Presence of the Lord. Afterwards, she thought about how I was, in her words, "chivalrous and generous" because I opened her car door and then purchased roses for all the ladies from an elderly woman trying to make some extra income. Joanna said, "That touched my heart," and she enjoyed our time of prayer and fellowship.

Intrigued, yet having no thoughts about a potential relationship, Joanna had a major chat with God that evening. "God, You know I've been stabbed in the back by professed Christians, and they even prayed curses against me. Who is this guy? Is he really your servant or is he Mr. Joe Slick?"

God responded, "He's my servant." She knew she'd heard clearly, so she accepted my Facebook request, then sowed money into the ministry several times. It was my job to follow up with donors, so I sent an email, then called to thank her for her donation. We chatted, and over several months, became good friends, and prayed for one another's requests.

Joanna thought back on the way we'd met and said, "I liked that we became friends and I genuinely appreciated his friendship. As a friend, David was quick to be there for people in need. On Thanksgiving, my little nephew was critically sick and I messaged David to keep us in prayer. He called me *during his family's Thanksgiving dinner* to pray. It struck me he was a thoughtful, kind, and serious prayer warrior, and it was refreshing to have such an incredible friend on my side."

I too appreciated that Joanna and I had become good friends over the months. It began to dawn on me that there was no denying, Joanna was amazing. I'd never met someone on such a parallel path as mine. She wasn't like many single women I knew who seemed to just be looking for a husband. I liked that she had her eyes on her calling.

In February of 2013, I was scheduled to preach a healing service in San Diego. Joanna amazed me when, after finding out I was coming to San Diego, she took the initiative to schedule several meetings where I could share the prison ministry vision. I thought, *she actually cares about inmates receiving the Word of God.*

Her explanation of why she took action was simple. "I was shocked to find out that there are over 2,000 inmates waiting for a Bible, and many of these for up to three years!" Joanna understood the need for action. If the inmates were to get Bibles, people needed to spread the word, and she was willing to do just that where she lived. She was a woman of her word, which I found impressive, and she followed through in setting up speaking engagements for me.

Joanna had been an international ministry singer and speaker, powerfully used by the Lord, until she was exposed to toxic mold and almost died. When planning the service, I asked her to sing. "That was a divine moment for me," she said. She knew at the time I asked her that God was using it to launch her back into the singing ministry. She told me, "Little did I know that what awaited me in that small San Diego church would alter the course of my destiny."

The day of the healing service began in dramatic fashion. I was up at 4:30 a.m. and had a freak accident. As I was coming down the stairs, it felt as if someone pushed my left foot out from under me. I heard a crack as I hit the floor. Excruciating pain shot through my foot and leg, so severe that I passed out for a few seconds. When I came to I started fiercely praying in tongues over my foot.

How could I break my foot on the day of a healing service and the day Joanna was coming out to sing? I was furious. Not on my watch! I thought, and continued praying.

I was staying at a friend's home who heard all the commotion and saw the magnitude of the injury. Immediately the two of us prayed, aggressively contending for healing. I *commanded* the bones to shift back into their proper alignment. Nothing happened. My foot throbbed. I sent out an SOS text message to key prayer warriors I knew. I decided to stand on my seemingly broken foot, as an act of faith, and had my friend take a picture. I don't recommend everyone try that at home, but I was determined that I wasn't hobbling into a healing service wearing a cast.

After 45 minutes of praying, I felt the glory of God descend and rest on my foot. Then my foot literally shifted back into its proper position before our eyes! Sensing God's peace fill the room and the pain dramatically decrease from a level nine or ten to a two or three, I laughed.

"We just got the victory," I proclaimed, "and it's going to be a great service tonight."

Remaining vigilant to hold on to my healing, I rested in the Presence of the Lord. The swelling decreased, but the purple, black and blue bruising increased, and a small bone still protruded. I contended for the rest of my healing and although some of the pain lingered, by the time the service began I was walking as if nothing had happened 12 hours earlier.

We arrived early at the church to meet Pastors Dane and Elizabeth and their team for prayer, and it was then my thoughts turned to Joanna. As I excused myself from the group, I turned around and there she was walking through the door. Our eyes locked and for the first time in 25 years, I felt a spark.

What? What is this? I don't get sparks!

Seven months had passed since I'd seen this woman and I couldn't believe what I saw. Joanna looked vibrant, healthy, and incredibly beautiful. My eyes went to her hair, long with soft waves, and I also noticed those very attractive boots she was wearing.

Shake it off! I thought. *This doesn't happen to me.* I respectfully greeted her with a friendship hug. As she looked at me, she averted her eyes. Did she have a spark too? *Get it together, David!* I told myself again. I tried convincing myself that this spark only seemed to happen because of my broken foot trauma. *Am I in denial?* I wondered.

That evening I was struck by how humble, loving, and servant-oriented Joanna was as she ministered. She looked regal as she prayed, tender and kind, and I was drawn to the love of God flowing through her. When I experienced yet another spark, I thought, *What? NO! This is ridiculous.* Earlier a friend of mine at the service had told me that Joanna was "the one" which dumbfounded me. I felt like I was experiencing warfare, first with the foot, and then with this situation with Joanna.

The last time I'd preached here God had rocked the house with all kinds of incredible healings and miracles and people were expecting the same. As I looked out at the audience, I felt no Presence of God. No anointing. No leading of the Holy Spirit. I read the keynote verse for the teaching. It was dead as a doornail. I read it again. It was even deader. I looked at Joanna and she looked away, then she suddenly got up and left. This service was in trouble.

God, I thought, *what's going on? Speak to me, quicken a verse, give me a word of knowledge, something please!* Nothing came. I closed my notes and said, "God's not in the sermon I had planned tonight. We're going to wait on the Lord to see what He wants to do." Then, Joanna returned, and after catching her eye, I asked her to come up and sing.

She smiled, took the mic and started speaking fluent Hebrew, translating into English. *What?? She speaks Hebrew??* She broke into beautiful acapella song and the Presence of God came in like a flood. I continued praying and praising as people wept, falling on their knees, praising God with hands lifted up in worship. I was speechless.

In the midst of the Presence of God descending, a third spark happened as I looked at Joanna. God pierced through a crack in my heart at that moment. People were getting set free of demonic bondages, inner healing was taking place, and God showed me Joanna was one of the most incredible spiritual warriors I'd met. That excited me! Then a memory came to me, of a discussion I'd had in prison with God about wanting a wife who could sing acapella.

Joanna tells of that evening that she too had observed my life and the way I ministered to others. "David's name means 'Beloved of God.' We know that in Acts 13:22 King David is referred to as 'a man after God's own heart' and this describes what I see in David." Prior to the meeting she had asked the Lord for gift ideas that would honor me and, in her words, "would cause him to be speechless from feeling so blessed." She said, "After that prayer, the idea came to me to ask my chocolatier to create one of her exquisite chocolate art pieces for David. I brought his gift of honor to the meeting and awaited God's timing to present it."

"I also asked the Lord for a powerful Presence of God when I sang, that would knock David off his rocker. Little did I know how God would answer my prayers! When I arrived at the church, I saw him. Our eyes locked and I had a spark." Just like I had, Joanna also tried to deny the spark, and in her words, "I pretended it wasn't there, all the while wondering, hmmm…is he attracted to me too?"

She instructed herself to stay focused, for she was here to minister. When Joanna realized there was no anointing on the preaching, she said, "The Holy Spirit prompted me to go pray in the bathroom. I start doing warfare prayer and commanding the Angels of the Lord into the house and releasing an open Heaven of God's Presence into the room."

The service lasted three and a half hours that night! We prayed for people, cast out demons and many received all kinds of healings. No one wanted to leave, and their faces were filled with joy and the glory of the Lord. I realized that the inner and physical healings God did that night were effortless, instant, and at an unusually deep level. The atmosphere shifted when Joanna began to speak in Hebrew, translate into English, and then sang acapella. It was as if God wanted me to see something powerful about us ministering together. Heaven was released. The last time I remember this level of the tangible Presence of God was in 1990 when the Glory of God filled the prison cell and Jesus appeared.

Joanna described giving me the special gift she had brought. "As we wound down at the end of the night, I had the opportunity to give David his gift. I couldn't wait to see the look on his face as he received his incredible chocolate master work of art! It felt great to be able to honor and bless him because he blesses so many others."

For the first time in over 20 years, someone had managed to render me speechless. I was in utter shock and disbelief at the incredible gift of honor Joanna had bestowed upon me. It was a box made out of dark chocolate with truffles inside. The box's lid was made into a large chocolate eagle head (the symbol of the prison ministry) and brushed with edible gold. The level of detail and thoughtfulness was utterly amazing. I couldn't believe it.

After that evening of serving the Lord together, I couldn't quit thinking about this woman. *Joanna and I get along effortlessly by phone. She prays like a seasoned warrior. She seems to know more about prophetic intercession and spiritual warfare than I do. She carries the tangible Presence and love of God like few people I've met. And she isn't difficult on the eyes either! Why haven't I noticed this before? Hmmm....*

I continued down the list. *We flow effortlessly together during ministry time. Our gift mixes complement each other.* The more I thought about it, we seemed to fit together like two puzzle pieces. We fell in love in the ensuing months during our "chocolate wars." I had a wonderful chocolatier in Kansas City who told me "I've met my match" as he prepared numerous competing chocolate gifts!

Joanna fit beautifully into my family and I loved hers. God not only confirmed that I had met my life partner, but He sped things up and before long I was thinking, *I'm going to propose.* I thought long and hard about how and then the idea of a hot air balloon proposal took hold of me. Up, up and away we went. I was excited. She had no clue. I popped the question at 400 feet. She said yes and it was settled that the two of us would become one.

Joanna and I have been ministering together for some time, teaching on identity and the importance of understanding our position as sons and daughters of the King of Heaven. Joanna crowns ladies 'princesses of the King of Heaven' and once they receive this revelation into their hearts, their lives are transformed.

The Lord has me knight men as 'knights of the King of Heaven' using a Solomon sword and a similar thing occurs. Joanna said, "David because we're King's kids we should believe God to provide for a royal wedding."

I thought for a minute and agreed, "Let's do it. This is what we teach others." We prayed and sought the Lord together using the "prayer of agreement" and we sensed several things. First, a supernatural peace, next, that Heaven had heard our prayer. Finally we sensed that because this idea originated in Heaven, it was the will of God for our lives, and that our job was to contend in prayer that it might be done in Earth as it already was in Heaven.[85]

We announced our engagement. Immediately, my Jewish former prisoner friend in Florida who blessed me with a laptop upon my release from prison said, "How can I send you a wedding gift in advance?" Joanna set up a wedding kitty at a bank for us. My Jewish friend made the first deposit. We later discovered it would prove to be exactly 10 percent of what we needed. Others outside the Body of Christ began blessing us. The majority of our wedding needs were taken care of three ways: by people who had been touched through our lives, by God's favor giving us deep discounts, and by

---

85   Matthew 18:19-20, 1 John 5:14-15, Matthew 6:10

Joanna and I saving for six months before the wedding.

One of the many skills God developed in Joanna through her secular job includes event-planning. The relationship capital she carried with service providers and facilities was nothing short of astounding. Through a unique series of events, along with Joanna's skill set, God provided for our royal wedding at a yacht club overlooking the water for less than the price of a backyard wedding, including royal invitations and wedding favors for those who attended. He also gave us an incredible first class honeymoon via a family member who provided eight days at one of his royal condos in Maui overlooking the water.

God truly bestowed upon us a royal wedding where I beheld the woman of my dreams in all of her glory and beauty as she walked down the aisle towards me. As I gazed at her, I was overwhelmed and remembered Proverbs 18:22, **"He who finds a wife finds a good thing and obtains favor from the LORD."** I realized the Lord's great blessing. Incredibly grateful I thought, *this is Joanna, my wife, my love.*

Journey Insight

Proverbs 18:22 says, "He who finds a wife finds a good thing and obtains favor from the LORD." Twenty-five years earlier, I had prayed for a wife who could sing acapella, was a seasoned warrior, and walked in the love of God. I was committed to remain sexually pure until marriage. I later learned Joanna had made the same commitment more than 15 years earlier. We both remained sexually pure until our wedding night. God was faithful. He honored His Word by bringing me the love of my life. Are there any areas of your life that have not been honoring to God? He's waiting for you to put Him first so He can bless you.

79

VIRTUAL CHURCH MEDIA

The Journey Continues

After five years of running Eagle Heart Fellowship, I felt myself wearing down physically. Tiredness led to discouragement, discouragement to disillusionment, and disillusionment to disgust. I preached on Friday nights, went home and uploaded videos to YouTube. Then I designed cover art and burned audio CD's from the service to hand out through the week to people who didn't attend.

Where is the lasting fruit of all this? I wondered continually. *Am I just going through the motions? Is God testing me?* I needed to know.

While praying one afternoon, I cried out to God, "Lord, if I'm doing what You called me to do, then where's the growth, where's the lasting fruit that Jesus said pleased Him in John 15:16? I have hosted the Holy Spirit for five years in this church. We have small numbers, maybe 20-40 people. I'm confused. Your Presence and power show up in every gathering. The Word is preached in power. You confirm Your Word by healing the sick. Devils are coming out of people and the captives are being set free. We even see deaf ears opening up and people throw away their hearing aids. Metal that was placed by surgeons is bending and even disappearing in people's backs and the pain leaves instantly. But instead of the church growing, the numbers remain the same."

I continued to cry out to God about this matter. "Other five-fold ministers from around the area come to this church, not to minister but to receive. They say they get fed the Word here and re-filled with the Holy Spirit here, like no other place in Kansas City. They say this place is like a spiritual filling station. But, where is the growth?"

"I spend every weekend uploading videos teachings. For what reason? We have several hundred teaching videos in our account but we only have a few hundred subscribers. If I've missed you, if I'm off track, just tell me. I'll even quit the ministry and go get a secular job, attend church, pay tithes, give offerings, and support a ministry to which You send me. Otherwise, please tell me what this is all about. I need to know where the Romans 8:28 God of the Bible is, the God who is faithful to cause all things to work together for good to those who love Him."

After I presented my case, and completed my tantrum, I waited His response. There was a pause, and then with absolute clarity the Holy Spirit spoke just two words in response, *"VIRTUAL CHURCH!"*

Surprised by these words, I pondered their possible meanings. Suddenly a download of information came flowing into my mind from Heaven. In a matter of what couldn't have been more than seconds, the Holy Spirit showed me how, through Virtual Church, the Gospel would go around the globe. This would be possible through a variety of technologies, some yet to be invented, but many of which were already in people's hands. The Gospel was literally beaming into their mobile phones, computers, televisions, tablets, laptops, and other hand-held or wearable devices. Their eyes and ears were held in rapt attention to the broadcasts.

The people I was shown were literally all over the planet, represented a variety of ethnic and religious backgrounds, and were eager to learn about Jesus. Their faces reflected their spiritual hunger and satisfaction. The majority of these people were living in under-developed and developing third-world nations. Again the two words were repeated, this time, softer as they trailed away, *"Virtual Church…"*

I was astonished! The feeling of discouragement dissipated as realization settled in that God did have a purpose for all I was doing. I asked Him, *God, how is a global ministry going to spring forth from our small congregation in Independence, Missouri?* The Holy Spirit reminded me of Zechariah 4:10 (NLT): **"Do not despise these small beginnings, for the LORD rejoices to see the work begin…"**

Even though I was confident I'd heard from Heaven, I still needed to "test the spirits" (1 John 4:1-6) on this experience. I went to the computer to research what was shown and spoken to me about Virtual Church. I spent the next 36 hours on and off the computer. I was astounded and intrigued at what I discovered.

This was March of 2014, just a couple of weeks after Joanna and I had first realized we were interested in each other. Before I went to prison in 1989 my cell phone weighed 8 ½ pounds. It was shaped like a giant brick with a handle and had a whopping 90-minute battery life. It dialed and hung up. The new bag phone was just coming out, but I was arrested before upgrading. When I was released from prison just five years earlier in 2009 my cell phone weighed only 8 ounces. It accessed email and in an emergency could visit a website in a matter of only a few minutes. In fact, one out of every 100 cell phones could perform these functions at that time. Five years later 72 out of 100 cell phones had internet access. The majority of these offered high-speed access, enabling owners to watch YouTube videos with little buffering. This was a 7200 percent increase and internet speeds on phones had increased by nearly 2500 times. As I continued to research I discovered that:

- 2.5 billion people now had high-speed internet access.

- Nearly seven billion cell phones were active on the planet. Forty-four percent of these accessed the internet the month prior, and this number was growing daily.

- More than 80 percent of Asia was now online. These countries represent nearly 43 percent of the world's population. Only a fraction of these believed in Jesus. Many had never even had the opportunity to hear about Him.

- More than 90 percent of the Middle East was now online. These are primarily Muslim countries where it is illegal to preach about or receive Jesus at the risk of losing your freedom, or in some areas, your head.

- The United States is no longer ranked in the top 10 fastest internet speeds in the world. Although we have an amazing infrastructure here, the rest of the world has shot past us in many technological areas.

The statistics went on and on. I was astounded at the wisdom of the Lord. He was preparing the last day's evangelism and discipleship of *nations* through the avenue of His *virtual churches*. The final words of Jesus to His disciples rang in my spirit, **"Go therefore and make disciples of all the nations, baptizing them in the name of the Father and of the Son and of the Holy Spirit teaching them to observe all things that I have commanded you; and lo, I am with you always, even to the end of the age. Amen."** (Matthew 28:19-20)

God, Your desire and command to take the Gospel to the nations, can now be accomplished on a worldwide scale through Your idea from before the foundation of the world -- The Virtual Church. I was mesmerized as the revelation became clear of what He had planned. *Each person attending a virtual church will have access to a pastor teaching them on their mobile device or on their home computer!*

I learned that there is only one pastor for every 100,000 people in some third world countries. In the United States, we have one pastor for every one hundred people. Suddenly I saw how the Romans 8:28 God had led me down a path of His choosing even though for the last five years I had no idea where it was leading until He spoke the words that changed the ministry: **"Virtual Church."**

I further realized this surge in technology and access to virtual church enabled people around the world to think for themselves by simply clicking a mouse, or giving a voice command search to ask about Jesus on the internet. Evangelism and discipleship in the 21st century would look completely different than we'd ever seen before in all world history. The physical church gatherings would continue and be necessary while God's virtual church would arise around the world overnight! And just as there were many physical churches, there would also come many virtual churches overnight.

Daniel prophesied, in the last days **"...knowledge shall increase"** (Daniel 12:4). Contemplating this, I knew the century we live in is often referred to as the Age of Technology or the technological revolution. *God, You blessed us to see more technological advancements in the last 100 years than in the previous 6,000 years combined!*

As Christians, we can either lead, follow or be left behind. We can either harness the power of the Internet to make things happen, watch things happen or wonder, what happened? I decided to step out of the boat and walk on these hardly charted waters with Jesus. Little did I know that the next thing God would do would occur in a jet at 30,000 feet. On a business trip, God positioned me next to an attorney who had just returned from his first mission trip to India and was rethinking his whole purpose on Earth. We had a great conversation about him, and then he asked, "What do you do?"

My thoughts immediately turned towards the virtual church media vision, and so to a perfect stranger I began to explain. He cocked his head and said, "That's very interesting. I think that's the direction God is taking ministries at this hour to reach the nations in an accelerated way. When we land, I'm going to send you an email that I believe will help you."

As promised, he sent the email. It contained a link connecting me with an organization that had an incredible online platform. This encounter with the attorney led to having our own fully-licensed, online discipleship platform, offering unlimited spiritually-nourishing videos for kids, children and adults in almost every sub-category imaginable, i.e., marriage, parenting, pastoring, relationships, finance, spiritual growth, etc. These were now accessible to people around the world through VirtualChurchMedia.com.

Moreover, we could instantly make available any of our videos in our YouTube account that we'd recorded over the previous five years, on our Virtual Church Media channel through our portal. *God, You are truly causing all things to work together for good!* What I didn't know was that this was just *the small beginning...*

Journey Insights

Zechariah 4:10 says, "Do not despise these small beginnings, for the LORD rejoices to see the work begin..." I decided to step outside of the boat into the uncharted waters of launching a virtual church. It was a small beginning, but it was a beginning that would open unimaginable doors. What ideas has the Lord given you that you need to step outside of the boat?

80

EMF'S, SMART METERS, AND CELL PHONES

The Journey Continues

Joanna and I moved to Newport Beach, California, embarking on our life together as one. We were full of hopes, dreams, and plans to continue ministering together as we built a life unto God.

But in January 2015, only 60 days into our marriage, as we were praying into an opportunity to launch our first TV broadcast, I began having unexplained health problems involving among other things, the cervicals in my lower neck. These began locking up, causing extreme tightness, and then my feet became sore and inflamed. I'd never had health problems like these. My energy levels dropped. Then the headaches began. Chest pain followed. It was incredibly odd, as if I was having a heart-attack. The left side of my neck around the carotid artery area, and the top of my head, nose, and lips became numb at times. Then the numbness expanded to a few of my front teeth. My mind was racing! *Is this psychosomatic?* Joanna and I were increasingly concerned.

Then I noticed a pattern. When I left the house for several hours, the symptoms would slowly diminish or even leave. Usually, within minutes of arriving back home, these symptoms would return, quickly, and with a vengeance. Was there something in the house? Was I allergic?

The nights were the worst. On a couple of occasions, it felt like I was fighting for my life. Joanna, who is a valiant prayer warrior, contended with me. We didn't know what to pray. We called other prayer warriors. They began interceding while at the same time, I had bizarre images popping into my mind of dying in a hospital room to what was written on my tombstone!

Whatever was attacking me from the spirit realm was also capitalizing on whatever was taking place in the natural. But it was evident to me that this principality didn't know me. None of the images or thoughts being projected into my mind were past strongholds. I was in a new region. I knew this entire experience had something to do with the TV broadcast and our arrival into Orange County, California to preach the Gospel with signs and wonders.

The Holy Spirit directed me to attend a service where a prophetically gifted minister was speaking. After the service, he came over to me and said, "The Lord shows me that you've been hit by dirty electricity, because of the Glory of God that resides within you. It's the real electricity from Heaven, Holy Spirit electricity that will change things on the earth. I see God is about to bring forth a glory light from within your spirit that will bring corporate healing and miracles in services where He sends you. When you overcome this attack of dirty electricity sent to incapacitate you, and *you will,* the true healing and miracle ministry to which God has called you will spring forth." My heart was encouraged at his words!

Joanna kept praying and the Holy Spirit spoke two words, *"Smart Meters."* Joanna had never heard of a smart meter so she went on an Internet fact-finding mission. "David! This is it!" She had my attention. "These new devices are being added by Electric companies in California and they're being rolled out across the United States. The smart meters pulse emissions every two to three seconds, 24 hours a day, sending data to the electric company." The health problems people were reporting shortly after a meter was installed on their house were staggering. Some of the symptoms mirrored what I was experiencing and we felt we were on the right track.

Joanna called the property manager and we discovered six smart meters hidden behind a locked case on one side of our living space just beneath my office. We later discovered that our Wi-Fi hotspot located next to my working desk was adding emissions into my body. More research revealed that a Wi-Fi broadcast signal next to a smart meter actually pulls the smart meter emissions out of the air and then broadcasts these emissions into the room. We then discovered another bank of 10 smart meters secreted behind a second locked box 30 feet away.

The information just kept coming. We had a cell phone booster signal given to us by the phone company to reduce dropped calls while a cell tower in the area was being repaired. I inadvertently stored this booster under my bed. Also, when using our new cell phones they emitted high levels of emissions directly into our heads. The cumulative effect of ALL these exposures sent my body over the edge. Who knew?

Joanna was working her job away from the house and I was working from home. Thank God she wasn't exposed to the same levels. But, for me, this proved to be the perfect storm. The Holy Spirit directed us to call a well-respected chiropractor in the area, who specializes in EMF exposures. He said, "David, you don't have a heart problem and you aren't having a stroke. You are simply blown out, like thousands of others walking around, who don't know it."

"What do you mean by blown out?" I asked.

"Come in my office and we'll reset your system. You have EMF Exposure, and your system is on overload."

The next day he tested me, and sure enough, in his words, I was completely blown out. Within a few minutes, he was able to reset my system using technology he had developed. Instantly my body posture improved. The pain in my back and inflammation in my feet began to dissipate. The headaches went away. Numbness in my face, nose and teeth disappeared. Within a few days, I was feeling almost normal.

He recommended we test our house. We took a device to measure for emissions. They were off the charts. We made some adjustments, trading out the Wi-Fi for hard wires to our computers. The management had the smart meters covered with protective shields. We hard wired our smart TV, and a few others things. I had no idea so many things that have been released in the information age was also exposing us to harm.

We only received the answers to the cause and wisdom for what to do *after* Joanna began asking God with expectancy and determination. I realized this same wisdom applies to every type of health problem, marriage problem, work, business, or relationship problem we encounter in life. God is there, waiting for us to ask. **"and whatever we ask we receive from him, because we keep his commandments and do what pleases him"** (1 John 3:22 ESV).
[86]

Journey Insights

James 1:5-7 (NLT) says, "If you need wisdom-- if you want to know what God wants you to do-- ask him, and he will gladly tell you. He will not resent your asking. But when you ask him, be sure that you really expect him to answer, for a doubtful mind is as unsettled as a wave of the sea that is driven and tossed by the wind. People like that should not expect to receive anything from the Lord." Are you praying in hidden doubt or expectant faith? If you need a word of knowledge, ask God and He will answer.

---

[86] I encourage you to take a moment to ask God for wisdom on a matter that has come to mind while reading my story in this chapter. James 1:5-7 (NLT) says, **"If you need wisdom-- if you want to know what God wants you to do-- ask him, and he will gladly tell you. He will not resent your asking. But when you ask him, be sure that you really expect him to answer, for a doubtful mind is as unsettled as a wave of the sea that is driven and tossed by the wind. People like that should not expect to receive anything from the Lord"**.

81

REACHING MILLIONS FOR CHRIST

The Journey Continues

As I looked back over my life, the realization hit me how God prepared me for what would later become necessary. Not only had I traveled to several Arab countries as a teenager, but I was raised Jewish and Armenian. I had an understanding of the middle-eastern culture, an appreciation for its wonderful people, and an awareness of the continual religious conflicts that arose.

Once I met Joanna, our hearts united to reach the lost regardless of people groups. We made the commitment that no matter what is required or where it takes us, we're following God. As we began to research broadcasting opportunities, we felt the Lord lead us to a Christian network owned by a middle-eastern follower of Jesus named Dr. Joseph. He ran a thriving TV network and God quickly united our hearts in our desire to reach the lost. Recognizing the Lord calling us to broadcasting as our next step, we asked Joseph to relate how he came about owning the network.

"Ah, David and Joanna, I would be happy to share, for God has done a mighty work in my life." We rejoiced and were captivated as his journey unfolded.

He was raised a Christian in Egypt, a Muslim nation. As a child, Joseph was severely persecuted and as a result he became angry at God, along with his father. Choosing to go the way of the world with his singing gift, he hit the nightclubs and eventually became well-known with many hit songs on the radio. He settled into a lavish lifestyle of drinking, smoking, drugs, and partying.

A friend from the night clubs had a powerful conversion experience in an underground Egyptian church. He relentlessly invited Joseph to his Bible study. Finally Joseph joined him, and he had a stunning vision. He saw his life full of darkness and sin, yet how his life could be with Christ, full of light and purpose. The scene suddenly changed. Joseph saw a Roman soldier brutally whipping a man who was wearing a crown of thorns. Joseph cried out to the Roman soldier, "Stop! Why are you whipping this man?" The snarling Roman soldier turned and it was Joseph who had been wielding the whip!

As his guilt crushed down on him, he realized that Jesus willingly took his punishment. The Presence of God flooded into the room and Joseph fell to his knees, weeping. Immediately he accepted Jesus into his heart, completely turning from his old lifestyle, and attending church every night for the next year!

Joanna and I were riveted, listening to his story. Joseph said, "It was a challenging time when I was required to serve my mandatory year in our Egyptian military. I went against my father's advice, handing out Bibles, and I was arrested. I faced life in prison or the death penalty for illegally evangelizing. Eventually they placed me in a pit, alone, where I was beaten and tasered on my private parts by several Muslim military personnel for hours each day."

I was, of course, keenly interested in his prison time, comparing it to many of the challenges I'd faced for almost 20 years. I did not, however, face torture. Joseph continued sharing the details that led him to being in California, with a Christian network.

"One day they came and yanked him me out of the hole. They put a machete to my neck."

"Denounce your Jesus," his captors demanded. "Repeat the Muslim prayer and make Allah your god, or die now!" Joseph said his first thought was, *Lord, can I just denounce you publicly but really keep you in my heart?*

He heard a voice, **"If you deny me before men I will deny you before my Father in Heaven."** Joseph remembered reading this in Matthew 10:33 and knew he could never denounce Jesus. So he asked the Lord if there was another way out of his persecution. The voice of the Lord said, "Tell them you will become a Muslim if they can answer just one question. Tell them, if not, they have to let you live."

He turned to the Muslim terrorists, "I will become the greatest Muslim preacher in all of Egypt if you can answer me just one question!"

They paused, looked at each other, and slowly took the machete' away from his throat. "Okay, what is your question?"

The Lord spoke to Dr. Joseph again, "Ask them to tell you three good things that Mohammed did during his whole life, that are written anywhere in the Koran or the Hadith." Joseph repeated this question to the terrorists and waited. Dumbfounded, the terrorists couldn't come up with one good thing that Mohammad had done.

This infuriated them and they argued amongst themselves. Finally, one of the terrorists said, "Kill him anyway!"

One of the others intervened, "We can't kill him. We can't answer his question. We have to let him live." So they broke his leg instead and threw him back in the pit. The following day a military sergeant, who was secretly a Christian, happened to arrive, heard about Joseph, and rescued him.

Years later God called him to America to start a small TV ministry. He did so on a shoestring budget, broadcasting in both Arabic and English. The TV network continues to grow and now reaches 120 million homes on five continents, 24 hours a day with the love of Jesus. It became clear to Joanna and me that God was leading us to share His love with the Muslim people, and we didn't have to wait long.

Journey Insights

Are you the "Roman Soldier beating Jesus" with your mouth, your actions, and your heart? The Apostle Peter started sinking in the water and cried out to Jesus for help. Jesus immediately put him back into the safe boat. Cry out to God and let Him show you your heart.

82

GREEN LIGHT FOR TV BROADCASTING

The Journey Continues

In March of 2015, Joanna and I were given the green light and launched our first weekly TV Broadcast on Dr. Joseph's network. The Holy Spirit gave us the name, "In His Presence, Where ALL Things Are Possible!" and our primary focus was to help others enter into God's Presence, where God meets them, and then He does the rest.

We arrived at the TV studio a little nervous, not knowing what to expect for our first one-hour live broadcast. *This is overwhelming,* I thought. *People in Iran, Iraq, Pakistan, South America, Nigeria, Australia, Canada, Europe, and several other Middle Eastern countries will be listening and watching.*

Taking Joanna's hand and speaking as softly as I could, I said, "You realize, don't you, that the amount of people that will hear us will be at least a thousand times larger than any audience to which we've ever spoken?"

"Maybe this is what the Lord means in Deuteronomy 1:11 about the God of our fathers increasing us a thousand times, and blessing us as he has promised!" She smiled as did I.

Squeezing her hand I said, "This really is a defining moment in our lives." A holy fear and responsibility quieted us.

Joanna had some theater training while living in Finland but neither of us had any live TV experience, let alone broadcasting into foreign countries. I repeated to myself, *one shot, no retakes, and speak for an hour.* Both of us were aware that we would either sink or swim and knew we had to keep our eyes on Him. The Holy Spirit reminded me of the Apostle Paul's words:

"For I determined not to know anything among you except Jesus Christ and Him crucified. I was with you in weakness, in fear, and in much trembling. And my speech and my preaching were not with persuasive words of human wisdom, but in demonstration of the Spirit and of power, that your faith should not be in the wisdom of men but in the power of God." (1 Corinthians 2:2-5)

Then the Holy Spirit prompted us to pray that He would give us a "global mindset." Over the years, I'd learned the importance of obeying God's promptings no matter how small. We agreed, prayed, and then stepped onto the set, curious as to what would happen next.

Sitting in my chair, I counted six cameras, then noticed a seventh one suspended from the ceiling. At least three were facing my direction. The first five minutes of this live broadcast I wasn't quite sure where I should be looking. Every 90 seconds or so a crew member would run behind one of the cameras and point to it as if to say, speak to this one, you novice! *Why couldn't we have been trained?* I thought.

Everything was happening so quickly. At times I felt like I was drowning; almost grasping for words. I silently called out to God in my weakness, fear, and inner trembling, and then the Holy Spirit came and helped. We were suddenly able to minister with the peace and power of God.

I spoke in Spanish at one point during the broadcast, connecting culturally with the South American listeners. Then, the owner of the network translated into Arabic during our prayer and healing time. The power and Presence of the Lord only increased as Joanna played the piano and sang the songs of Heaven in English and Hebrew. Then the Holy Spirit prompted me to share the testimony of the large open air meetings in Nigeria and I repeated the few words I'd learned in the Igbo language, Jesus Metromacha! Jesus Metromacha! [87]

The power of God coursed through the set. People from around the world began calling with their prayer requests as God touched them in their homes. We stepped off the set exhausted and the whole experience was a little surreal.

How is this kind of ministry possible? I thought. By this time, Joanna and I together had over 40 years of combined ministry experience, but TV was different than speaking in church settings. The Lord spoke to my heart that it didn't matter, for it was His same precious Holy Spirit anointing every true ministry regardless of the venue.

"Joanna, did the Lord just trust us to reach more people in a single broadcast than in all our previous years of ministry combined?"

"He did, David, He did." She was serious and it was clear to both of us that God caused our first broadcast to be a success, in spite of our lack of training, as people were ushered into His Presence, Where ALL Things are Possible!

The Lord had graciously entrusted my wife and me with several ministry opportunities. We had the privilege of hosting a monthly local service, of speaking around the nation in churches, of assisting with the Bible ministry

---

87   Much to our surprise we later realized that five languages were represented in this single broadcast as God gave us a global mindset to reach his people around the world.

to prisoners, and of airing a weekly television broadcast via satellite, cable, and through online outlets around the world.

The vision of Virtual Church Media that the Holy Spirit gave just 18 months earlier had been birthed by the Lord and continued to grow. *God, You've shown me over the years that if You speak it, You are well able to bring it to pass.*

Journey Insights

In one moment, we went from a hosting small congregation to being in the homes of millions of people world-wide. Our journeys of life led us into preparation for this moment. Are you letting God prepare you through the journey? He's waiting for you.

83

THE KING'S CROWN

The Journey Continues

In 2015, the Bible ministry to prisoners was struggling for financial support. The Tree of Books vision the Lord gave me for this ministry in a Leavenworth Penitentiary prison cell nearly 25 years earlier was powerful and much needed. The current lack of finances to get Bibles to prisoners left me mystified and broken.

God, You said that we're to remember those in prison as if bound with them.[88] *Jesus told us that every time that we did something for the prisoner, that we did it unto Him personally!*[89] *How can this die, God? Why aren't people supporting this fruitful Bible ministry? My life was changed and I saw many inmates who were radically changed by receiving a study Bible.*

I don't get it.

Without a Bible I wouldn't have known You. I wouldn't have been set free from my own sinful ways. I wouldn't have been able to maneuver behind bars, and I would have relied on what people said instead of what You say! Look at how many people have worked sacrificially to help keep Bibles going into prisons…Patricia, Barb, Jeff, Elaine, Koren, Nanette, Angelina, Chip, Robert, Mom, Dad, Jody, Kent, Mary, Terri, Manny, Monnette, Dan, and so many others!

Please help me understand, God.

Reflecting on the previous five years, only one church where I'd preached or shared my testimony had actually supported Heart of America Prison Ministries. In fact, a couple of churches had taken up offerings while I spoke, promising they would be using a portion of the funds for our Bible ministry, then we never received anything! I sought the Lord asking Him what the next steps were. No answers came. I went to sleep hurt, frustrated, and somewhat flustered at the lack of interest from the Body of Christ for this area of God's heart, the prisoners who needed and had requested a Bible.

At exactly 4:35 a.m. I awoke from a very clear and vivid dream indicating God's continued love for the prisoners. The dream opened with me looking through a box of my 83-year-old mother's letters, determining what to

---

88 Hebrews 13:3
89 Matthew 25:36-41

discard and what to keep. I picked up a hand-written letter from my mother to a well-respected international television ministry. The letter, which had never been sent, was dated more than *a decade ago* and requested financial help to obtain Bibles for prisoners.

In the dream I noticed the back of the envelope was covered with hundreds of tiny social security numbers, representing the ID number of each prisoner who was still waiting for their leather-bound study Bible. As I turned the paper over, like an accordion, it sprang into the shape of a three-dimensional *King's Crown*. The social security numbers were on the inside of the crown, and my mother's unsent words on the outside.

God showed me in this dream His heart of compassion for the prisoners who were waiting for their study Bibles. The Father's heart rose up in me in the dream, along with the unanswered cry of my mother's heart, and then I awoke. Back when I was in Springfield, 1995-98, I was with a former prisoner named Geoff, who had actually directed my mother to write that letter. Geoff had helped fund that ministry, spent countless hours with the pastor and his wife, and saved them from losing their multi-million dollar property when a balloon payment came due. He told my mother to contact them and mention his name. She wrote the letter, but instead of it going in the mail, it inadvertently got placed in a box. We may have forgotten about it but the Lord didn't, which He showed me in the dream 18 years later.

When I awoke, I followed up to obey the Lord. I sent an email sharing the dream and asking for wisdom and guidance. No response ever came. I believe when I meet the leaders of this ministry one day and relate the dream and history in person, the Lord will redeem the time.[90] We may have missed our day of visitation but God showed us another way.[91]

My good friend, Jeff Gay, was now at the helm as the president of Heart of America Prison Ministries. We were motivated by the power of the dream. We were re-inspired and pressed into the Lord remembering the Bible taught, **"…for nothing can hinder the LORD from saving by many or by few"** (1 Samuel 14:6 ESV). I once calculated, during my 20 years behind bars, that I spent about 1,000 hours a year in the Word, which represents 20,000 hours of study. This was another thing about which I spoke with the Lord.

Lord, thank You for transforming my life as I read Your Word. It helped immensely having a durable Bible with commentary, dictionary, study notes, concordance, maps, etc. In fact, God, You've shown me numerous prisoners with similar testimonies, who've received one of these quality Bibles.

---

90   Ephesians 5:16
91   Luke 19:44

Jeff and I then prayed specifically about the need, but this time with resolve and confidence. We knew that through intense study and much use, the higher-quality Bibles wouldn't fall apart as a paperback does. The Holy Spirit highlighted the main difference between the 2000 prisoners on our Bible waiting list – who waited up to two years for their Bible - and the majority of Christians in the free world. *The prisoner actually takes the time to read their Bible, often for hours and hours a day.* Prisoners need a high quality Bible more than the average Christian on the outside.

Jeff and I brought our case on behalf of the prisoners before the courtroom of Heaven. We sensed God's gavel slam as His verdict was decreed on the prisoner's behalf. The first thing God did was provide unusual deals on first-quality study Bibles. A $60 Study Bible for $10 that was 83 percent off. An $80 Study Bible for $15, which was 79 percent off. We were used to paying about $20 wholesale, and around $5 shipping and handling for these four pound Bibles. The special prices that were falling into our laps were very unusual and would only last a few days.

The next thing God did was raise people up to take advantage of this window of donation opportunity. Jeff would share the temporary price we were able to purchase at and I'd contact people at the direction of the Holy Spirit. The first time I sent out four simple text messages. Within 24 hours all four people responded.

"Yes David, I'll donate 25, here's my credit card for $250."

"Sure, put me down for 30 Bibles."

Another called, "Forty Bibles for me!"

The fourth said, "Yes, I'll buy 70 Bibles."

Next, the Holy Spirit prompted me to send out a shipping opportunity to several people at $5 per Bible. Text messages came back, "I'll pay the shipping for 10 Bibles."

Another replied, "Twenty Bibles."

"Put me down for 100 Bibles, I'm sending $500."

Every time we sought the Lord, people responded. The hand of God doesn't move without prayer. God wants us to seek His face daily. We have true authority to the degree we are in relationship with the King. I thought of something I'd heard for years: *No prayer, no power. Little prayer, little power. Much prayer, much power.* Jeff and I bombarded Heaven together almost every day by phone. As we sought God, Bibles began to flow through the ministry to the prisoners again.

At the time of this writing Heart of America is providing Study Bibles in more than 1,300 state and federal prisons. It seems we always have a waiting list of over 1,000 which simply speaks to the massive work God is doing behind bars, drawing hearts to His. With financial support and hands-on help, we all are Helping Change Lives…One Bible at a Time!

Many have asked how they can help change a life. If you'd like to make a difference in a prisoner's life, like someone did for me, go to heartprisonministries.org now. You can make a one-time donation or enroll in our *Raise up 12 Disciples behind Bars* Monthly Giving Program, for a $25 monthly donation.[92] As you read this, I believe Jesus has these men on His mind. In fact, their numbers are written on the inside of His crown: **"And the King shall answer and say unto them, Verily I say unto you, Inasmuch as ye did it unto one of these my brethren, even these least, ye did it unto me"** (Matthew 25:40).

Journey Insights

"Yet you do not have because you do not ask" (James 4:2-3). My life was transformed by God as I read the Bible, and having a Bible with commentary, dictionary, study notes, concordance, maps, etc. helped me tremendously. Have you read the Bible, asked Jesus into your heart, and asked the Holy Spirit to fill and baptize you? If not, now's your time! I encourage you to get your Bible, and ask God to help you understand it. Get ready for an amazing journey.

---

92   To donate online visit heartprisonministries.org; to donate by check, sent to Heart of America Prison Ministries, P.O. Box 1685, Independence Missouri, 64055

84

THE JOURNEY CONTINUES

Life can move at a snail's pace, or at the speed of a jet ride, but the main thing is the direction we're headed. At the end of the day, is our destination Heaven or hell? God has a destiny for you! It is filled with victory and divine accomplishment, born from faith and favor. Our lives were never meant to be filled with only disappointment and discouragement, and we were not created to be saddled by fear and failure.

You are called to greatness! You are meant to journey through life enjoying freedom, whether in prison chains or out in the world. And if you're reading this, it's not too late.

I am standing firmly on the soil of freedom after having survived 20 years in federal prison. My jet ride to hell came to a screeching halt the moment I met Jesus in a prison cell. That day I accepted the free ticket that God offered me and I began my journey to freedom.

God brought to mind a powerful illustration that I once witnessed from a prison guest speaker years ago. The audience was asked, "Do any of you want this hundred dollar bill?" They all said, "yes!" The speaker smashed and wadded it up, asking the same question. Their response was still, "yes!" He stomped on it, and they still held out their hands for it. He spit on it and stomped again. Why was their answer still, "YES! YES! YES!"? The intrinsic worth was not changed by anything that happened to the bill. Its value did not change, nor has yours. You are still incredibly valuable to God.

Whether you're behind bars or not, God is inviting you to allow Him to love you and to have fellowship with Him. It is why you were created. Have you done this before, but your relationship with Him has drawn cold, powerless, and fruitless? Have you never before made the decision that will change your life? Either way, You can make that decision, or renew that decision, right now. Just go to Him and ask. He loves you in spite of anything and everything. Your journey to freedom can begin now by simply receiving His love.

Long ago I began my own jet ride to hell when I made wrong choices. My journey to freedom, "my ticket out," began by a simple choice.

★

Father, You valued me during my jet ride down and through my crash. I was headed to hell yet You met me and led me to a point of decision, and You helped me say "YES" to You.

You taught me to be about Your business wherever I am. You've refined me, trained me, and partnered with me to minister behind prison walls and now throughout the world.

You've developed patience within me and absolute trust in You, God, and in Your goodness. I've learned to hold fast to the profession of my faith, and having done all, to still stand.

Thank You for teaching me forgiveness for the injustices done to me, and that You can use all to accomplish Your sovereign will.

Father, I praise Who You are and Who You want to be for every reader. You met me in prison, completely reversing the course of my life. I lift up each reader to You now, for You alone see where they've been, where they are, and where You want to take them. Fear, sadness, and hopelessness is not their destiny. You love us right where we're at, but You love us too much to leave us there. You love us before we change, and You love helping us change. You loved us first and we get to say yes to You.

Give them the courage, God, to release their life to You. Help them, as You helped me, and continue to help me, with every detail of life.

For those who don't know You at all, God, I ask You to gather them into Your arms as they pray the prayer of salvation, that will change their destiny forever.

For those who are on their way, but have gotten lost somehow amidst life's issues, I pray that You bring them back to the main highway with You as their source and passion.

And God, for those Who are leading the way for others, I ask You to revive and refresh them as they journey with You.

Together, God, I thank You for this amazing journey of freedom we are all on, for You, God our King and our God, You are the Way, the Truth, and the Life for each of us. And together, we lift up the prisoners, those bound who so deeply need our prayers and Your touch.

In Jesus' Name, Amen.

★ ★ ★

ADDENDUM

Prayer Help

How to Accept Jesus - *Sinner's Prayer*.

"Heavenly Father, I come to You as I am in need of a Savior. Today I turn from my sins and turn to Jesus. I believe He died on the Cross, was buried in the tomb, and on the third day He was supernaturally raised from the dead.

Jesus, cleanse me with Your shed blood, make me clean, and heal my wounded soul. I break all ties with Satan, his influences, all negative and evil people, and demons. Jesus, I ask you now to remove sins and demonic strongholds. I fully give You my life, and I fully receive Yours into my spirit, soul, and body in Jesus' Name. Holy Spirit, I invite You to come in and take full residence in my heart. Amen."

Prayer for Holy Spirit Baptism

"Heavenly Father, I thank You for the gifts You have freely given to me so I can walk in Your love and power. You said in Luke 11:13, "If you then, being evil, know how to give good gifts to your children, how much more will your Heavenly Father give the Holy Spirit to those who ask Him!" Based upon Your Word, I ask You from my heart for the Holy Spirit baptism of fire, power and love now in Jesus' mighty Name.

I repent of anything I have been in agreement with against this gift. I also ask You to give me my personal prayer language of tongues, so I can pray to You in secret and see Your power released in, through and around me in public. By faith now, I fully expect to experience this empowerment for service from You and I fully expect to speak in other tongues now in Jesus' Name. Amen."

Now spend a few minutes with the Lord. If you can, just lift your hands in the air like a child reaching up to his Heavenly Father and allow the Holy Spirit to fill you afresh.

A new prayer language will often come up from your belly and begin to bubble forth through your lips and mouth when you do this. This language may also come while you lie down and pray like it did with me years ago. If you allow the Holy Spirit to have freedom with your mouth in the same way you allowed the enemy in days gone by, your whole life and the atmosphere around you will be transformed as Heaven fills you. Go ahead, take some time alone with the Lord.

How to Receive the Holy Spirit's Empowerment for Ministry

Heavenly Father, you said that we could be baptized with the Holy Spirit and FIRE. Based on your promises, I want everything that you have for me. I desire to be baptized with the Holy Spirit fire empowerment that will burn up everything inside me that will hinder me in my walk with Christ or your people. So I ask you now in faith to "Fill me with the Holy Spirit and FIRE! I receive now." Spend a few minutes with the Lord as He visits you.

Prayer for Deliverance from Deferred Hope

"Lord, I recognize my need for deliverance from deferred hope. I ask You now in the Name of Jesus to set me free from every stronghold of the enemy in my life. I humbly yet boldly ask for complete deliverance from the enemy's mindset, spiritual forces, and words that have been spoken into my life.

I believe Your promises concerning my life and will accept no compromise. I want all You have for me. Father, show me Your faithfulness in some way today, and in the days ahead, so that I might know You are with me. I thank You for a fresh injection of hope right now, in Jesus' Mighty Name. Amen."

Now, let me pray for you, just as that dear saintly woman calmly prayed for me when I was in Leavenworth, nearing the end of my sentence:

"Deferred hope, I name you and break you off of this life right now in Jesus' Name. I command you to depart from them and never return. In its place, I release a desire fulfilled from the Lord right now over your life, which the Bible says is like a tree of life. I speak the shed blood of Jesus Christ between you and the adversary of your soul, and I release a blessing of perseverance upon you now.

By the authority of Jesus' Name, I release renewed vision and the mind of Christ to fill your mind now. I speak full restoration of hope to your soul from this point forward. Amen."

Prayer for Your Loved One's Salvation

"Lord Jesus, You are the great Liberator. You set the captives free. I believe that (_____name of your loved one) will come to know You personally. I come against the attempts of hell to derail Your call upon their life.

Lord, I ask You to speak to _____ in dreams in the night. Visit him/her with Your tangible Presence and love. Send others to speak Your words of life into his/her heart. Convict _____ of sin during the day and draw them to You in the late hours of the night. Even when he/she shows no sign of change, even when _____ speaks words that cause me to doubt, I will hold fast to Your promises by faith in your Word. I believe You are working in him/her, despite anything said and/or what I see. Apprehend and captivate _____ with Your love, Father. Let _____ be a living miracle, a testimony of Your power to transform a life. Thank You for the miracle that is about to happen with _____. I believe that nothing is impossible with You. I pray this prayer and proclamation in the all-powerful Name of Jesus. Amen."

Daily Prayer Covering for You and Your House

I found this prayer next to a copy machine in the law library in the 1990's. I'm not usually a fan of written prayers but I've shared this one for 25 years. There's something about it that seems to fire up my inner spirit man EVERY time I pray it out loud. The author is unknown; maybe the Holy Spirit wanted it this way.

I use it as a jump start in the morning to help get into God's Presence. When I come across a word in the prayer that ignites my spirit, I leave the written prayer, and allow the Holy Spirit to lead me with Heaven's specific words for the day. This could go on for a few seconds, minutes, or even longer.

Be encouraged to pray this **out loud** daily for thirty days and see how your prayer life and spiritual walk with Jesus is transformed. Watch what the Holy Spirit does once you are sparked and His engine of prayer within you takes over.

Daily Prayer Covering

I encourage you to speak this out loud:

"Heavenly Father, I pray this prayer in the power of the Holy Spirit. In the Name of Jesus Christ I bind, rebuke, and bring to no effect all division, discord, disunity, strife, anger, wrath, murder, criticism, condemnation, pride, envy, jealousy, gossip, slander, evil speaking, complaining, lying, false teaching, false gifts, false manifestations, lying signs and wonders, poverty, fear of lack, fear spirits, murmuring spirits, complaining spirits, hindering spirits, retaliatory spirits, deceiving spirits, religious spirits, occult spirits, witchcraft spirits (including Jezebel, Delilah, and Apollyon), and spirits of the Antichrist.

I bind all curses that have been spoken against me. I bless those who curse me and pray blessings on those who despitefully use me. I bind all spoken judgments made against me, and judgments I have made against others. I bind the power of negative words from others, and I bind and render useless all prayers not inspired by the Holy Spirit; whether psychic, soul force, witchcraft, or counterfeit tongues that have been prayed against me.

I am Your child. I resist the devil. No weapon formed against me shall prosper. I put on the whole armor of God. I take authority over this day, in Your Name, Jesus. Let it be prosperous for me. Let me walk in Your love, Lord.

The Holy Spirit leads and guides me today. I discern between the righteous and the wicked. I take authority over Satan and all his demons, and those people who are influenced by them. I declare Satan is under my feet and shall remain there all day. I am the righteousness of God in Christ Jesus. I am God's property. Satan, you are bound from my family, my mind, my body, my home, and my finances. I confess that I am healed and whole. I flourish, am long-lived, stable, durable, incorruptible, fruitful, virtuous, and full of peace, patience and love. Whatsoever I set my hands to do shall prosper, for God supplies all my needs. I have all authority over Satan, all demons, and beasts of the field.

God, I pray for the ministry You have for me. Anoint me for all You have called me to do for You. I call forth divine appointments, open doors of opportunity, God-ordained encounters, and ministry positions.

I claim a hedge of protection around myself, my spouse and my children (_____insert names) throughout this day and night. I ask You, God, in the Name of Jesus, to dispatch angels to surround me, my spouse, and my children today. Put them throughout my house and around our cars, souls and bodies. I invoke angels to protect my house from any intrusion and to protect my family and me from any harmful demonic or other physical or mental attacks. I ask this prayer in the Name of Jesus. Amen."

How You Can Change a Life, One Bible at a Time

The Lord directed us to create a program entitled, *"Raise Up 12 Disciples Behind Bars."* With a donation of only $25 a month, Heart of America is currently able to provide a first-quality leather or simulated leather, Bible that retails for $50-80. These Bibles are delivered directly to the prisoner at mail call, just like I received in 1990 which helped change my life.

If you sense the Holy Spirit is prompting you to help change a life with a Study Bible, please join our *"Raise up 12 Disciples Behind Bars"* Bible Program. You can also make a one-time donation online: **www.HeartPrisonMinistries.org**, or send a check to:

Heart of America Prison Ministries
P.O. Box 1685,
Independence, MO 64055.

Thank you for helping change lives…*One Bible at a Time!* The prisoners who will receive their Bible will also thank you in person on that special day each of us completes our journey to freedom and arrives in Heaven with Jesus!

ADDITIONAL INFORMATION

PRISON TERMINOLOGY

BOP: Bureau of Prisons

CCO: Community Corrections Officer

Cop Out: Formal request used by inmates to get things done by staff.

Count or Count Time: Every prison counts the inmates a few times a day. In the federal system, 4pm and 10pm are the nationwide times for "count." On the weekends, it's 10am, 4pm and 10pm. Inmates report to their bunks while the guards count the population.

Drop a dime: Ratting on someone.

All Day: A life sentence, as in "I'm doin' all day."

Beef: 1. A criminal charge, as in "I caught a burglary beef in Philly." 2. A problem with another convict, as in "I have a beef with that guy in Block D."

Brake fluid: Psychiatric meds

Bug: A prison staff member considered untrustworthy or unreliable.

Buck Rogers Time: (Early to mid-20th century) A parole or release date so far away that it's difficult to imagine.

Cell Warrior: An inmate that puts on a tough front or runs their mouth when locked in their cell, but is submissive or cowardly when interacting with other prisoners in the open.

Chin Check: To punch another inmate in the jaw to see if he'll fight back.

"Chomo" (or "Cho-Mo"): Child molester

Chow time: Time to eat

Clear count: When the count is submitted and the numbers match and all inmates are accounted for.

CO: Corrections Officer

Convict: A convict, in most cases, may abide by the rules, but only because they want to avoid additional aggravations or frustrations. Yet if he believes breaking a rule would be in his interest, he will make his choice and live with the consequences. A convict would never cooperate with a staff member in some kind of deal to spare himself (i.e. snitch, trade another prisoner for reduced punishment). Convicts often have an air of defiance. He may suppress that defiance even though he feels it coursing through his veins. (See Inmate for comparison.)

Diesel Therapy: A lengthy bus trip or transfer to a far-away facility, or even an incorrect destination, used as punishment or to get rid of troublesome inmates. Diesel Therapy can last for weeks, or even months at a time, for the prisoner being punished.

Dry-Snitching: To inform on another inmate indirectly by talking loudly about their actions or behaving suspiciously in front of correctional officers; supply general information to officers without naming names.

FCC: Federal Correctional Complex

FCI: Federal Correctional Institution

FPC: Federal Prison Camp

Four piece or four-piece suit: A full set of restraints, composed of handcuffs, leg irons and waist chain, and security boxes to cover the restraints' key holes.

Four Points: When guards discipline a prisoner by placing him on his back naked, cuffed, and shackled to four corners of a slab of cement in solitary confinement.

FTC: Federal Transfer Center

Grandma's or Grandma's House: A prison gang's headquarters or meeting place, or the cell of the gang leader.

Hacks: Prison guards

Heat Wave: The attention brought to a group of inmates by the action of one or a few, as in "Joe and John got caught with contraband, and now the whole tier is going through a heat wave."

Hole: (The hole), an isolation (segregation) cell, used as punishment for the most paltry of offenses as well as serious offenses.

House: Prisoner's cell or living area

Iron Pile: Weight, weightlifting equipment

Hold your mud: To resist informing or snitching even under threat of punishment or violence.

In the car: In on a deal or a plan, or group of guys who work out or hang out together.

Jacket: An inmate's information file or rap sheet; an inmate's reputation among other prisoners.

Jack Mack: Canned mackerel or other fish available from the prison commissary. Can be used as currency with other inmates or placed in a sock and used as a weapon.

Jewelry: Ankle bracelet or some other electronic monitoring device worn by an offender leaving prison on probation or parole. His jewelry is a sort of "get-out-jail" token.

Juice Card: An inmate's influence with guards or other prisoners. "He should have gone to the hole for that, but he's got a juice card with one of the guards."

Inmate: An inmate by definition usually will quickly give up another inmate to save his own skin, even if he is guilty of the behavior. Convicts often identify inmates by their quick willingness to engage in conversation with staff members, and consider them to suffer from the "Stockholm-Syndrome,"[93] where they identify more with their

---

93 A psychological phenomenon ... in which hostages express empathy and sympathy and have positive feelings toward their captors, sometimes to the point of defending and identifying with the captors. These feelings are generally considered irrational in light of the danger or risk endured by the victims, who essentially mistake a lack of abuse from their captors for an act of kindness. [source: Wikipedia]

captors than with others who share their captivity. To call a convict an inmate, and vice versa, can easily be considered an insult or a form of disrespect in many cases, and have consequences in certain prisons. (See Convict for comparison.)

Keister: A verb referring to the act of smuggling in contraband, like cigarettes, by inserting items into your anus.

Killing your number: Prison slang for serving one's time or getting out on parole.

Kite: A contraband letter.

Leg-Rider: Slang for a person who sucks up to the police, as in, "humping the officer's leg," in an attempt to get favors.

Lock-down: When prisoners are confined to their cells.

LOP: Low on Potential, "He's a LOP."

MCFP: Medical Center for Federal Prisoners

Monkey Mouth: A prisoner who goes on and on about nothing.

Ninja Turtles: Guards dressed in full riot gear. Also known as "hats and bats."

No Smoke: To follow staff's orders without resisting or causing any problems, as in "He let the guards search his cell, no smoke."

Old School: The way prisons used to be, particularly more respect given to fellow prisoners, less informing, less horseplay. "He's an old school convict," meaning stand up or raised right.

PC: Protective Custody; also as in "He's a PC case", meaning weak or untrustworthy.

Peels: The orange jumpsuit uniforms worn by prisoners in some facilities.

Pepsi Generation: Newer, younger prisoners, who lack respect for "old school" ways.

Potting: Prison slang for throwing or dumping a bucket of excrement on a correctional officer.

Prison Wolf: An inmate who is normally straight on the outside, but engages in sexual activity with men while incarcerated.

Punk: Derogatory term meaning homosexual or weak individual.

Rabbit: An inmate who is normally a history of escape attempts or has plans to try to escape.

Rapo: Anyone with a sex crime; generally looked down on by convicts.

Rat/Snitch/Stool Pidgeon: n., informant. v., to inform, tell on others to cops.

REC: Recreation Yard, e.g. an area for inmates to walk around or get exercise.

Road Kill: Cigarette butts picked up from roadsides by prison work crew. They're brought back to the facility and the collected tobacco is rerolled with toilet paper to smoke.

Sally Port: Entryway that is secure and controlled where guards enter the institution.

Segregation: A disciplinary unit, used for minor and major offenses, where prisoners are kept apart from the main population and denied most all privileges, e.g. Solitary Confinement.

Shake-down: Search done by guards of a prisoner's cell, prisoners, or an area of the prison.

Shank/Shiv: Homemade knife. A sharp or pointed implement used as a knife-like weapon. A shank or shiv can be anything from a glass shard with fabric wrapped around one end to form a handle, to a razor blade stuck in the end of a toothbrush.

SHU: Special Housing Unit (same as segregation, solitary confinement, the hole)

SIS: Special Investigating Supervisor

Solitary Confinement: Form of imprisonment where an inmate is isolated from human interaction, except staff. (See (the) hole, segregation, SHU.)

Store: Commissary, where a prisoner may purchase food, health, or welfare items; an inmate who has a stash of commissary items he sells to other inmates for an increased price. Stamps or bags of coffee purchased from the commissary are used as a form of prison currency and repayment.

Tag/Write-up: Infraction of institution rules that results in an incident report written by a guard against a prisoner.

Turned out: Use someone for your own ends. Generally means to be cajoled or forced into homosexual acts; also, turn out a guard, turn him to "pack" (pack drugs) for you.

U.A.: Urinalysis (urine test)

USP: United States Penitentiary

Wolf Tickets: To talk tough or challenge others, without any intent to back it up with action or violence, as in "He's just selling wolf tickets."

CONTENTS BY CHAPTER

Arrested

Addendum

Endorsements, *Continued from the front*

David carries an anointing, that transcends nationalities and positions in life, to reach out to all. God prepared him early in life to understand, appreciate, and communicate with people in all walks of life in America and throughout the world. He has experienced the Middle East culture since a young boy, visited Arab countries and Israel, and been exposed to the Mexican culture. He speaks Spanish, was born in America, is half Armenian, and through his freedom journey, he's developed Christ's heart for humanity.

Dr. Joseph Nassralla
Founder of the Cross TV Network
Reaching 120 million homes on five continents

David Hairabedian has chronicled an amazing and entertaining story of God's dealings that apply to every reader. You will be emotionally captured by his adventure and educated in the "school of hard knocks" from which David successfully graduated. Enjoy!

Hal Linhardt
Founder and Director
Kansas City Evangelists' Fellowship, HalLinhart.com

The question, "how then shall we live?" has been answered in David Hairabedian's life journey. He's learned the secret to walking with God and communing with Him, bringing God's Presence into all of life regardless of circumstances. It's been my joy to witness David's experiential discovery of our hope-filled God Who transforms lives of despair into miraculous hope.

Bob Hartley
Founder Deeper Waters Ministries
Advisor to business, church and world leaders
CEO Hartley Group, BobHartley.org

After 28 years in prison ministry, I know what kind of book it takes to reach men and women inside the walls. Constantly searching for books to recommend, I found Jet Ride to Hell, Journey to Freedom a writing of great impact that will have a lasting effect on them.

Bill Corum
Founder Prison Power Ministries
Author of The Ultimate Pardon, BillCorum.com

Jet Ride is a triumph. David has given us an eagle view far past his crash and into a fascinating redemptive journey. During 30 years of friendship and working with Heart Prison Ministries, I've seen David's relentless pursuit of sharing salvation, restoration, and healing for all. Obstacles and hardships merely fuel his fire to focus on the Father's business. Somewhere along the line, the Lord stops us all to do a reality check. This book captures David's crash landing that erupted in a white-hot fire for God.

Elaine Hart
20 year Former KC Chiefs Cheer Director
Former CEO Youth America, Inc., FatherNotes.com

David Hairabedian's book, *Jet Ride to Hell, Journey to Freedom*, is a powerfully riveting testimony full of marvelous modern day miracles! Like Saul's road to Damascus conversion, David's is a life changing story that will forever impact the reader! If there were one book besides the Bible that I would recommend handing to all your unsaved loved ones, this would be it!

Greg Petty
Author, International Speaker
Consultant to over 1000 financial planners

I have said of David Hairabedian for the last 22 years, "David will rush in where angels fear to tread." It's a quality of faith and character that endears him to the Lord and shapes a magnificent destiny. Hearing his wife Joanna sing, I saw the same strength.

Pastor Ed Jones

Nothing is more entertaining than hearing of people whose lives have been radically transformed by Jesus Christ. David's story will have you on the edge of your seat as you hear about a man who encountered Jesus in a maximum security prison and is now being used to change the world.

I have had the privilege of sitting under much of David's teachings, and he has a powerful spirit of wisdom and revelation on his life. It is amazing to see God take society's worst cases and turn them into society's GREATEST hope. David's book will set you on fire for Jesus and give you hope for the hardest heart to be saved.

Josh McDonald
Evangelist, International House of Prayer, Kansas City
JoshMacDonald.org

David is one that God has called out of bondage to be a deliverer. He knows what it's like when God breaks the chains of imprisonment. Jet Ride to Hell, Journey to Freedom is an instrument in the hands of God that will make it into the hands of those called to freedom in Christ. Many prison ministries will benefit from this amazing work.

Wade Hankins
President, Apostolic Developments, Inc.
ApostolicDevelopments.com

This compelling book will hold you spellbound. You will follow David's heart journey from prison hell to freedom. To some degree you can apply this to your own journey in life. When you are free in Christ you are truly free indeed.

Diane Wendell, C.N.
Nutrition Plus Wellness Center
www.npwellnesscenter.com

David's journey mirrors the agony and the ecstasy of the life of Joseph in so many ways as he went from dungeon to destiny. Joseph's profound statement to his brothers who betrayed him is also the story of David, "You intended to harm me, but God intended it for good to accomplish what is now being done, the saving of many lives" (Genesis 50:20 NIV). Joseph's willingness to forgive his brothers saved a nation; David's willingness to forgive many brothers is now affecting many nations!

This radical book gives hope to those in prison, and to those on the outside who are imprisoned within themselves. For 20 years, David was constantly tested yet he came out of prison leaning on his Beloved, and the exploits have only just begun!

Linda Valen
Ministry Director, Master Potter Ministries
www.masterpotter.com

When I arrived as chaplain at the Federal Correctional Institution in Englewood, Colorado, in 1991, I found a bitterly divided church. It wasn't unusual for that time. Some claimed that spiritual gifts had ceased with the early church. Others boldly practiced those gifts. The leader of the "cessationists" was an extremely charismatic and gifted young man. He went on to pastor a large church when he left prison. Unfortunately, he is back behind bars on a new case.

The articulate young man who represented the charismatics was David Hairabedian. He was bold. Full of faith. Truly caring about other people – but not afraid to confront them with the truth, even when it hurt. And he was often given supernatural insight into peoples' lives. At times, I was a little uncomfortable with what he was doing. Yet I always felt his respect and support, which was not the case with all the inmate leaders in the church. He had a submissive heart.

We spent hours together talking and praying, and at times ministering to others. Occasionally God's supernatural work – like demonic deliverances – ruffled feathers among prison administrators, especially psychologists. The Catholic chaplain didn't hide his disdain for David. But try as they might, they were hard-pressed to find fault with his personal life. He demonstrated Jesus as consistently as I've seen in prison. When he got out, he moved smoothly into ministry. I had the great privilege of preaching in one of his meetings. David has walked the talk, living out what he preaches. I pray this book would encourage many – especially those incarcerated – and release many into supernatural ministry.

Loren VanGalder
aspiritualfather.com

Simply stated, the Holy Spirit operating through David helped transform my life and continues to transform lives throughout the world. God planted David in my path throughout my incarceration in the US Federal BOP (Bureau of Prisons). From Waseca, MN to Florence, CO to Leavenworth, KS… I just couldn't shake this guy and I praise God for it every single day.

I have personally witnessed David lead dozens of disciples into God's Kingdom, leaving transformed individuals, prison revivals, and the Glory of God in his wake. I am honored and blessed beyond measure to have David as an amazing friend and Spiritual mentor.

David is a heavily anointed man of God and teaches with authority and conviction. God touches and heals hearts wherever he goes and, undoubtedly, God will use "Jet Ride to Hell …Journey to Freedom" as a powerful medium to break the chains of physical, emotional, psychological, and, most importantly, spiritual bondage in the lives of all those who are blessed to come in contact with it.

Clark A. Swihart
CEO and Founder, CAS Enterprises, Inc.
Author, "Breaking the Chains – an Exodus to a New Genesis"
www.facebook.com/TestimonyofGodsDeliverance

When I first met David in 2011, we discovered that we both had a relationship with the same prophet in Nigeria. We began funding together large crusade meetings held in that nation. Jet Ride to Hell Journey to Freedom is an adventure that will inspire many in all walks of life. For the believer, this will strengthen your faith. For the unbeliever, this will lead you to faith. To many young people, this book will be wisdom to keep them from incarceration. For the incarcerated, this is a message of hope.

Pastor Dan Jensen
President and Founder Shekinah Glory Fire Ministries

RESOURCES BY DAVID C. HAIRABEDIAN

Booklets and e-booklets by David

- 7 Deadly Diseases of the Tongue, e-book, $4.99 (booklet $4.99)
- What the Bible Really Says about the Subject of Tongues, e-book $4.99 (booklet $4.99)
- Hearing God 25 Different Biblical Ways, e-book, $4.99 (booklet $4.99)
- Points to Ponder, e-book, $4.99 (booklet $4.99)
- Freedom from Hope Deferred, e-book, $4.99 (booklet $4.99)
- A Spiritual Key for Every Healing, e-book, $4.99 (booklet $4.99)

Audio CD Series by David

- Freedom from Bondage, 6 CD Audio Series, $40
- God's Angels, 4 CD Audio Series, $25
- Jezebel, Recognizing, Combatting, and Overcoming, $30
- The Super 7's, 10 CD Audio Series, $50
- The Names of God, 6 CD Audio Series, $35
- Prayer and Warfare, 4 CD Audio Series, $25
- The Tabernacle Series, 6 CD Audio Series, $40
- David's Testimony, Single Audio Message, $10

Purchasing Bibles for Prisoners

Study Bibles are $50. For every Bible purchased we will also send the same quality Bible to a prisoner on our Bible waiting list through Heart of America Prison Ministries. To support online or learn more about how you can help *Raise up 12 Disciples Behind Bars,* visit: www.HeartPrisonMinistries.org. Checks can also be mailed directly to Heart of America Prison Ministries, P.O. Box 1685, Independence, MO 64055. A $25 donation represents Helping Change one life behind bars through our Bibles to Prisoners program.

The examples used in this book are compilations of stories from actual situations. Names, facts, and issues have been altered to protect confidentiality. Internet addresses (blogs, websites, etc.) in this publication are offered as a resource to you. Though we do our best to recommend reliable resources, please understand that we cannot be responsible for any information presented once you leave our websites.

Cover art: Emily Lam

ACKNOWLEDGMENTS

My acknowledgments are two-fold. I have an immense appreciation to those who have helped birth this book. But even more so, my gratitude runs deep for those who have helped me have a reason to write my autobiography. A simple thank you isn't enough when people have invested sacrificially into your life, and helped make you a better man. I cannot mention everyone, but you know who you are.

To those who helped specifically with this book, I'm grateful. Pastors Ed and Dawn, you helped immensely during the early editing phases of this book. To my sister, Carron, I appreciate how you helped recount factual details from my childhood. To the many advance copy readers, your keen insight was tremendously respected. Jackie, your laser professional editing focus added great life to the book (ChristianBookDoctor.com). Elaine, you took the ball through every line of the enemy's defense, into the red zone, and then as a team we ran across the goal line for a touchdown. To my love, Joanna, your insight and support has been invaluable and your involvement has been particularly enjoyable.

To the many prison chaplains who serve G.O.D. first and the B.O.P. (Bureau of the Prisons) second, thank you. Your tireless work on behalf of inmates, regardless of your faith, often goes unappreciated, but God sees. Chaplains Loren, Mike, Pat, Harvey "One Love," and Chaplain Susan, you went above and beyond. Prison mailroom workers, thanks for extra efforts to get prisoners their Bibles from Heart of America Prison Ministries. Ministers and ministries going in personally or donating materials, you've transformed many lives.

To my friends and family who worked in the Bible ministry and stood by my side throughout this life-journey, you are heroes. The list is endless of those who spent endless hours investing in the lives of prisoners, writing newsletters, shipping Bibles, raising funds, coordinating card writing campaigns, and much more: Koren, Jeff, Kent, Dan, Patricia, Barb and Nanette; Elaine, Mary, Colleen, Ray, Pam, Tammy and Ben; Vic, Susan, Diane, Doctor G., Judy, Jim and Barbie; Wes and Debbie; Dominick and Priscilla; Jerry and Christine; Michael and Dawn; Terri, and others. To our attorney who incorporated us for free in 1997. Gin, you expressed God's heart by securing Bibles for inmates at exceptional prices. Diana, when we desperately needed your talents as a webmaster, when few had discovered the world wide web, you donated your services. Bob and Charlotte, your substantial donation made it possible to begin purchasing Bibles in quantity.

To the donors who helped fund the purchase of discipleship materials for inmates, and for the hundreds who wrote thousands of Christmas cards over the years to fight despair with a kind word, thank you. Chip, your donations strengthened the foundation of HEART and enabled us to mail in 1,000 Bibles. Richard and Melanie, your faithfulness year after year made a monumental difference. My great (anonymous) Texas friends, you helped get Bibles to prisoners for more than a decade. To every gracious private donors, you helped with life-impacting orphanage donations and the debt free automobile for ministry events upon my prison release. Pauly, you knew I needed that laptop that I've used for countless hours of writing. You all share in the harvest of this ministry (1 Samuel 30:24).

To my 78-year-old spiritual father, you sacrificially mentored me weekly the first five years after my prison release. You made a difference that only eternity will tell its true impact. Thank you for your love, prayers, teaching, encouragement, correction, and for rebuking me when needed while you shared and imparted wisdom from your 40 years in ministry and travel to the nations.

Isaiah 61:1

"The Spirit of the Lord GOD is on Me, because the LORD has anointed me to preach good news to the poor. He has sent me to bind up the brokenhearted, to proclaim freedom to the captives and release for the prisoners."

Psalm 146:7

"He upholds the cause of the oppressed and gives food to the hungry. The LORD sets prisoners free."

Matthew 6:33

"But seek first his kingdom and His righteousness, and all these things will be given to you as well."